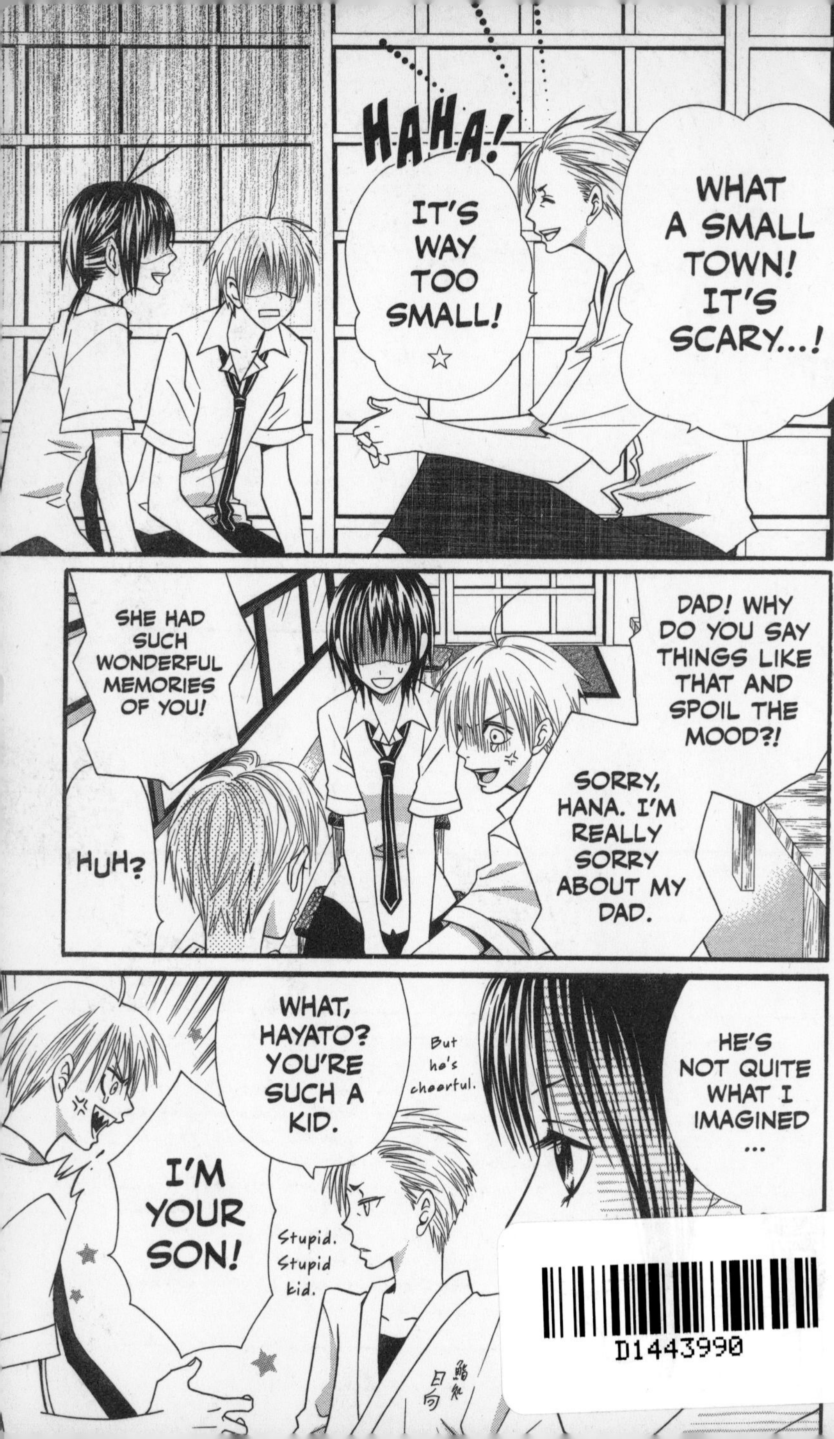
WHAT A SMALL TOWN! IT'S SCARY...!
HAHA!
IT'S WAY TOO SMALL! ☆
DAD! WHY DO YOU SAY THINGS LIKE THAT AND SPOIL THE MOOD?!
SORRY, HANA. I'M REALLY SORRY ABOUT MY DAD.
SHE HAD SUCH WONDERFUL MEMORIES OF YOU!
HUH?
HE'S NOT QUITE WHAT I IMAGINED...
But he's cheerful.
WHAT, HAYATO? YOU'RE SUCH A KID.
Stupid. Stupid kid.
I'M YOUR SON!

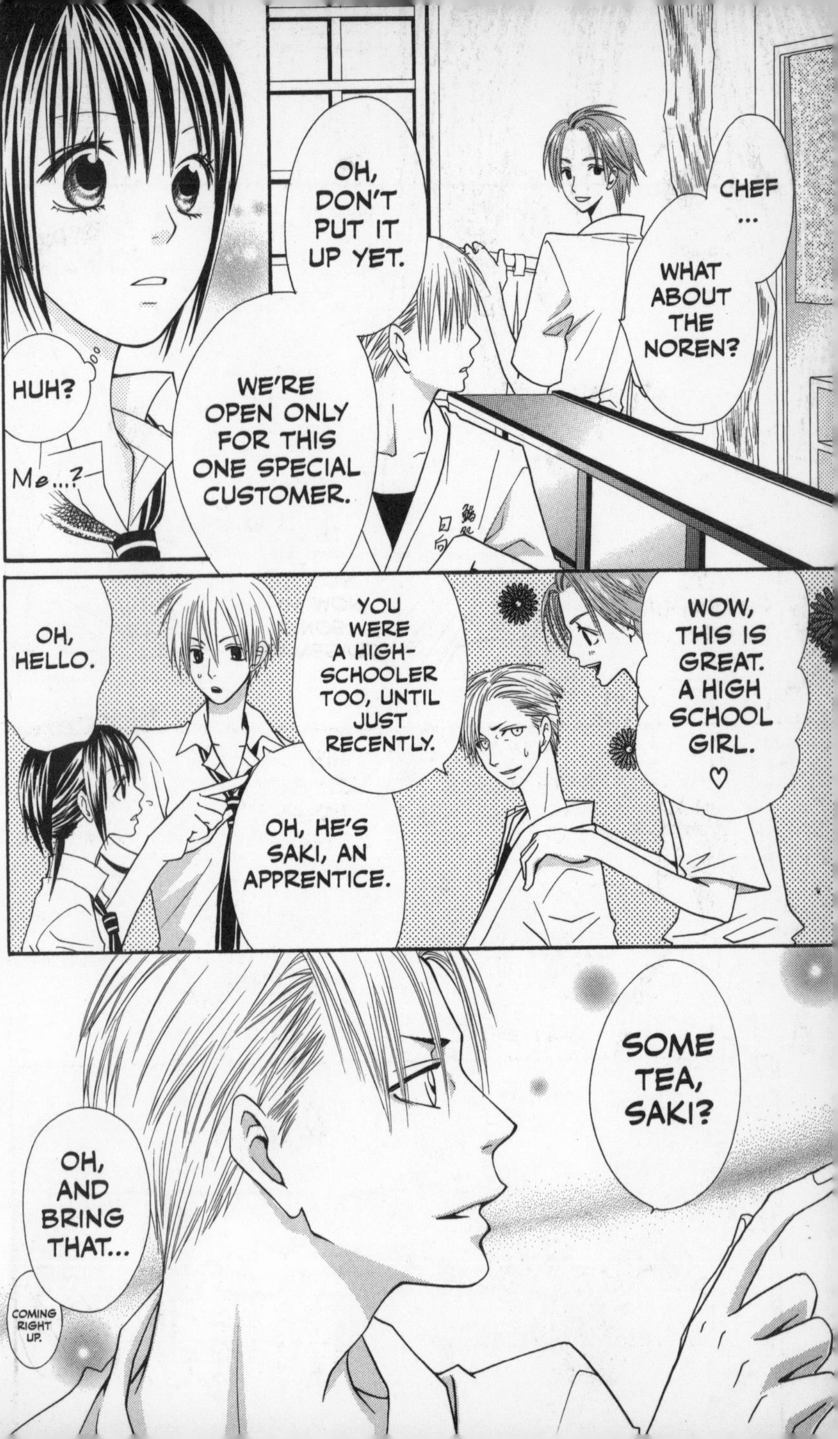
CHEF ... WHAT ABOUT THE NOREN?
OH, DON'T PUT IT UP YET.
WE'RE OPEN ONLY FOR THIS ONE SPECIAL CUSTOMER.
HUH?
Me...?
WOW, THIS IS GREAT. A HIGH SCHOOL GIRL. ♡
YOU WERE A HIGH-SCHOOLER TOO, UNTIL JUST RECENTLY.
OH, HE'S SAKI, AN APPRENTICE.
OH, HELLO.
SOME TEA, SAKI?
OH, AND BRING THAT...
COMING RIGHT UP.

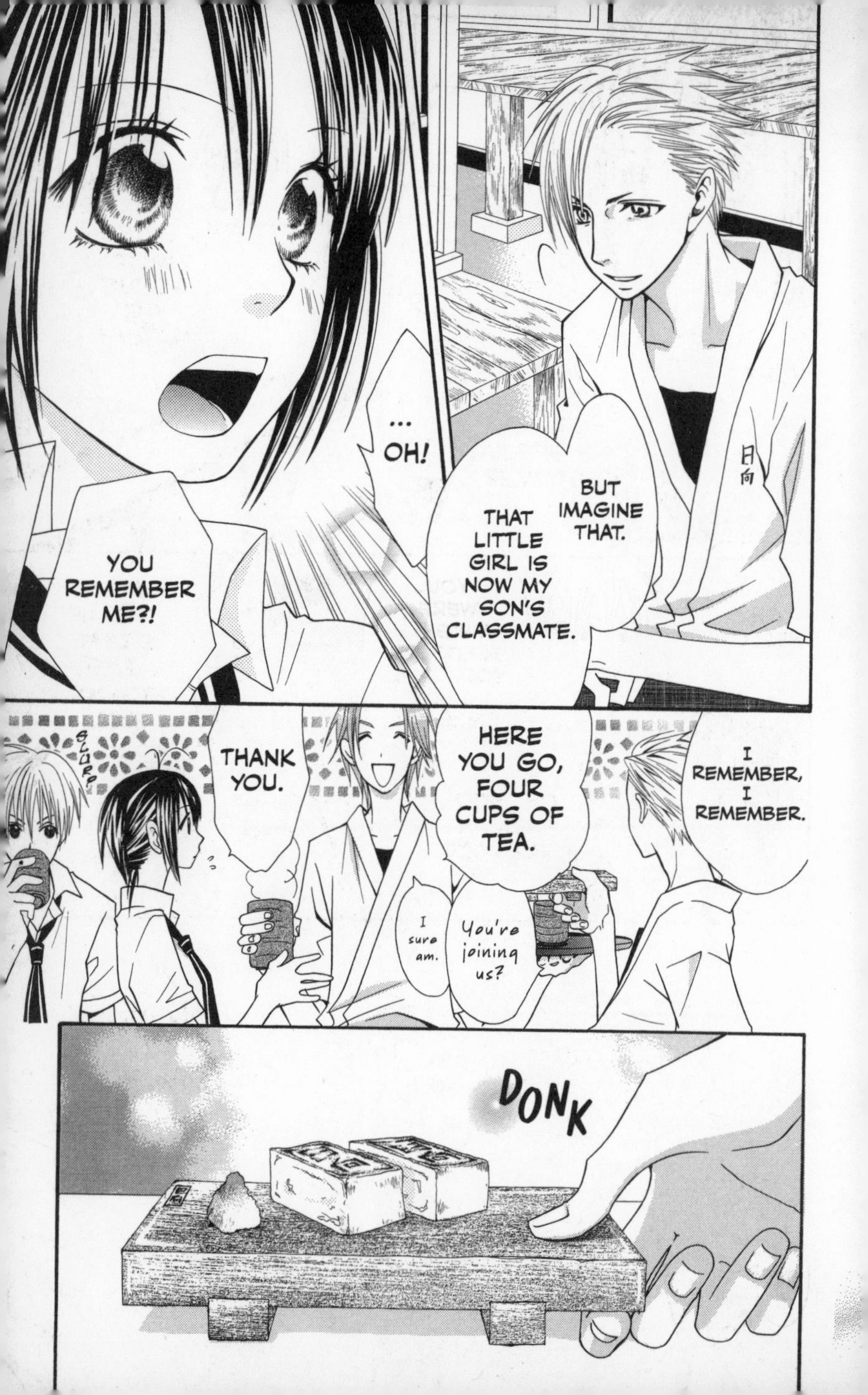
BUT IMAGINE THAT.
THAT LITTLE GIRL IS NOW MY SON'S CLASSMATE.
日向
... OH!
YOU REMEMBER ME?!
I REMEMBER, I REMEMBER.
HERE YOU GO, FOUR CUPS OF TEA.
You're joining us?
I sure am.
THANK YOU.
SLURP
DONK

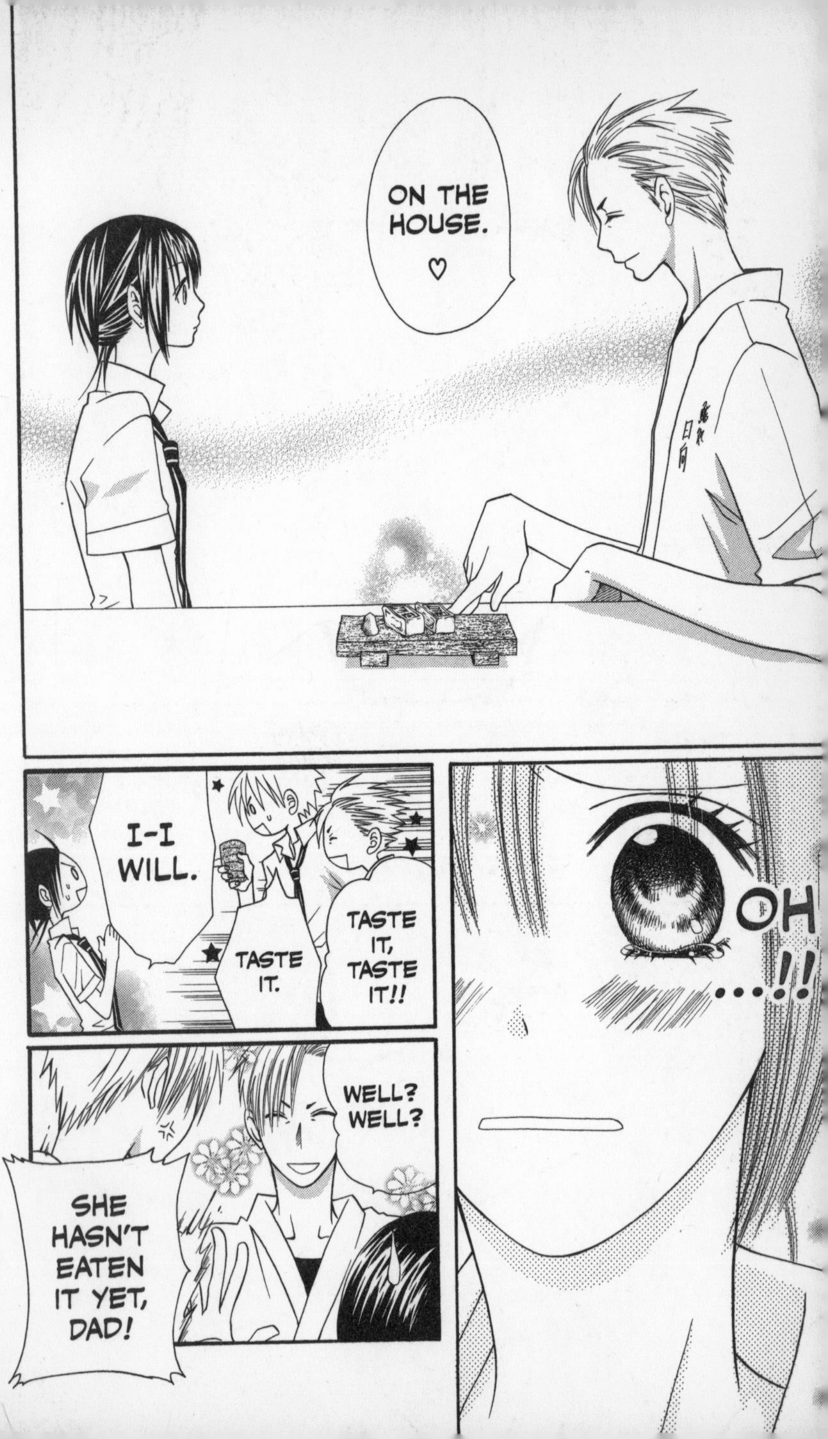
ON THE HOUSE. ♡
OH ...!!
TASTE IT, TASTE IT!!
TASTE IT.
I-I WILL.
WELL? WELL?
SHE HASN'T EATEN IT YET, DAD!

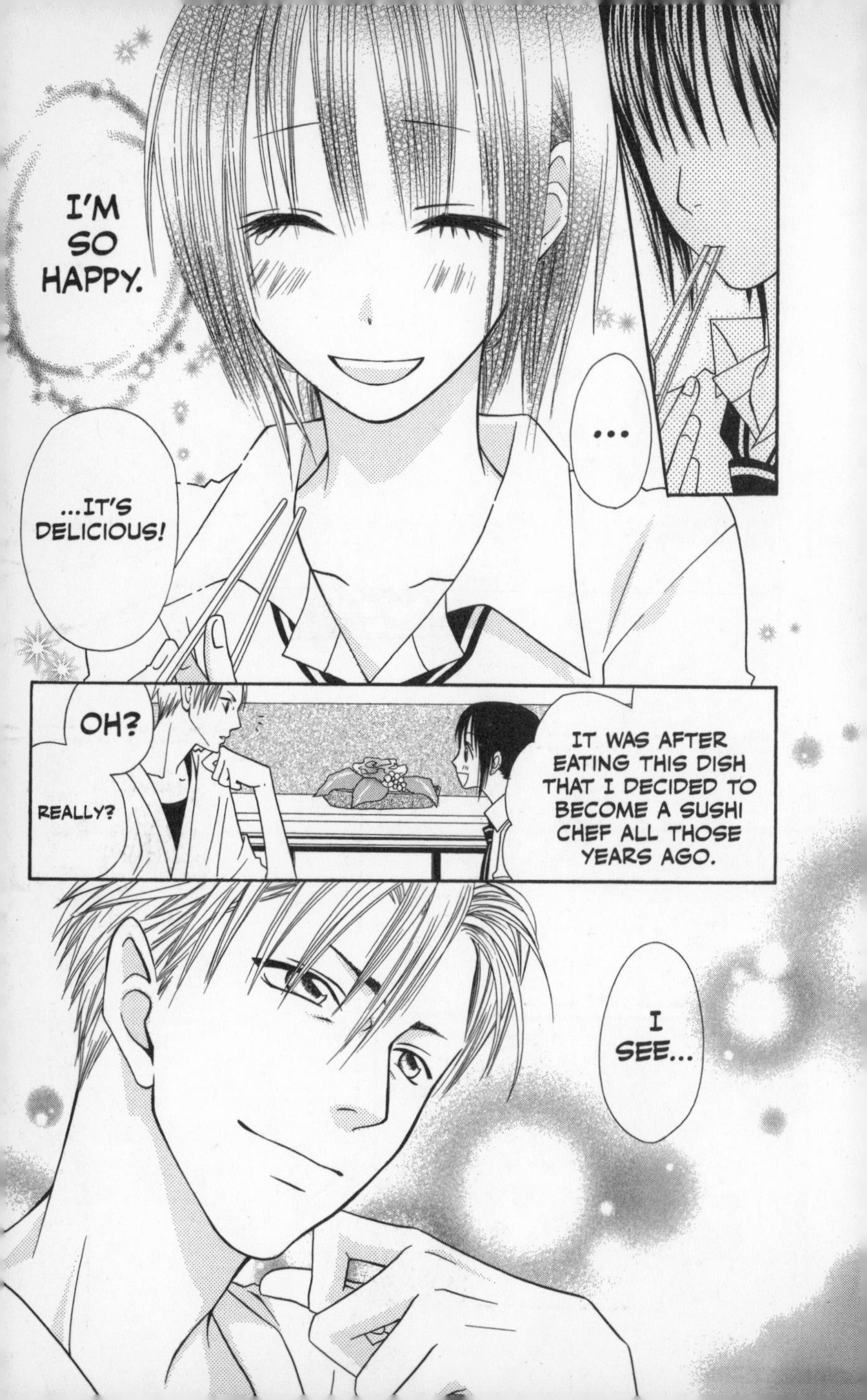
...
I'M SO HAPPY.
...IT'S DELICIOUS!
IT WAS AFTER EATING THIS DISH THAT I DECIDED TO BECOME A SUSHI CHEF ALL THOSE YEARS AGO.
OH?
REALLY?
I SEE...

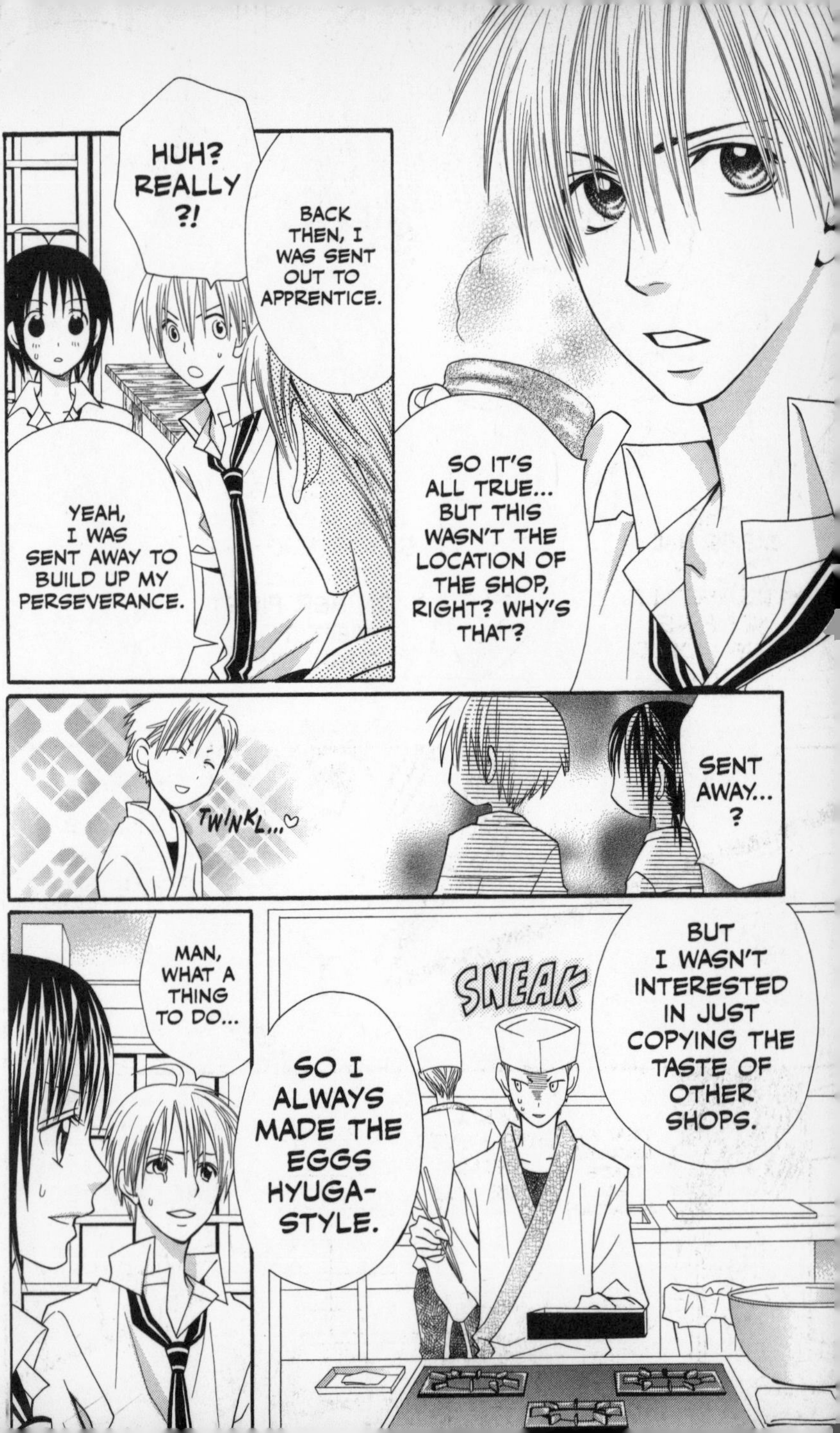
SO IT'S ALL TRUE... BUT THIS WASN'T THE LOCATION OF THE SHOP, RIGHT? WHY'S THAT?
BACK THEN, I WAS SENT OUT TO APPRENTICE.
HUH? REALLY?!
YEAH, I WAS SENT AWAY TO BUILD UP MY PERSEVERANCE.
SENT AWAY...?
TWINKL...♡
BUT I WASN'T INTERESTED IN JUST COPYING THE TASTE OF OTHER SHOPS.
SNEAK
SO I ALWAYS MADE THE EGGS HYUGA-STYLE.
MAN, WHAT A THING TO DO...

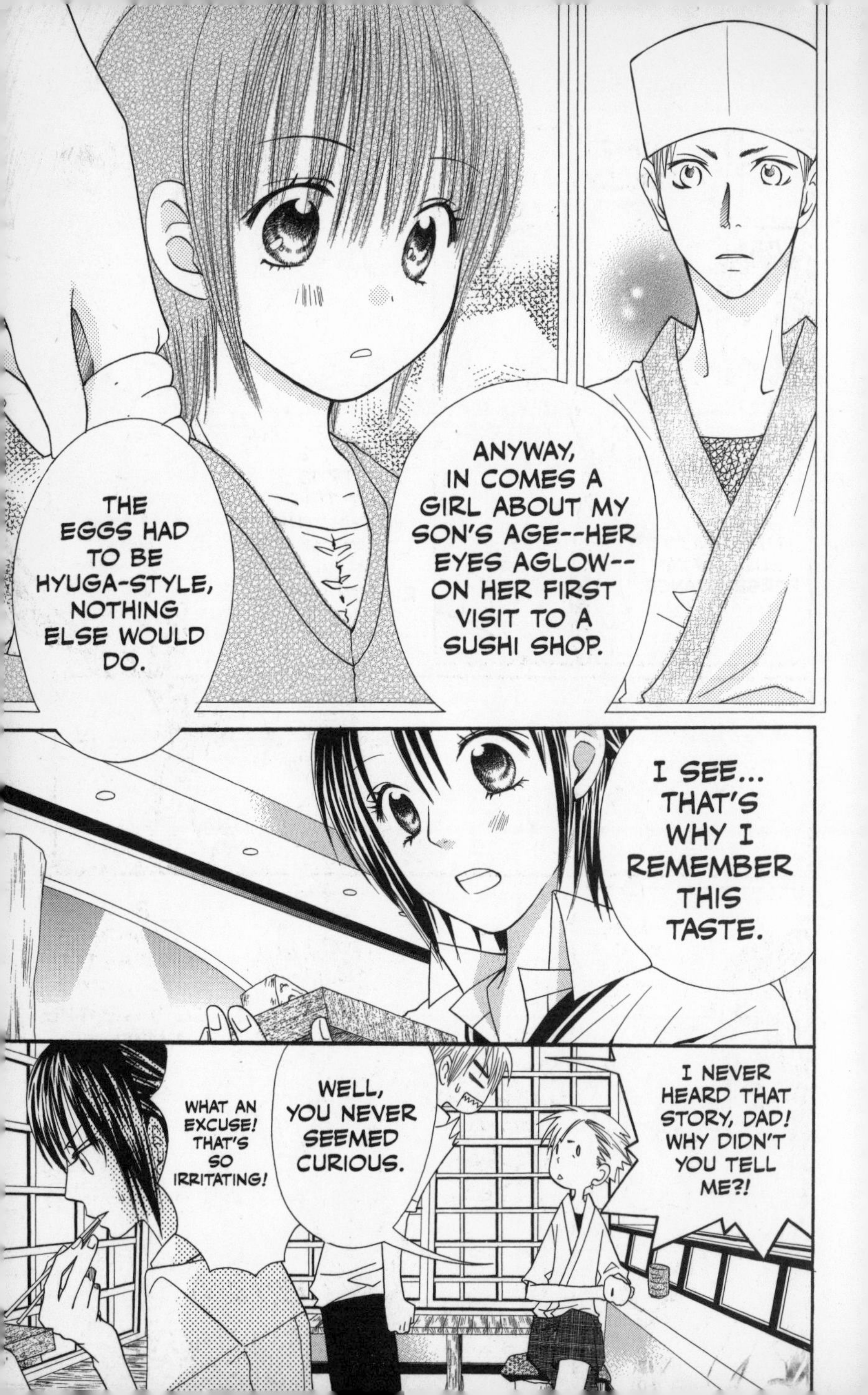
ANYWAY, IN COMES A GIRL ABOUT MY SON'S AGE--HER EYES AGLOW--ON HER FIRST VISIT TO A SUSHI SHOP.
THE EGGS HAD TO BE HYUGA-STYLE, NOTHING ELSE WOULD DO.
I SEE... THAT'S WHY I REMEMBER THIS TASTE.
I NEVER HEARD THAT STORY, DAD! WHY DIDN'T YOU TELL ME?!
WELL, YOU NEVER SEEMED CURIOUS.
WHAT AN EXCUSE! THAT'S SO IRRITATING!

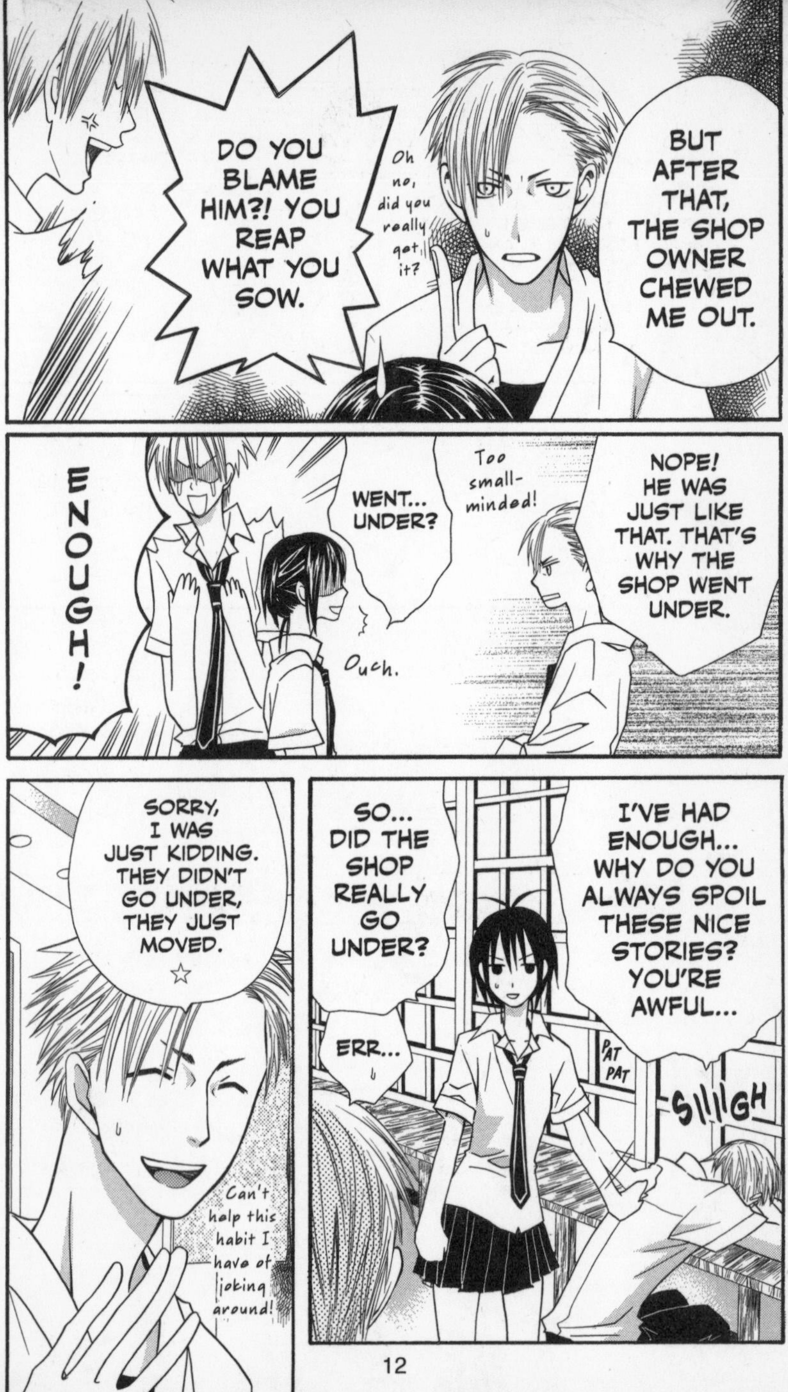
BUT AFTER THAT, THE SHOP OWNER CHEWED ME OUT.
Oh no, did you really get it?
DO YOU BLAME HIM?! YOU REAP WHAT YOU SOW.
NOPE! HE WAS JUST LIKE THAT. THAT'S WHY THE SHOP WENT UNDER.
Too small-minded!
WENT... UNDER?
Ouch.
ENOUGH!
I'VE HAD ENOUGH... WHY DO YOU ALWAYS SPOIL THESE NICE STORIES? YOU'RE AWFUL...
SO... DID THE SHOP REALLY GO UNDER?
PAT PAT
SIIIIGH
ERR...
SORRY, I WAS JUST KIDDING. THEY DIDN'T GO UNDER, THEY JUST MOVED. ☆
Can't help this habit I have of joking around!

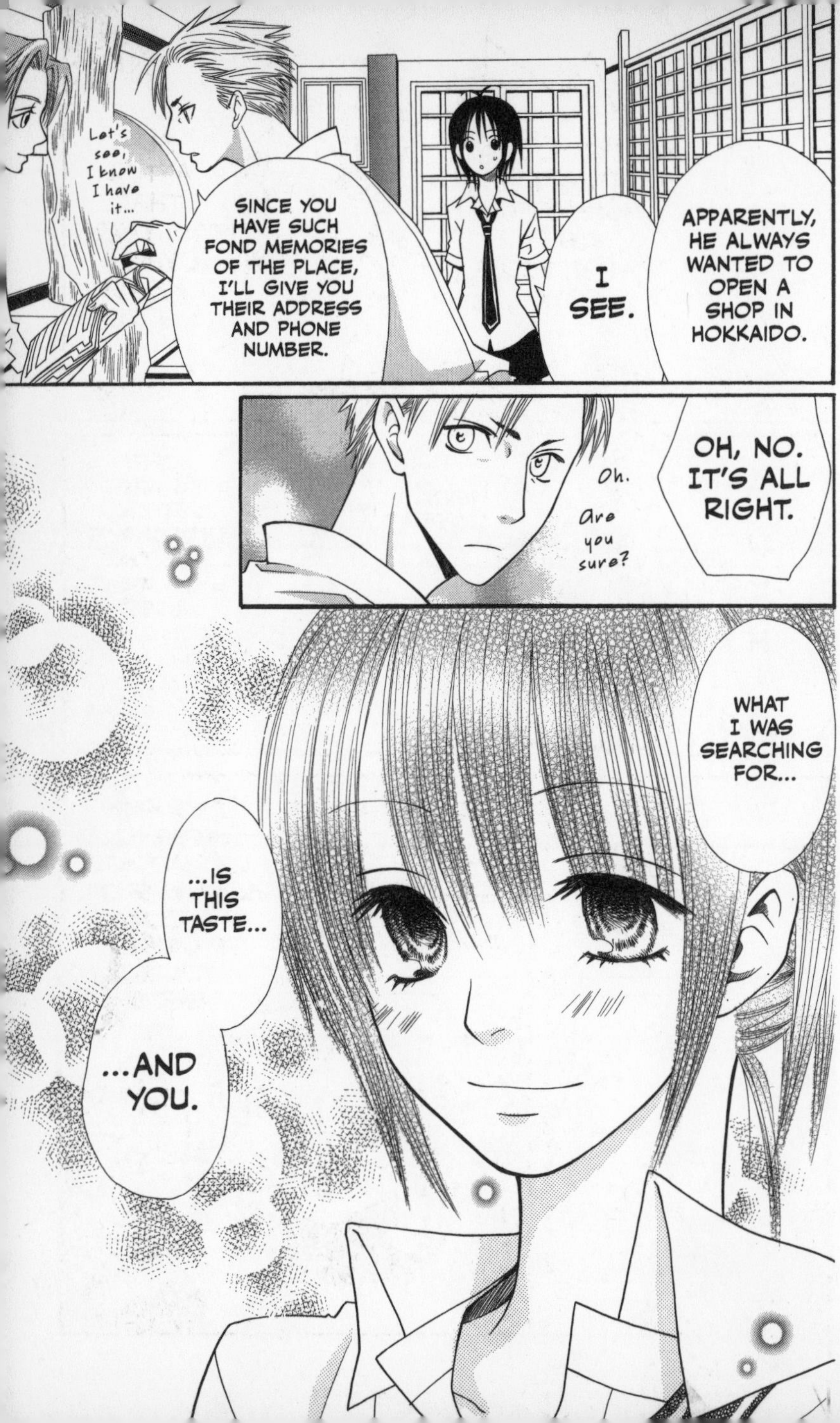
APPARENTLY, HE ALWAYS WANTED TO OPEN A SHOP IN HOKKAIDO.
I SEE.
SINCE YOU HAVE SUCH FOND MEMORIES OF THE PLACE, I'LL GIVE YOU THEIR ADDRESS AND PHONE NUMBER.
Let's see, I know I have it...
OH, NO. IT'S ALL RIGHT.
Oh.
Are you sure?
WHAT I WAS SEARCHING FOR...
...IS THIS TASTE...
...AND YOU.

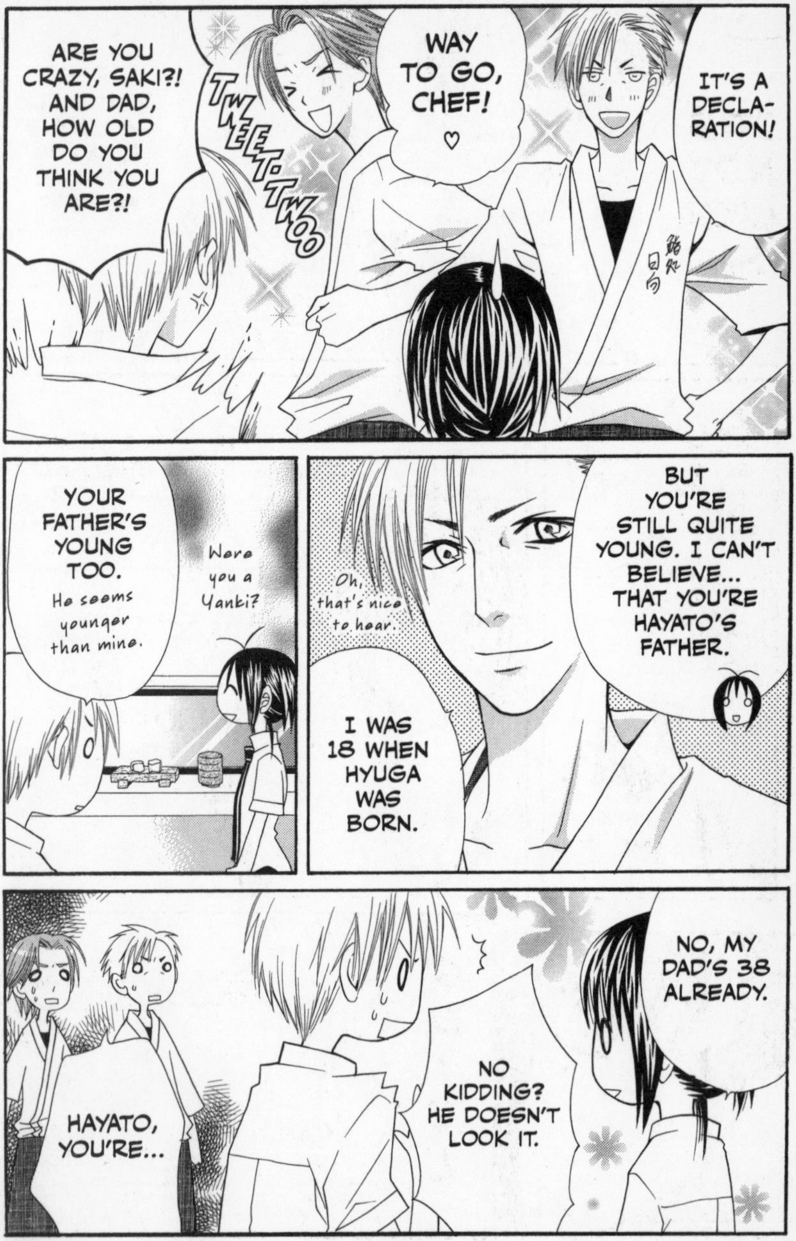

IT'S A DECLARATION!
WAY TO GO, CHEF! ♡
TWEET-TWOO
ARE YOU CRAZY, SAKI?! AND DAD, HOW OLD DO YOU THINK YOU ARE?!
BUT YOU'RE STILL QUITE YOUNG. I CAN'T BELIEVE... THAT YOU'RE HAYATO'S FATHER.
Oh, that's nice to hear.
I WAS 18 WHEN HYUGA WAS BORN.
YOUR FATHER'S YOUNG TOO.
He seems younger than mine.
Were you a Yanki?
NO, MY DAD'S 38 ALREADY.
NO KIDDING? HE DOESN'T LOOK IT.
HAYATO, YOU'RE...

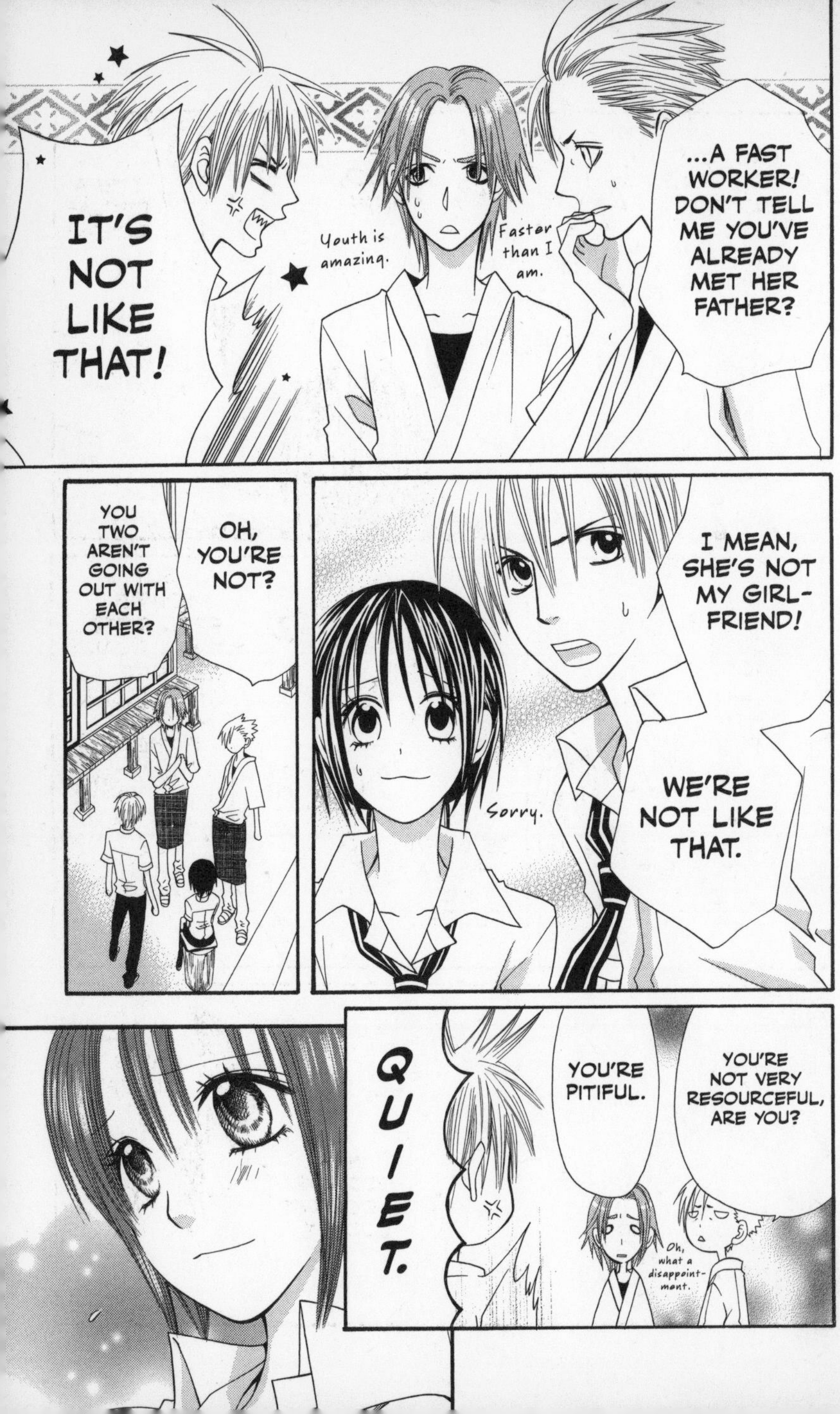
...A FAST WORKER! DON'T TELL ME YOU'VE ALREADY MET HER FATHER?
Faster than I am.
Youth is amazing.
IT'S NOT LIKE THAT!
I MEAN, SHE'S NOT MY GIRL-FRIEND!
WE'RE NOT LIKE THAT.
Sorry.
OH, YOU'RE NOT?
YOU TWO AREN'T GOING OUT WITH EACH OTHER?
YOU'RE NOT VERY RESOURCEFUL, ARE YOU?
YOU'RE PITIFUL.
Oh, what a disappoint-ment.
QUIET.

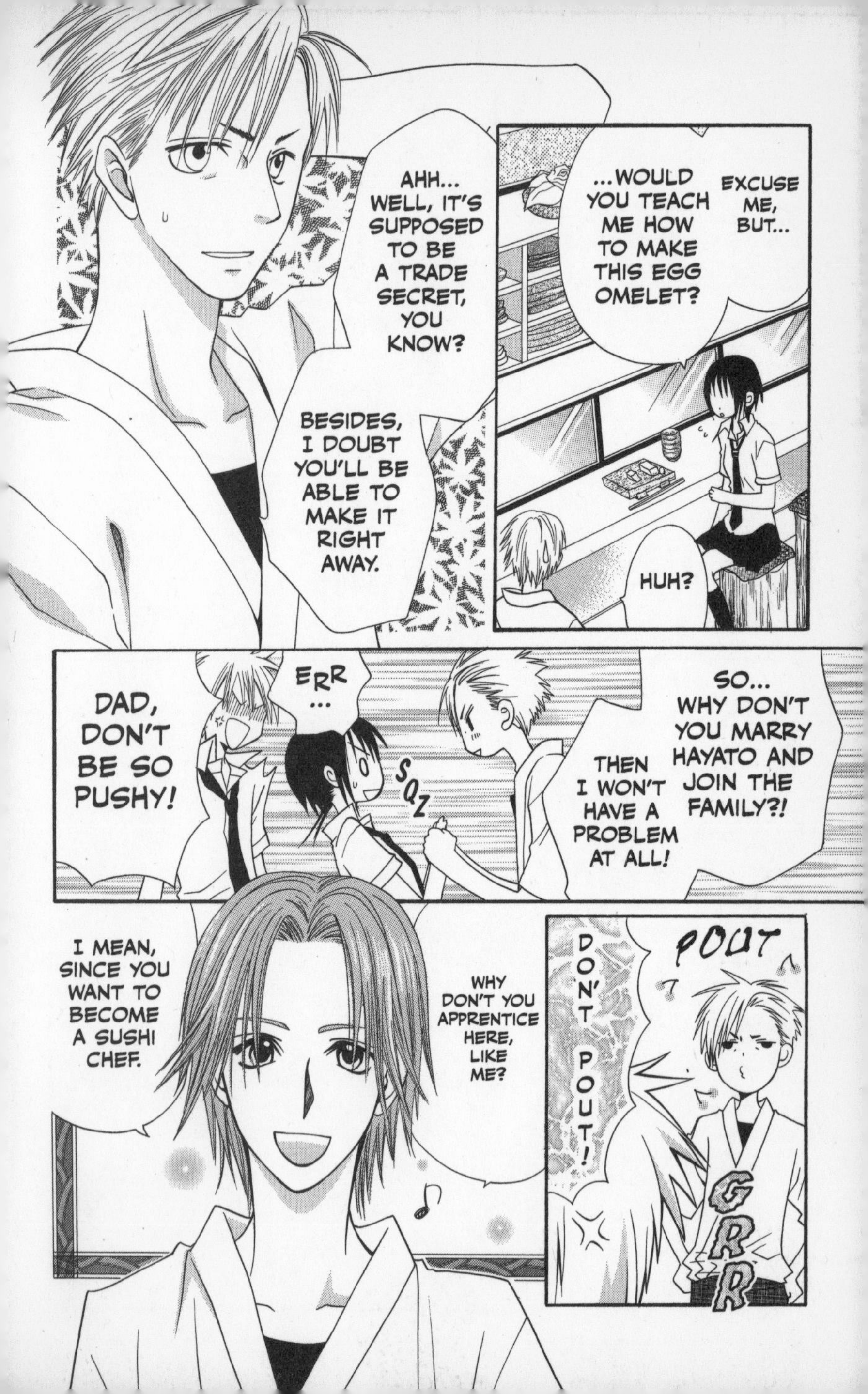
EXCUSE ME, BUT...
...WOULD YOU TEACH ME HOW TO MAKE THIS EGG OMELET?
HUH?
AHH... WELL, IT'S SUPPOSED TO BE A TRADE SECRET, YOU KNOW?
BESIDES, I DOUBT YOU'LL BE ABLE TO MAKE IT RIGHT AWAY.
SO... WHY DON'T YOU MARRY HAYATO AND JOIN THE FAMILY?!
THEN I WON'T HAVE A PROBLEM AT ALL!
SQZ
ERR...
DAD, DON'T BE SO PUSHY!
POUT
DON'T POUT!
GRR
WHY DON'T YOU APPRENTICE HERE, LIKE ME?
I MEAN, SINCE YOU WANT TO BECOME A SUSHI CHEF.

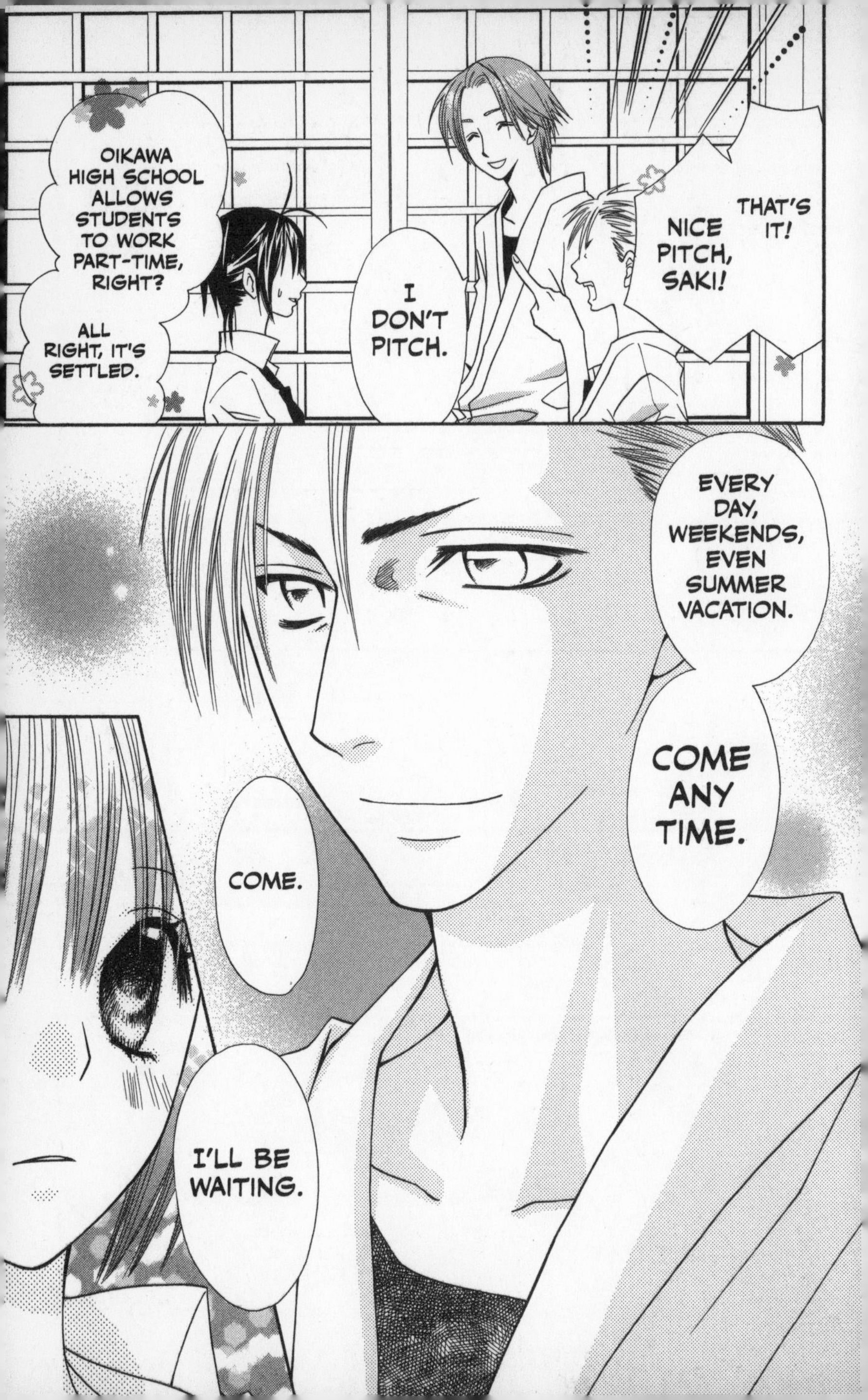
THAT'S IT!
NICE PITCH, SAKI!
I DON'T PITCH.
OIKAWA HIGH SCHOOL ALLOWS STUDENTS TO WORK PART-TIME, RIGHT?
ALL RIGHT, IT'S SETTLED.
EVERY DAY, WEEKENDS, EVEN SUMMER VACATION.
COME ANY TIME.
COME.
I'LL BE WAITING.

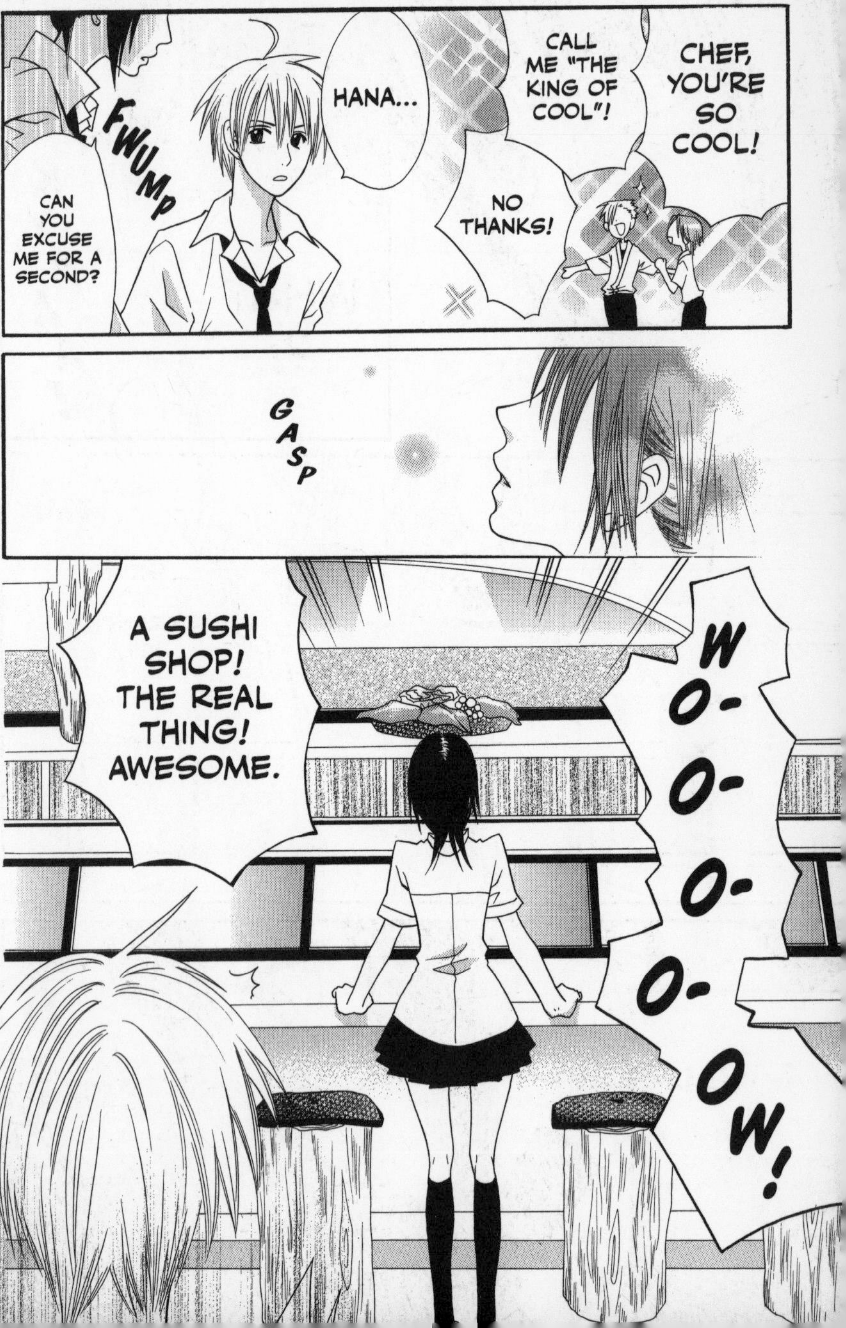
CHEF, YOU'RE SO COOL!
CALL ME "THE KING OF COOL"!
NO THANKS!
HANA...
FWUMP
CAN YOU EXCUSE ME FOR A SECOND?
GASP
WO-O-O-O-O-OW!
A SUSHI SHOP! THE REAL THING! AWESOME.

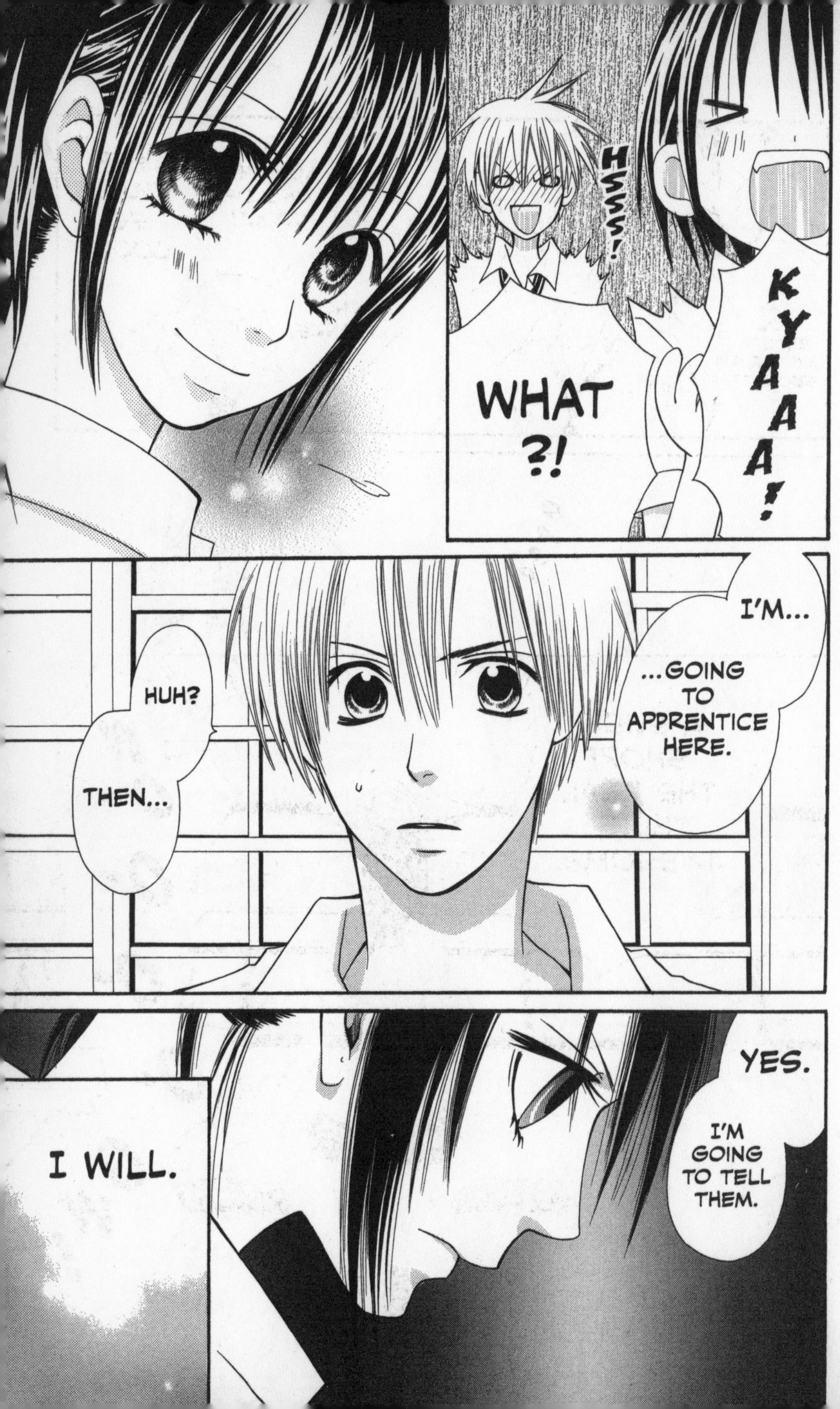
KYAAA!
HSSS!
WHAT?!
I'M...
...GOING TO APPRENTICE HERE.
HUH?
THEN...
YES.
I'M GOING TO TELL THEM.
I WILL.

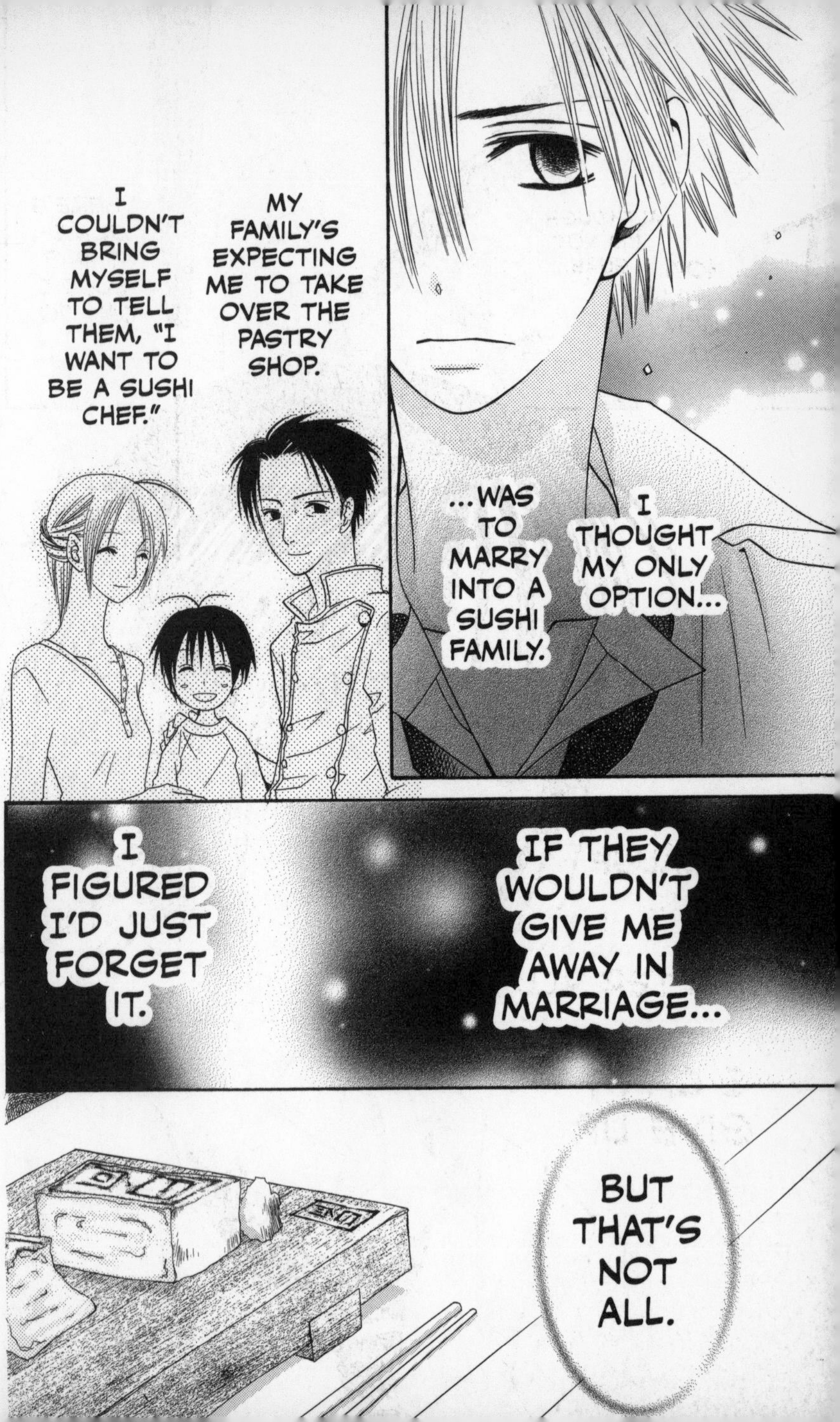
I THOUGHT MY ONLY OPTION...
...WAS TO MARRY INTO A SUSHI FAMILY.
MY FAMILY'S EXPECTING ME TO TAKE OVER THE PASTRY SHOP.
I COULDN'T BRING MYSELF TO TELL THEM, "I WANT TO BE A SUSHI CHEF."
IF THEY WOULDN'T GIVE ME AWAY IN MARRIAGE...
I FIGURED I'D JUST FORGET IT.
BUT THAT'S NOT ALL.

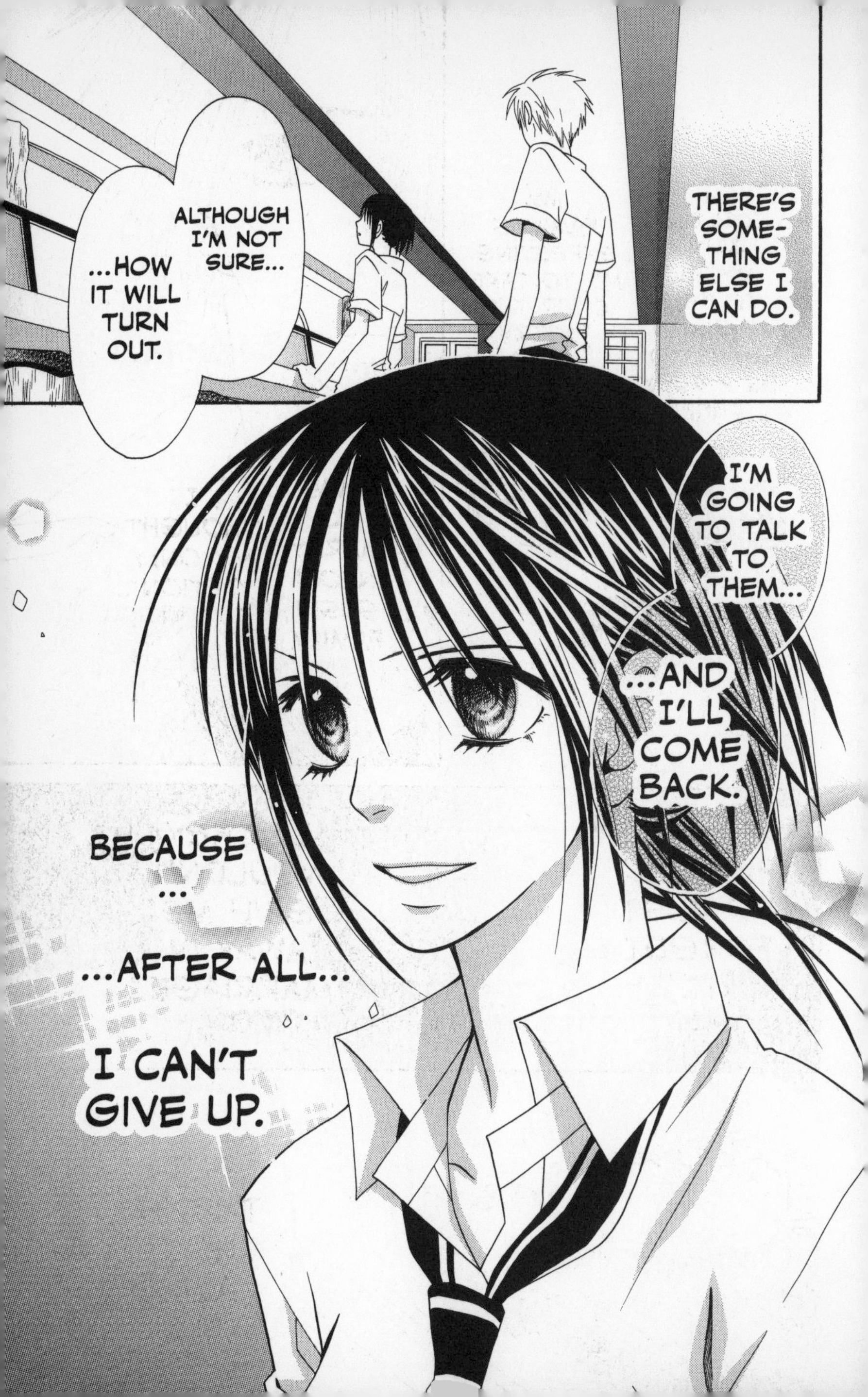
THERE'S SOMETHING ELSE I CAN DO.
ALTHOUGH I'M NOT SURE...
...HOW IT WILL TURN OUT.
I'M GOING TO TALK TO THEM...
...AND I'LL COME BACK.
BECAUSE...
...AFTER ALL...
I CAN'T GIVE UP.

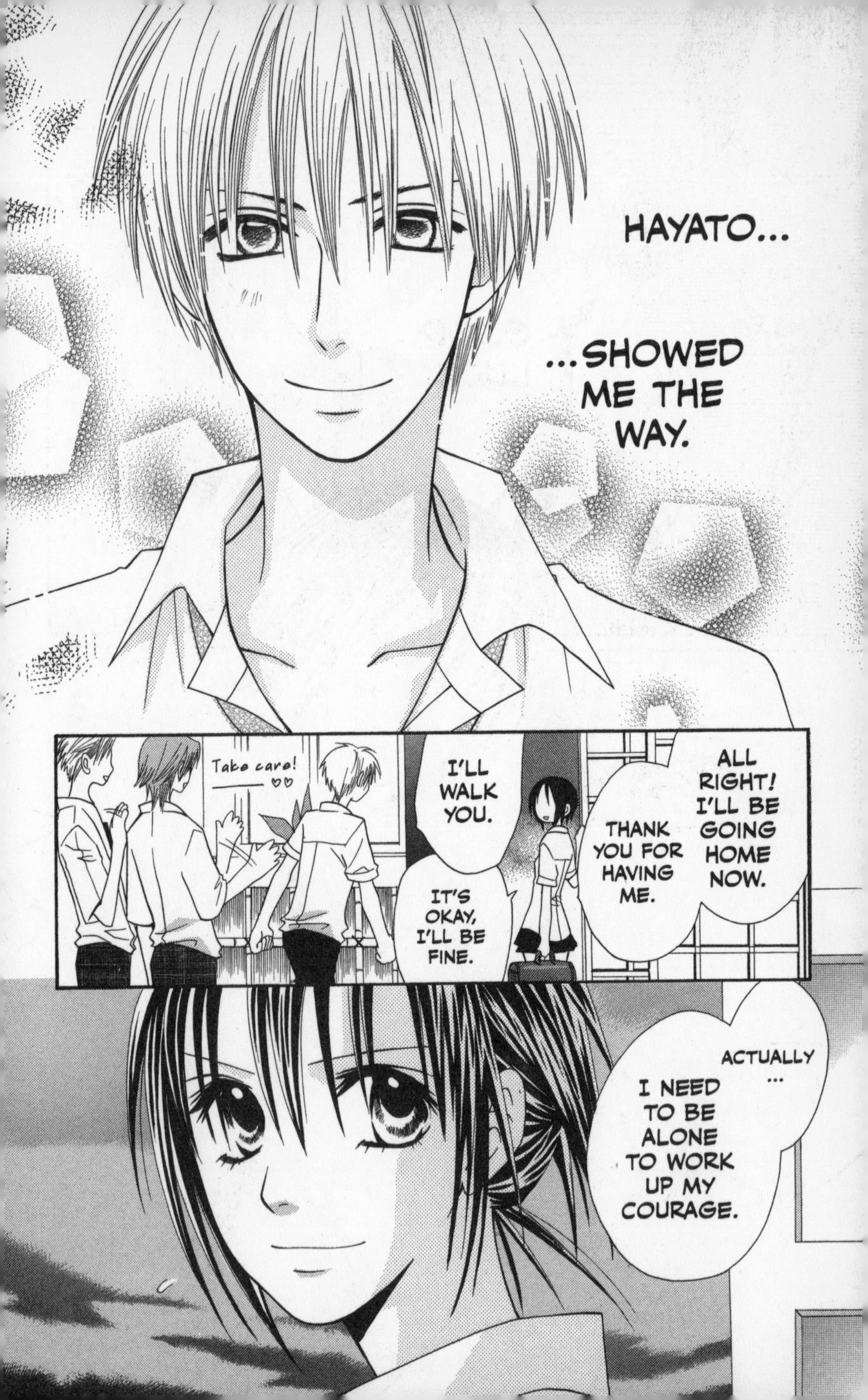
HAYATO...
...SHOWED ME THE WAY.
ALL RIGHT! I'LL BE GOING HOME NOW.
THANK YOU FOR HAVING ME.
I'LL WALK YOU.
IT'S OKAY, I'LL BE FINE.
Take care! ♡♡
ACTUALLY...
I NEED TO BE ALONE TO WORK UP MY COURAGE.

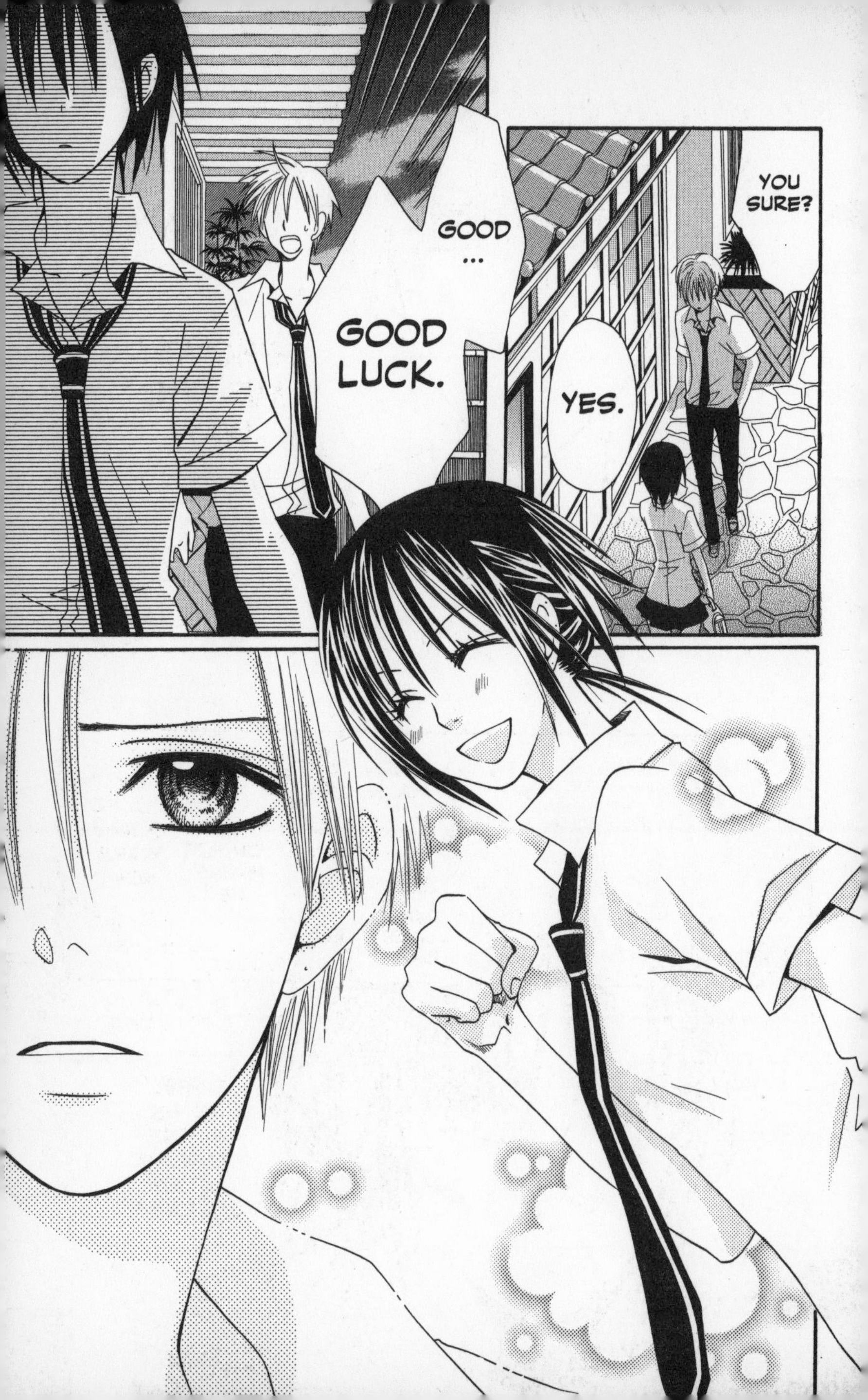
YOU SURE?
YES.
GOOD ...
GOOD LUCK.

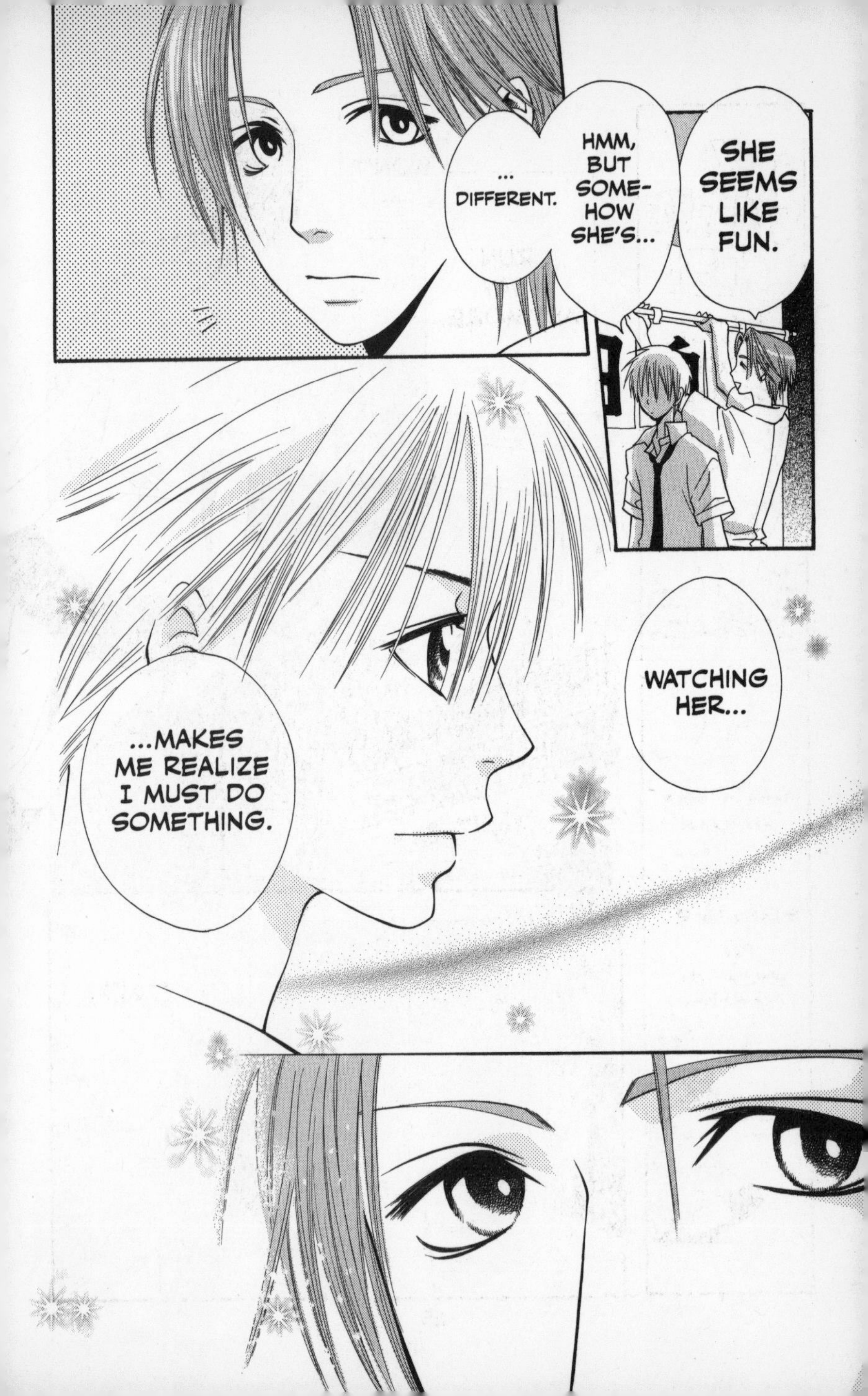
SHE SEEMS LIKE FUN.
HMM, BUT SOME-HOW SHE'S...
... DIFFERENT.
WATCHING HER...
...MAKES ME REALIZE I MUST DO SOMETHING.

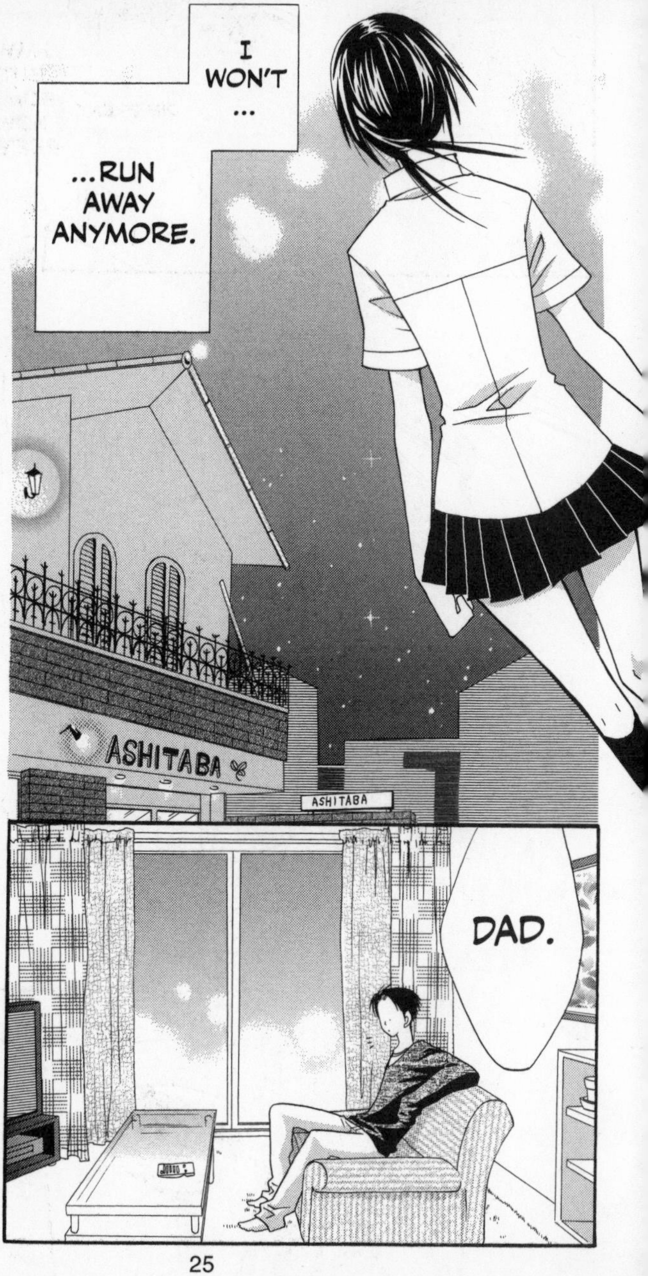
I WON'T ...
...RUN AWAY ANYMORE.
ASHITABA
ASHITABA
DAD.

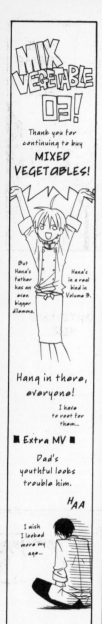

MIX VEGETABLE 03!

Thank you for continuing to buy **MIXED VEGETABLES!**

Hana's in a real bind in Volume 3.

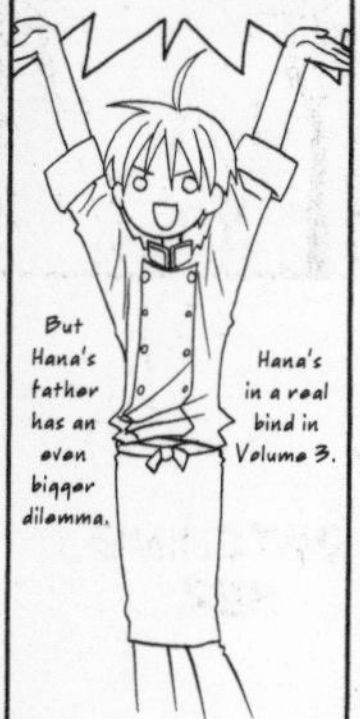

But Hana's father has an even bigger dilemma.

Hang in there, everyone!

I have to root for them...

■ Extra MV ■

Dad's youthful looks trouble him.

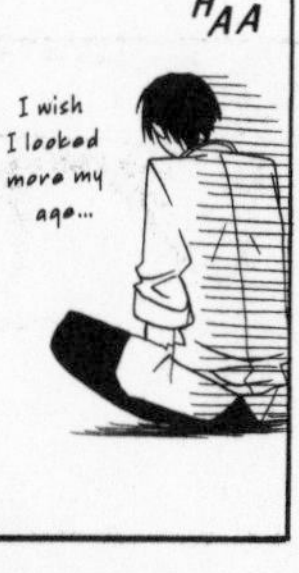
HAA
I wish I looked more my age...

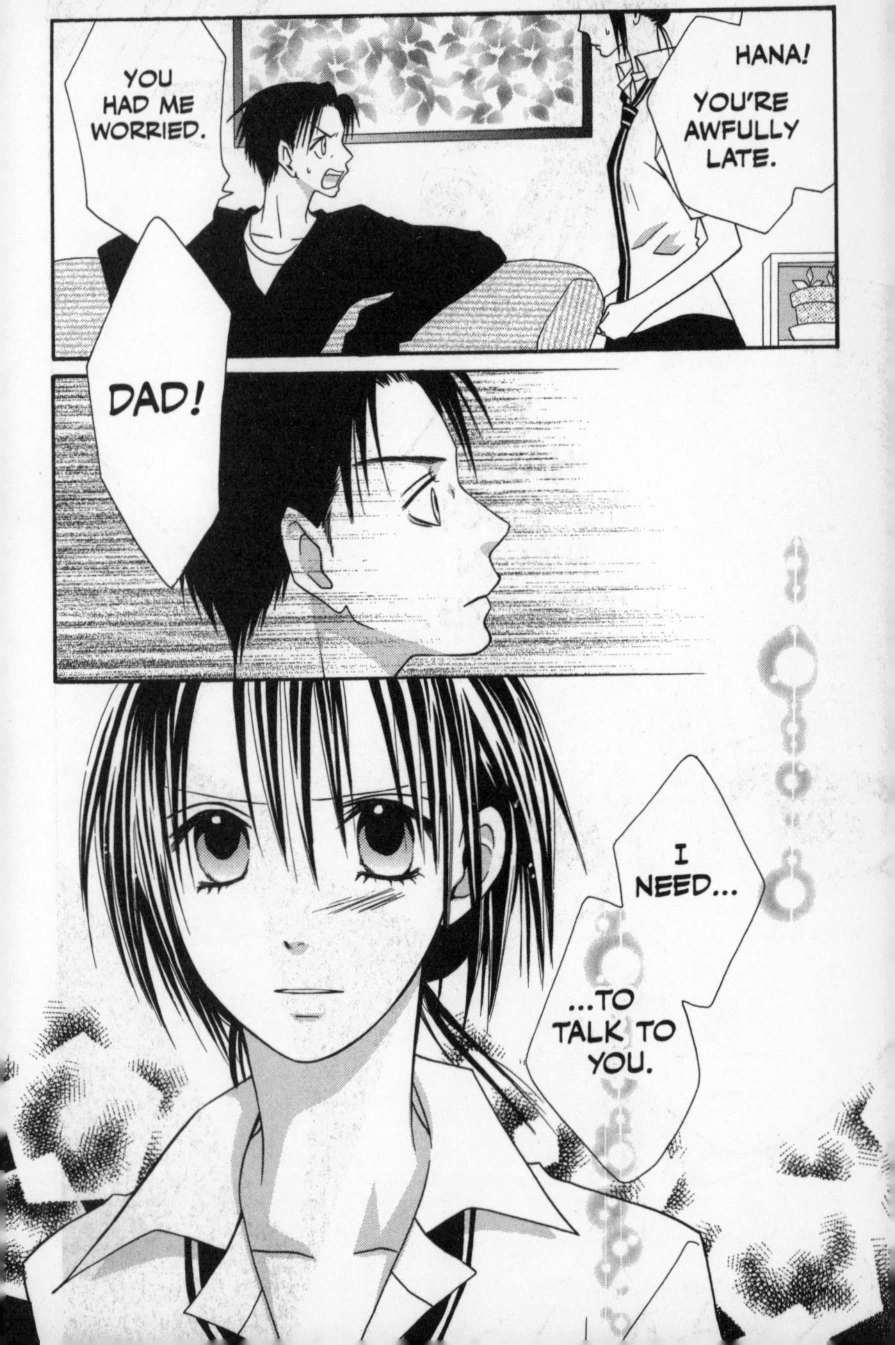
HANA!
YOU'RE AWFULLY LATE.
YOU HAD ME WORRIED.
DAD!
I NEED...
...TO TALK TO YOU.

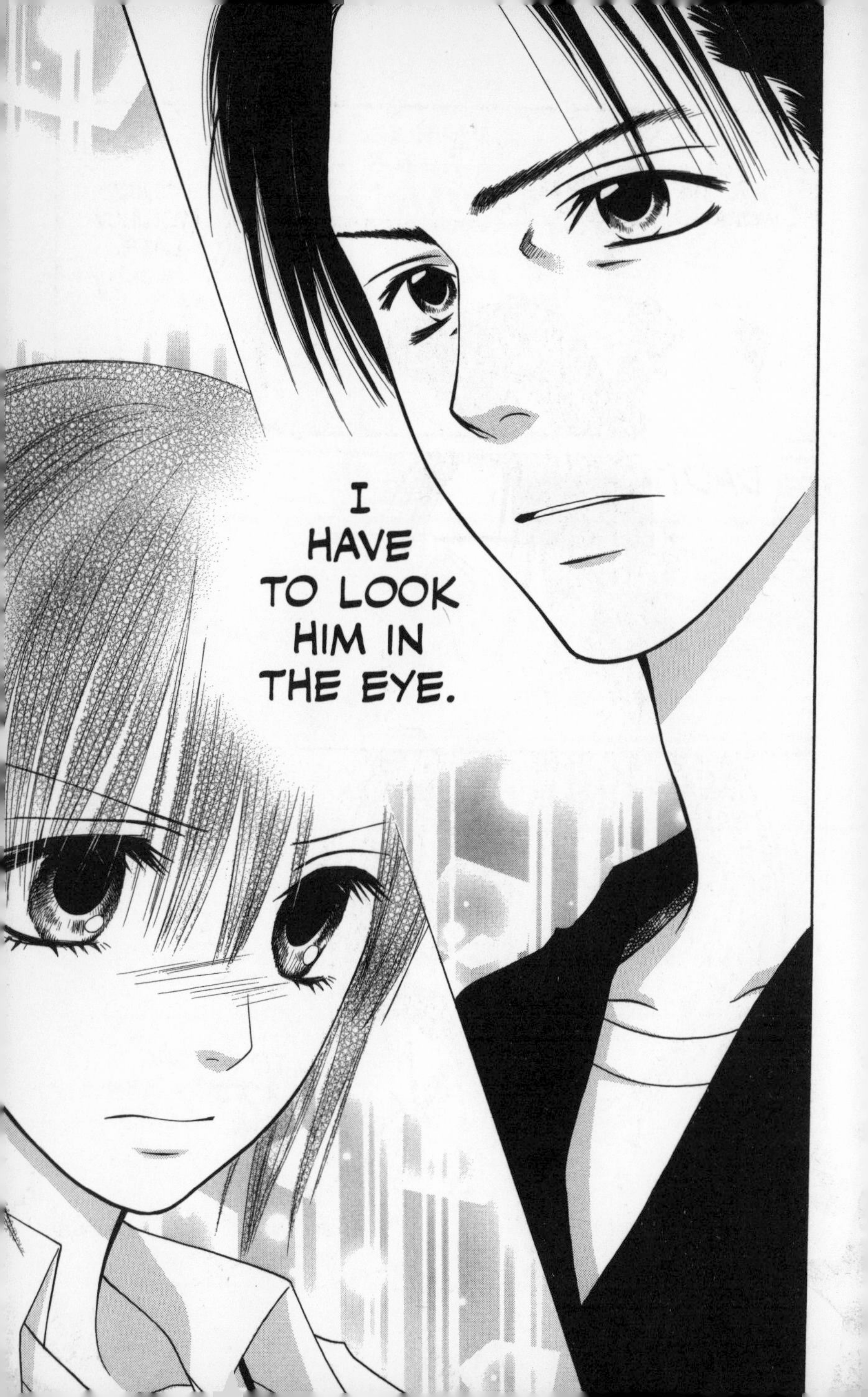
I HAVE TO LOOK HIM IN THE EYE.

SIDE DISH Mixed Vegetables 1

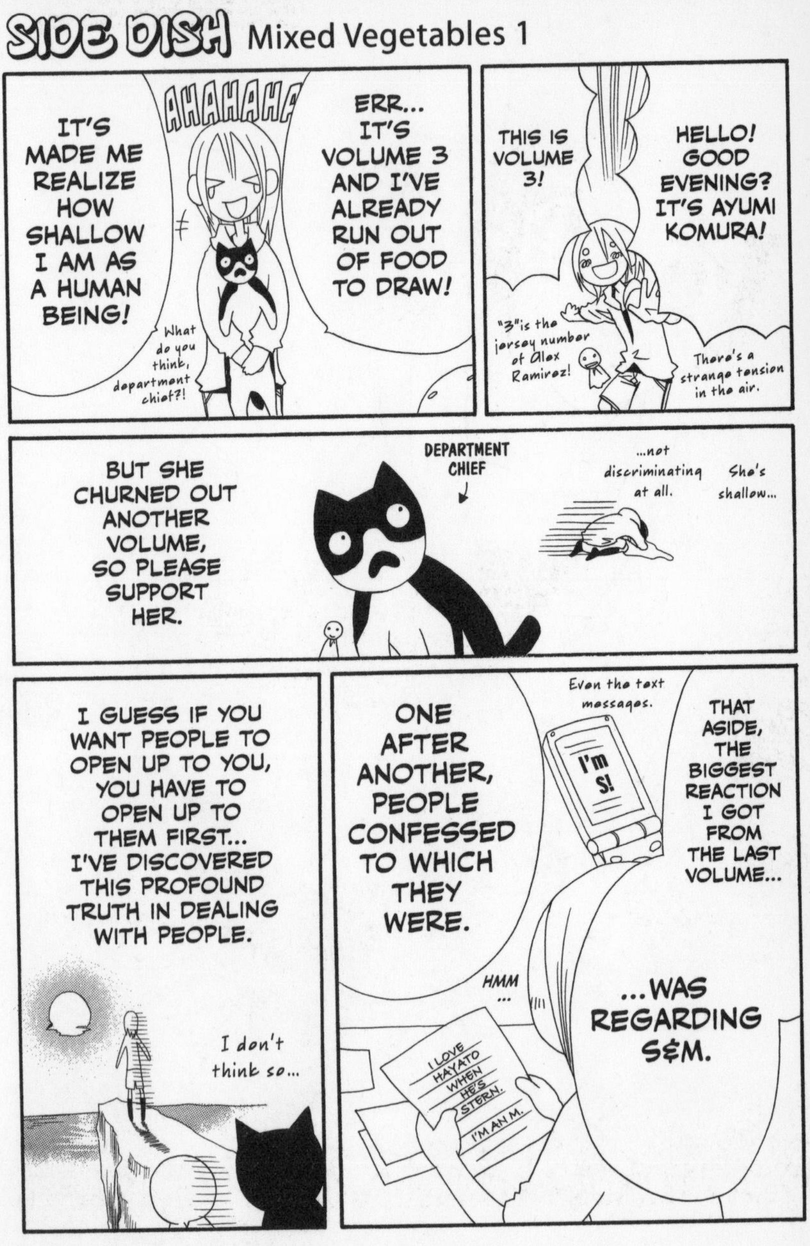
HELLO! GOOD EVENING? IT'S AYUMI KOMURA!
THIS IS VOLUME 3!
"3" is the jersey number of Alex Ramirez!
There's a strange tension in the air.
ERR... IT'S VOLUME 3 AND I'VE ALREADY RUN OUT OF FOOD TO DRAW!
AHAHAHA
IT'S MADE ME REALIZE HOW SHALLOW I AM AS A HUMAN BEING!
What do you think, department chief?!
She's shallow...
...not discriminating at all.
DEPARTMENT CHIEF
BUT SHE CHURNED OUT ANOTHER VOLUME, SO PLEASE SUPPORT HER.
THAT ASIDE, THE BIGGEST REACTION I GOT FROM THE LAST VOLUME...
Even the text messages.
I'm S!
ONE AFTER ANOTHER, PEOPLE CONFESSED TO WHICH THEY WERE.
...WAS REGARDING S&M.
HMM...
I LOVE HAYATO WHEN HE'S STERN.
I'M AN M.
I GUESS IF YOU WANT PEOPLE TO OPEN UP TO YOU, YOU HAVE TO OPEN UP TO THEM FIRST... I'VE DISCOVERED THIS PROFOUND TRUTH IN DEALING WITH PEOPLE.
I don't think so...

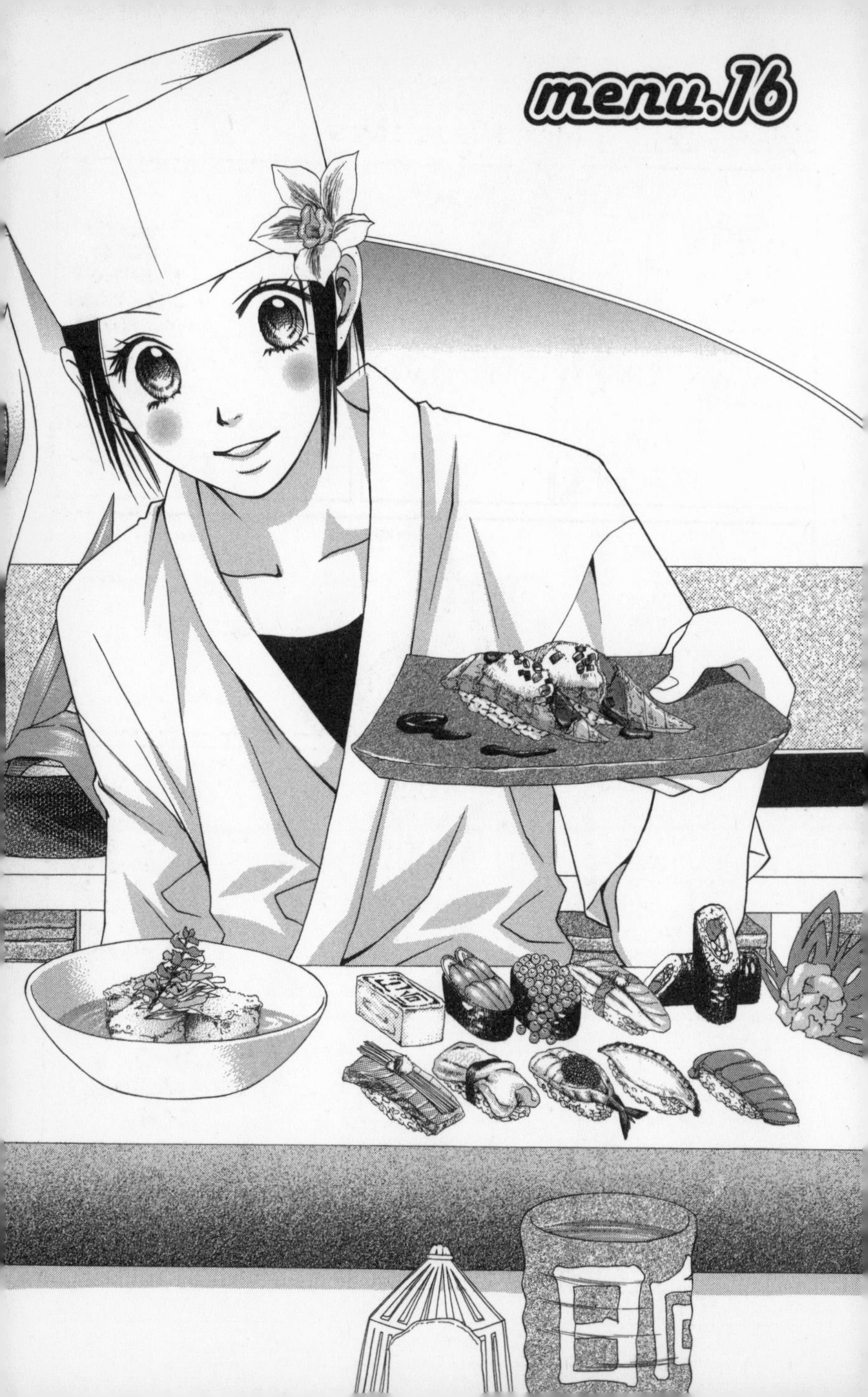
menu.16

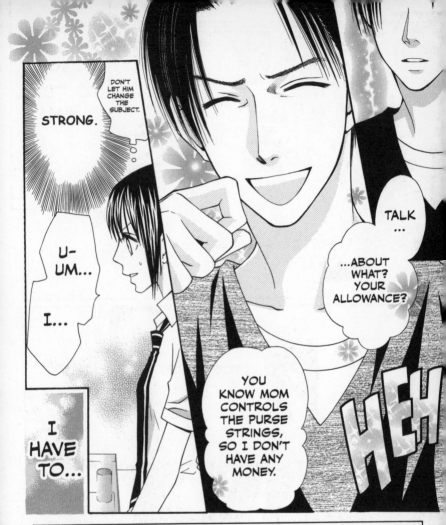

TALK ...
...ABOUT WHAT? YOUR ALLOWANCE?
YOU KNOW MOM CONTROLS THE PURSE STRINGS, SO I DON'T HAVE ANY MONEY.
HEH
DON'T LET HIM CHANGE THE SUBJECT.
STRONG.
U-UM...
I...
I HAVE TO...

menu 16

...What can I say? I was consumed with this part of the story and I was able to get totally involved with my drawings, so there's nothing I need to change or explain here.

So anyway, let me just ramble a bit. I'm not the type to associate a theme song with my works, but for chapters 16 through 18, I kept listening to a song so that I could keep my mind on my drawings. The lyrics were in English, and I listened without understanding the words. When I saw the translation, I was shocked that the song was very similar to my story.

This is probably my own personal feeling, so I won't mention the title of the song.

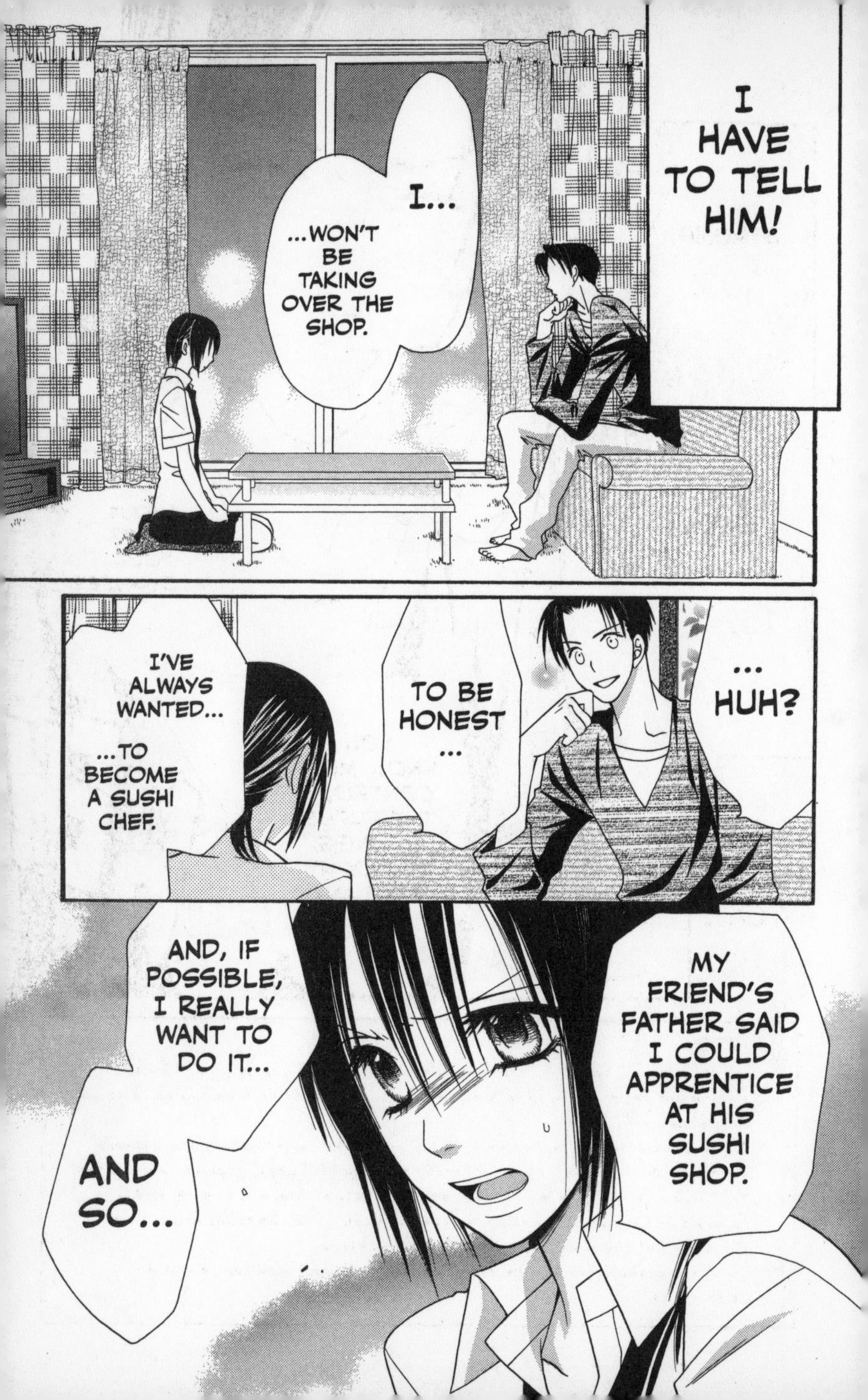
I HAVE TO TELL HIM!
I...
...WON'T BE TAKING OVER THE SHOP.
... HUH?
TO BE HONEST ...
I'VE ALWAYS WANTED...
...TO BECOME A SUSHI CHEF.
MY FRIEND'S FATHER SAID I COULD APPRENTICE AT HIS SUSHI SHOP.
AND, IF POSSIBLE, I REALLY WANT TO DO IT...
AND SO...

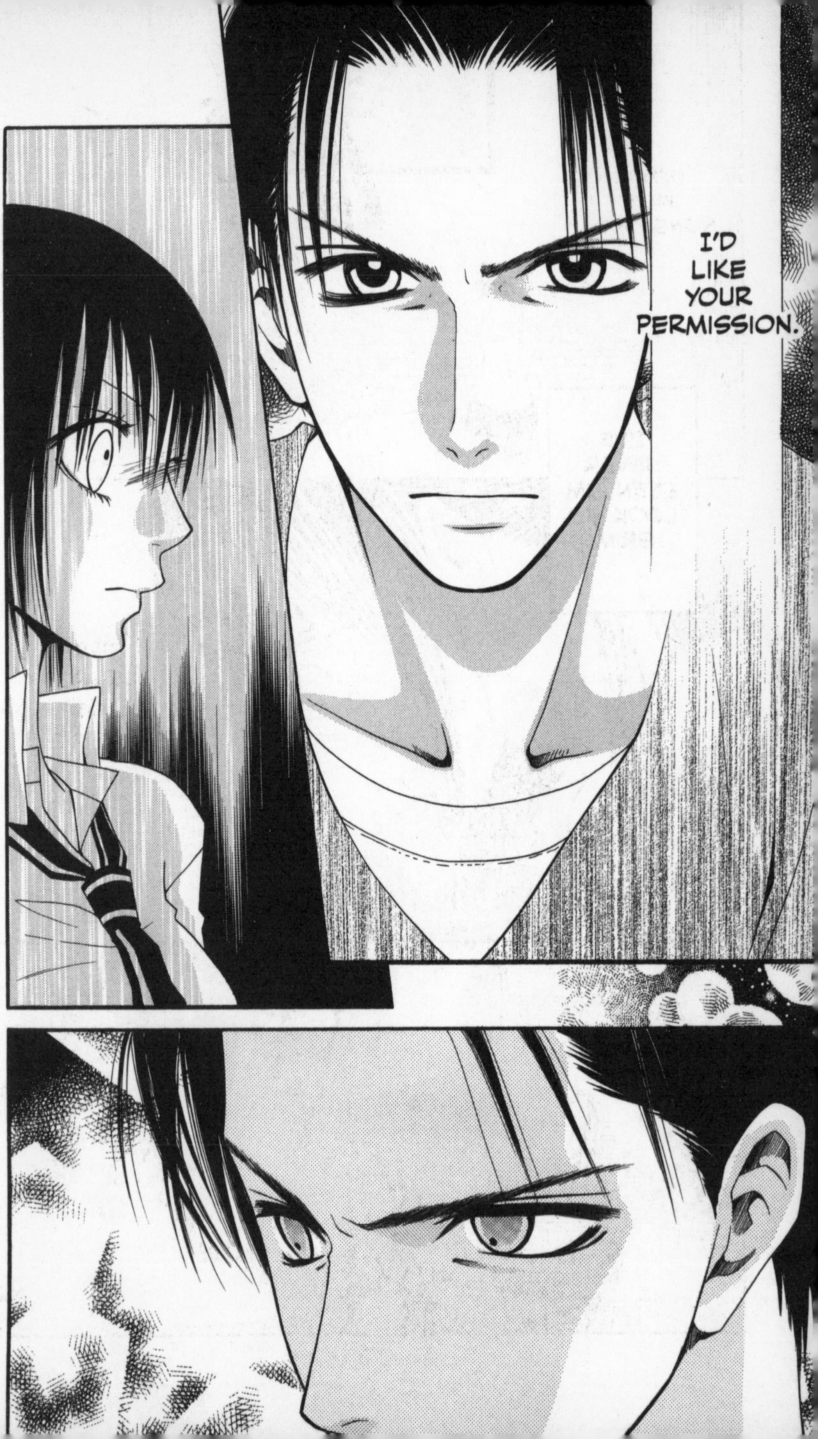
I'D LIKE YOUR PERMISSION.

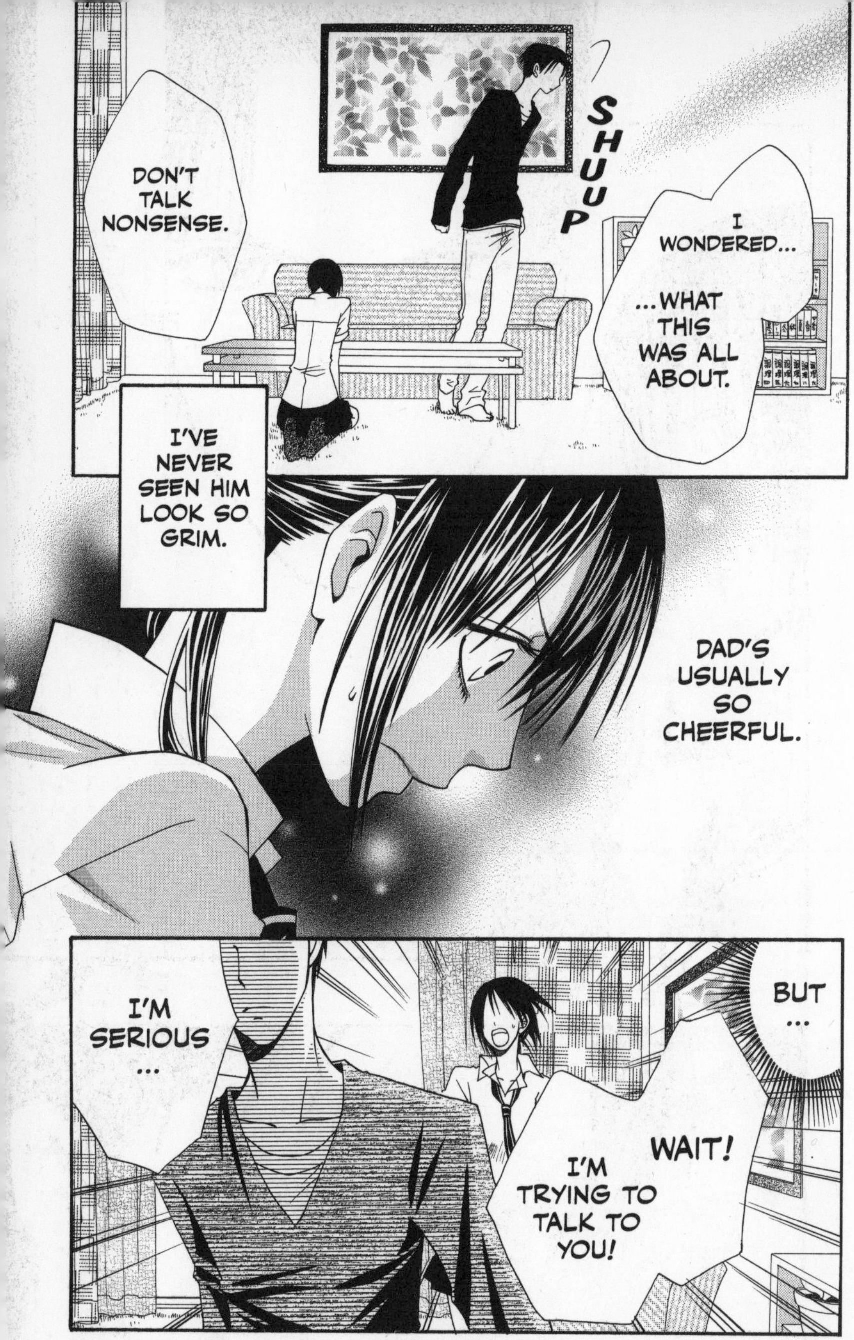
I WONDERED...
...WHAT THIS WAS ALL ABOUT.
SHUUP
DON'T TALK NONSENSE.
I'VE NEVER SEEN HIM LOOK SO GRIM.
DAD'S USUALLY SO CHEERFUL.
BUT ...
WAIT!
I'M TRYING TO TALK TO YOU!
I'M SERIOUS ...

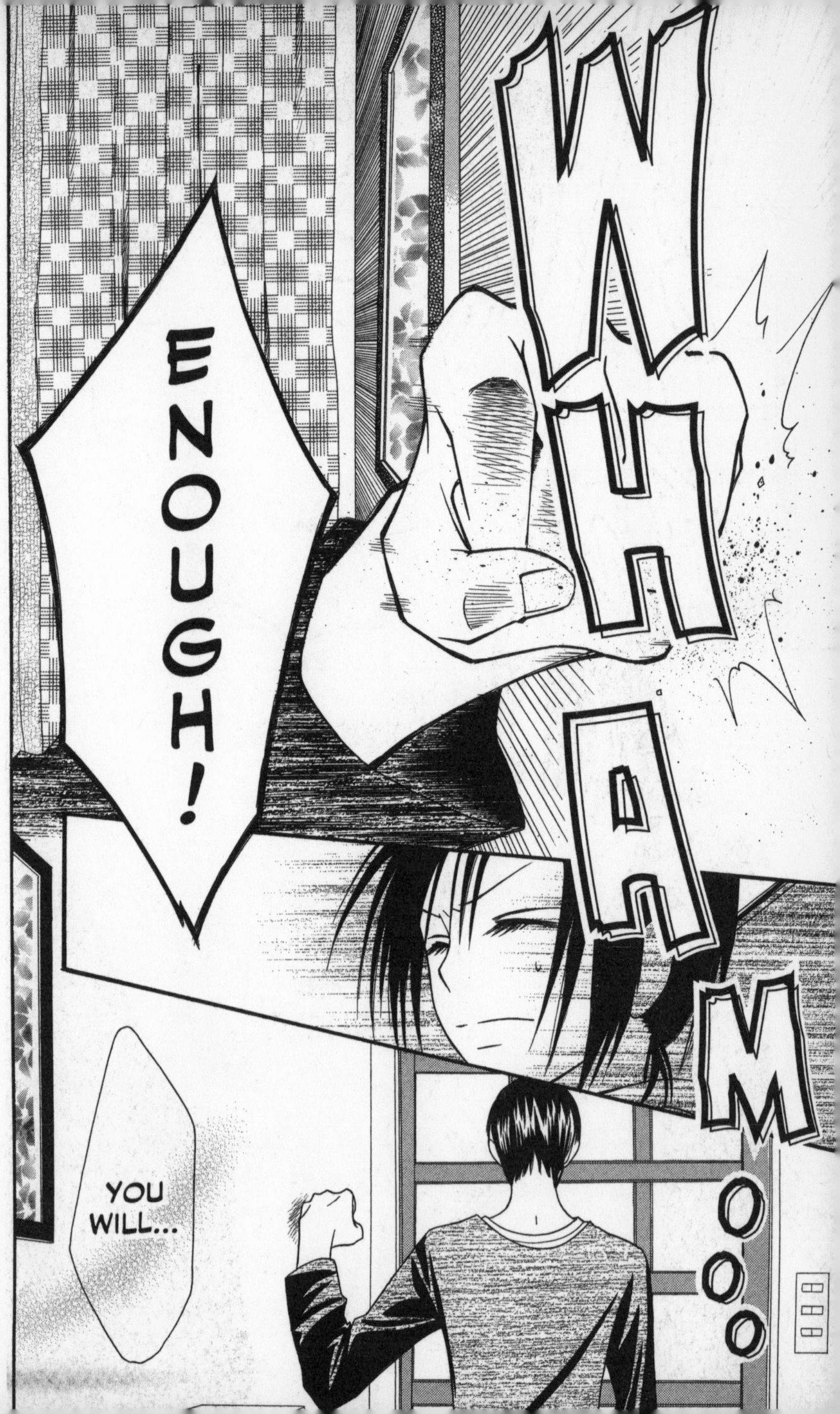
WHAM
ENOUGH!
OOO
YOU WILL...

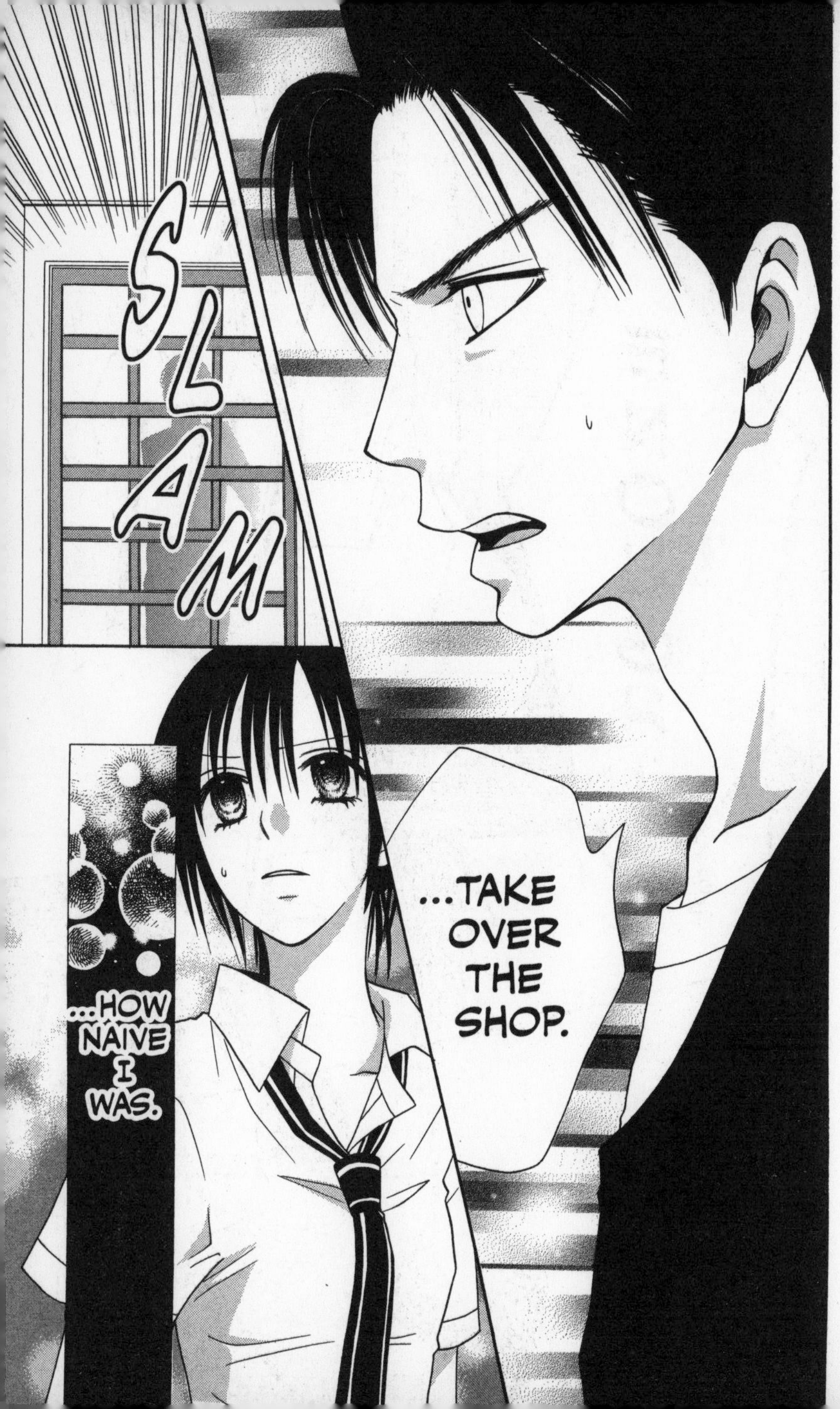
SLAM
...TAKE OVER THE SHOP.
...HOW NAIVE I WAS.

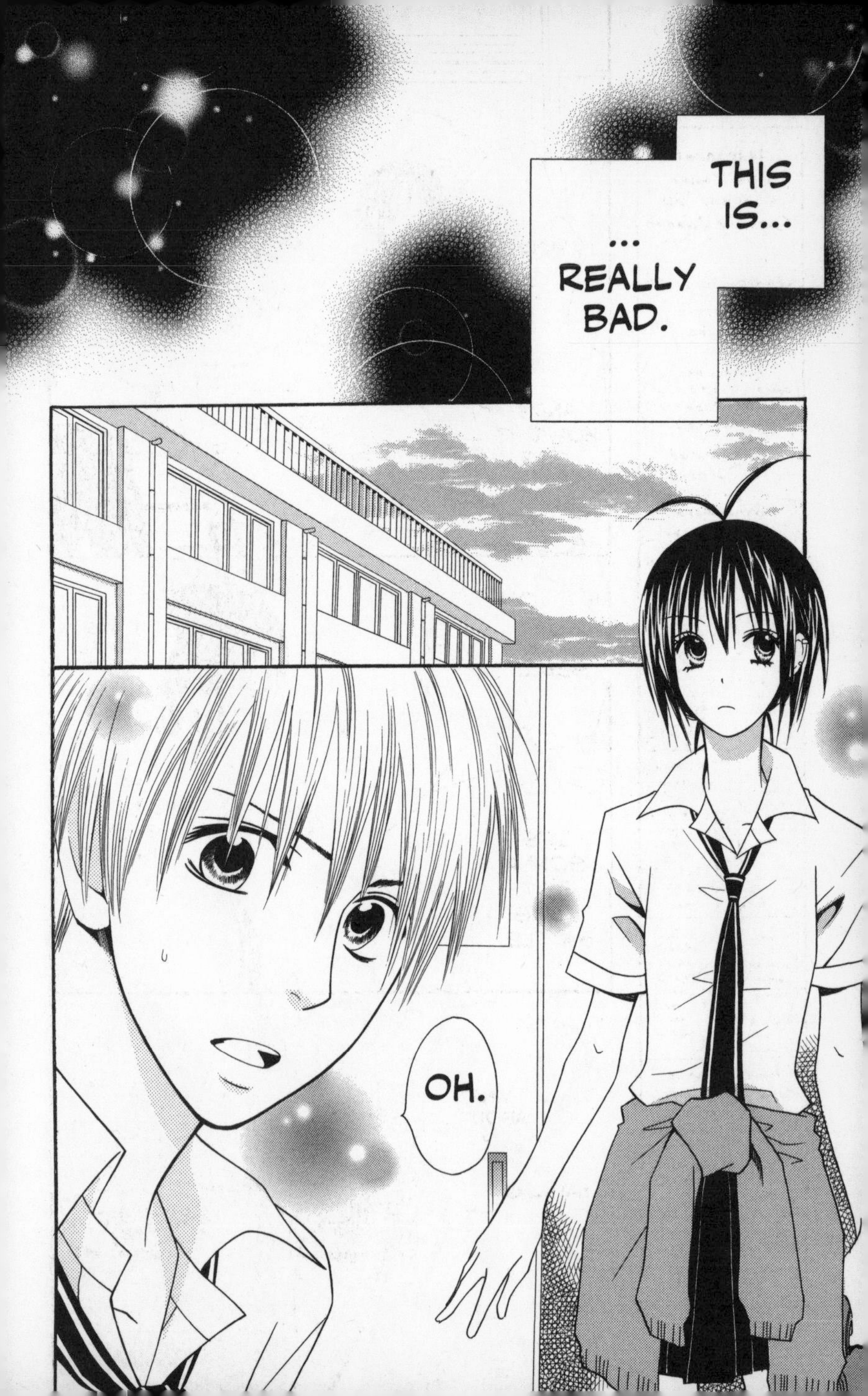
THIS IS...
...REALLY BAD.
OH.

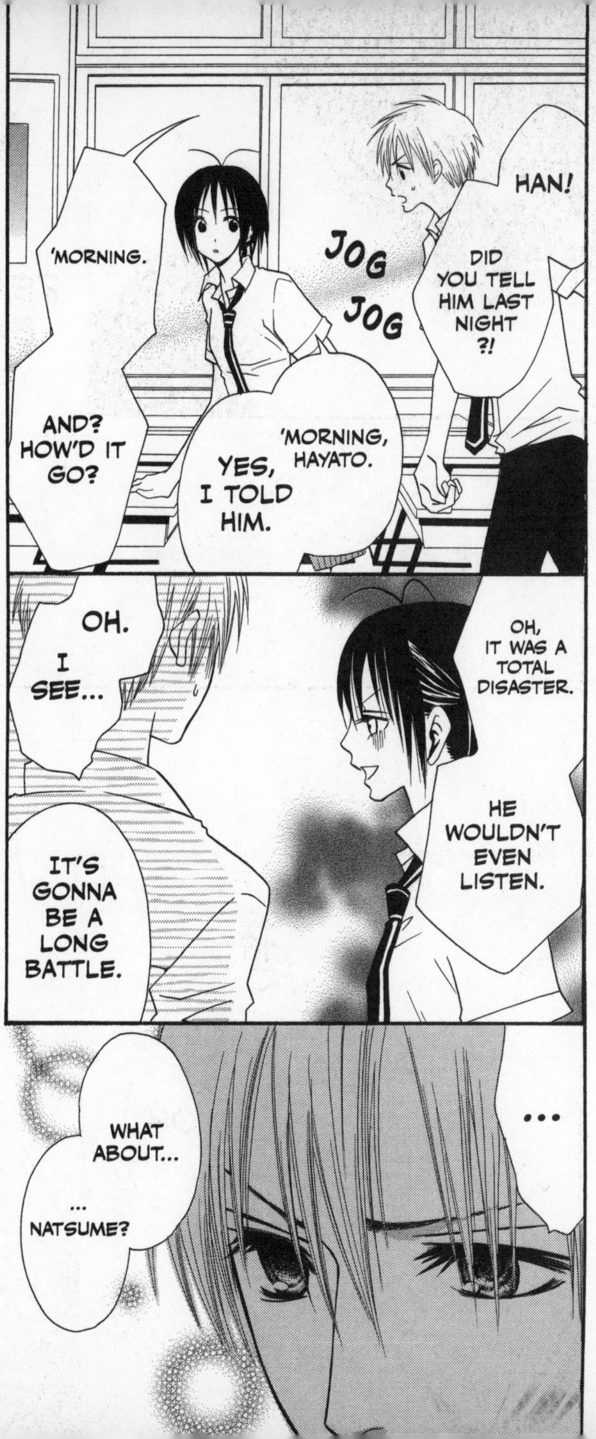
HAN!
DID YOU TELL HIM LAST NIGHT ?!
JOG JOG
'MORNING.
'MORNING, HAYATO.
YES, I TOLD HIM.
AND? HOW'D IT GO?
OH, IT WAS A TOTAL DISASTER.
HE WOULDN'T EVEN LISTEN.
OH.
I SEE...
IT'S GONNA BE A LONG BATTLE.
...
WHAT ABOUT...
... NATSUME?

Margaret New Manga Seminar '06 Seminar Report (?)

February 15, 2006 Seminar in Fukuoka

(Writers and editors get to meet face-to-face for discussions!)

I participated in the sessions.

Furthermore, I was a lecturer!

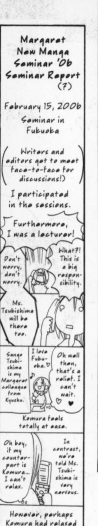

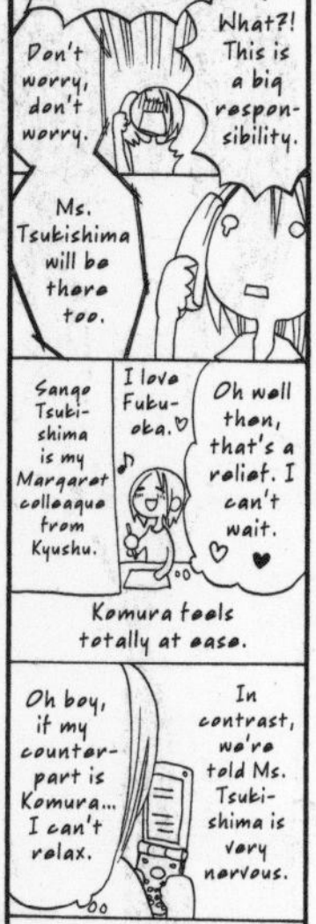
What?! This is a big responsibility.
Don't worry, don't worry.
Ms. Tsukishima will be there too.
Oh well then, that's a relief. I can't wait.
I love Fukuoka.♡
Sango Tsukishima is my Margaret colleague from Kyushu.
Komura feels totally at ease.
In contrast, we're told Ms. Tsukishima is very nervous.
Oh boy, if my counterpart is Komura... I can't relax.

However, perhaps Komura had relaxed too much. She suddenly had a nervous fit the day before departure, and that, combined with the fast-approaching deadline for her manuscript, meant she had to take her work with her to Fukuoka.

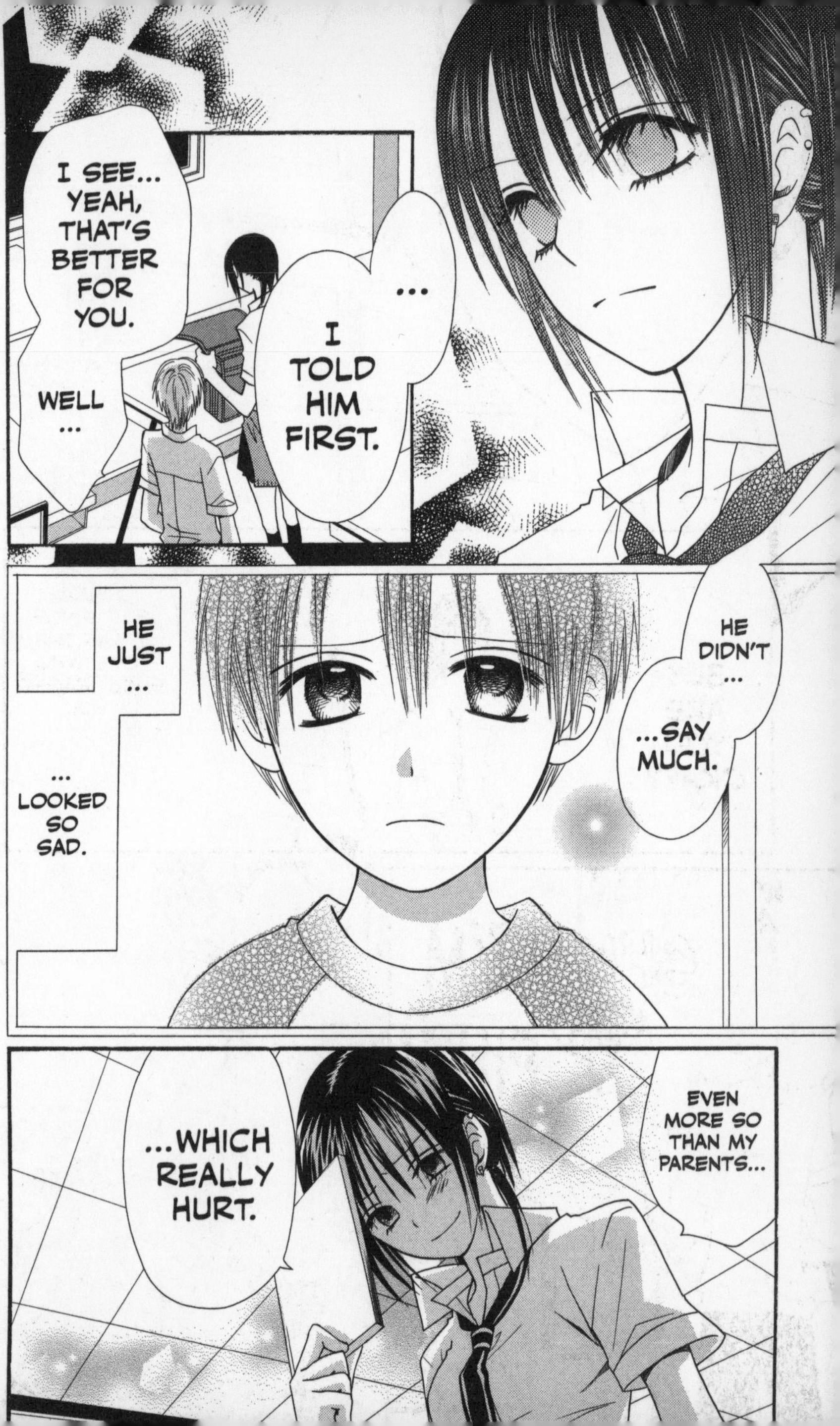
...
I TOLD HIM FIRST.
I SEE... YEAH, THAT'S BETTER FOR YOU.
WELL ...
HE DIDN'T ...
...SAY MUCH.
HE JUST ...
... LOOKED SO SAD.
EVEN MORE SO THAN MY PARENTS...
...WHICH REALLY HURT.

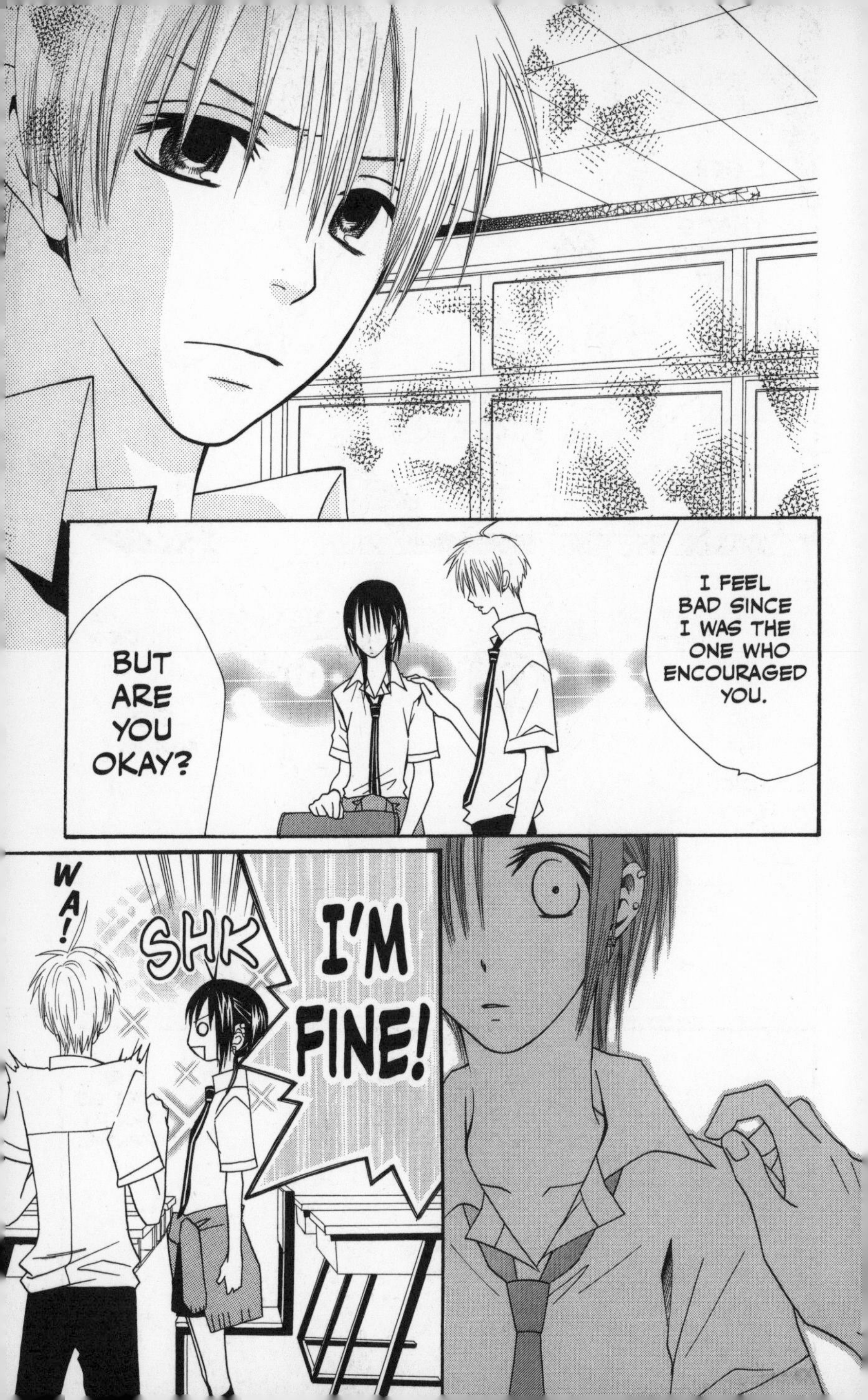

I FEEL BAD SINCE I WAS THE ONE WHO ENCOURAGED YOU.
BUT ARE YOU OKAY?
I'M FINE!
SHK
WA!

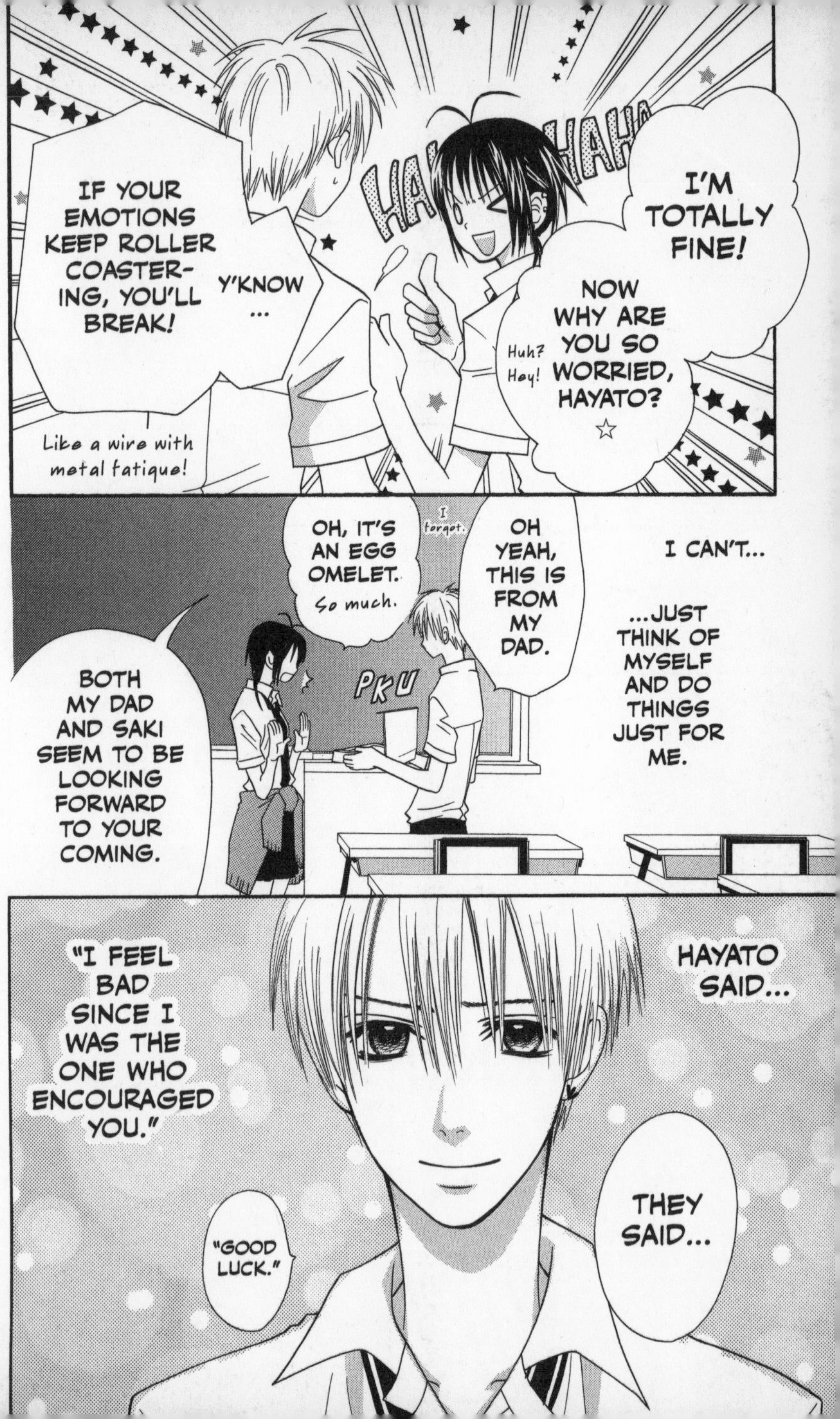
I'M TOTALLY FINE!
HAHAHA
NOW WHY ARE YOU SO WORRIED, HAYATO?
Huh? Hey!
Y'KNOW ...
IF YOUR EMOTIONS KEEP ROLLER COASTER-ING, YOU'LL BREAK!
Like a wire with metal fatique!
I CAN'T...
...JUST THINK OF MYSELF AND DO THINGS JUST FOR ME.
OH YEAH, THIS IS FROM MY DAD.
I forgot.
OH, IT'S AN EGG OMELET.
So much.
PKU
BOTH MY DAD AND SAKI SEEM TO BE LOOKING FORWARD TO YOUR COMING.
HAYATO SAID...
"I FEEL BAD SINCE I WAS THE ONE WHO ENCOURAGED YOU."
THEY SAID...
"GOOD LUCK."

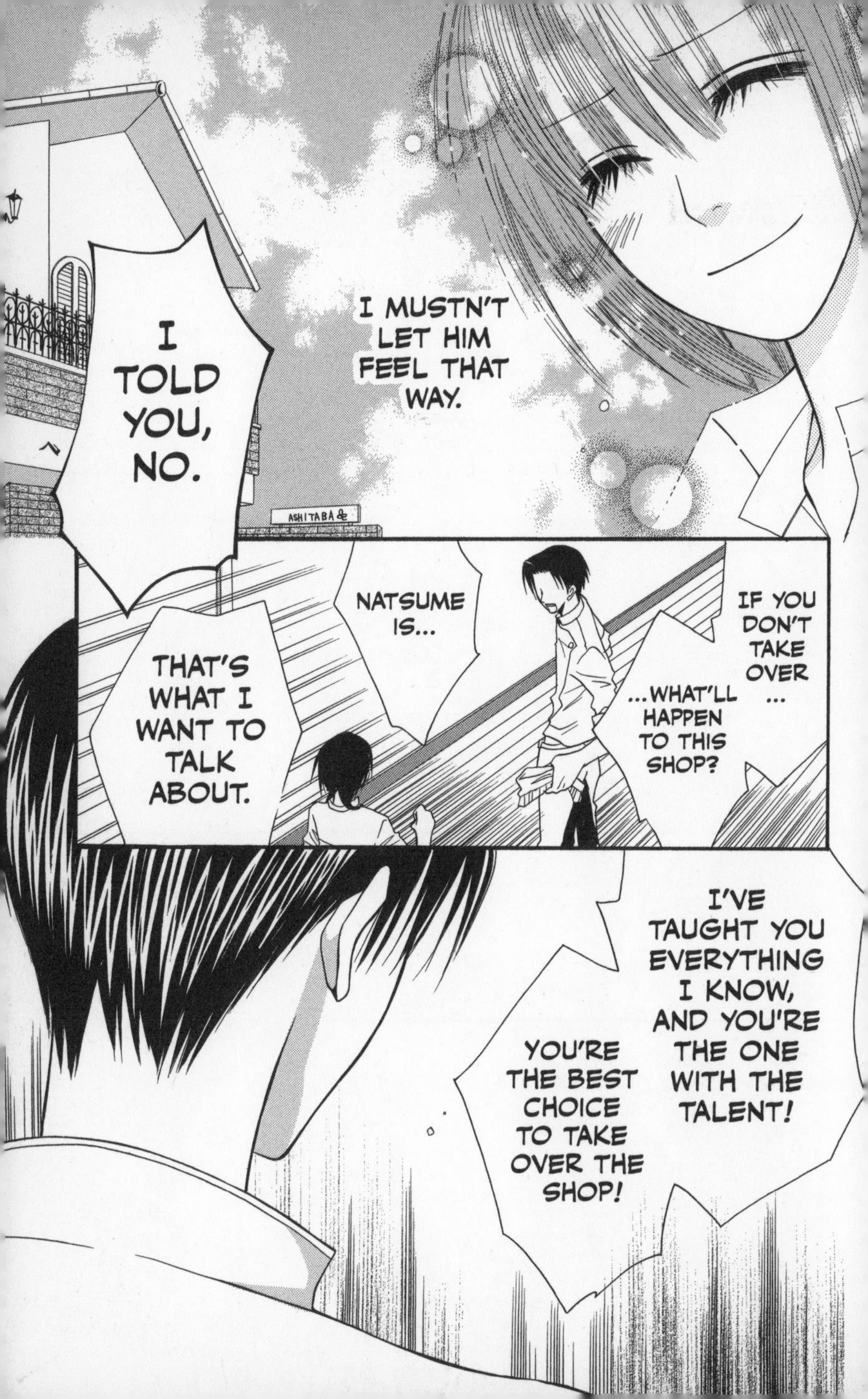
I MUSTN'T LET HIM FEEL THAT WAY.
ASHITABA
I TOLD YOU, NO.
IF YOU DON'T TAKE OVER ...
...WHAT'LL HAPPEN TO THIS SHOP?
NATSUME IS...
THAT'S WHAT I WANT TO TALK ABOUT.
I'VE TAUGHT YOU EVERYTHING I KNOW, AND YOU'RE THE ONE WITH THE TALENT!
YOU'RE THE BEST CHOICE TO TAKE OVER THE SHOP!

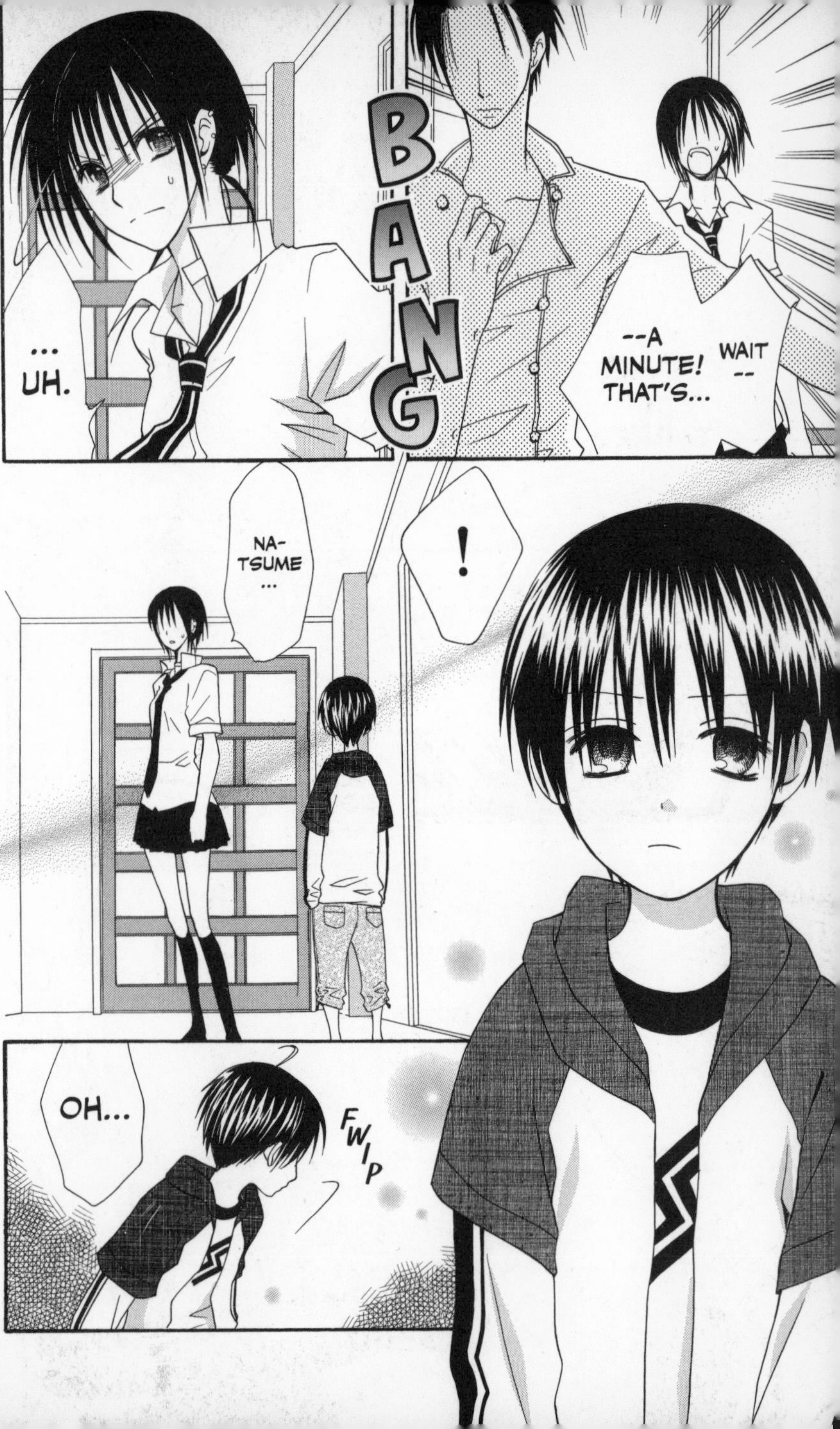
WAIT --
--A MINUTE! THAT'S...
BANG
... UH.
!
NA-TSUME ...
OH...
FWIP

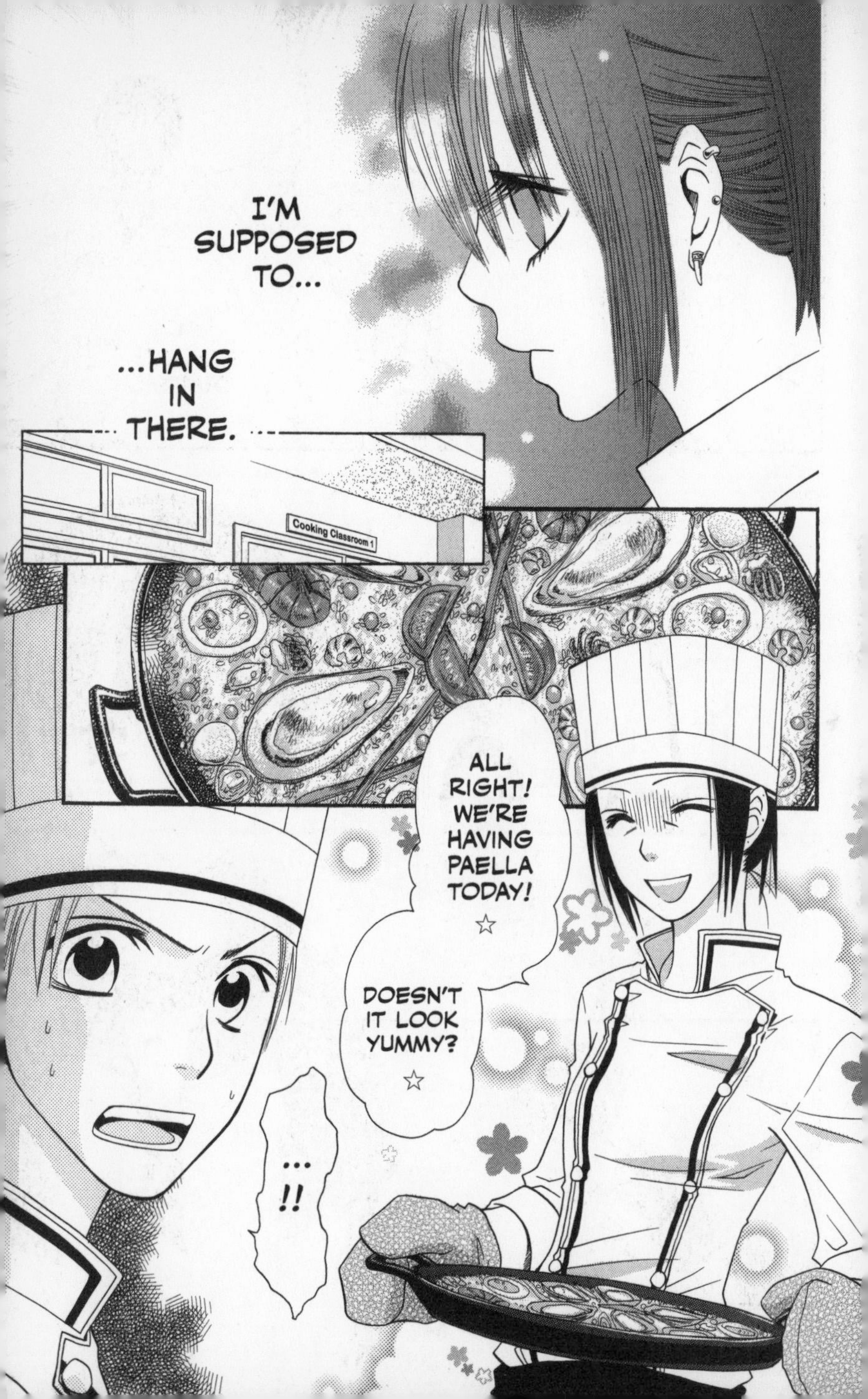
I'M SUPPOSED TO...
...HANG IN THERE.
Cooking Classroom 1
ALL RIGHT! WE'RE HAVING PAELLA TODAY! ☆
DOESN'T IT LOOK YUMMY? ☆
...!!

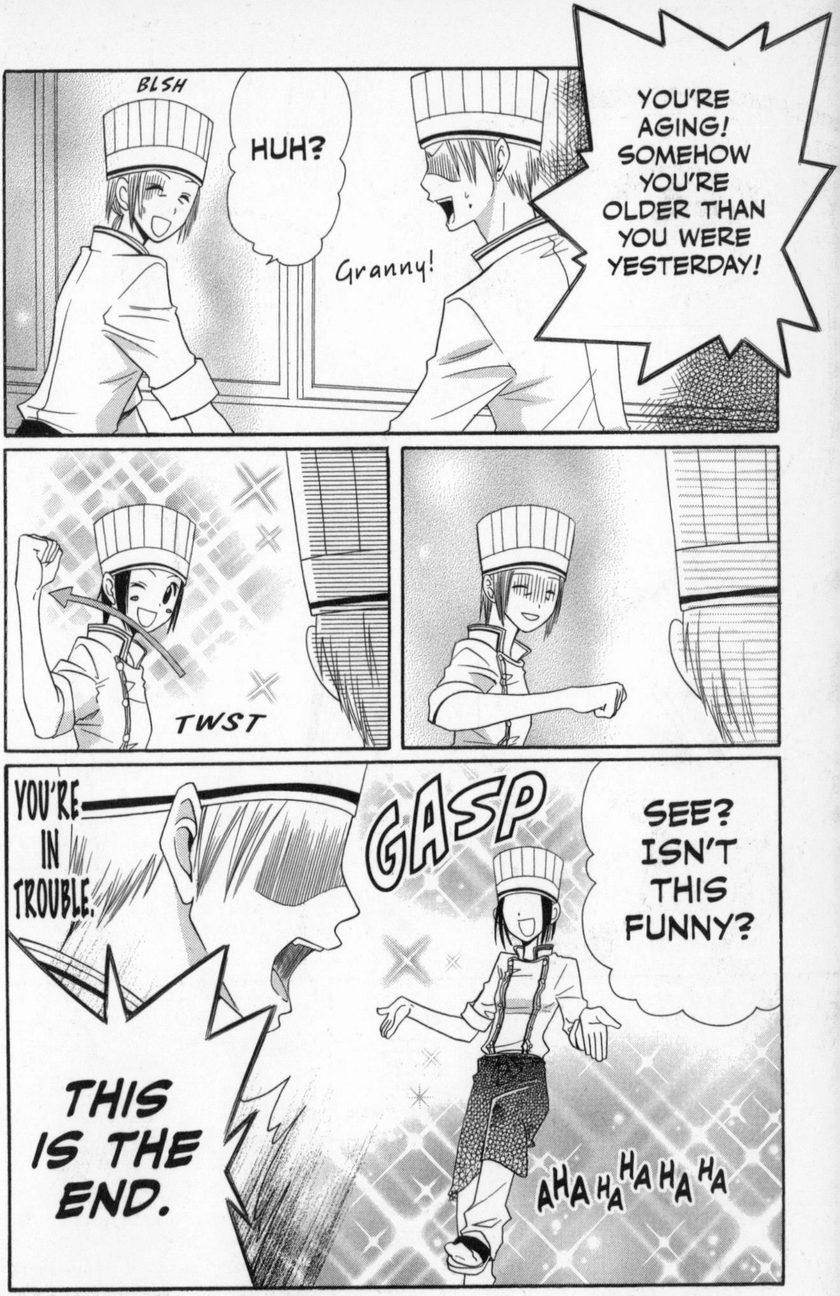
YOU'RE AGING! SOMEHOW YOU'RE OLDER THAN YOU WERE YESTERDAY!
Granny!
HUH?
BLSH
TWST
SEE? ISN'T THIS FUNNY?
GASP
YOU'RE IN TROUBLE.
AHA HA HA HA HA HA
THIS IS THE END.

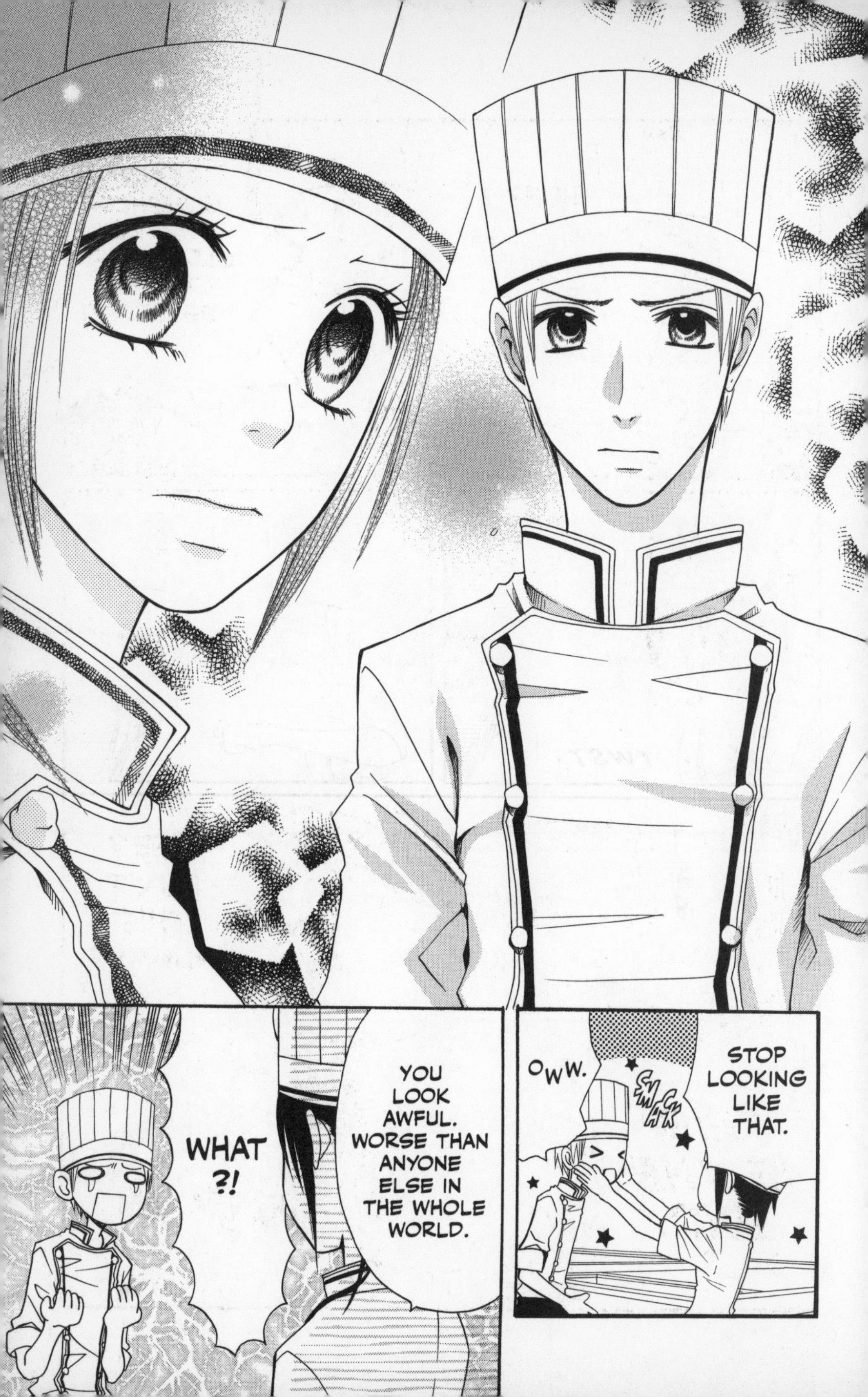
STOP LOOKING LIKE THAT.
SMACK
OWW.
YOU LOOK AWFUL. WORSE THAN ANYONE ELSE IN THE WHOLE WORLD.
WHAT?!

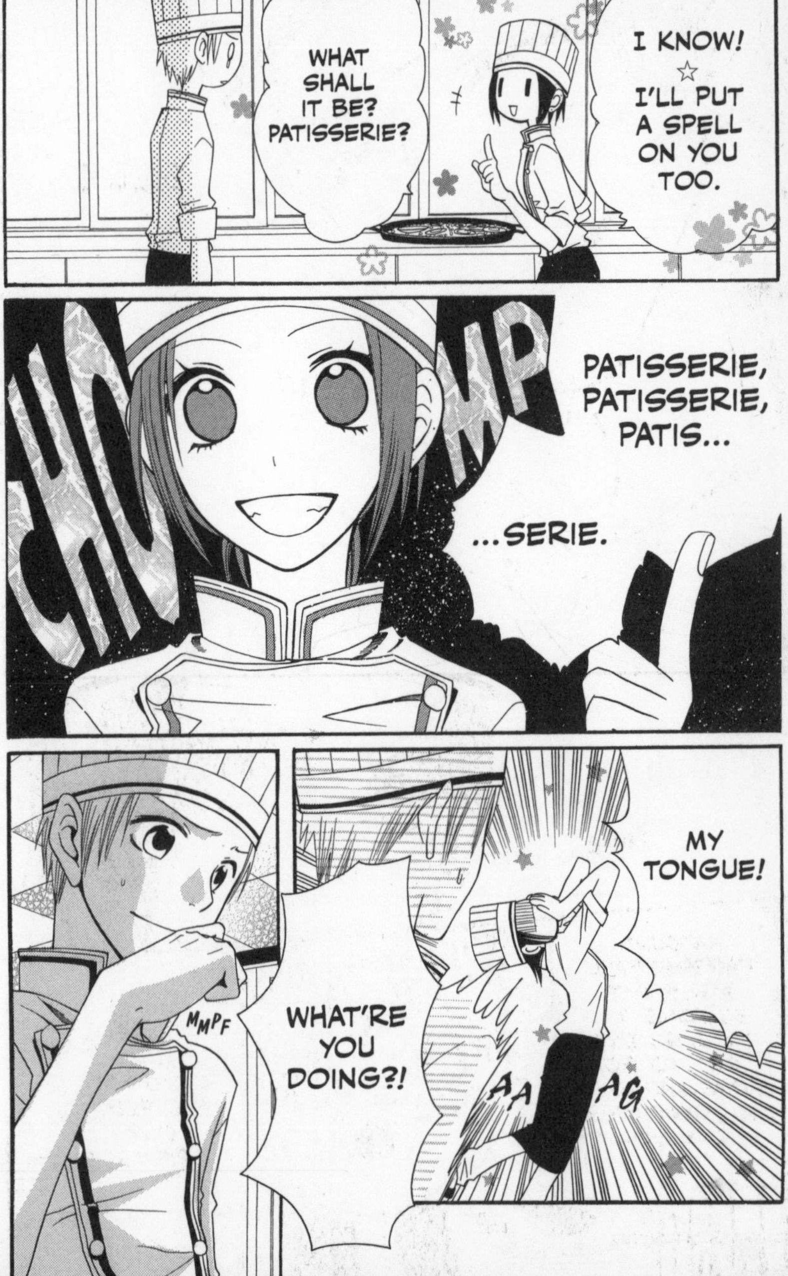
I KNOW! ☆ I'LL PUT A SPELL ON YOU TOO.
WHAT SHALL IT BE? PATISSERIE?
CHOMP
PATISSERIE, PATISSERIE, PATIS...
...SERIE.
MY TONGUE!
AAAG
WHAT'RE YOU DOING?!
MMPF

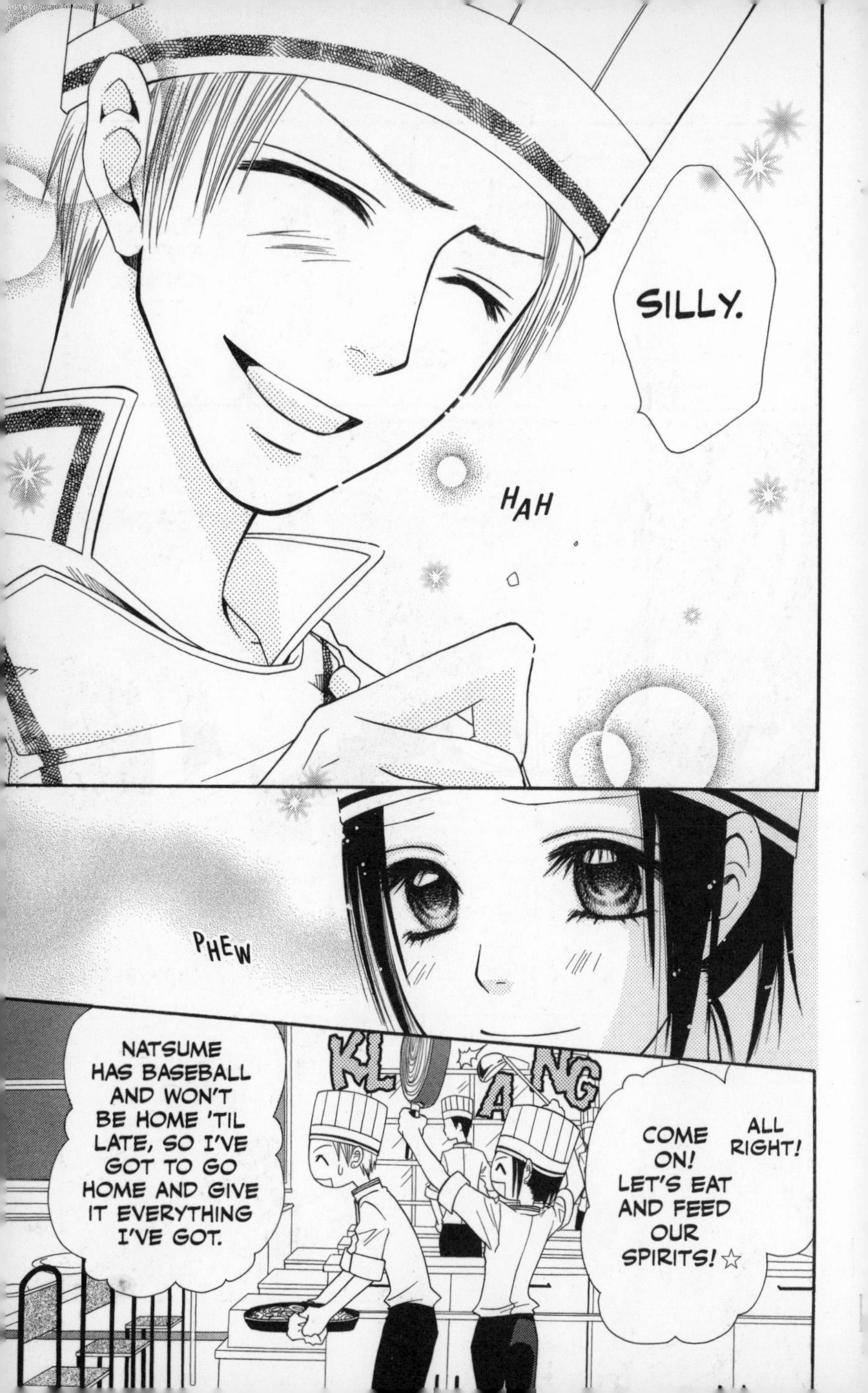
SILLY.
HAH
PHEW
KLANG
ALL RIGHT!
COME ON! LET'S EAT AND FEED OUR SPIRITS! ☆
NATSUME HAS BASEBALL AND WON'T BE HOME 'TIL LATE, SO I'VE GOT TO GO HOME AND GIVE IT EVERYTHING I'VE GOT.

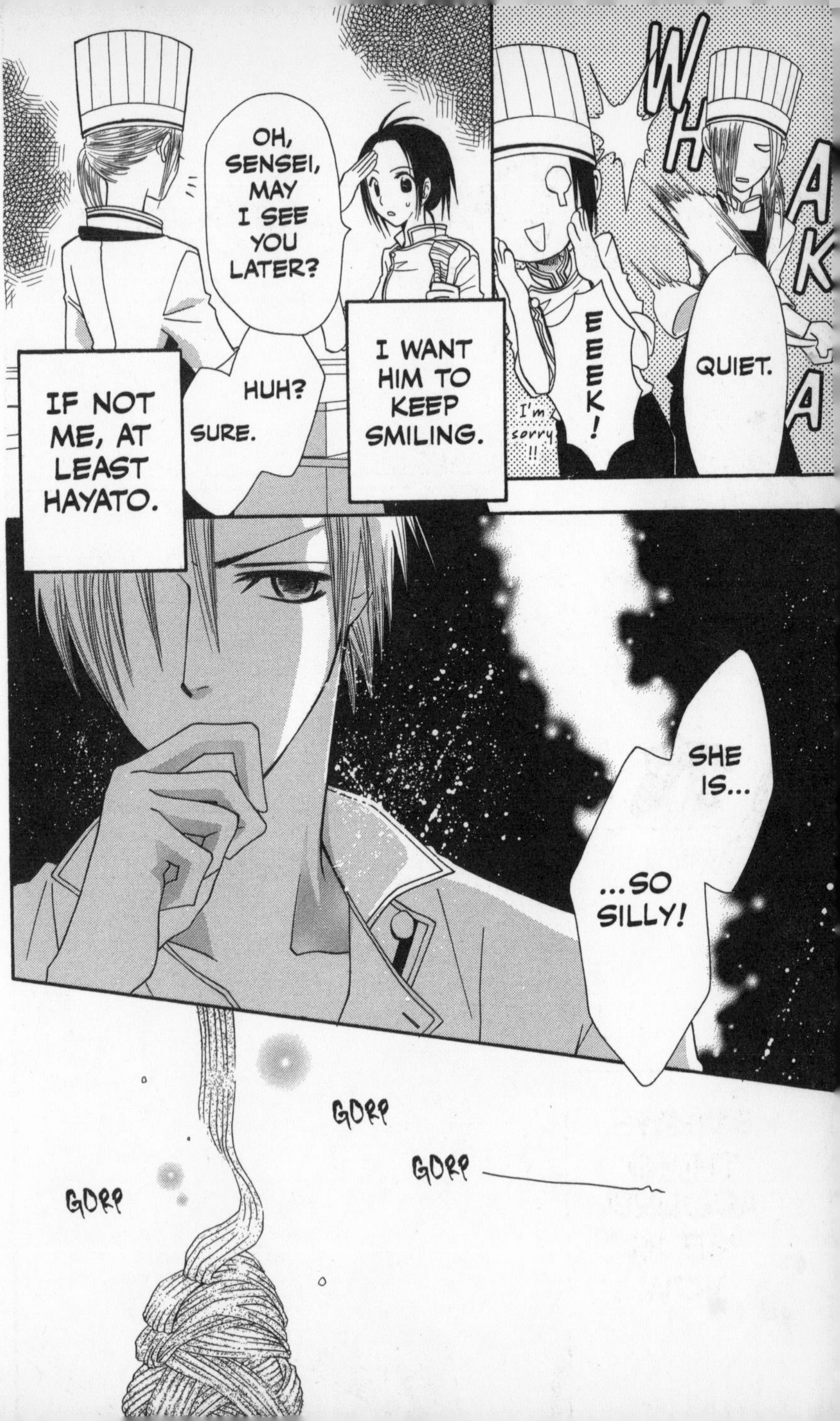
WHAKA
QUIET.
EEEK!
I'm sorry!!
OH, SENSEI, MAY I SEE YOU LATER?
HUH? SURE.
I WANT HIM TO KEEP SMILING.
IF NOT ME, AT LEAST HAYATO.
SHE IS...
...SO SILLY!
GORP
GORP
GORP

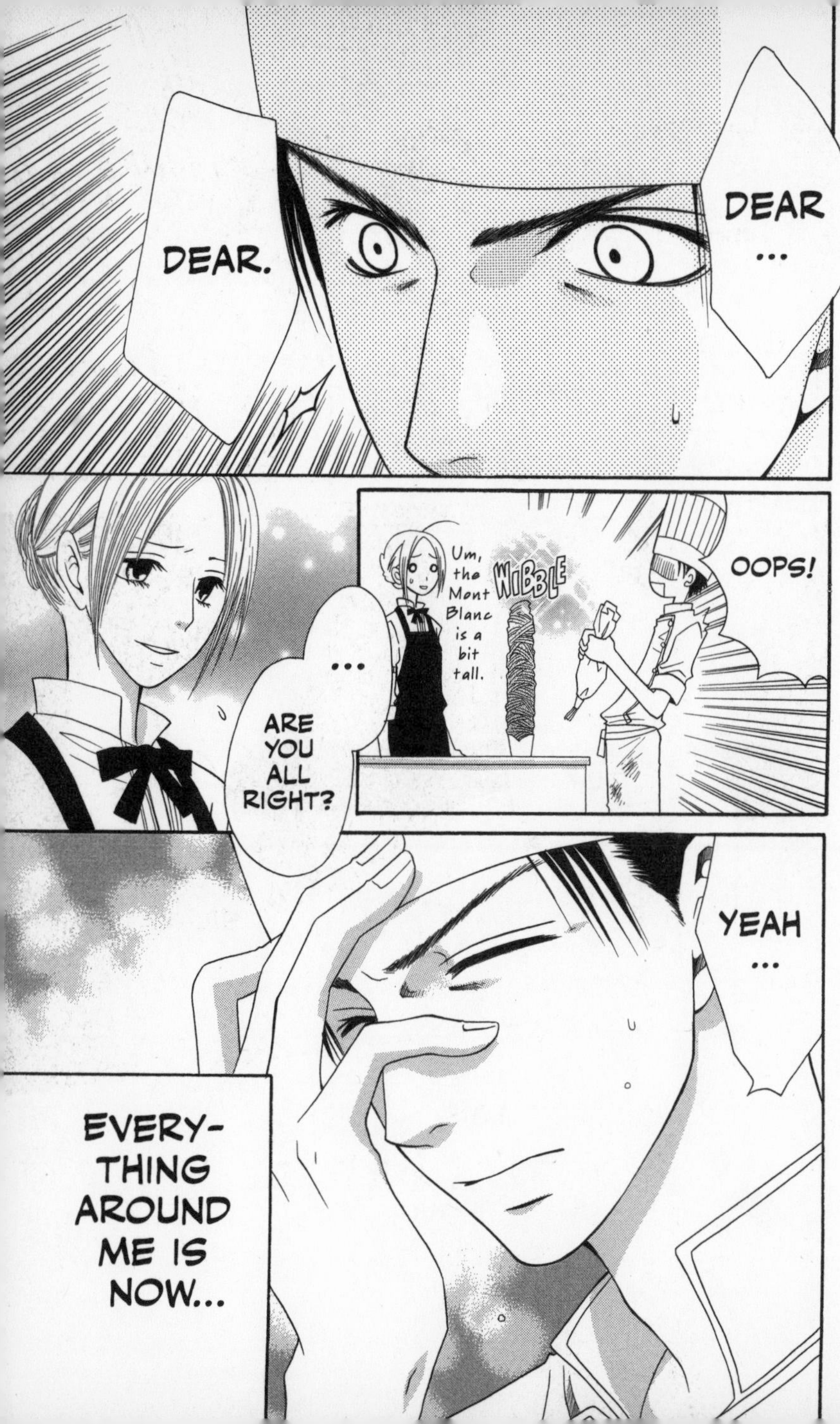
DEAR ...
DEAR.
OOPS!
WIBBLE
Um, the Mont Blanc is a bit tall.
... ARE YOU ALL RIGHT?
YEAH ...
EVERY-THING AROUND ME IS NOW...

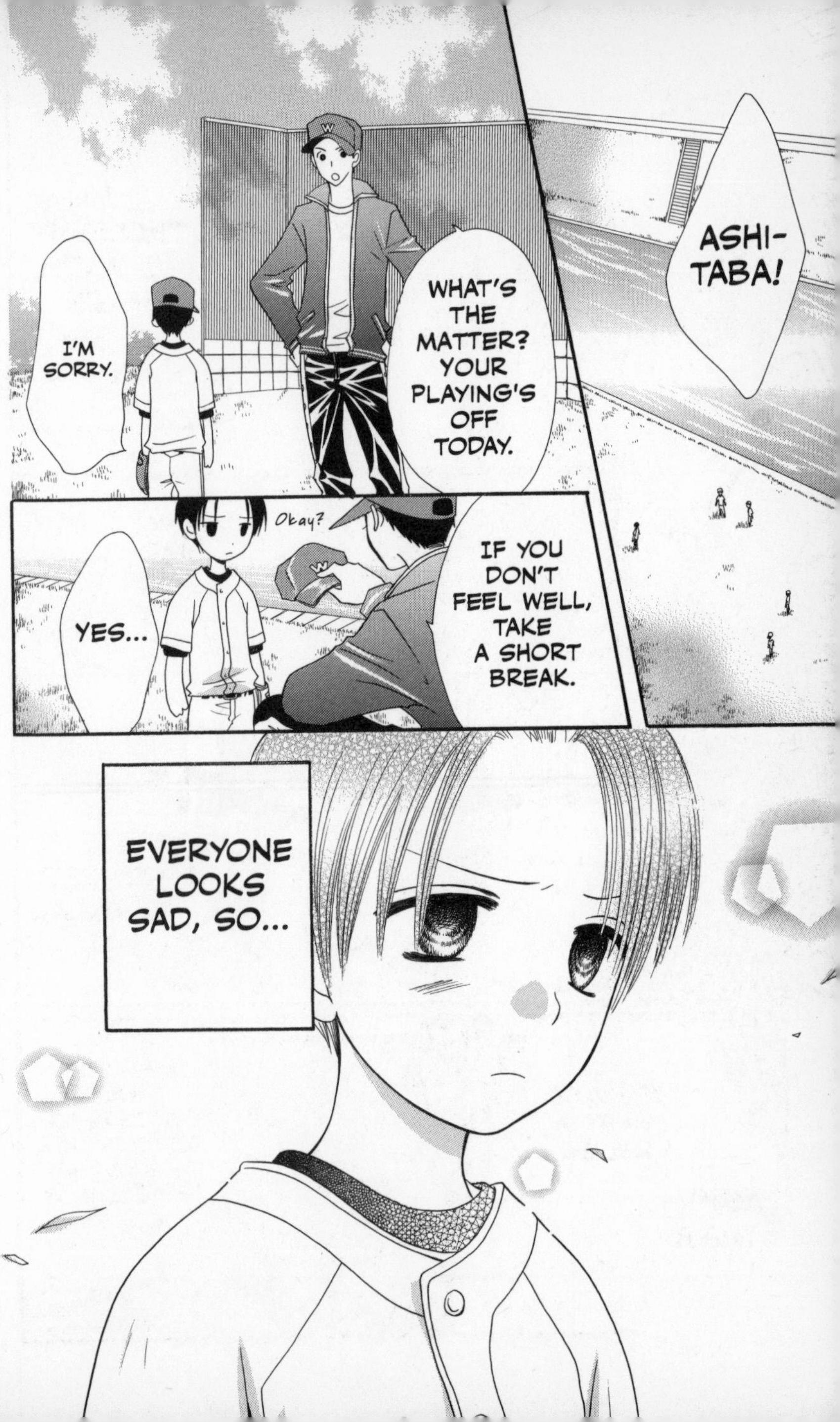
ASHI-TABA!
WHAT'S THE MATTER? YOUR PLAYING'S OFF TODAY.
I'M SORRY.
IF YOU DON'T FEEL WELL, TAKE A SHORT BREAK.
Okay?
YES...
EVERYONE LOOKS SAD, SO...

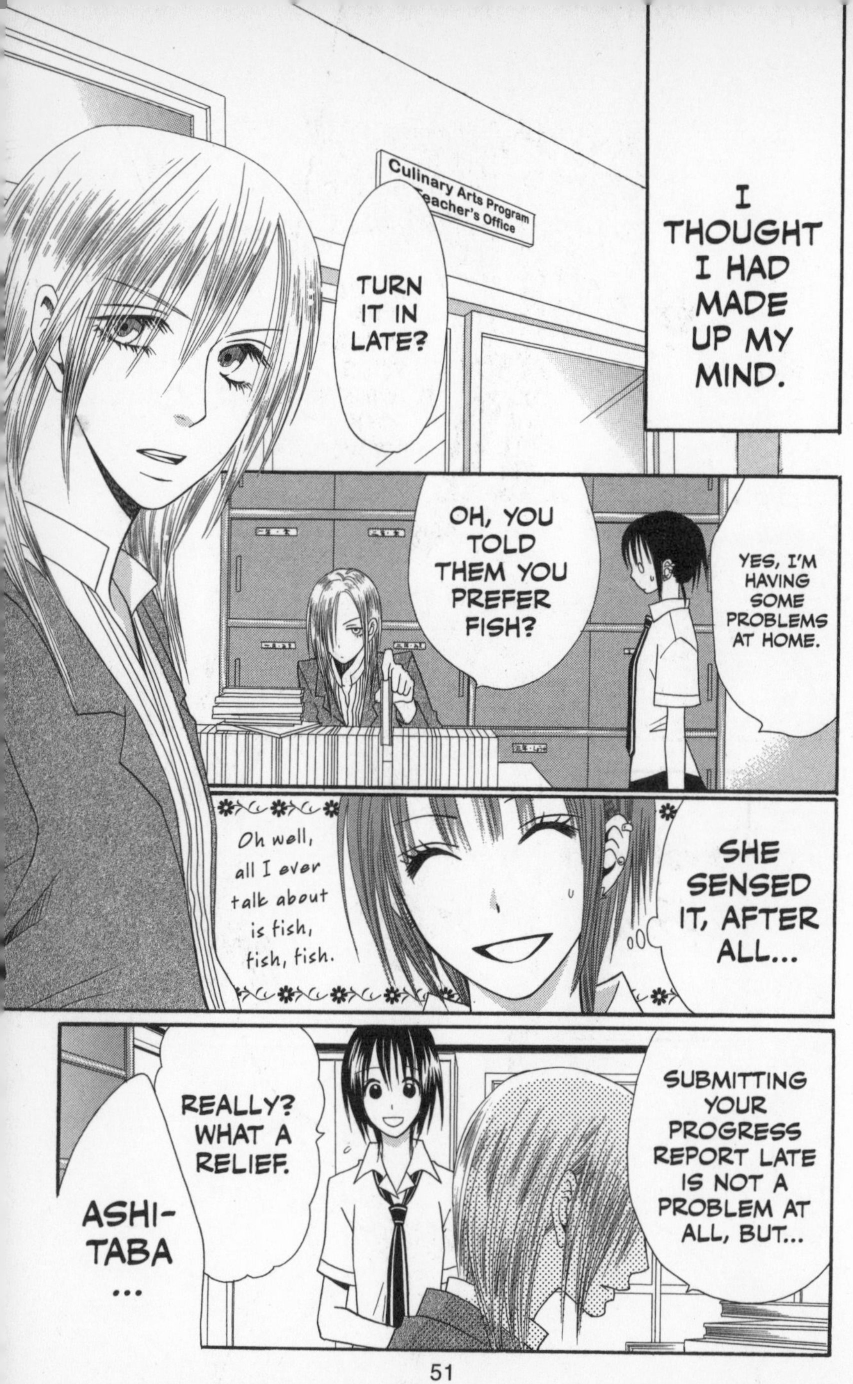
I THOUGHT I HAD MADE UP MY MIND.
Culinary Arts Program Teacher's Office
TURN IT IN LATE?
YES, I'M HAVING SOME PROBLEMS AT HOME.
OH, YOU TOLD THEM YOU PREFER FISH?
SHE SENSED IT, AFTER ALL...
Oh well, all I ever talk about is fish, fish, fish.
SUBMITTING YOUR PROGRESS REPORT LATE IS NOT A PROBLEM AT ALL, BUT...
REALLY? WHAT A RELIEF.
ASHI-TABA...

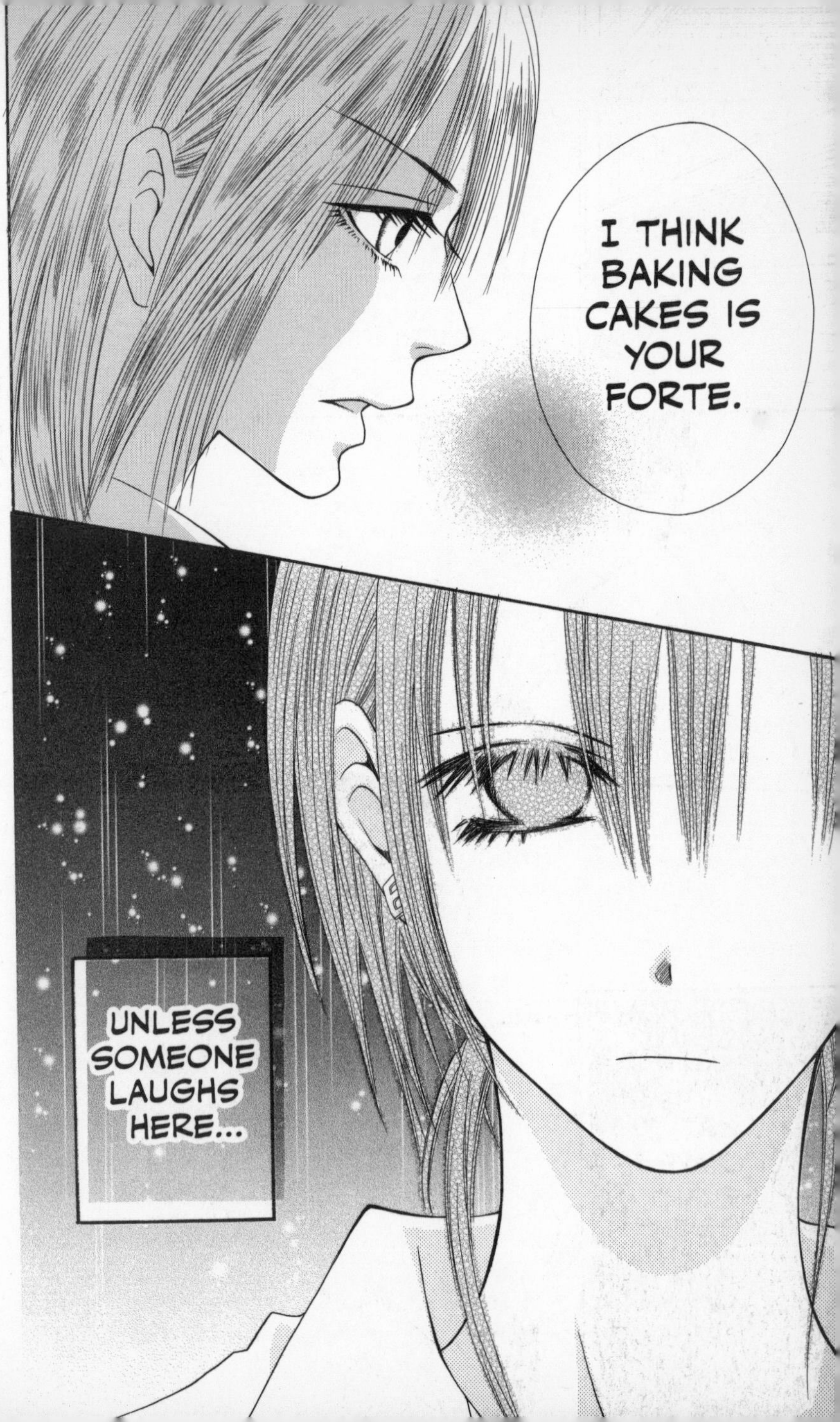
I THINK BAKING CAKES IS YOUR FORTE.
UNLESS SOMEONE LAUGHS HERE...

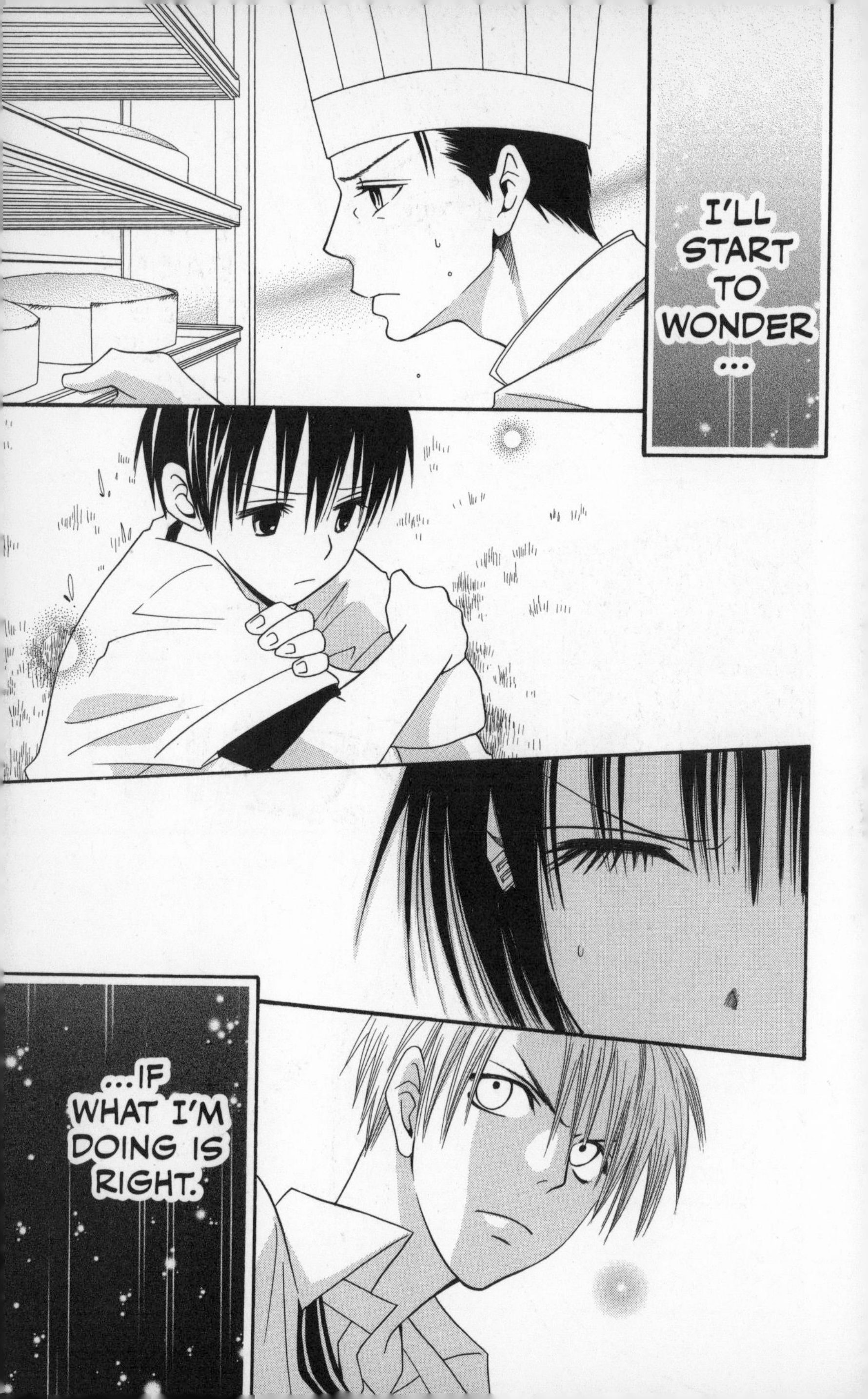
I'LL START TO WONDER...
...IF WHAT I'M DOING IS RIGHT.

SIDE DISH Mixed Vegetables 2

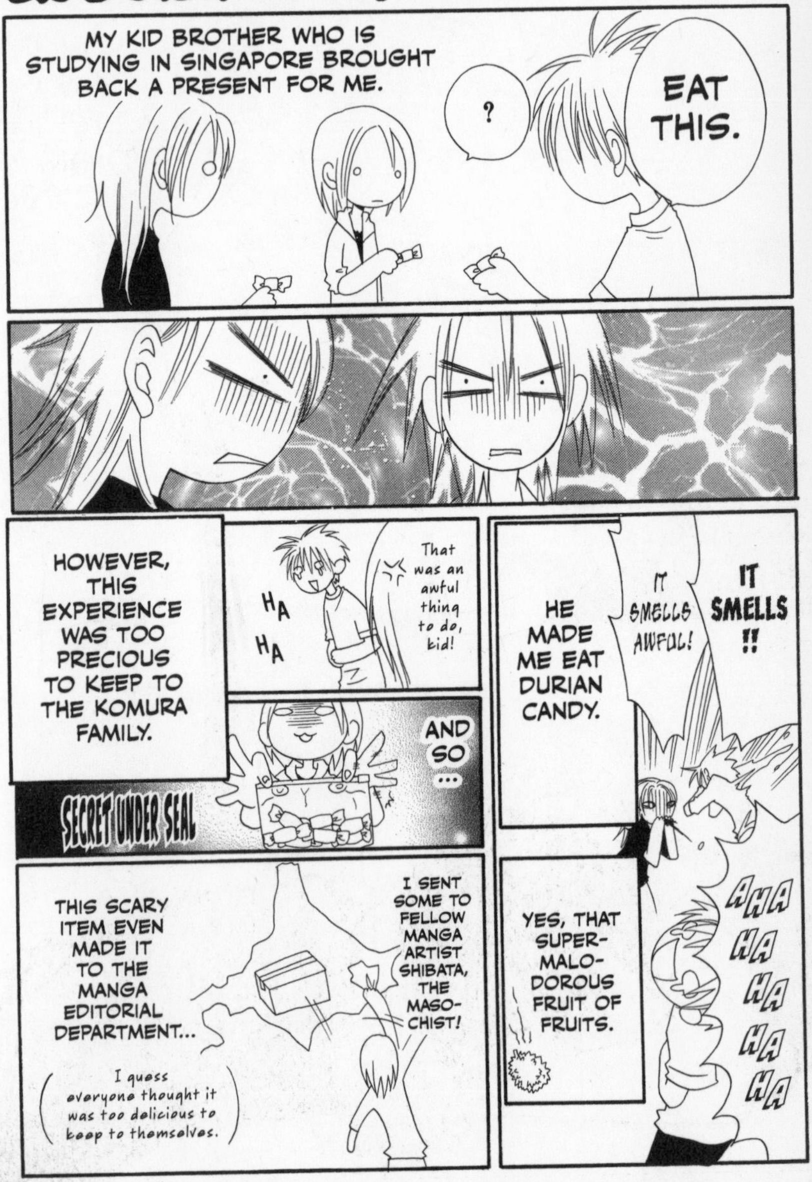

EAT THIS.
?
MY KID BROTHER WHO IS STUDYING IN SINGAPORE BROUGHT BACK A PRESENT FOR ME.
IT SMELLS !!
IT SMELLS AWFUL!
HE MADE ME EAT DURIAN CANDY.
That was an awful thing to do, kid!
HA HA
HOWEVER, THIS EXPERIENCE WAS TOO PRECIOUS TO KEEP TO THE KOMURA FAMILY.
AND SO ...
SECRET UNDER SEAL
AHAHA HA HA HA HA
YES, THAT SUPER-MALO-DOROUS FRUIT OF FRUITS.
I SENT SOME TO FELLOW MANGA ARTIST SHIBATA, THE MASO-CHIST!
THIS SCARY ITEM EVEN MADE IT TO THE MANGA EDITORIAL DEPARTMENT...
(I guess everyone thought it was too delicious to keep to themselves.)

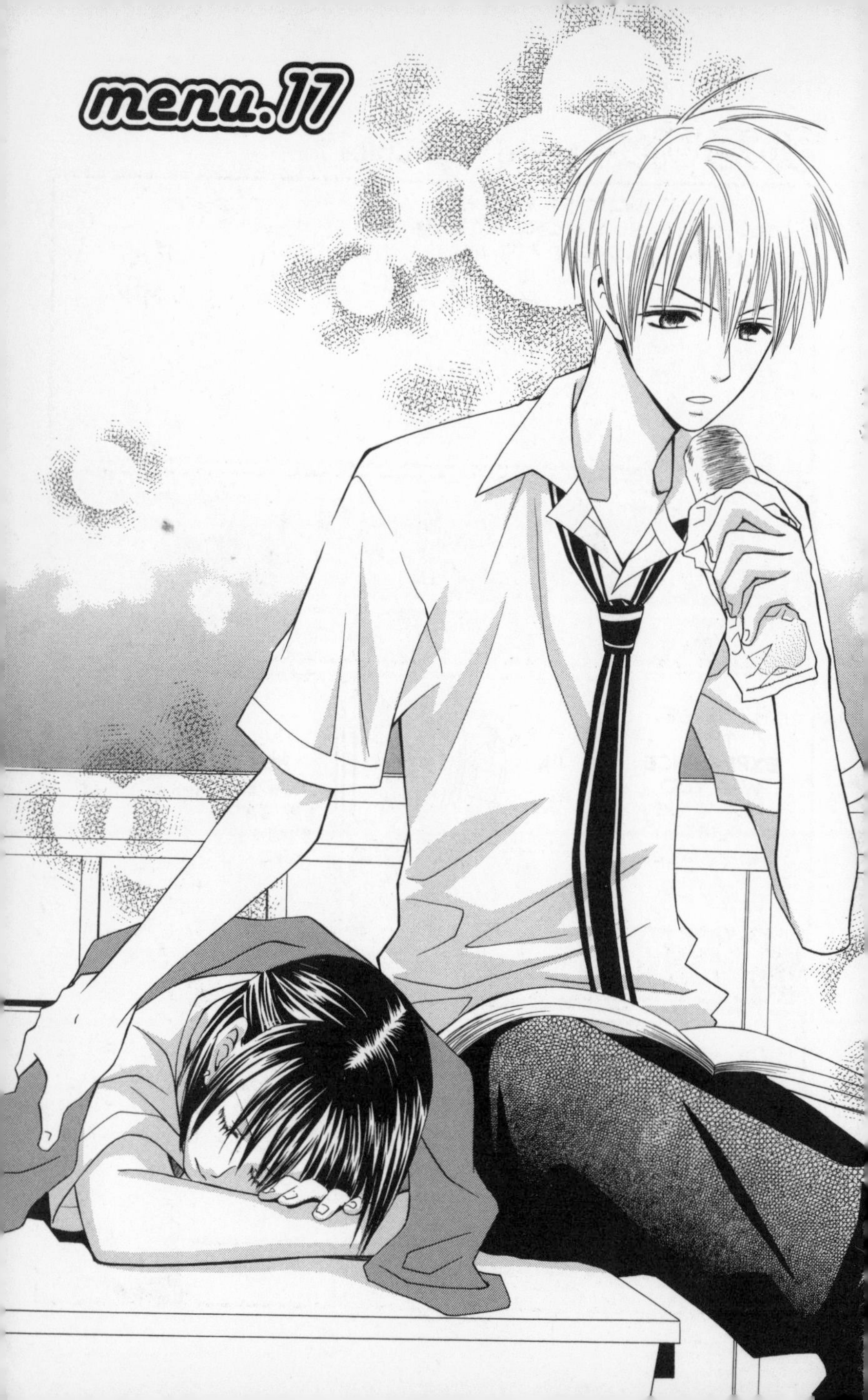
menu.17

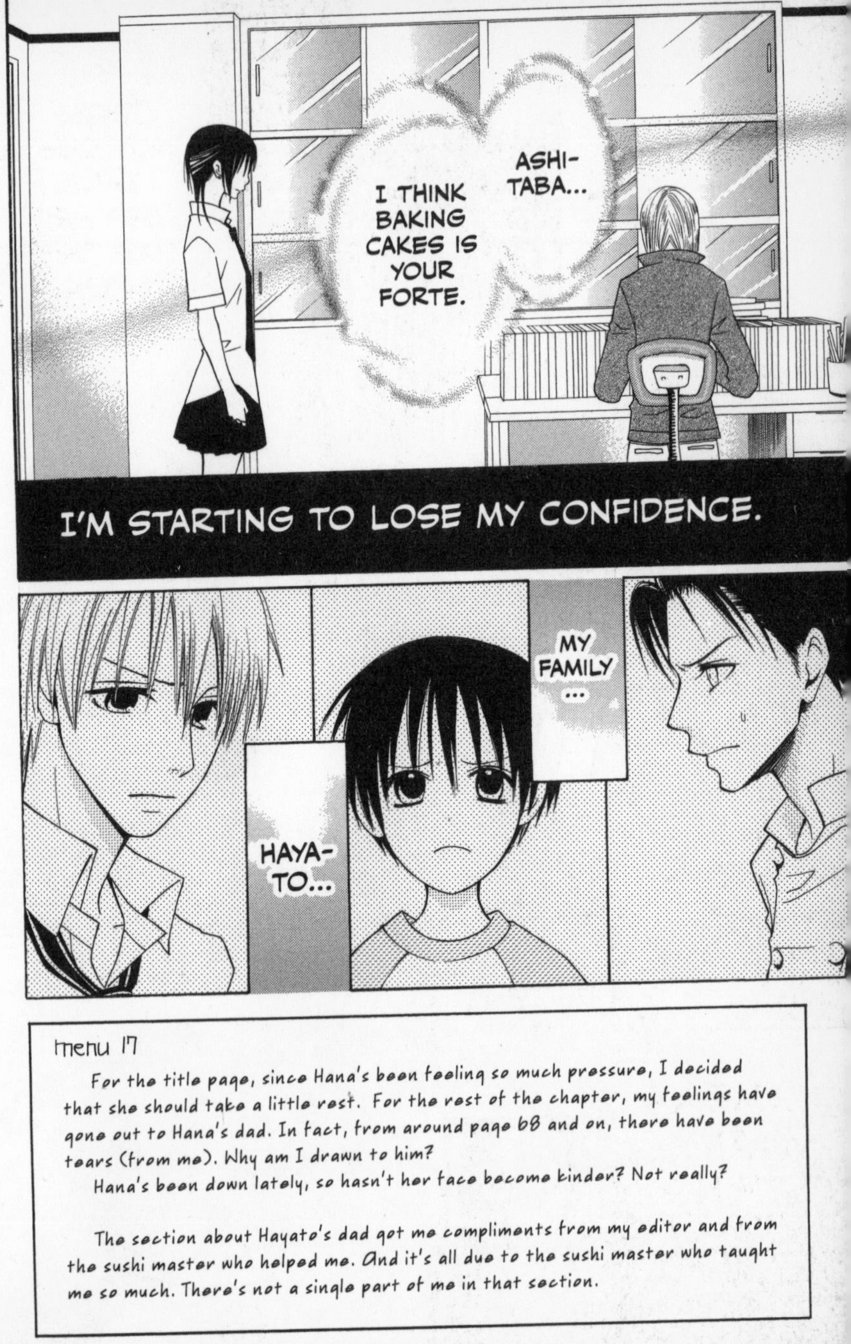
ASHI-TABA...
I THINK BAKING CAKES IS YOUR FORTE.
I'M STARTING TO LOSE MY CONFIDENCE.
MY FAMILY ...
HAYA-TO...

menu 17

For the title page, since Hana's been feeling so much pressure, I decided that she should take a little rest. For the rest of the chapter, my feelings have gone out to Hana's dad. In fact, from around page 68 and on, there have been tears (from me). Why am I drawn to him?

Hana's been down lately, so hasn't her face become kinder? Not really?

The section about Hayato's dad got me compliments from my editor and from the sushi master who helped me. And it's all due to the sushi master who taught me so much. There's not a single part of me in that section.

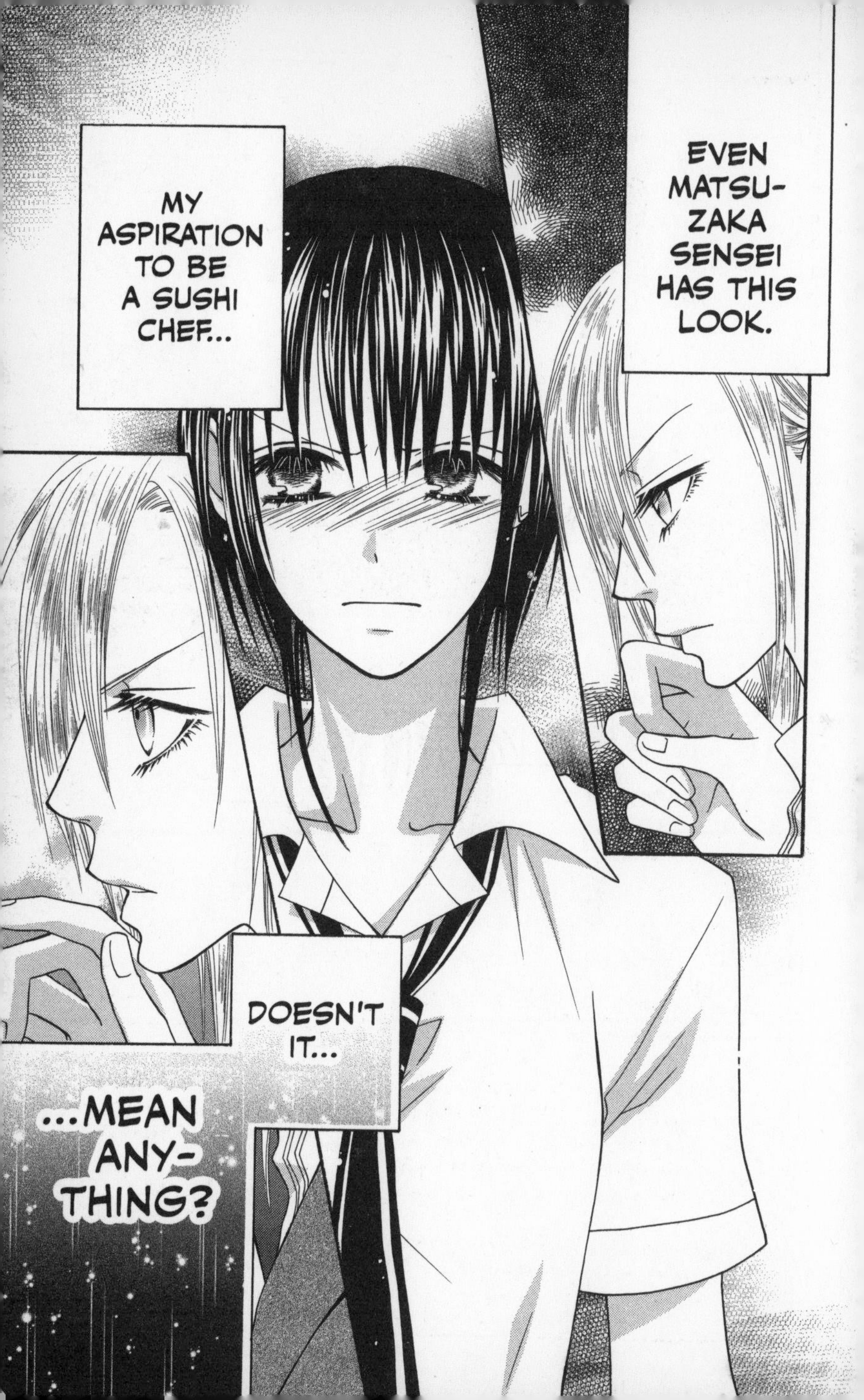
EVEN MATSU-ZAKA SENSEI HAS THIS LOOK.
MY ASPIRATION TO BE A SUSHI CHEF...
DOESN'T IT...
...MEAN ANY-THING?

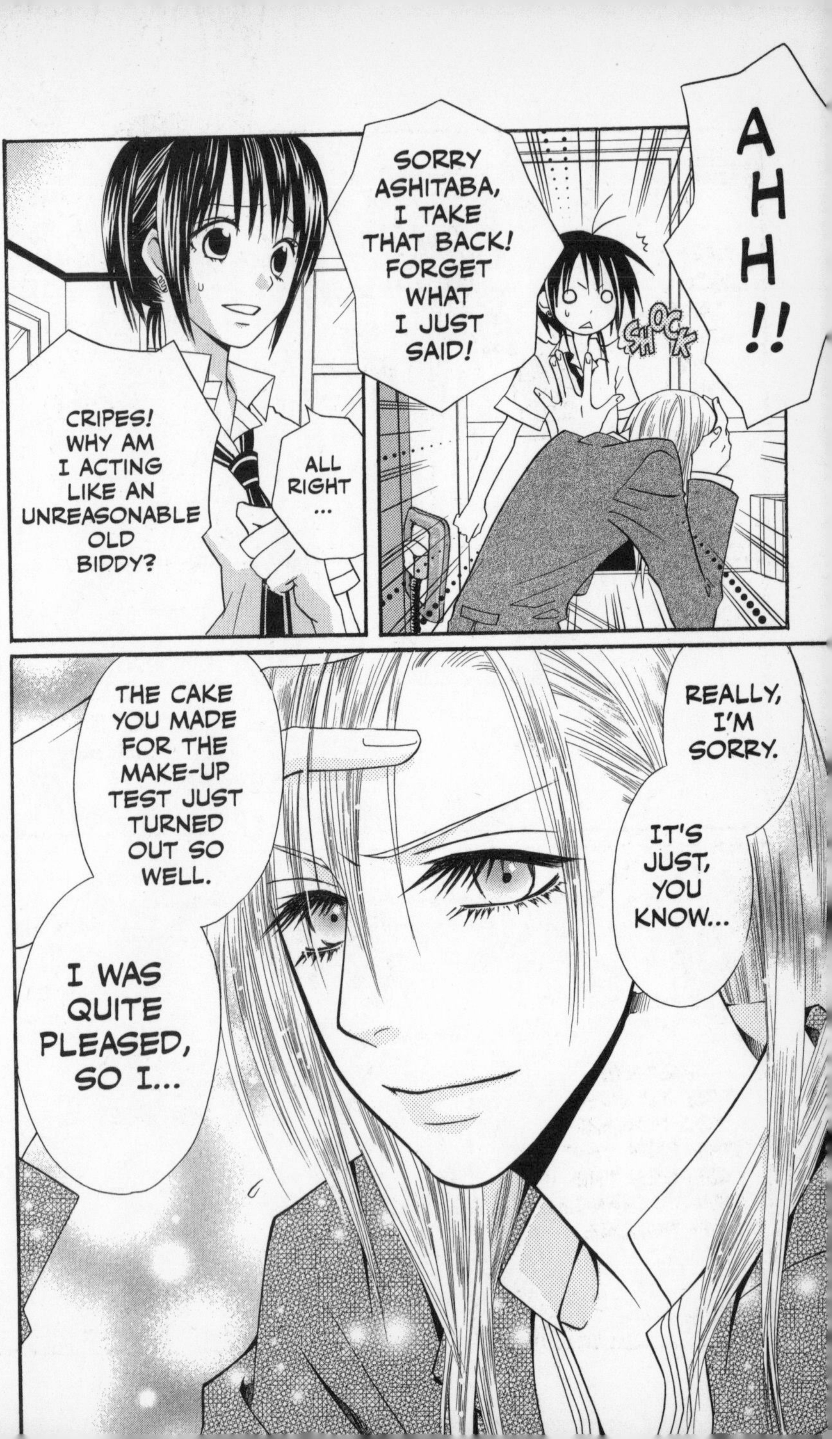
AHH!!
SORRY ASHITABA, I TAKE THAT BACK! FORGET WHAT I JUST SAID!
SHOCK
ALL RIGHT ...
CRIPES! WHY AM I ACTING LIKE AN UNREASONABLE OLD BIDDY?
REALLY, I'M SORRY.
IT'S JUST, YOU KNOW...
THE CAKE YOU MADE FOR THE MAKE-UP TEST JUST TURNED OUT SO WELL.
I WAS QUITE PLEASED, SO I...

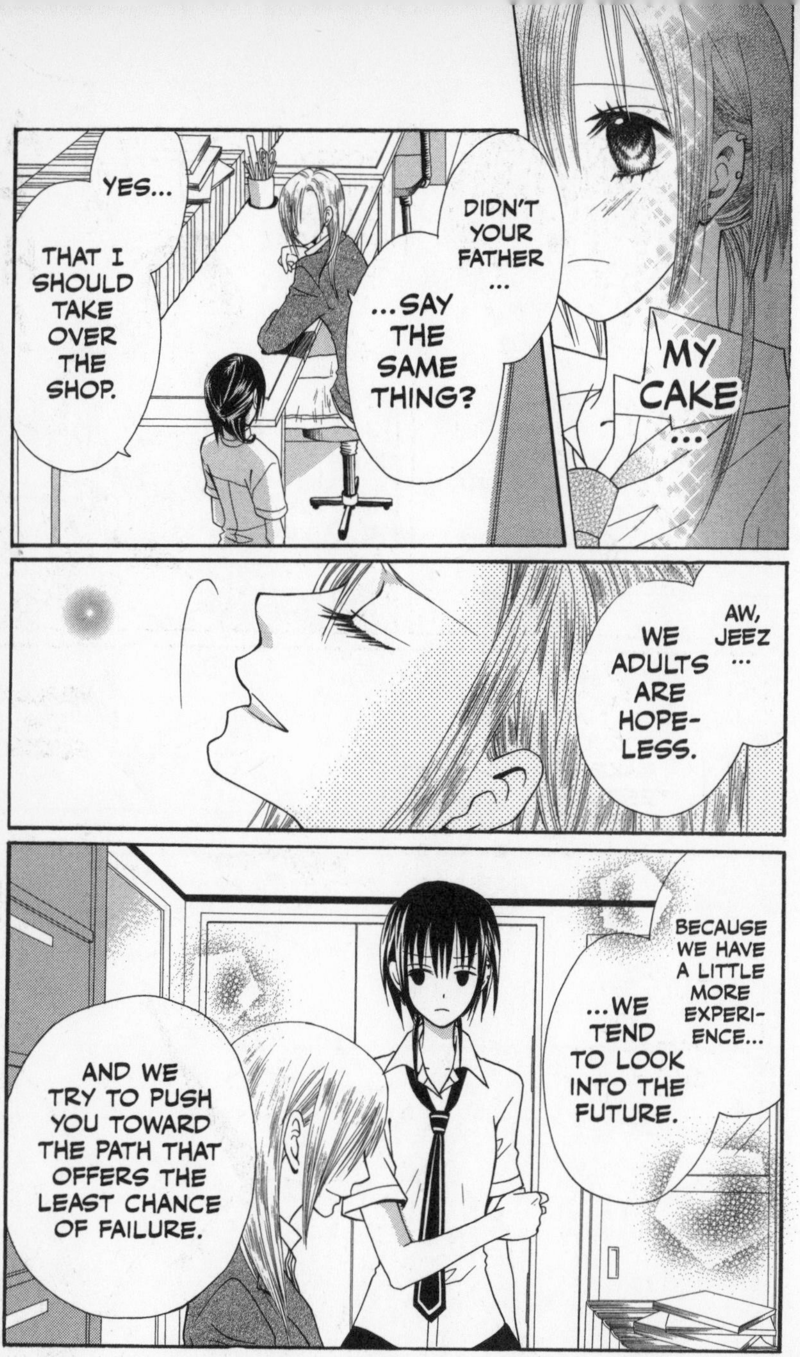
MY CAKE...
DIDN'T YOUR FATHER... ...SAY THE SAME THING?
YES... THAT I SHOULD TAKE OVER THE SHOP.
AW, JEEZ... WE ADULTS ARE HOPELESS.
BECAUSE WE HAVE A LITTLE MORE EXPERIENCE... ...WE TEND TO LOOK INTO THE FUTURE.
AND WE TRY TO PUSH YOU TOWARD THE PATH THAT OFFERS THE LEAST CHANCE OF FAILURE.

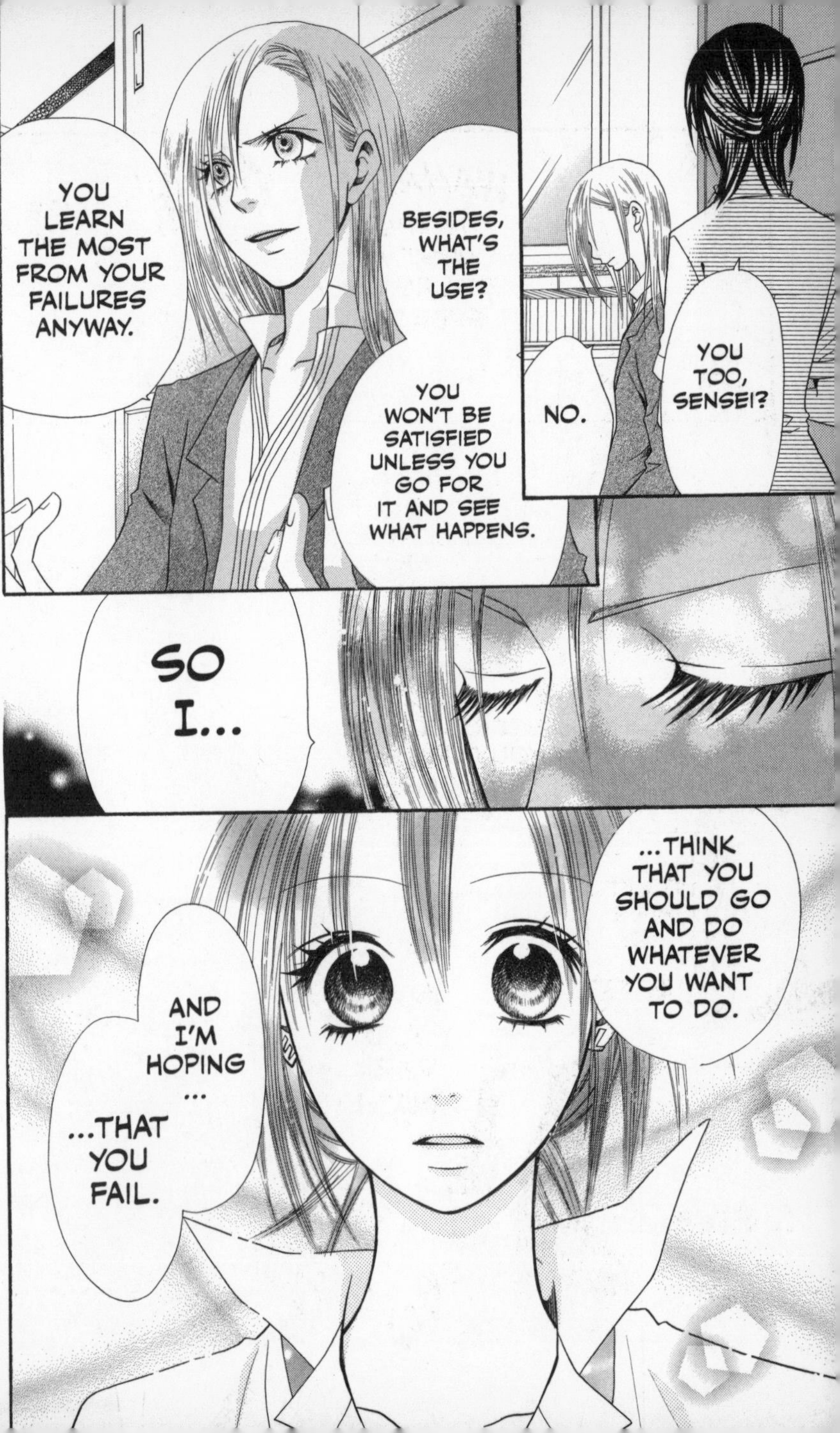
YOU TOO, SENSEI?
NO.
BESIDES, WHAT'S THE USE?
YOU WON'T BE SATISFIED UNLESS YOU GO FOR IT AND SEE WHAT HAPPENS.
YOU LEARN THE MOST FROM YOUR FAILURES ANYWAY.
SO I...
...THINK THAT YOU SHOULD GO AND DO WHATEVER YOU WANT TO DO.
AND I'M HOPING...
...THAT YOU FAIL.

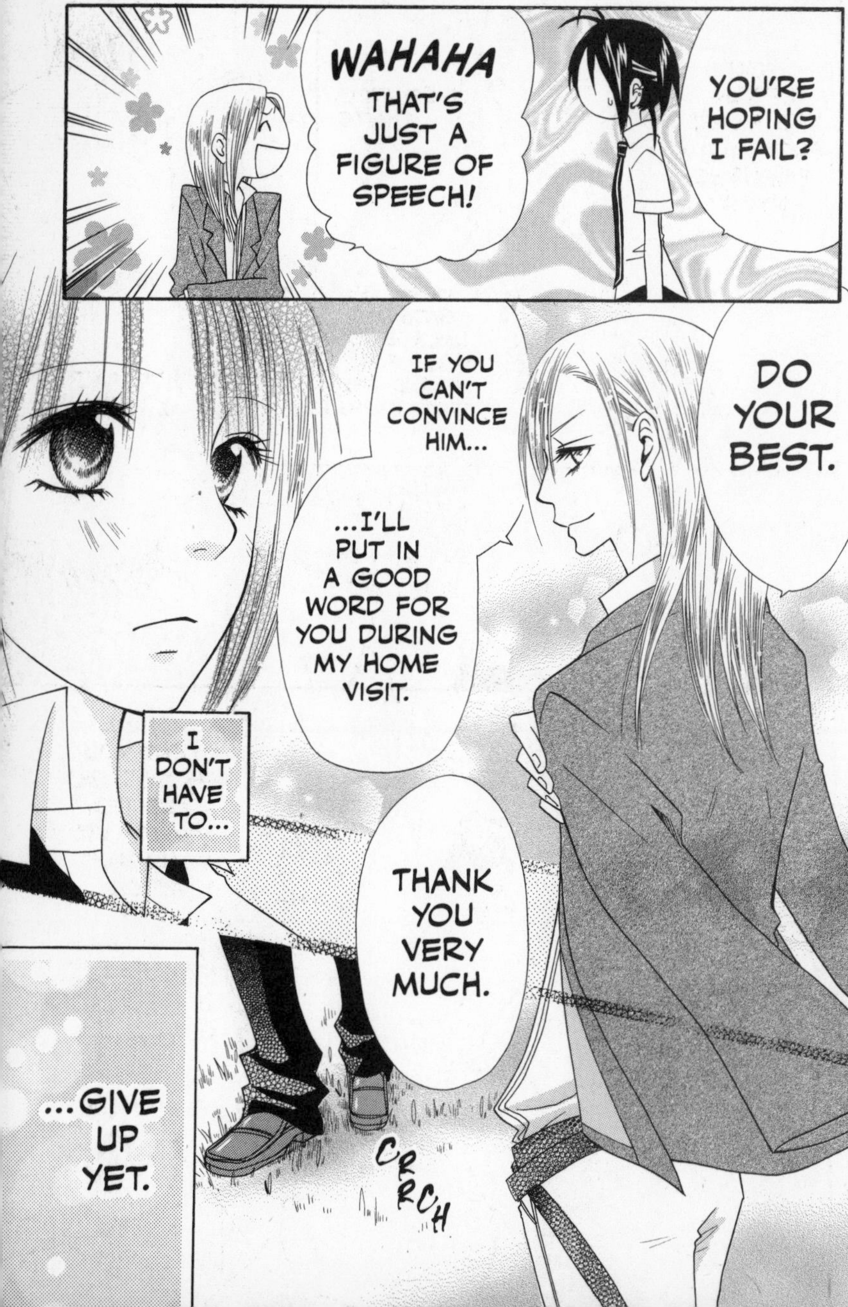
YOU'RE HOPING I FAIL?
WAHAHA
THAT'S JUST A FIGURE OF SPEECH!
DO YOUR BEST.
IF YOU CAN'T CONVINCE HIM...
...I'LL PUT IN A GOOD WORD FOR YOU DURING MY HOME VISIT.
THANK YOU VERY MUCH.
I DON'T HAVE TO...
CRRCH
...GIVE UP YET.

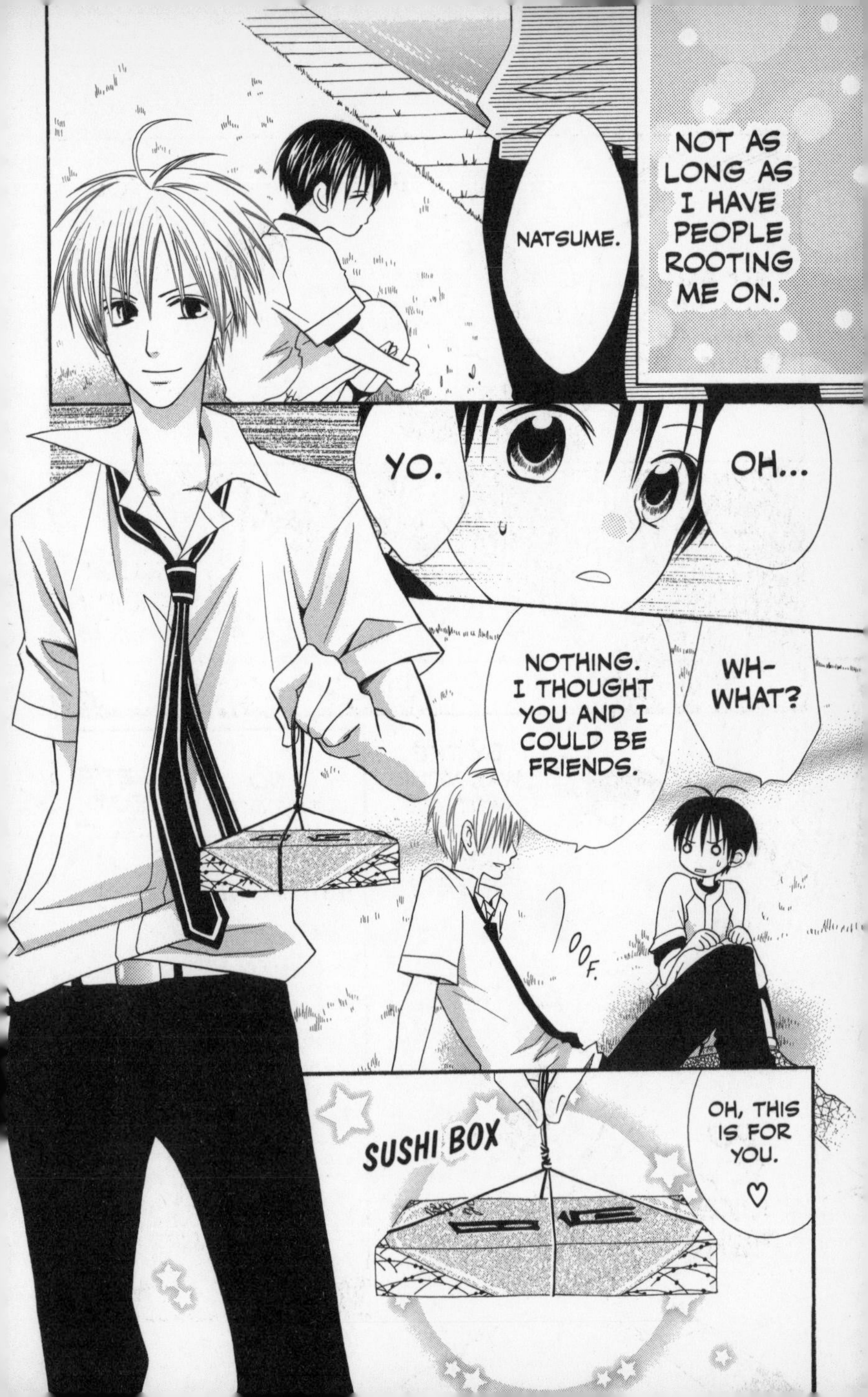
NOT AS LONG AS I HAVE PEOPLE ROOTING ME ON.
NATSUME.
OH...
YO.
WH-WHAT?
NOTHING. I THOUGHT YOU AND I COULD BE FRIENDS.
OOF.
OH, THIS IS FOR YOU. ♡
SUSHI BOX

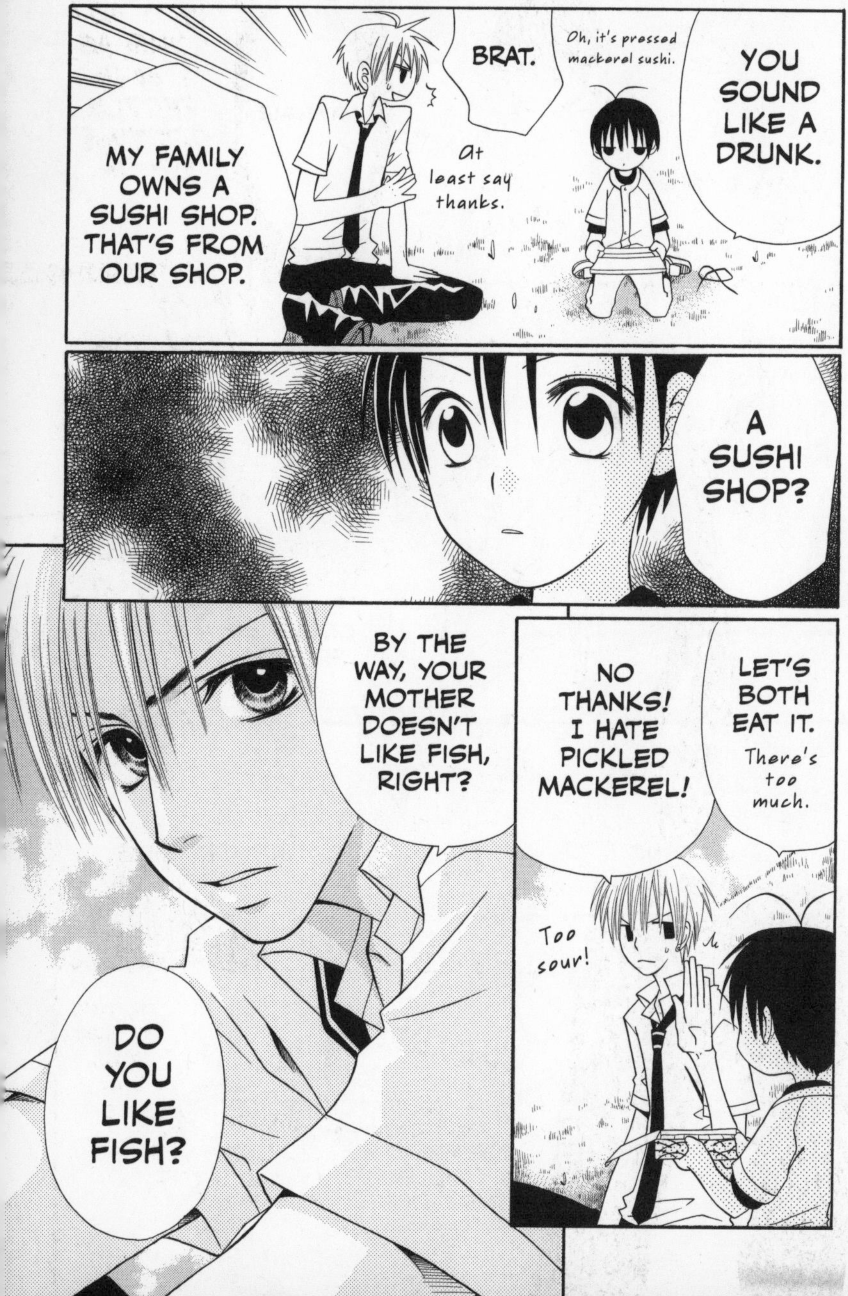
YOU SOUND LIKE A DRUNK.
Oh, it's pressed mackerel sushi.
BRAT.
At least say thanks.
MY FAMILY OWNS A SUSHI SHOP. THAT'S FROM OUR SHOP.
A SUSHI SHOP?
LET'S BOTH EAT IT.
There's too much.
NO THANKS! I HATE PICKLED MACKEREL!
Too sour!
BY THE WAY, YOUR MOTHER DOESN'T LIKE FISH, RIGHT?
DO YOU LIKE FISH?

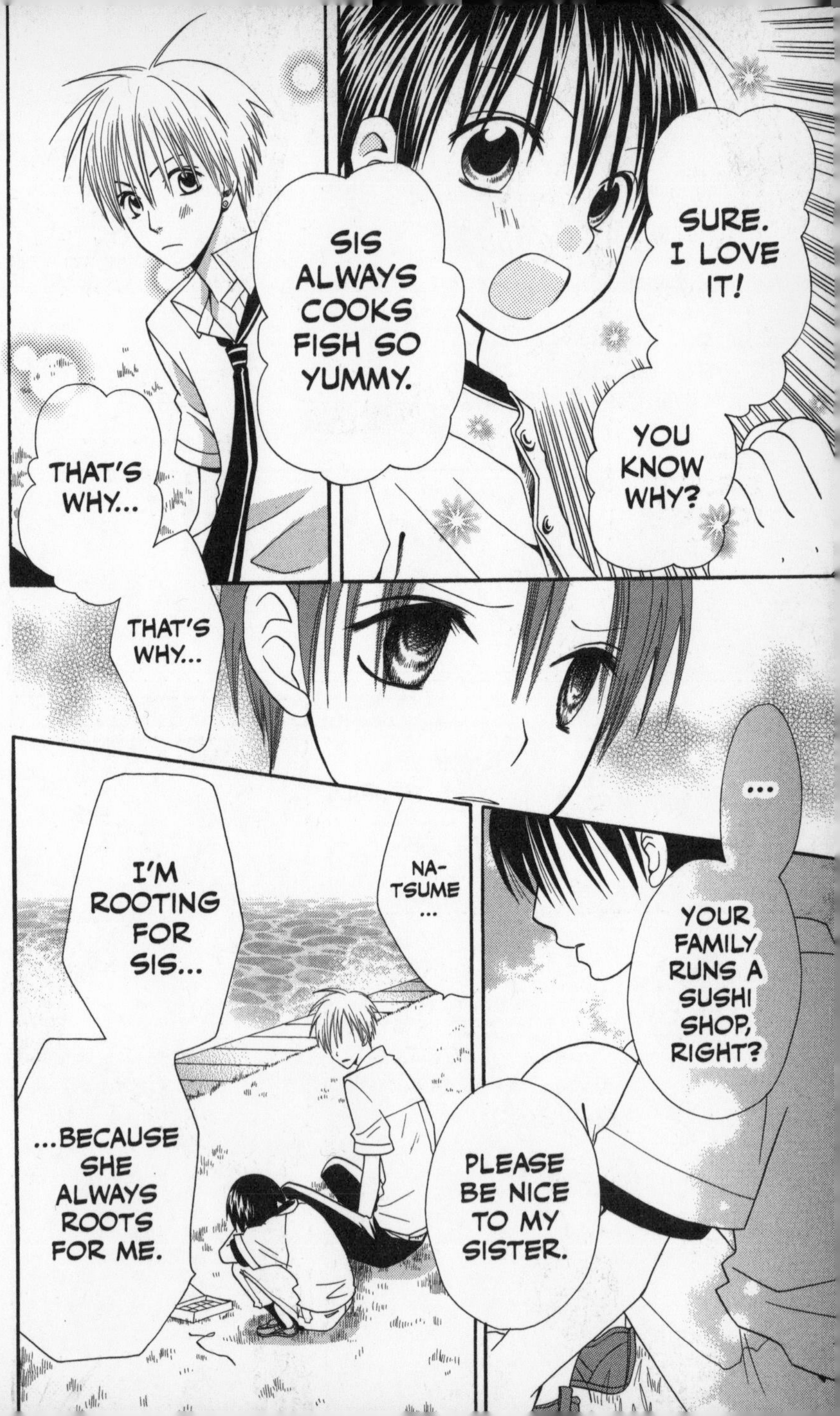
SURE. I LOVE IT!
YOU KNOW WHY?
SIS ALWAYS COOKS FISH SO YUMMY.
THAT'S WHY...
THAT'S WHY...
...
YOUR FAMILY RUNS A SUSHI SHOP, RIGHT?
PLEASE BE NICE TO MY SISTER.
NA-TSUME...
I'M ROOTING FOR SIS...
...BECAUSE SHE ALWAYS ROOTS FOR ME.

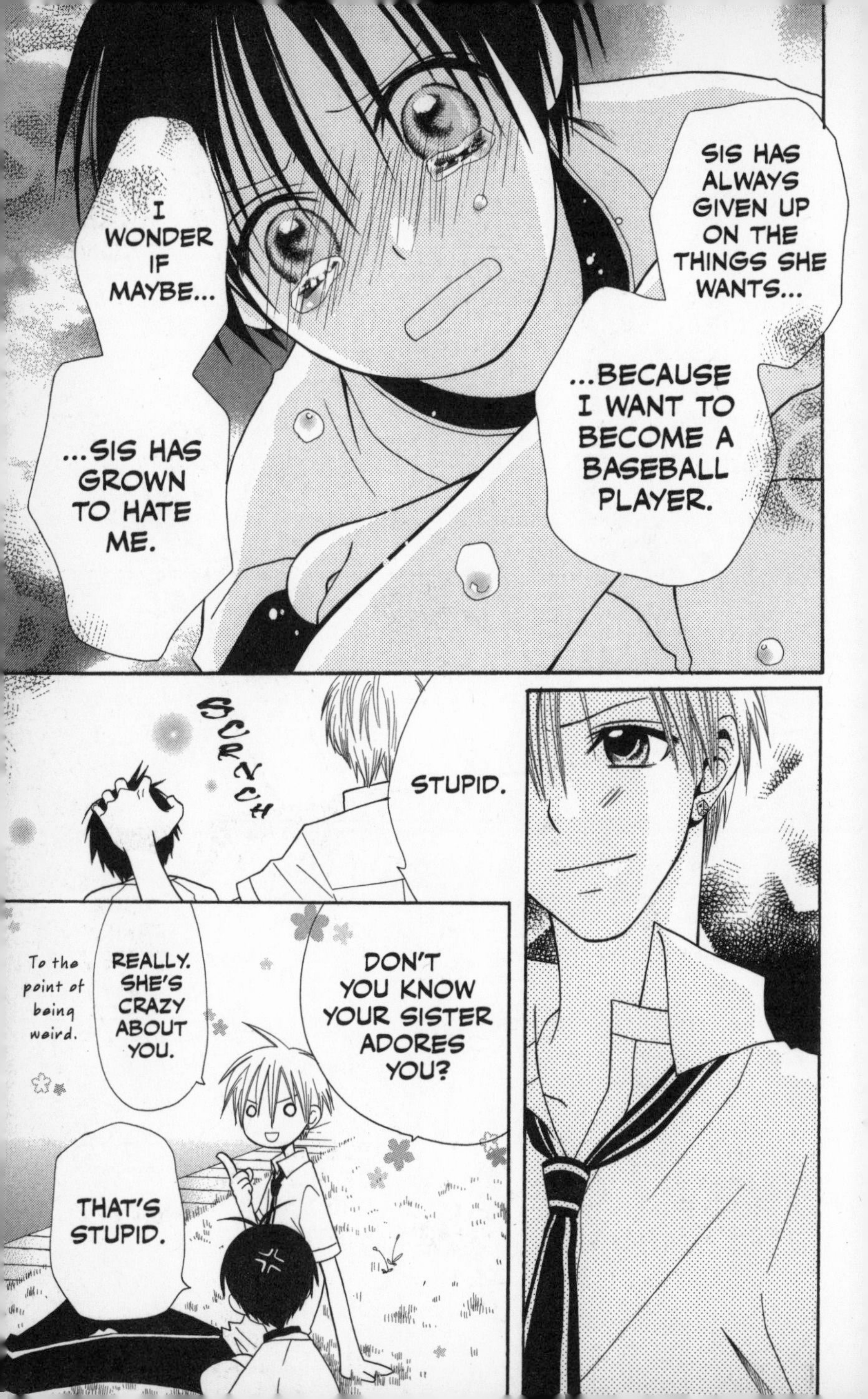

SIS HAS ALWAYS GIVEN UP ON THE THINGS SHE WANTS...
...BECAUSE I WANT TO BECOME A BASEBALL PLAYER.
I WONDER IF MAYBE...
...SIS HAS GROWN TO HATE ME.
SCRUNCH
STUPID.
DON'T YOU KNOW YOUR SISTER ADORES YOU?
REALLY. SHE'S CRAZY ABOUT YOU.
To the point of being weird.
THAT'S STUPID.

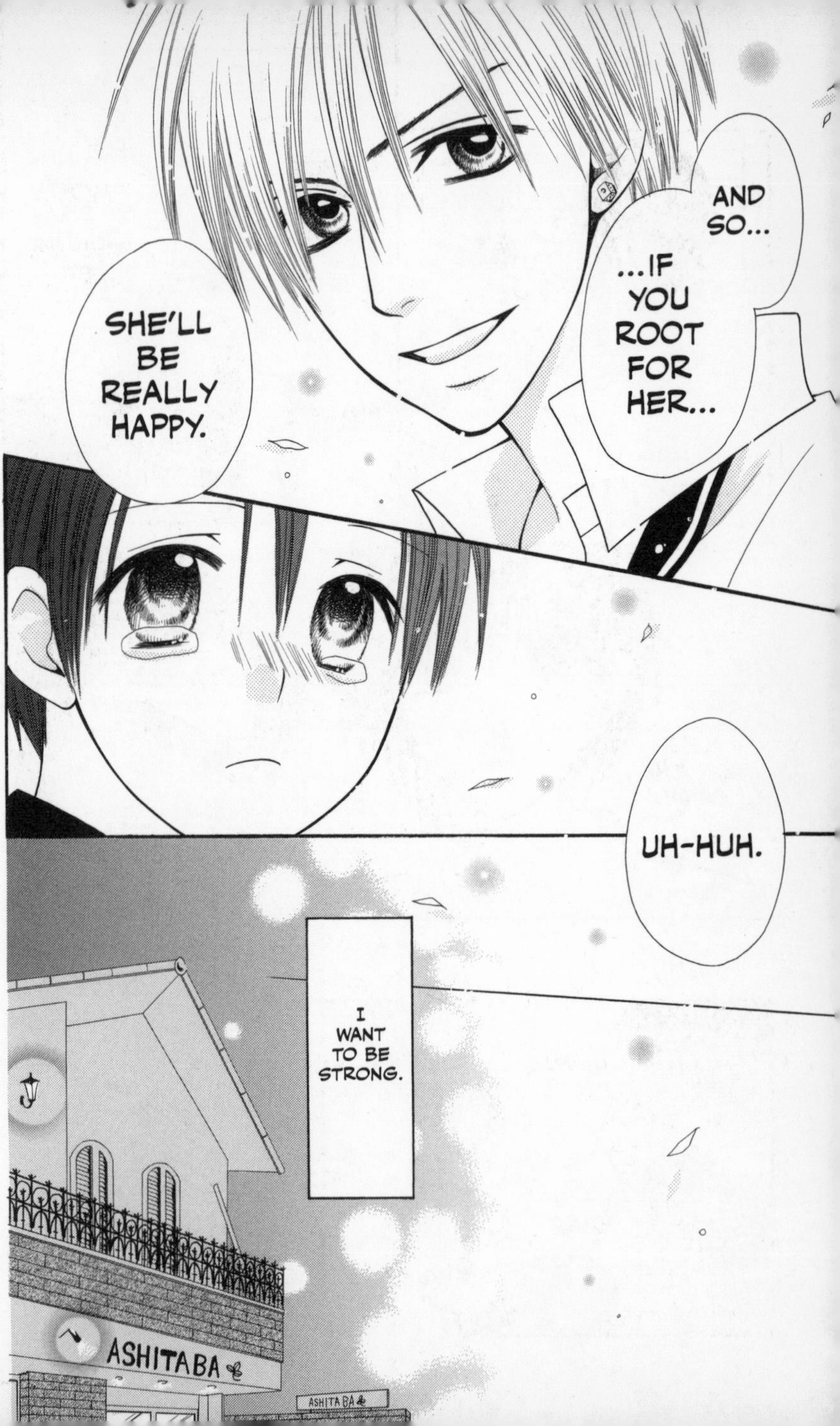
AND SO...
...IF YOU ROOT FOR HER...
SHE'LL BE REALLY HAPPY.
UH-HUH.
I WANT TO BE STRONG.
ASHITABA
ASHITABA

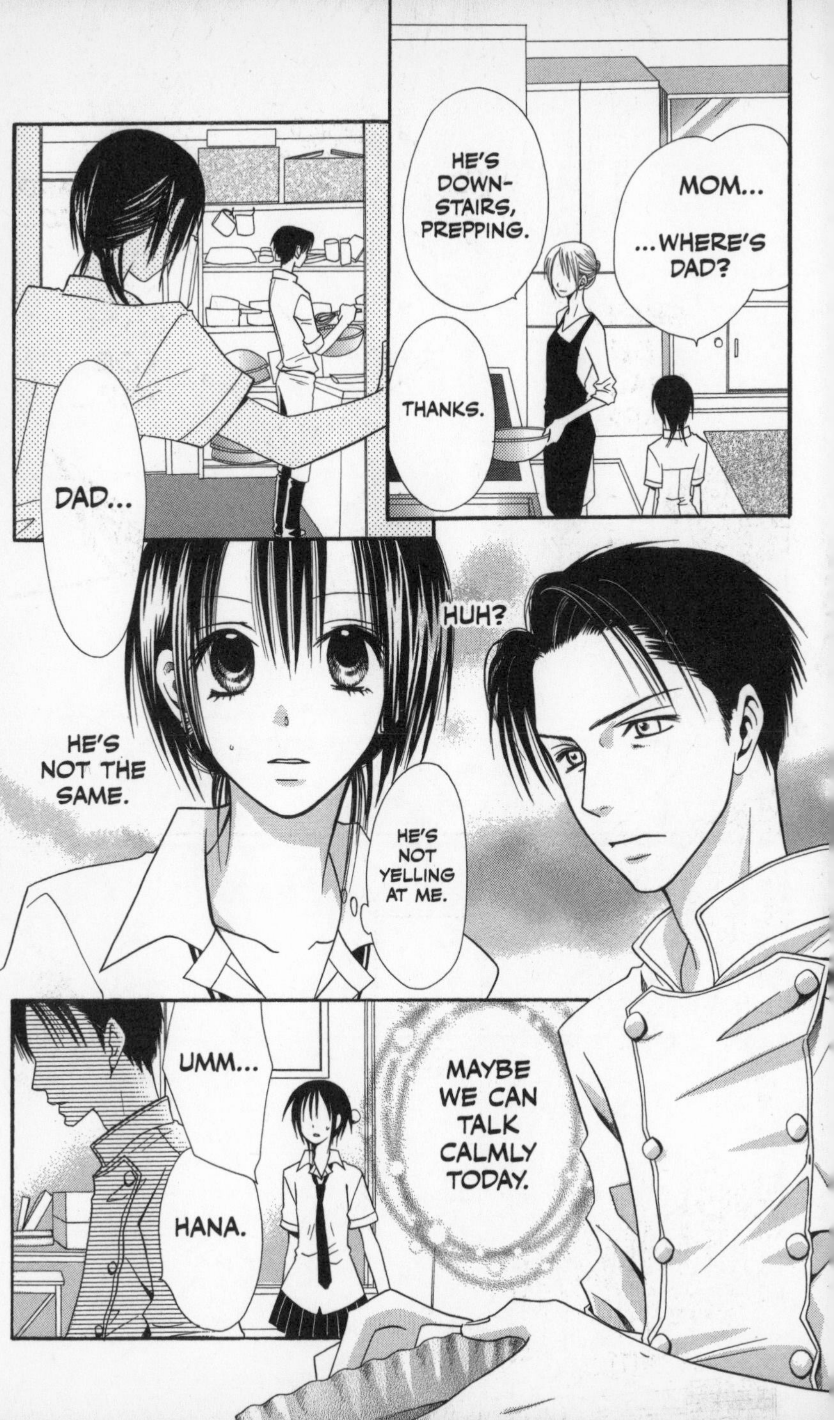
MOM...
...WHERE'S DAD?
HE'S DOWN-STAIRS, PREPPING.
THANKS.
DAD...
HUH?
HE'S NOT YELLING AT ME.
HE'S NOT THE SAME.
MAYBE WE CAN TALK CALMLY TODAY.
UMM...
HANA.

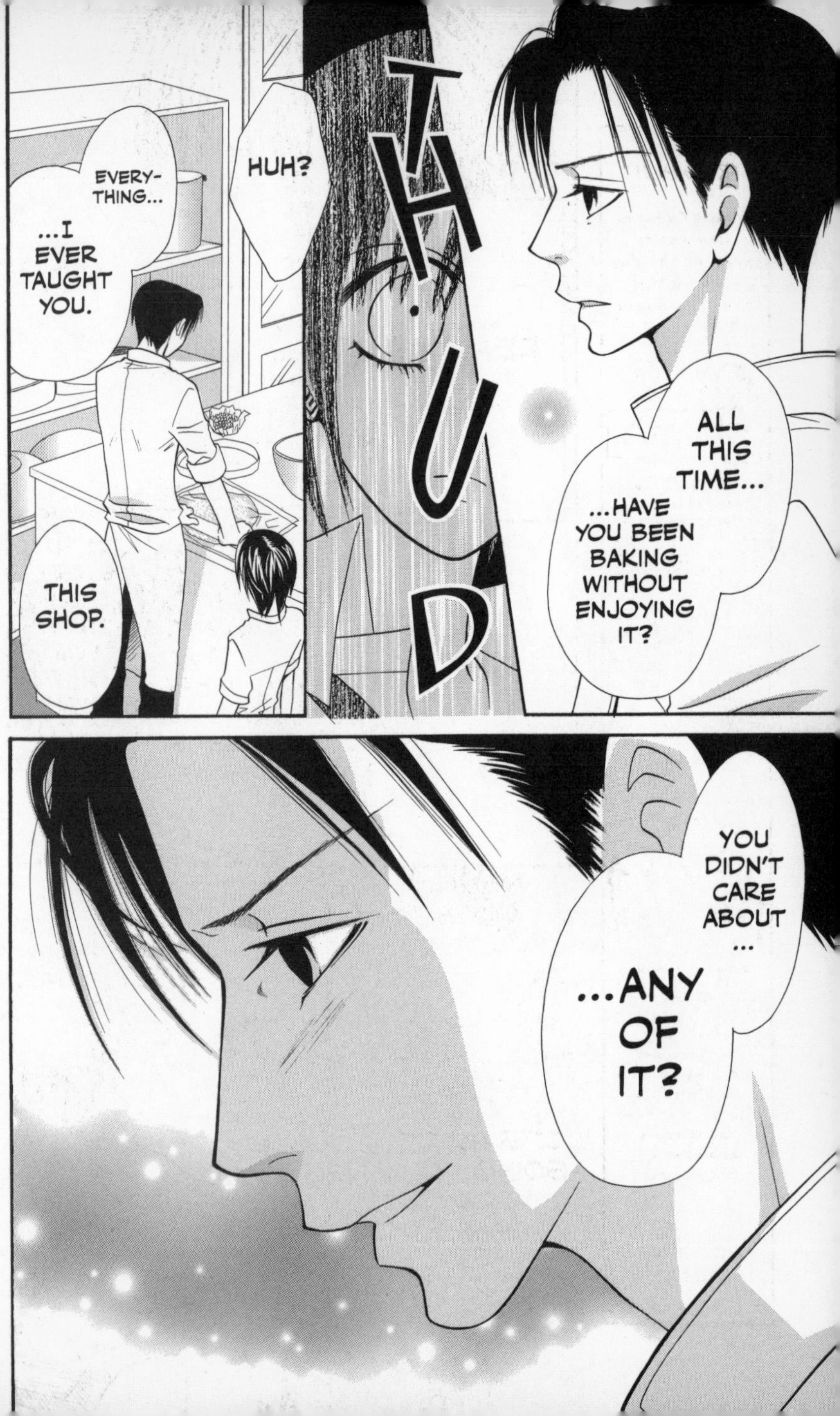
ALL THIS TIME...
...HAVE YOU BEEN BAKING WITHOUT ENJOYING IT?
THUD
HUH?
EVERY-THING...
...I EVER TAUGHT YOU.
THIS SHOP.
YOU DIDN'T CARE ABOUT ...
...ANY OF IT?

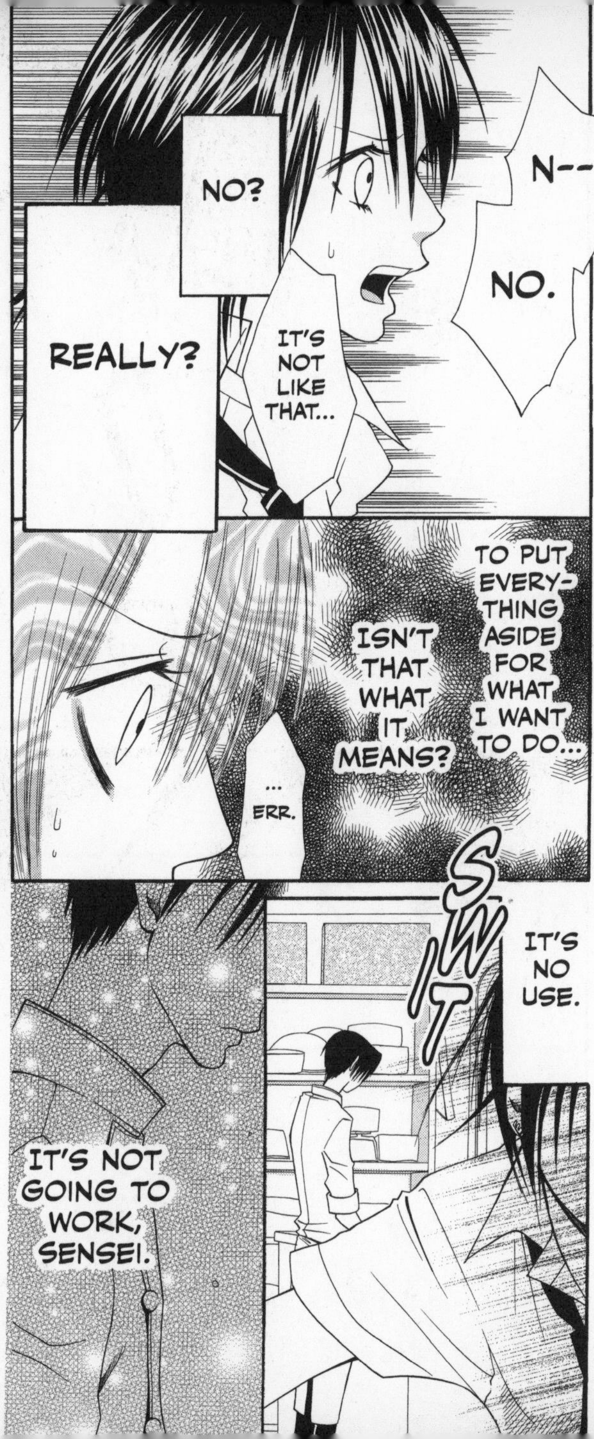
N--
NO.
NO?
IT'S NOT LIKE THAT...
REALLY?
TO PUT EVERYTHING ASIDE FOR WHAT I WANT TO DO...
ISN'T THAT WHAT IT MEANS?
... ERR.
SWIT
IT'S NO USE.
IT'S NOT GOING TO WORK, SENSEI.

Seminar Report 2!

Unlike Komura, who was so nervous the day before the seminar, Sango felt great.

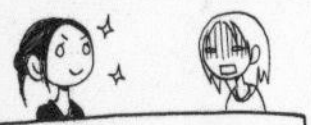

A comparison of the two during that time.

In any case, they decided to meet before the seminar and exchange notes, and the meeting had unexpected results.

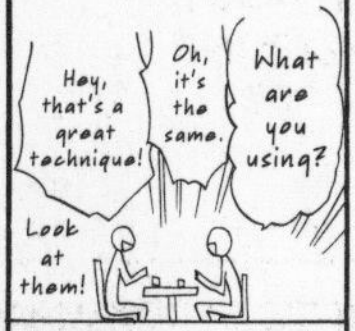
Hey, that's a great technique!
Oh, it's the same.
What are you using?
Look at them!

They talked about everything they planned to say at the lecture...

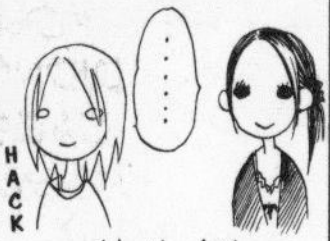
. . . . . .
HACK

...and both of them ended up lecturing with slightly sore throats!

But the lecture went very well and was very beneficial. I hope that the participants had as much fun as I did!

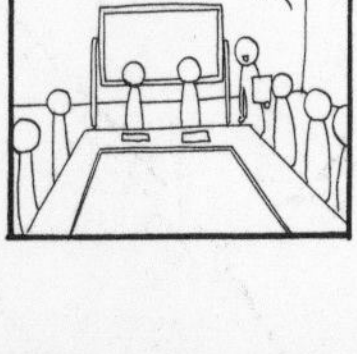

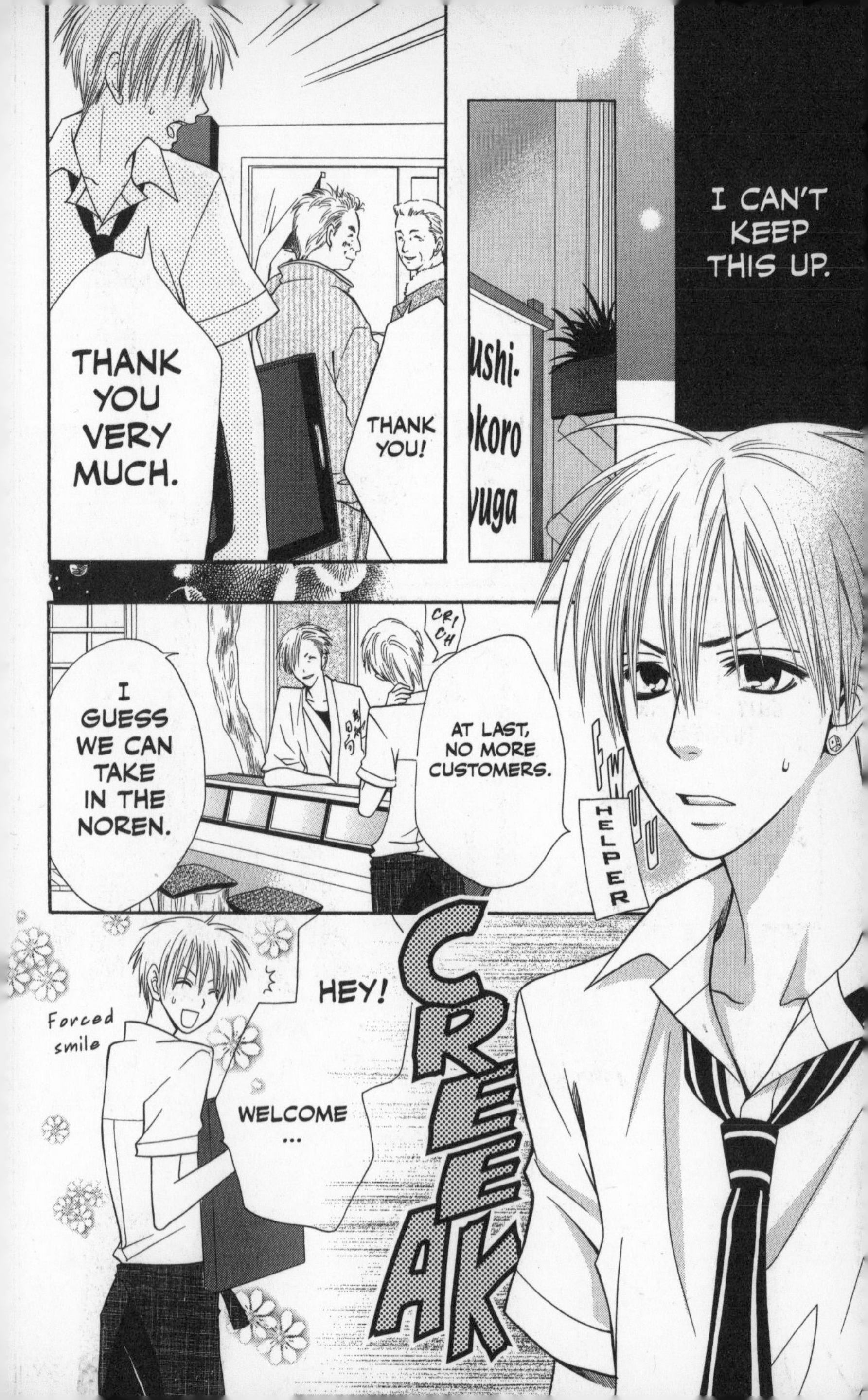

I CAN'T KEEP THIS UP.
THANK YOU!
THANK YOU VERY MUCH.
CRICH
AT LAST, NO MORE CUSTOMERS.
I GUESS WE CAN TAKE IN THE NOREN.
FWUU
HELPER
CREEAK
HEY!
WELCOME ...
Forced smile

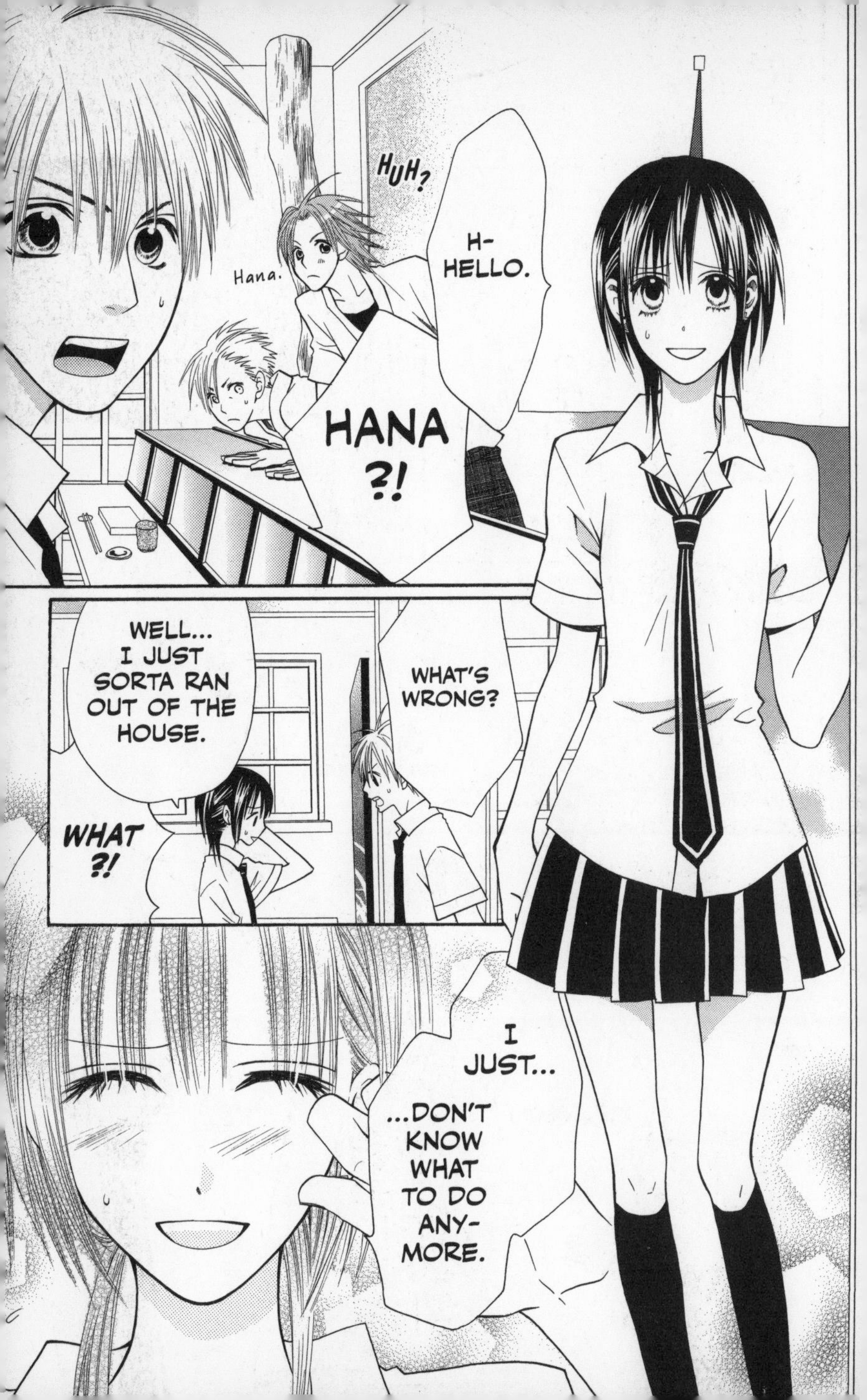
H-
HELLO.
HUH?
Hana.
HANA ?!
WHAT'S WRONG?
WELL... I JUST SORTA RAN OUT OF THE HOUSE.
WHAT ?!
I JUST...
...DON'T KNOW WHAT TO DO ANY-MORE.

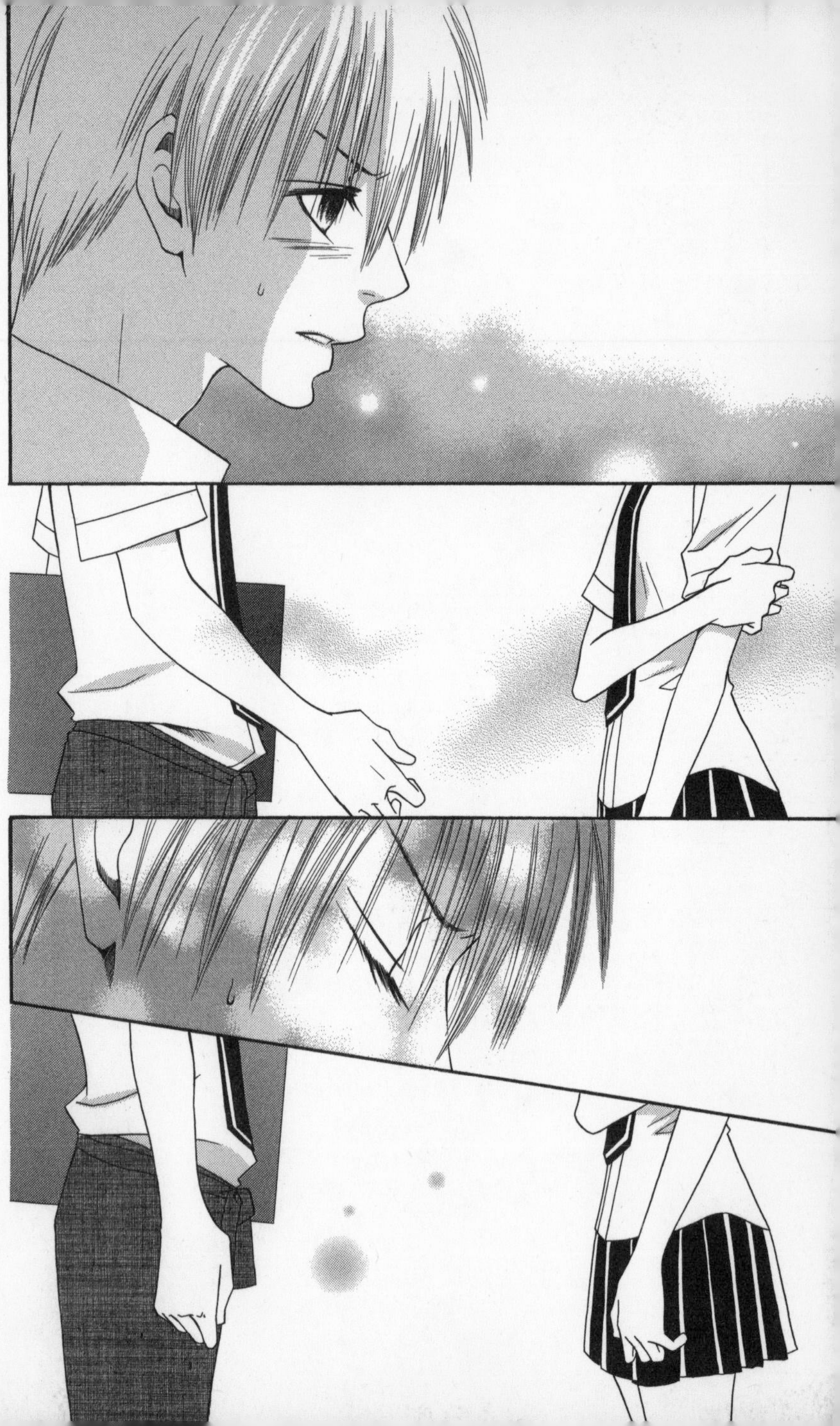

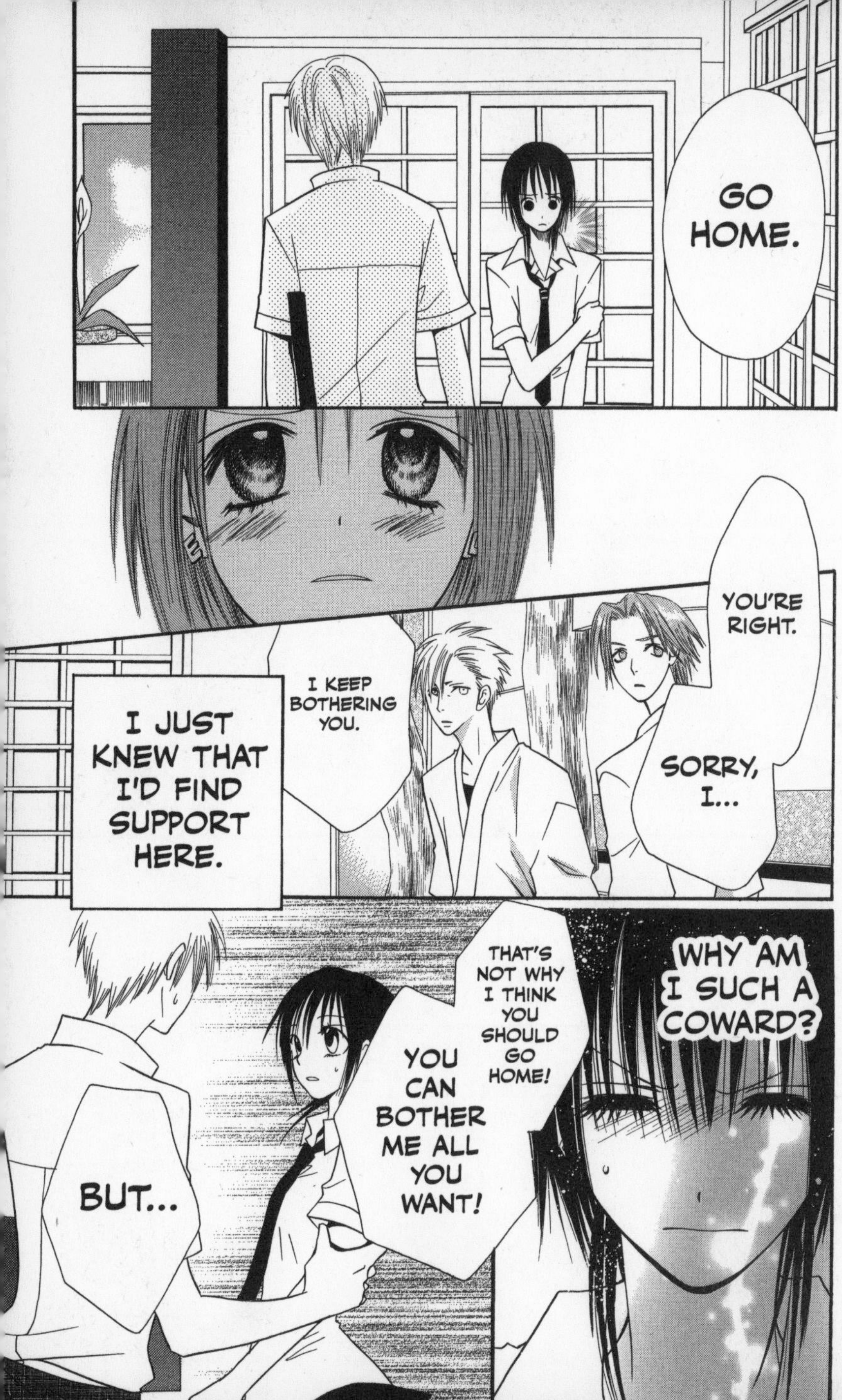
GO HOME.
YOU'RE RIGHT.
SORRY, I...
I KEEP BOTHERING YOU.
I JUST KNEW THAT I'D FIND SUPPORT HERE.
WHY AM I SUCH A COWARD?
THAT'S NOT WHY I THINK YOU SHOULD GO HOME!
YOU CAN BOTHER ME ALL YOU WANT!
BUT...

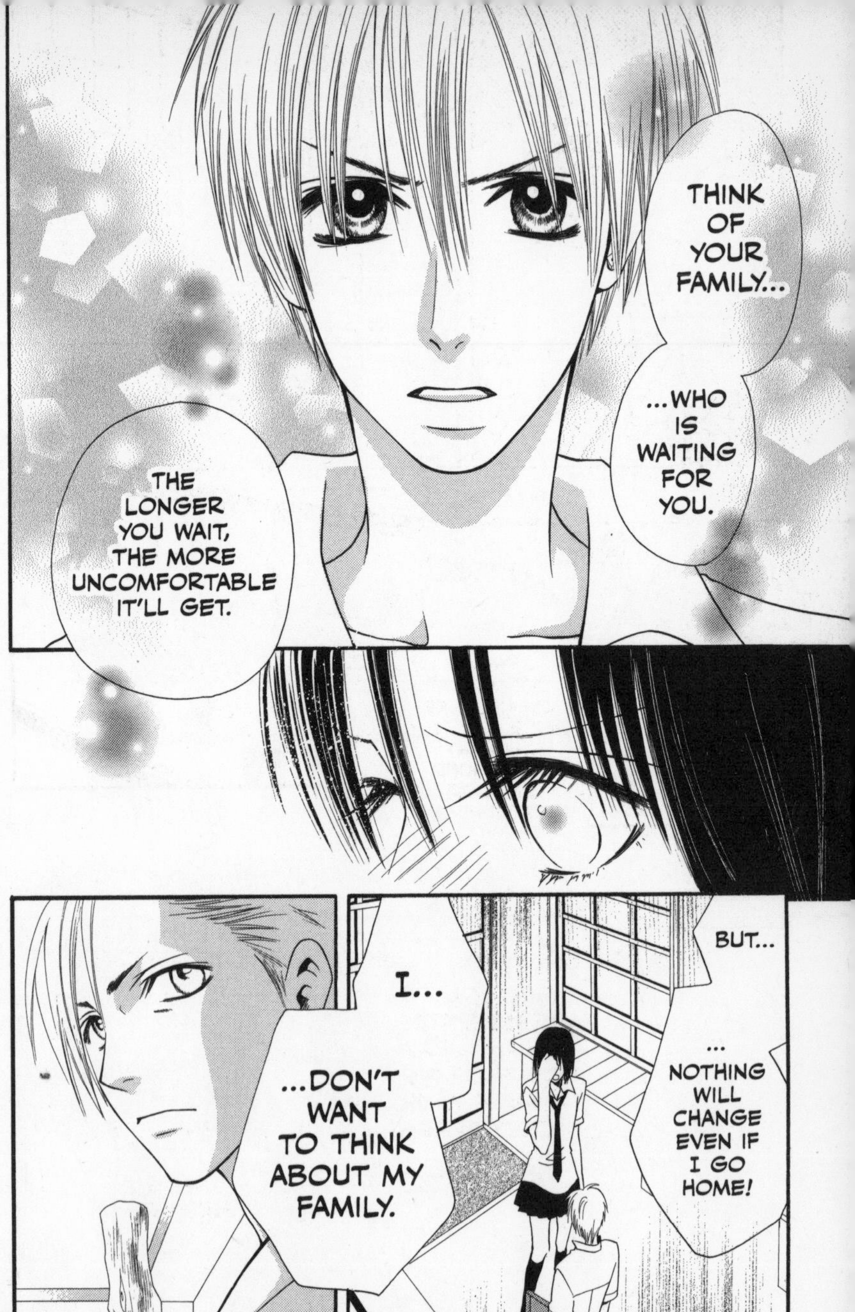
THINK OF YOUR FAMILY...
...WHO IS WAITING FOR YOU.
THE LONGER YOU WAIT, THE MORE UNCOMFORTABLE IT'LL GET.
BUT...
... NOTHING WILL CHANGE EVEN IF I GO HOME!
I...
...DON'T WANT TO THINK ABOUT MY FAMILY.

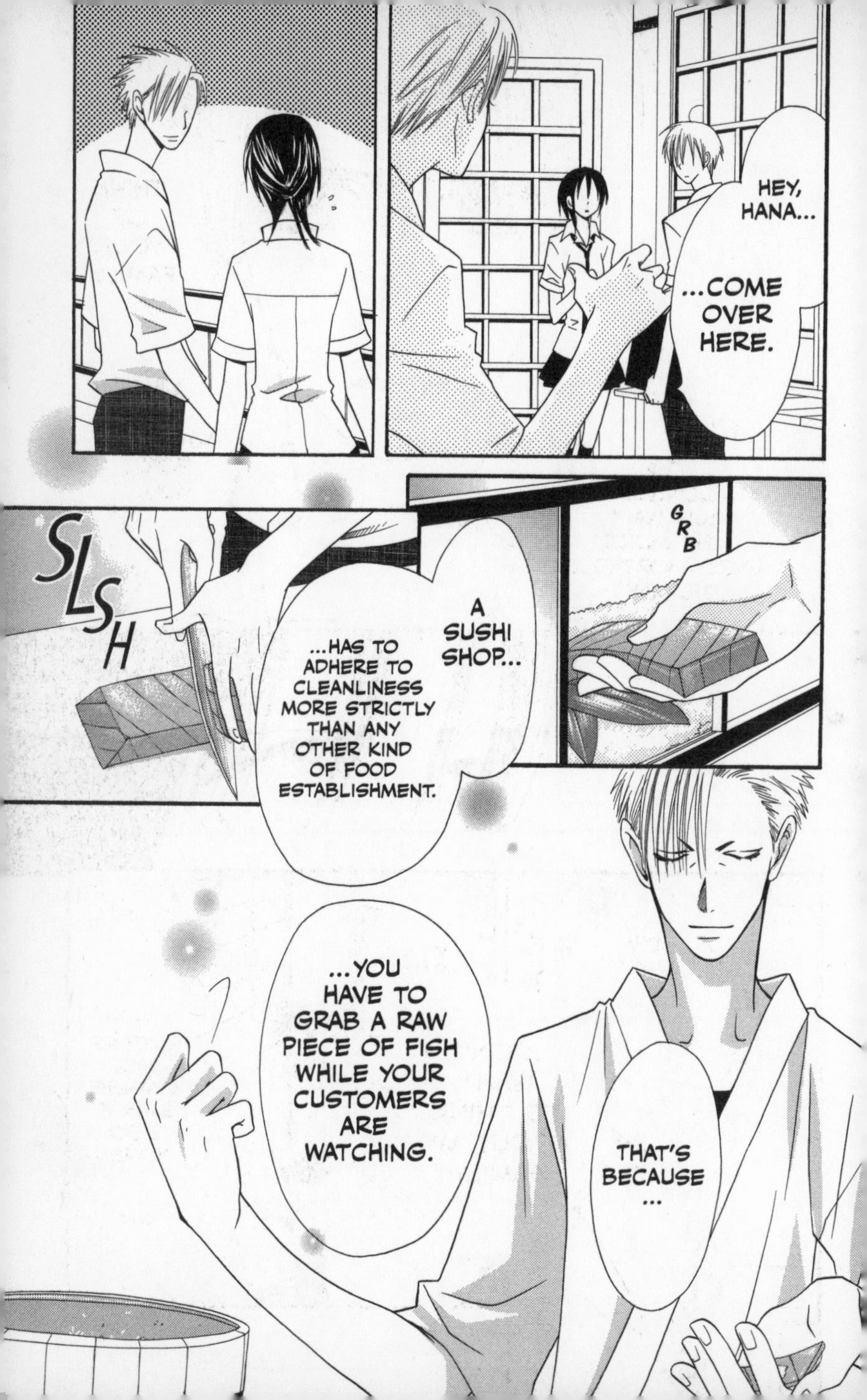
HEY, HANA...
...COME OVER HERE.
GRB
A SUSHI SHOP...
...HAS TO ADHERE TO CLEANLINESS MORE STRICTLY THAN ANY OTHER KIND OF FOOD ESTABLISHMENT.
SLSH
THAT'S BECAUSE ...
...YOU HAVE TO GRAB A RAW PIECE OF FISH WHILE YOUR CUSTOMERS ARE WATCHING.

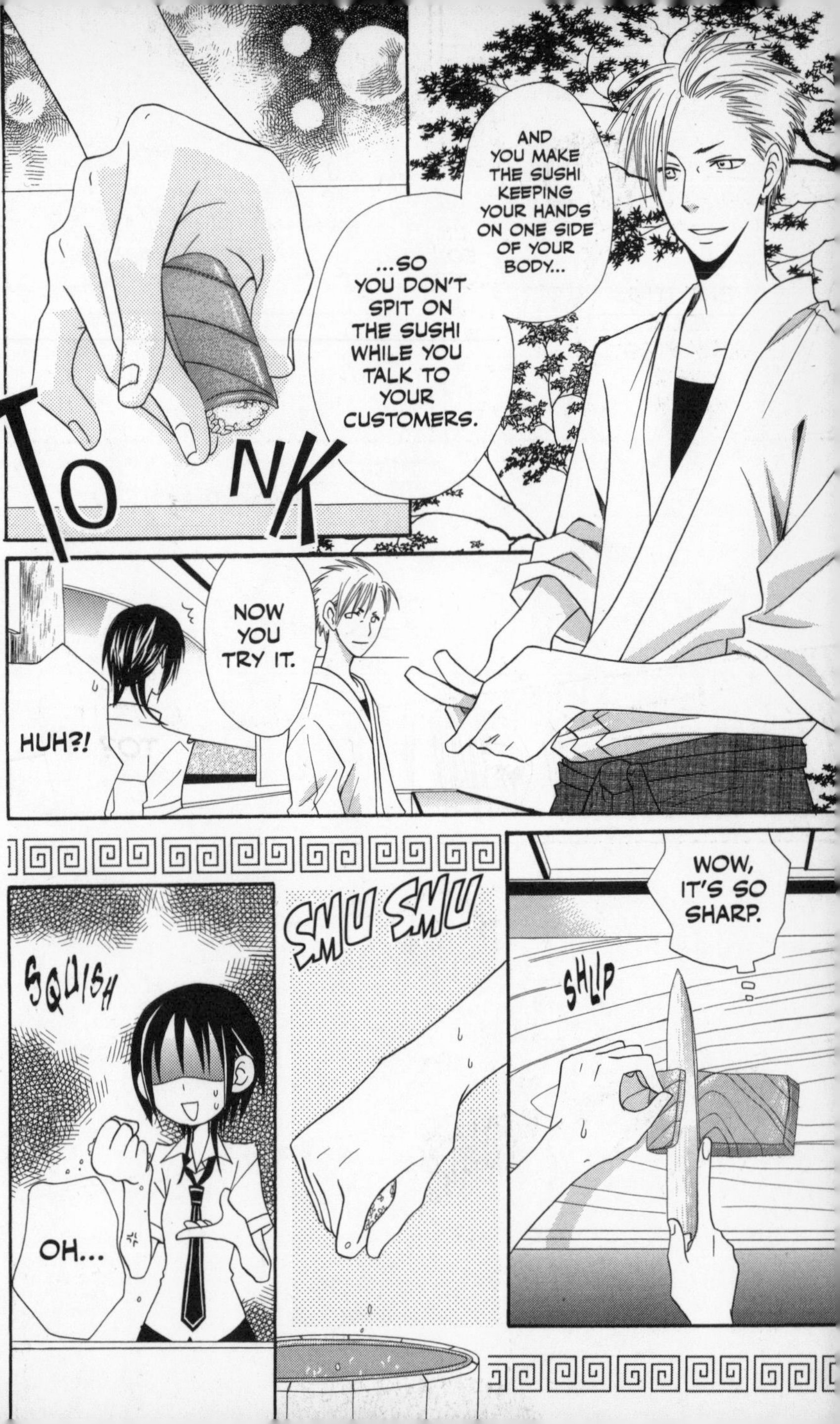
AND YOU MAKE THE SUSHI KEEPING YOUR HANDS ON ONE SIDE OF YOUR BODY...
...SO YOU DON'T SPIT ON THE SUSHI WHILE YOU TALK TO YOUR CUSTOMERS.
TONK
NOW YOU TRY IT.
HUH?!
WOW, IT'S SO SHARP.
SHLIP
SMU SMU
SQUISH
OH...

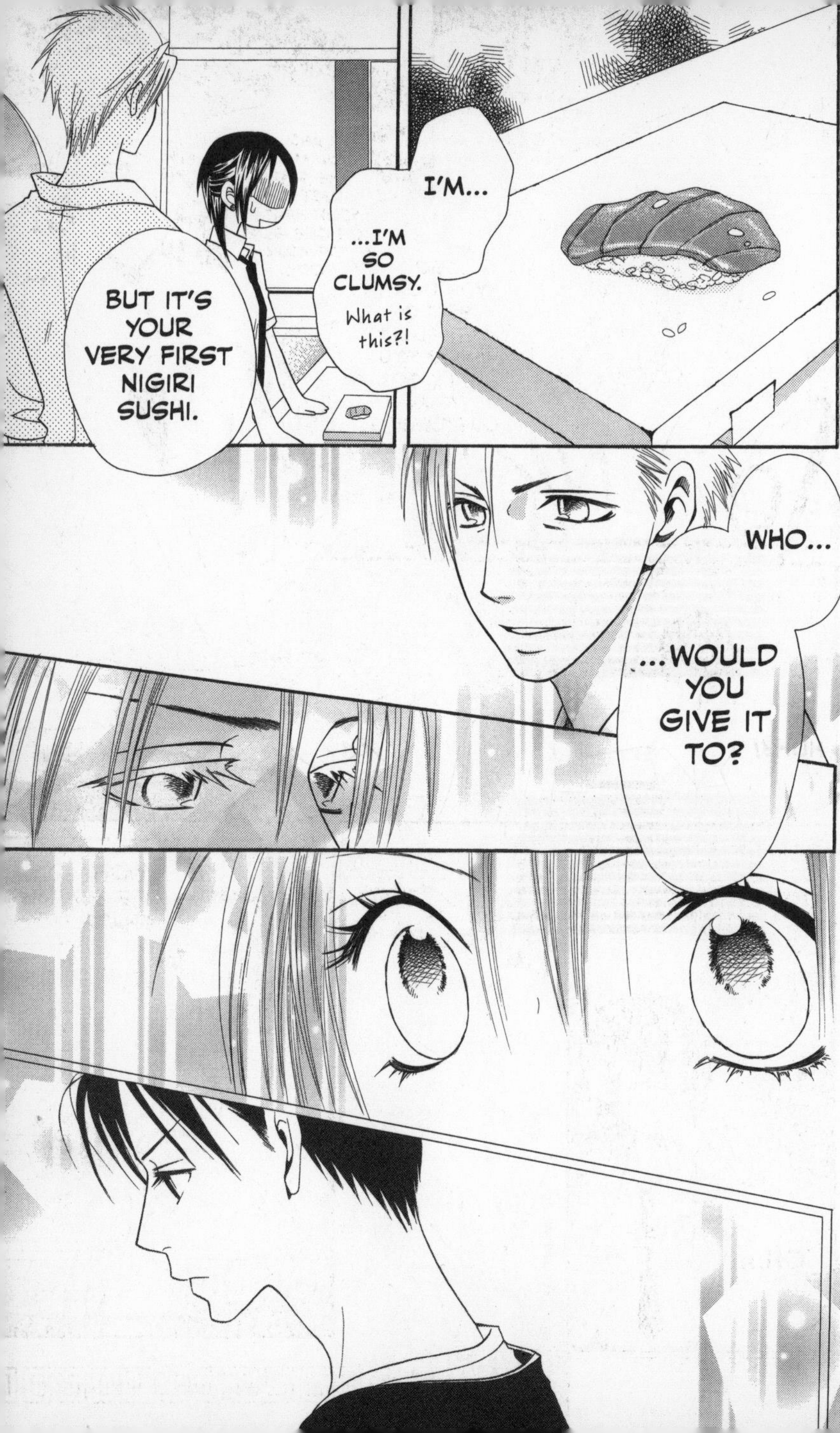
I'M...
...I'M SO CLUMSY.
What is this?!
BUT IT'S YOUR VERY FIRST NIGIRI SUSHI.
WHO...
...WOULD YOU GIVE IT TO?

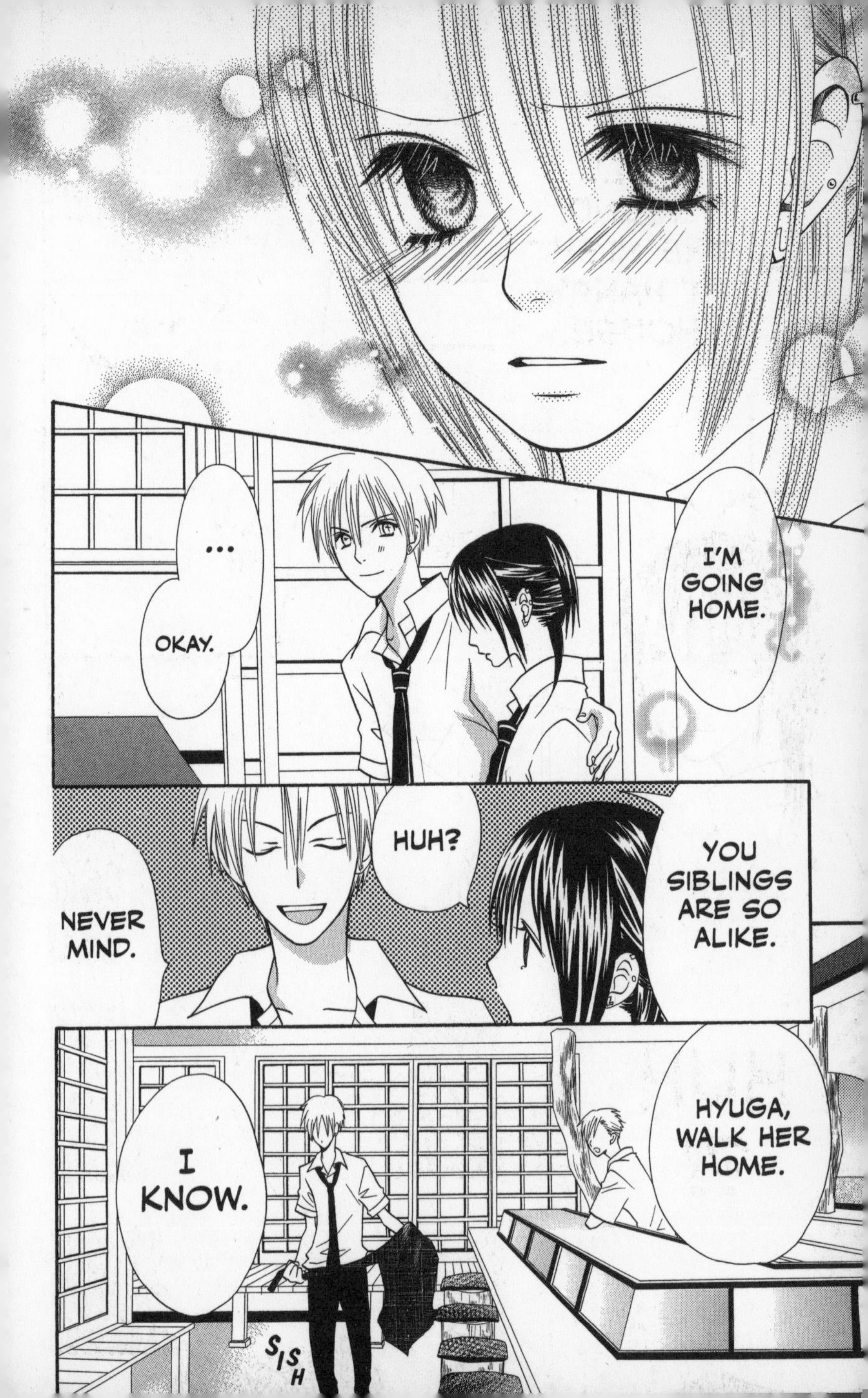
I'M GOING HOME.
...
OKAY.
YOU SIBLINGS ARE SO ALIKE.
HUH?
NEVER MIND.
HYUGA, WALK HER HOME.
I KNOW.
SISH

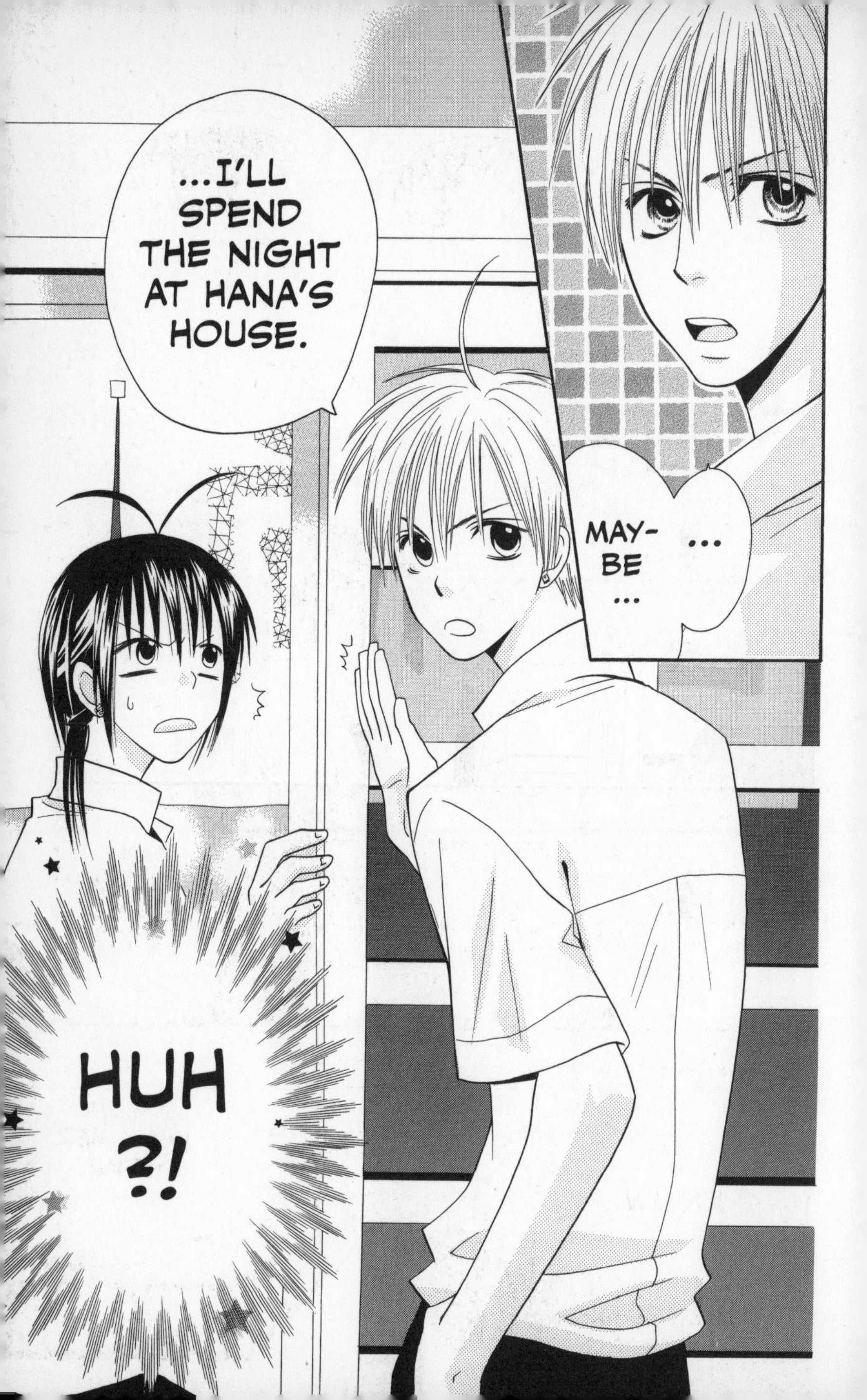
... MAY-BE ...
...I'LL SPEND THE NIGHT AT HANA'S HOUSE.
HUH ?!

SIDE DISH Mixed Vegetables 3

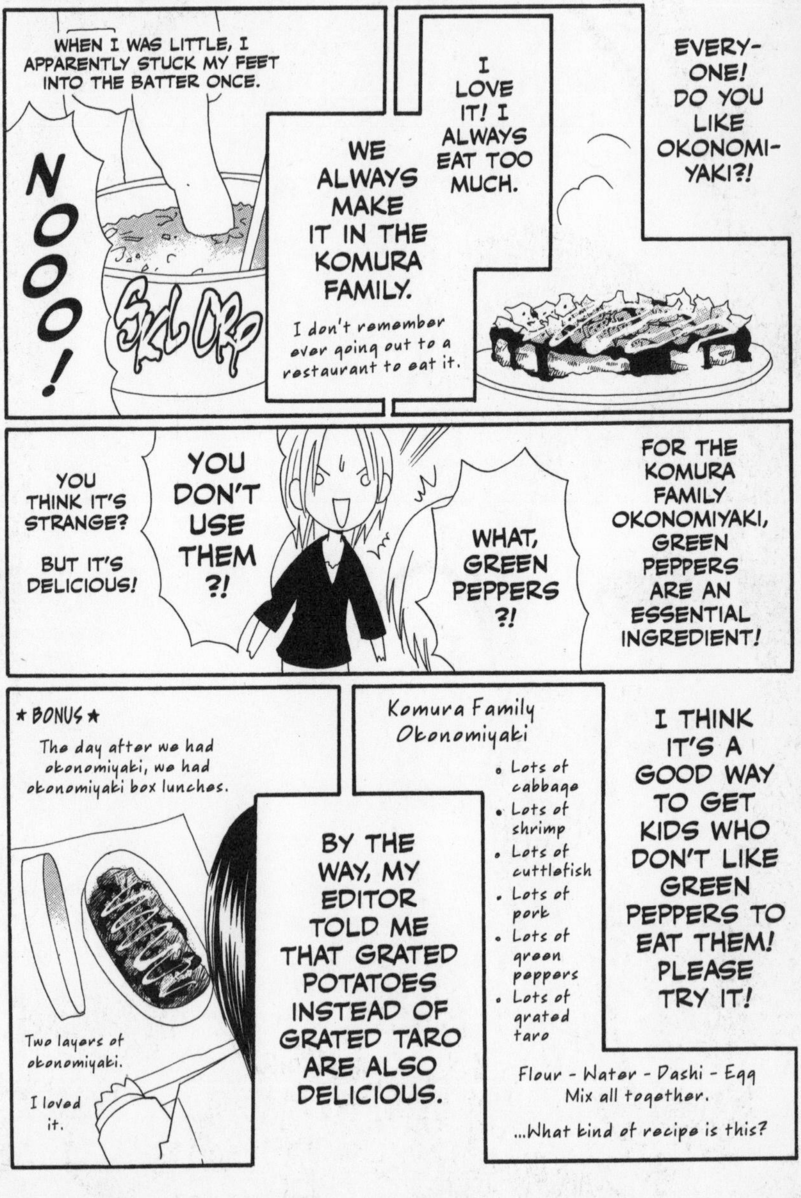
EVERY-ONE! DO YOU LIKE OKONOMIYAKI?!
I LOVE IT! I ALWAYS EAT TOO MUCH.
WE ALWAYS MAKE IT IN THE KOMURA FAMILY.
I don't remember ever going out to a restaurant to eat it.
WHEN I WAS LITTLE, I APPARENTLY STUCK MY FEET INTO THE BATTER ONCE.
NOOOO!
SKLORP
FOR THE KOMURA FAMILY OKONOMIYAKI, GREEN PEPPERS ARE AN ESSENTIAL INGREDIENT!
WHAT, GREEN PEPPERS?!
YOU DON'T USE THEM?!
YOU THINK IT'S STRANGE?
BUT IT'S DELICIOUS!
I THINK IT'S A GOOD WAY TO GET KIDS WHO DON'T LIKE GREEN PEPPERS TO EAT THEM! PLEASE TRY IT!
Komura Family Okonomiyaki
• Lots of cabbage
• Lots of shrimp
• Lots of cuttlefish
• Lots of pork
• Lots of green peppers
• Lots of grated taro
Flour - Water - Dashi - Egg
Mix all together.
...What kind of recipe is this?
BY THE WAY, MY EDITOR TOLD ME THAT GRATED POTATOES INSTEAD OF GRATED TARO ARE ALSO DELICIOUS.
★BONUS★
The day after we had okonomiyaki, we had okonomiyaki box lunches.
Two layers of okonomiyaki.
I loved it.

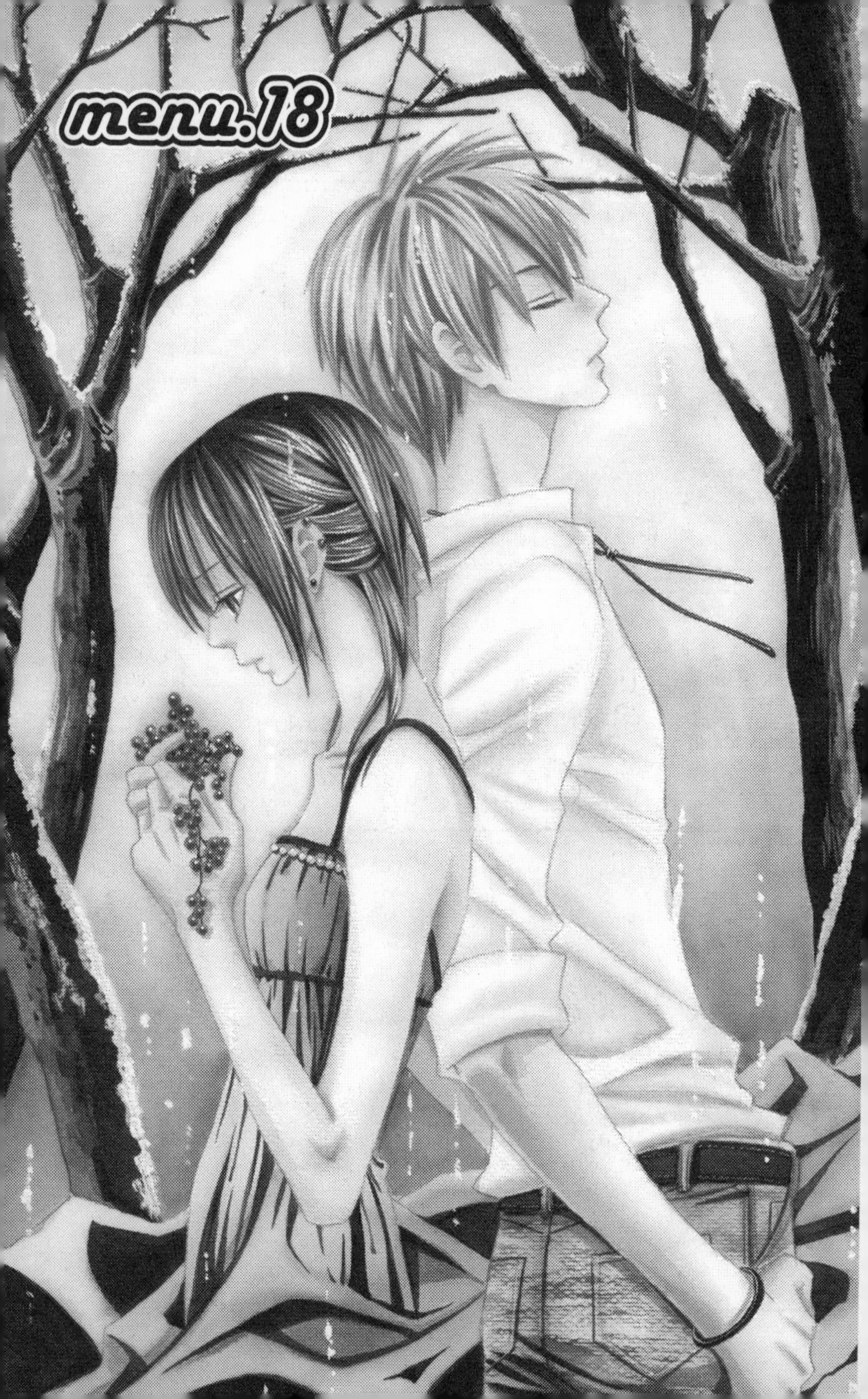
menu.18

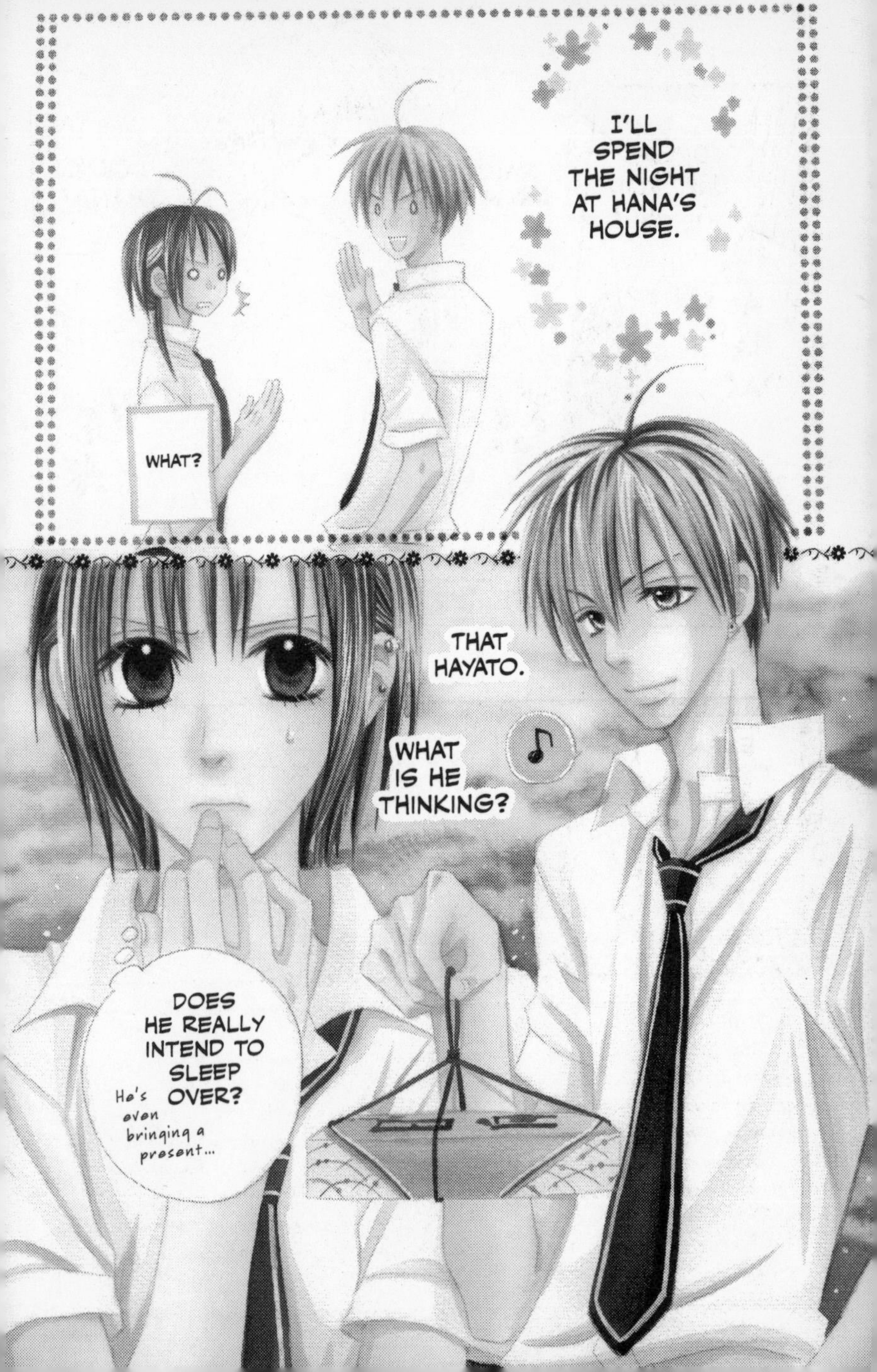
I'LL SPEND THE NIGHT AT HANA'S HOUSE.
WHAT?
THAT HAYATO.
WHAT IS HE THINKING?
DOES HE REALLY INTEND TO SLEEP OVER?
He's even bringing a present...

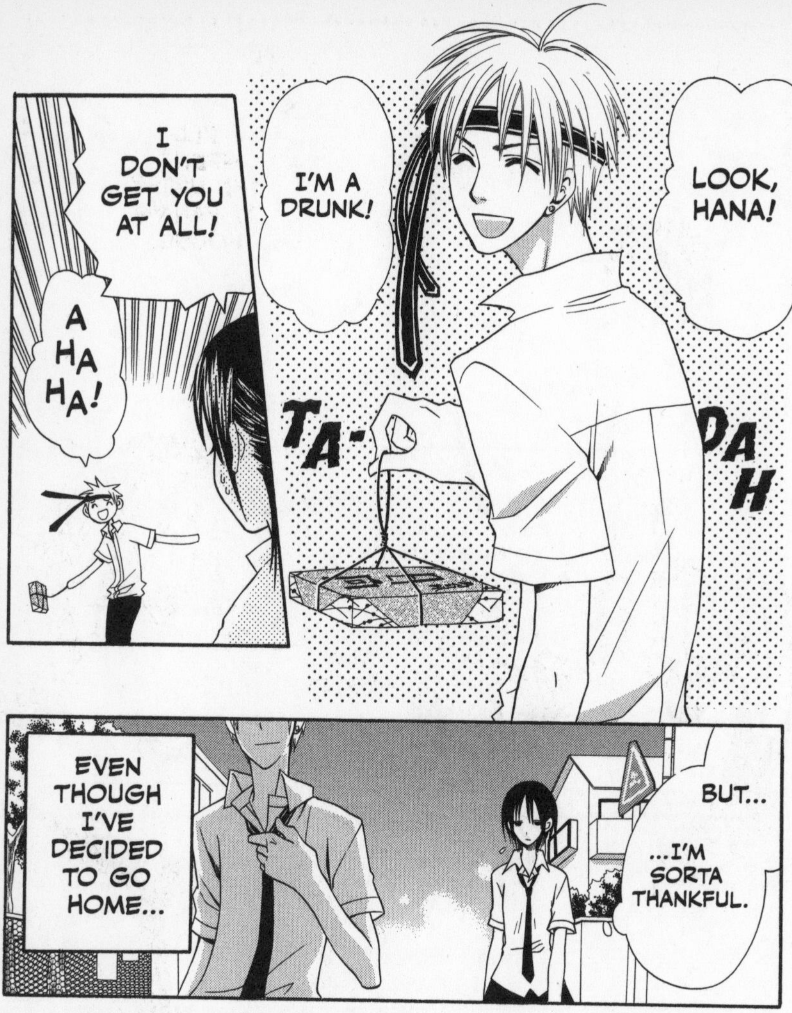
LOOK, HANA!
I'M A DRUNK!
TA-DAH
I DON'T GET YOU AT ALL!
A HA HA!
BUT...
...I'M SORTA THANKFUL.
EVEN THOUGH I'VE DECIDED TO GO HOME...

menu 18

They let me draw a color title page! I wanted the image to portray the idea that they're so close even though they're not face-to-face. I've really gotten into the story, and it's not just because I'm writing the story, but because the end result is due to the perseverance of all the characters.

And perhaps because I'm drawing furiously at full speed, I didn't notice anything even when my editor mentioned it during the storyboard reviews, or when people said the same thing after the magazine issue came out. But from about this point on, I think that the way I draw manga...changed a little bit.

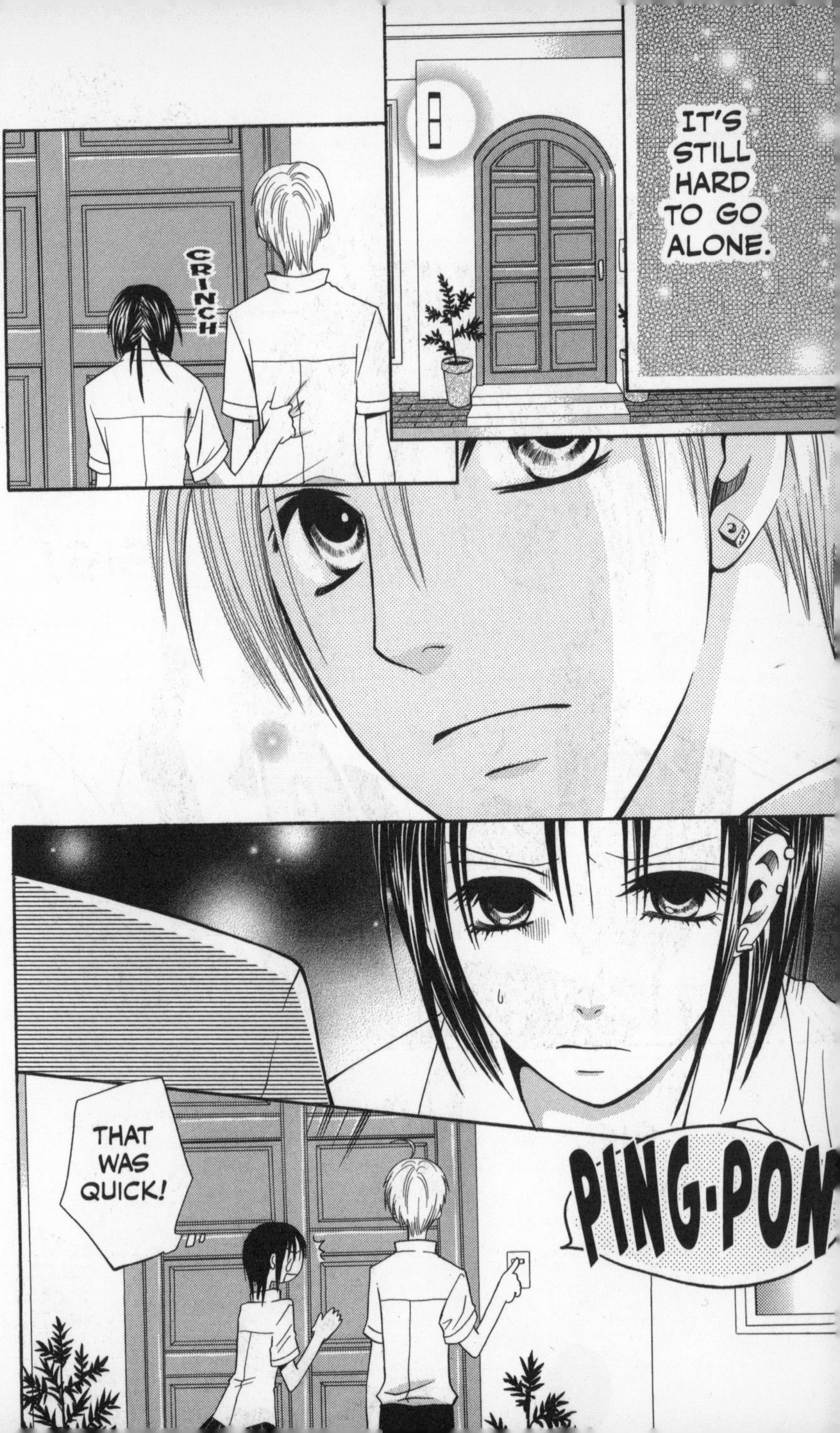
IT'S STILL HARD TO GO ALONE.
CRINCH
PING-PON
THAT WAS QUICK!

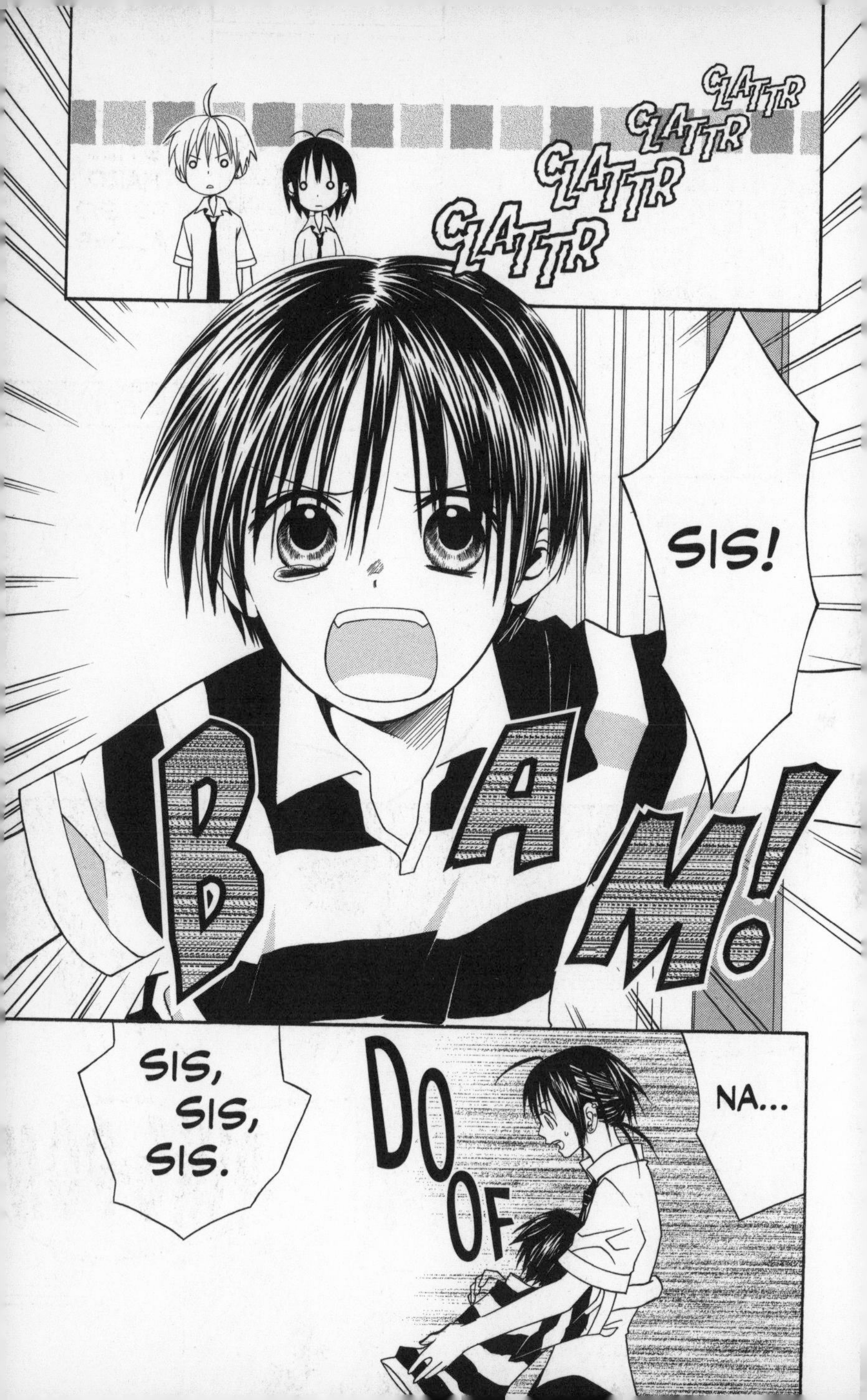
CLATTR
CLATTR
CLATTR
CLATTR
SIS!
BAM!
NA...
DOOF
SIS, SIS, SIS.

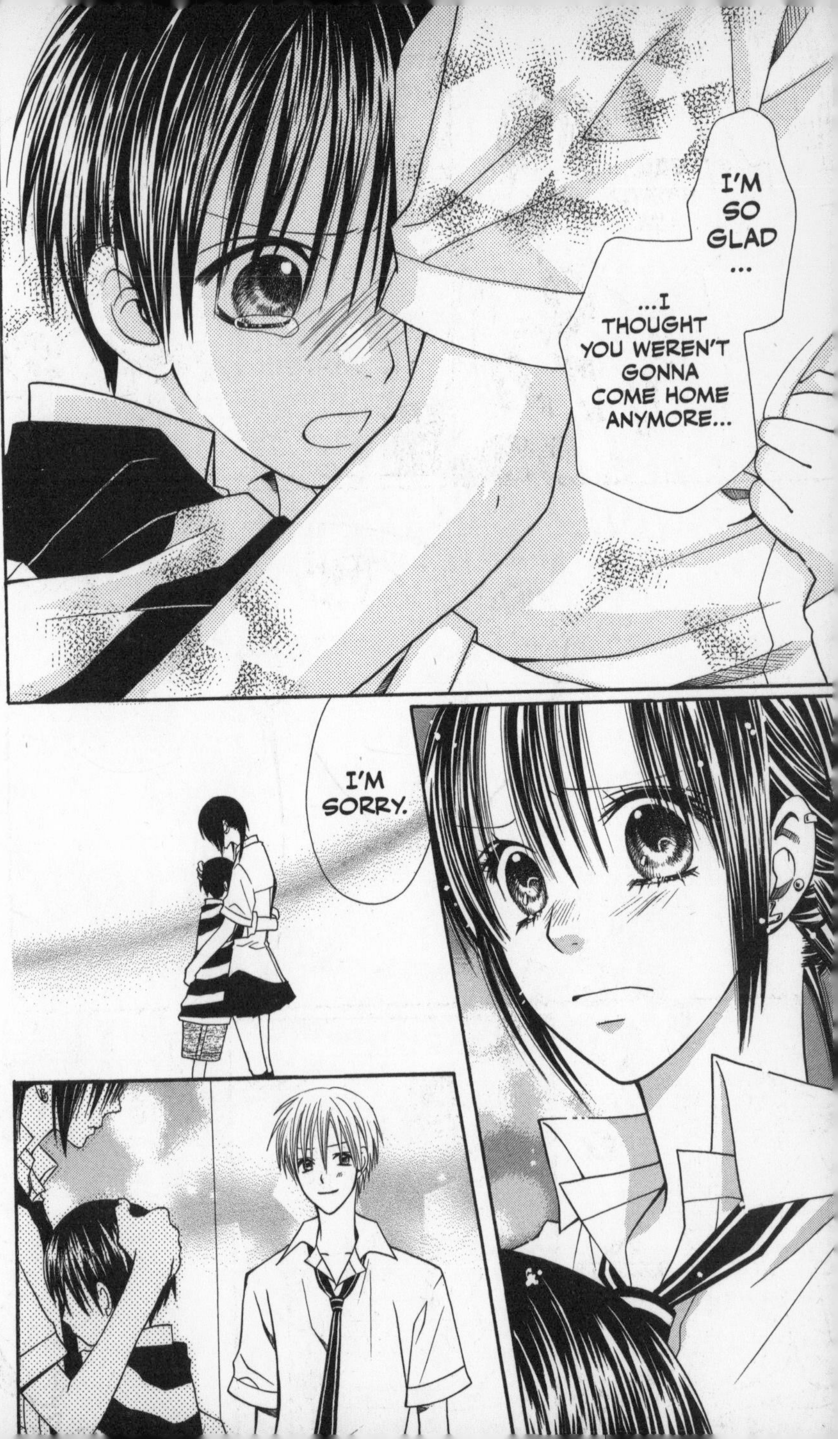
I'M SO GLAD ...
...I THOUGHT YOU WEREN'T GONNA COME HOME ANYMORE...
I'M SORRY.

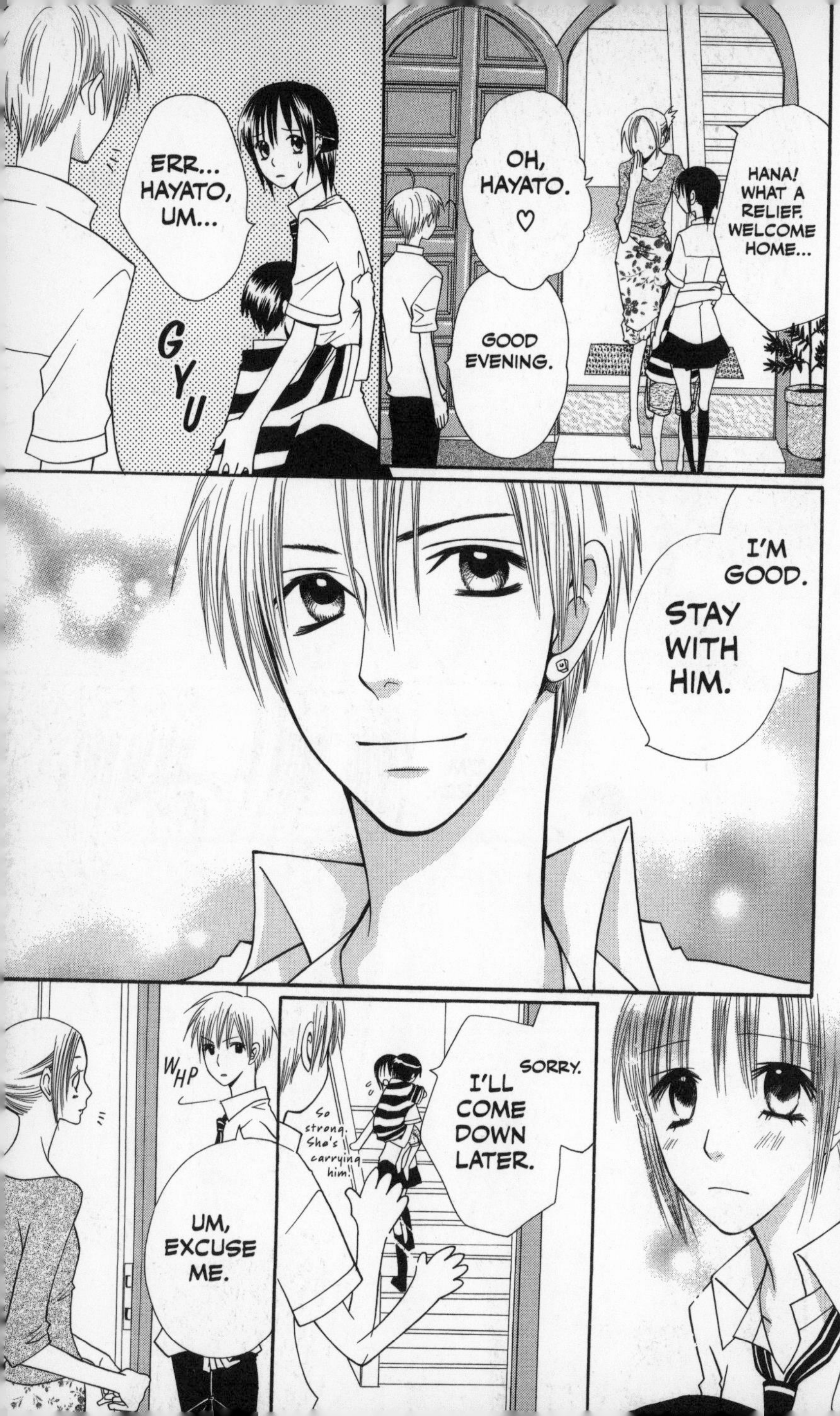
HANA! WHAT A RELIEF. WELCOME HOME...
OH, HAYATO. ♡
GOOD EVENING.
ERR... HAYATO, UM...
GYU
I'M GOOD.
STAY WITH HIM.
SORRY.
I'LL COME DOWN LATER.
So strong. She's carrying him.
WHP
UM, EXCUSE ME.

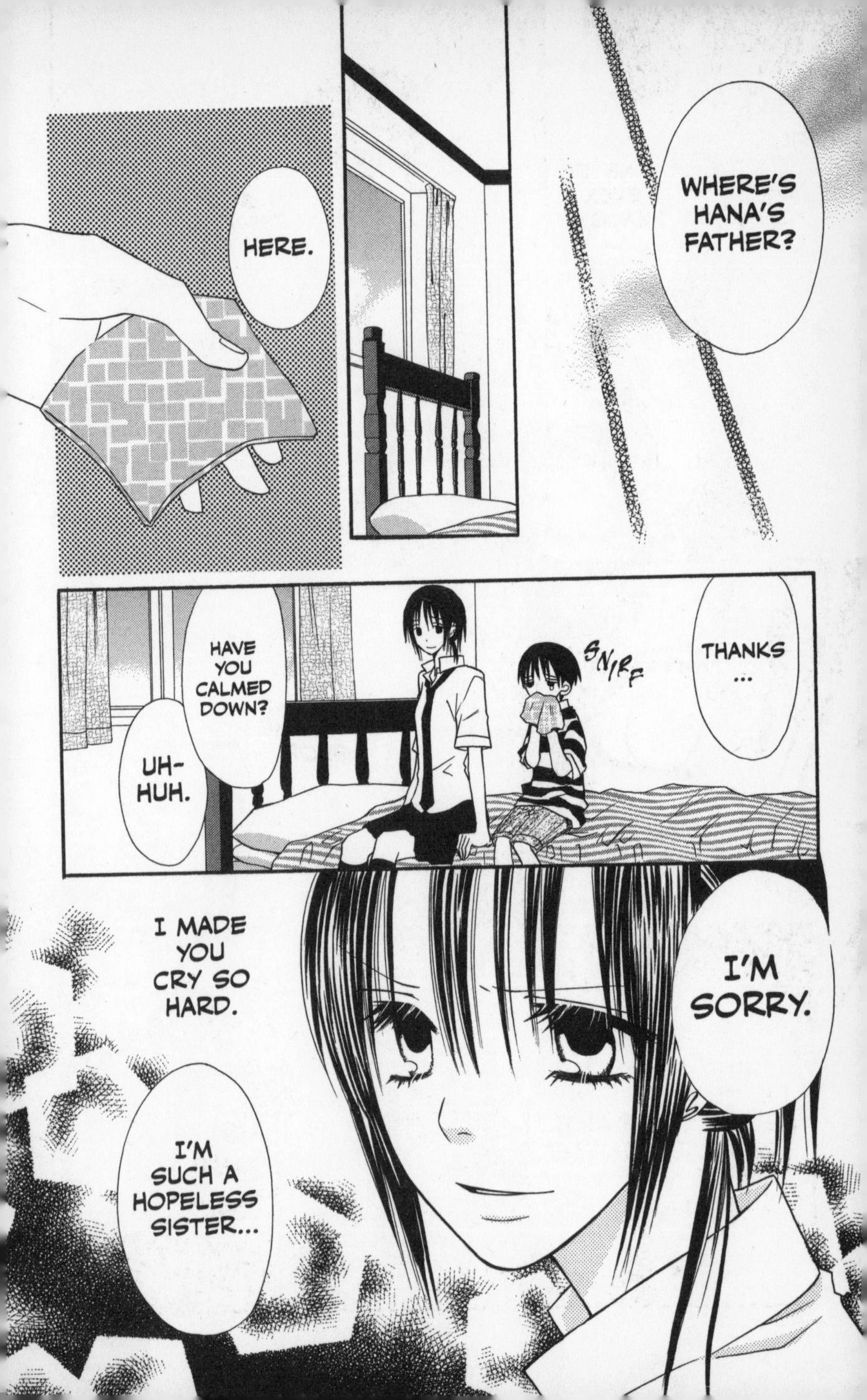
WHERE'S HANA'S FATHER?
HERE.
THANKS ...
SNIFF
HAVE YOU CALMED DOWN?
UH-HUH.
I'M SORRY.
I MADE YOU CRY SO HARD.
I'M SUCH A HOPELESS SISTER...

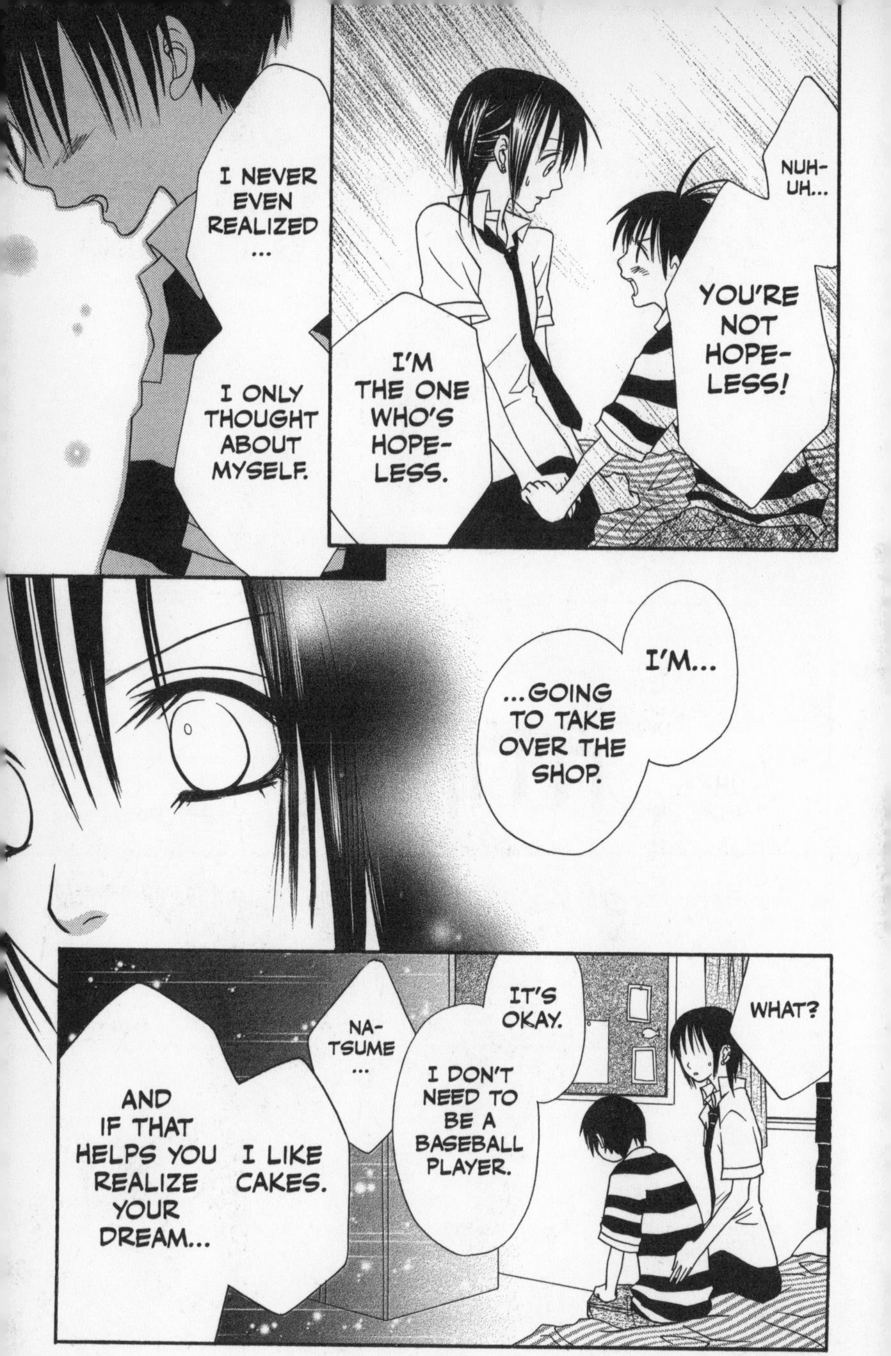
NUH-UH...
YOU'RE NOT HOPE-LESS!
I'M THE ONE WHO'S HOPE-LESS.
I NEVER EVEN REALIZED...
I ONLY THOUGHT ABOUT MYSELF.
I'M...
...GOING TO TAKE OVER THE SHOP.
WHAT?
IT'S OKAY.
I DON'T NEED TO BE A BASEBALL PLAYER.
NA-TSUME...
I LIKE CAKES.
AND IF THAT HELPS YOU REALIZE YOUR DREAM...

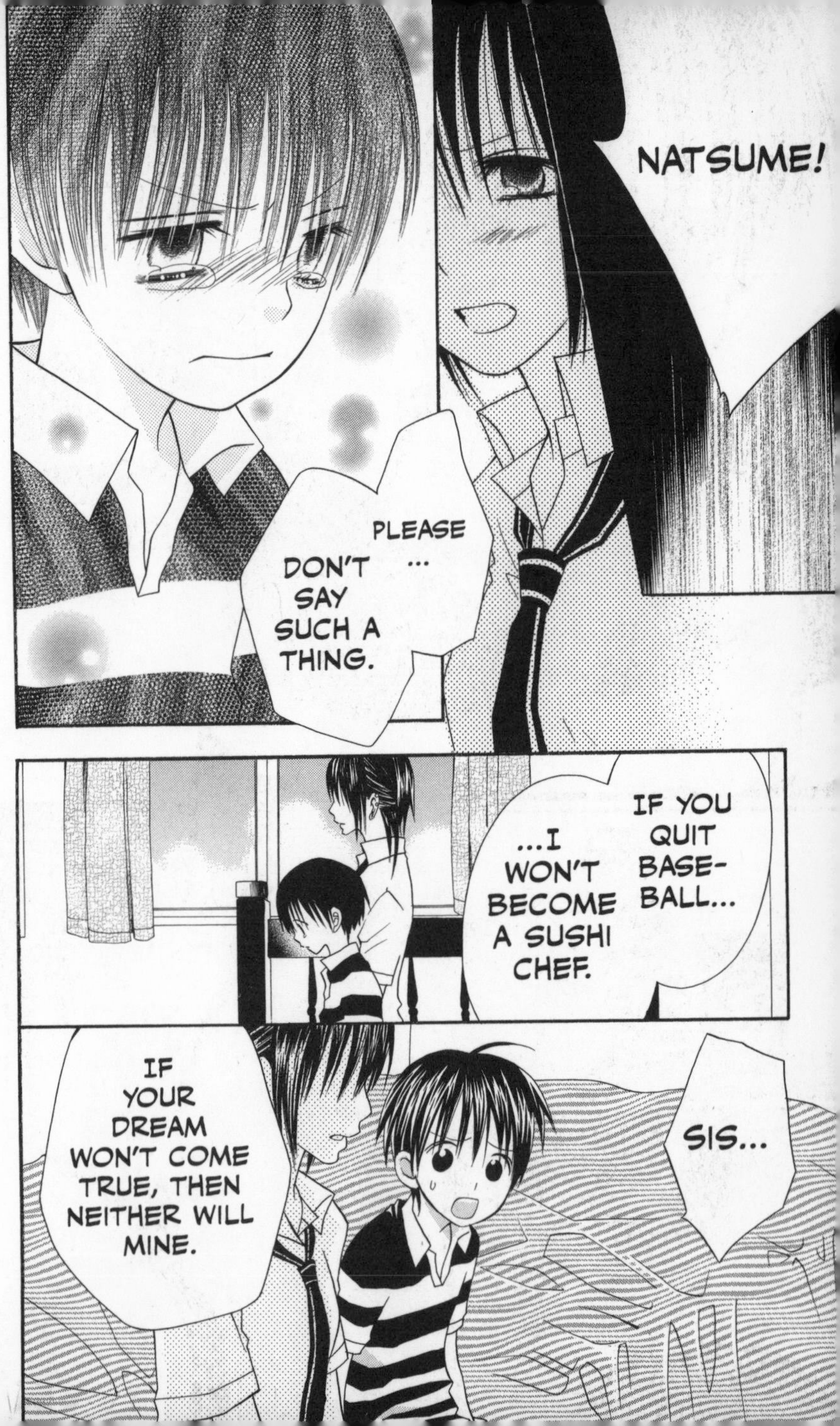
NATSUME!
PLEASE... DON'T SAY SUCH A THING.
IF YOU QUIT BASEBALL...
...I WON'T BECOME A SUSHI CHEF.
IF YOUR DREAM WON'T COME TRUE, THEN NEITHER WILL MINE.
SIS...

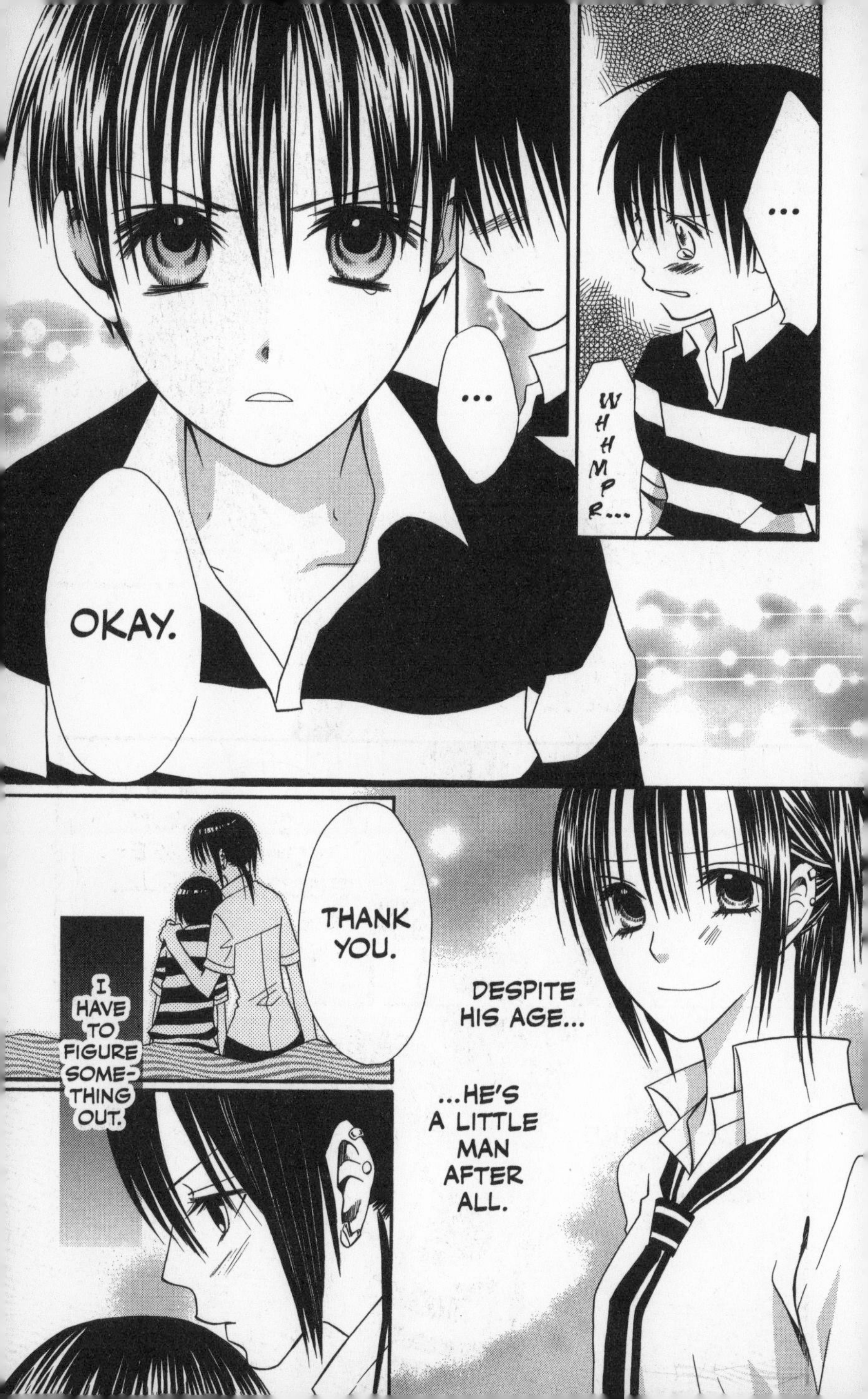
...
WHHMPR...
...
OKAY.
DESPITE HIS AGE...
...HE'S A LITTLE MAN AFTER ALL.
THANK YOU.
I HAVE TO FIGURE SOME-THING OUT.

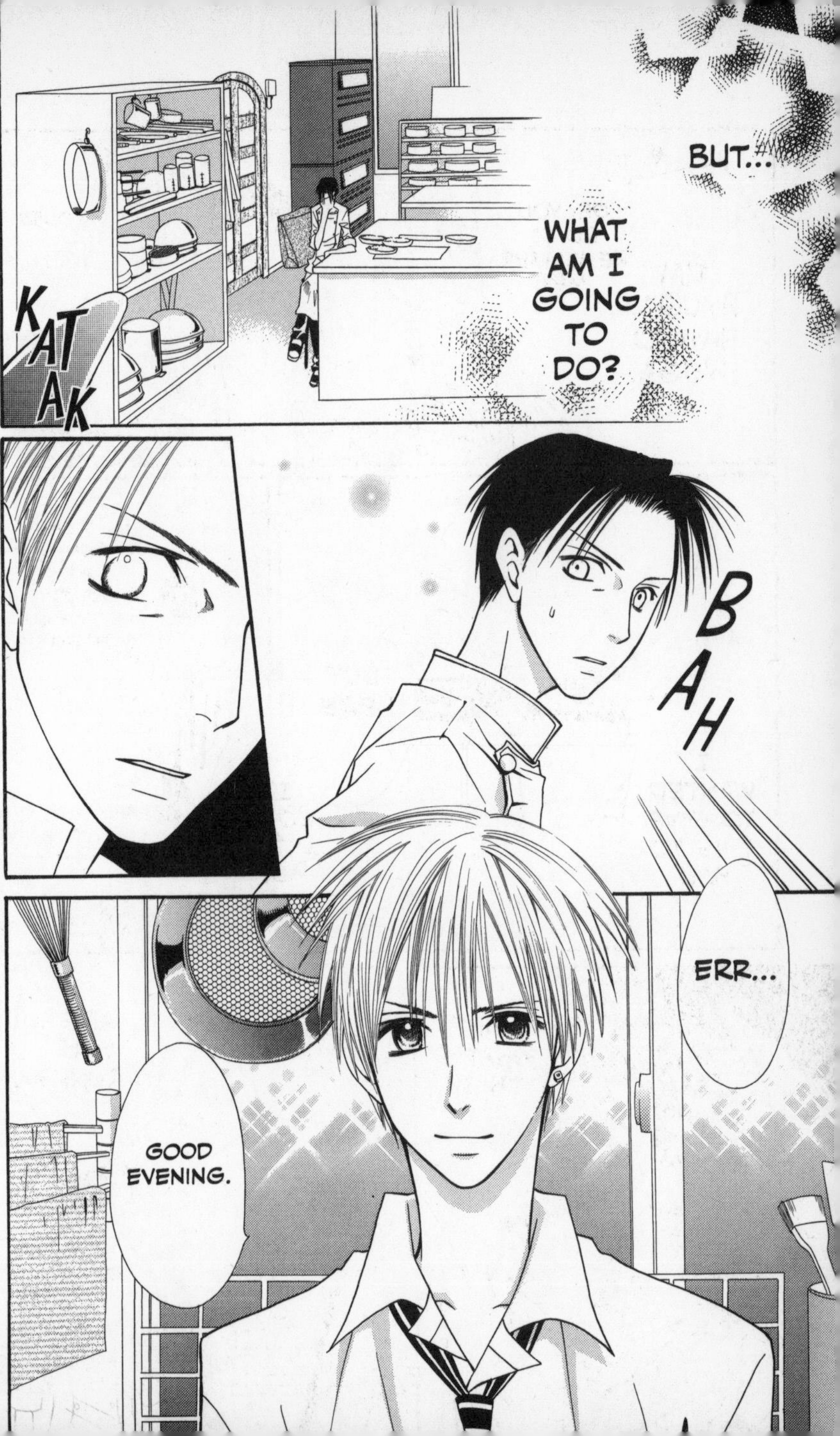
BUT...
WHAT AM I GOING TO DO?
KATAK
BAH
ERR...
GOOD EVENING.

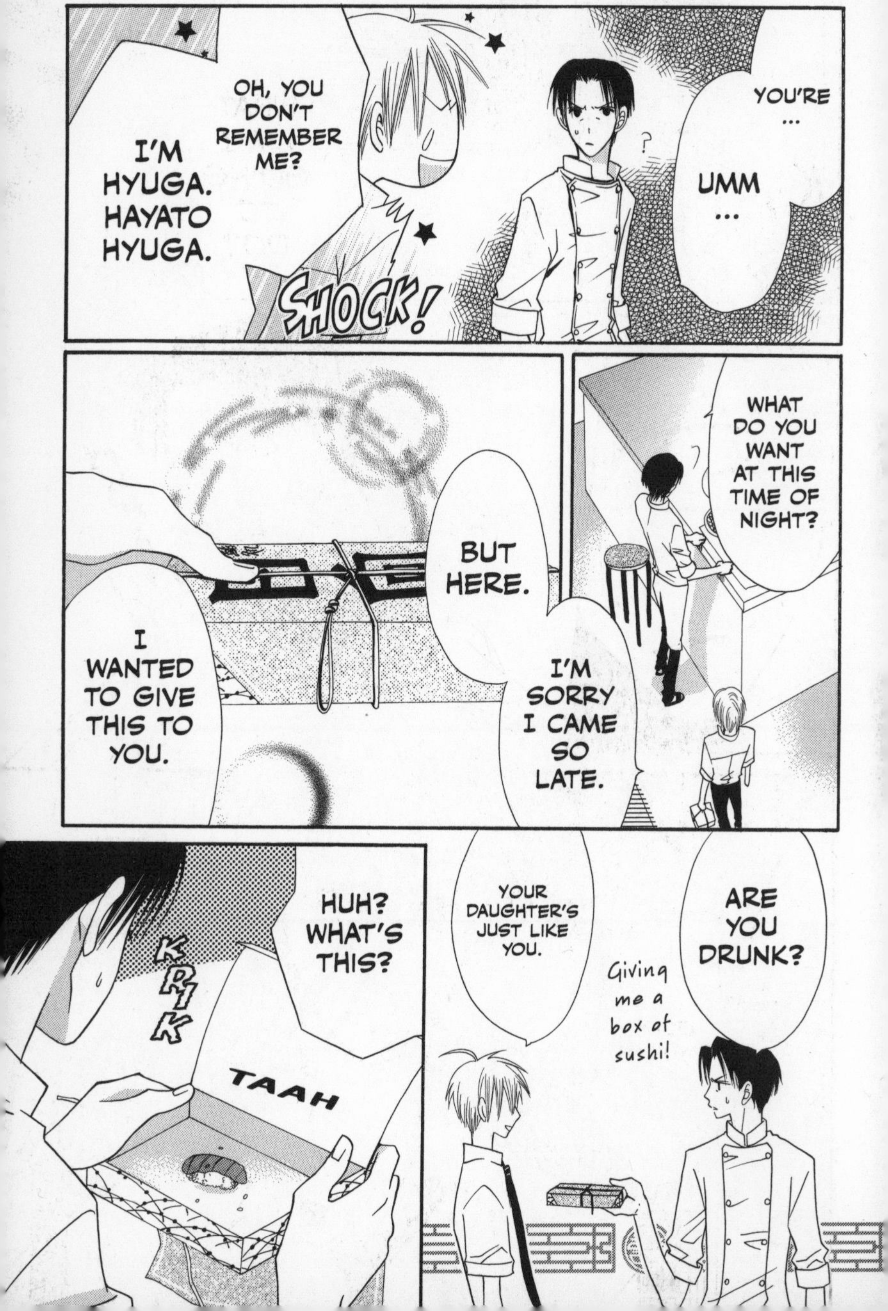
YOU'RE ... UMM ...
OH, YOU DON'T REMEMBER ME?
I'M HYUGA. HAYATO HYUGA.
SHOCK!
WHAT DO YOU WANT AT THIS TIME OF NIGHT?
I'M SORRY I CAME SO LATE.
BUT HERE.
I WANTED TO GIVE THIS TO YOU.
ARE YOU DRUNK?
Giving me a box of sushi!
YOUR DAUGHTER'S JUST LIKE YOU.
HUH? WHAT'S THIS?
KRIK
TAAH

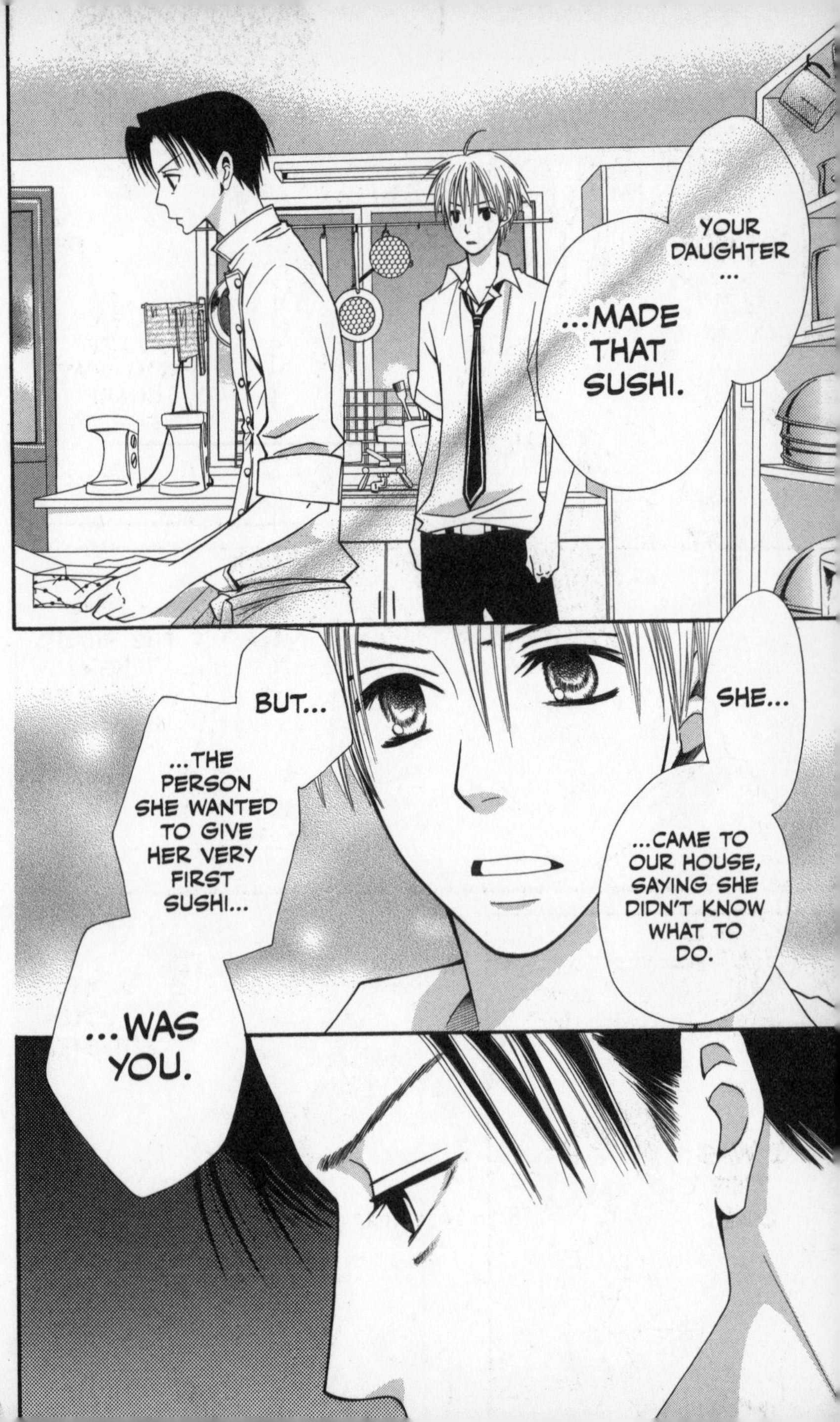
YOUR DAUGHTER ...
...MADE THAT SUSHI.
SHE...
...CAME TO OUR HOUSE, SAYING SHE DIDN'T KNOW WHAT TO DO.
BUT...
...THE PERSON SHE WANTED TO GIVE HER VERY FIRST SUSHI...
...WAS YOU.

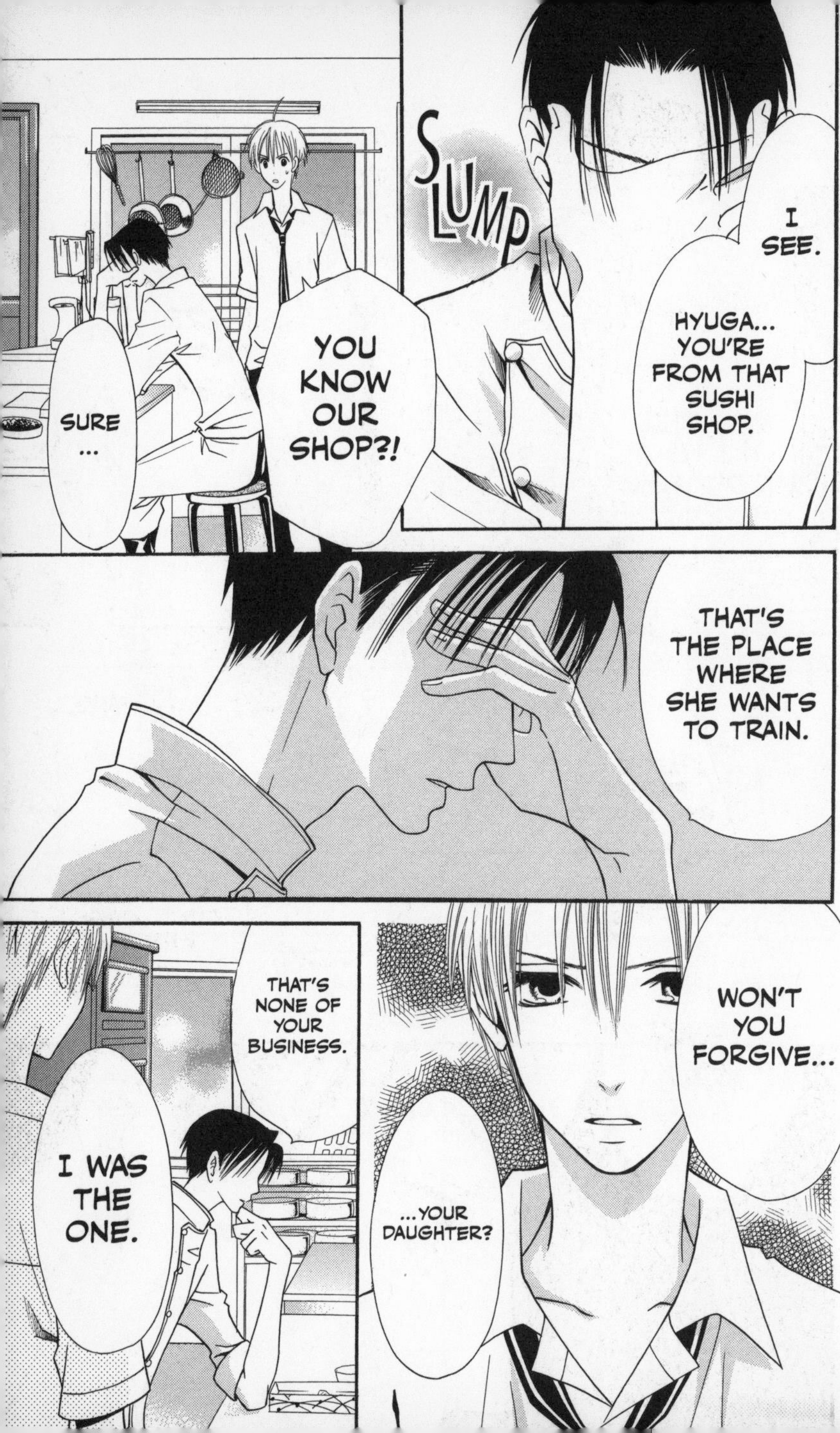
SLUMP
I SEE.
HYUGA... YOU'RE FROM THAT SUSHI SHOP.
YOU KNOW OUR SHOP?!
SURE ...
THAT'S THE PLACE WHERE SHE WANTS TO TRAIN.
WON'T YOU FORGIVE...
...YOUR DAUGHTER?
THAT'S NONE OF YOUR BUSINESS.
I WAS THE ONE.

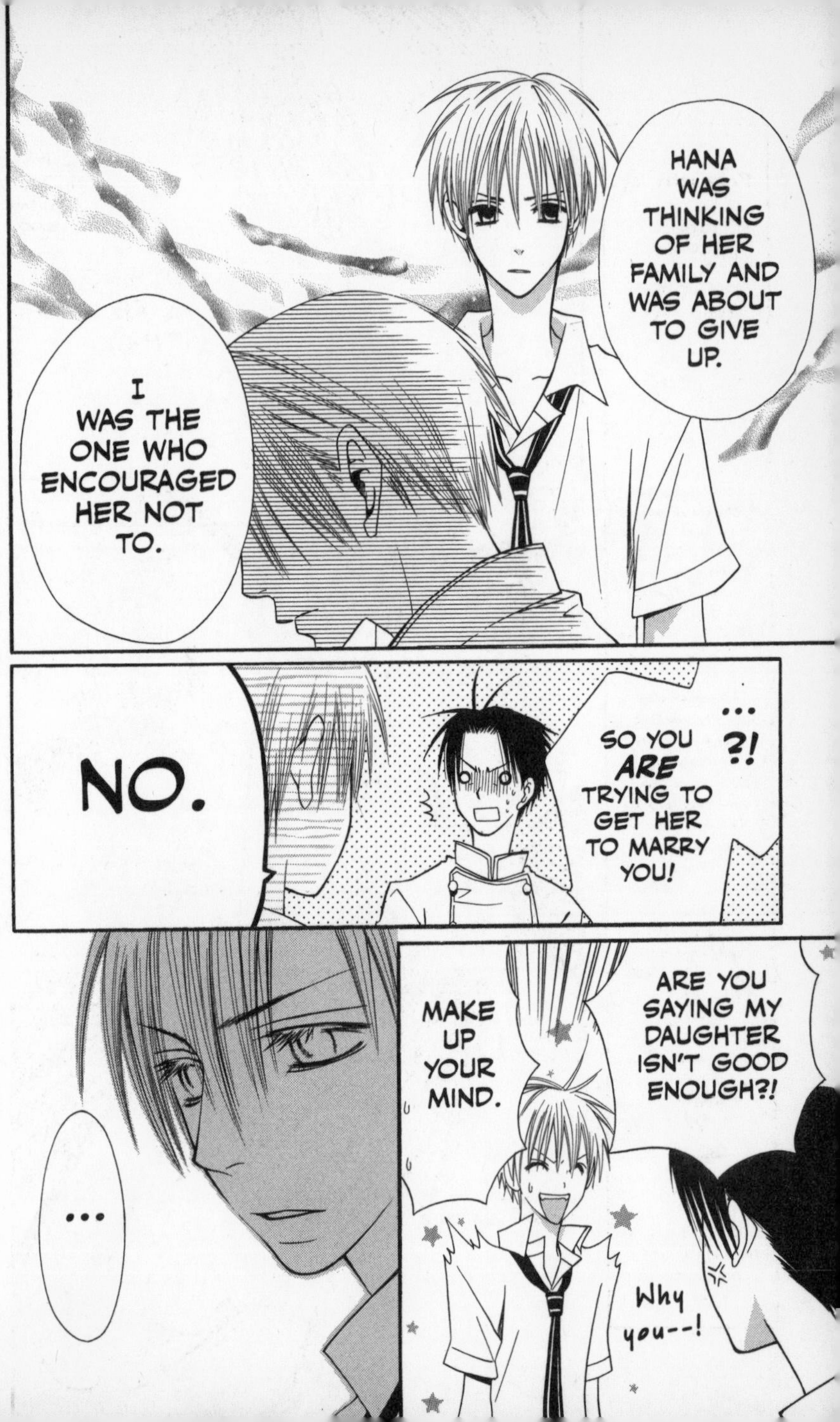
HANA WAS THINKING OF HER FAMILY AND WAS ABOUT TO GIVE UP.
I WAS THE ONE WHO ENCOURAGED HER NOT TO.
...?!
SO YOU **ARE** TRYING TO GET HER TO MARRY YOU!
NO.
ARE YOU SAYING MY DAUGHTER ISN'T GOOD ENOUGH?!
MAKE UP YOUR MIND.
Why you--!
...

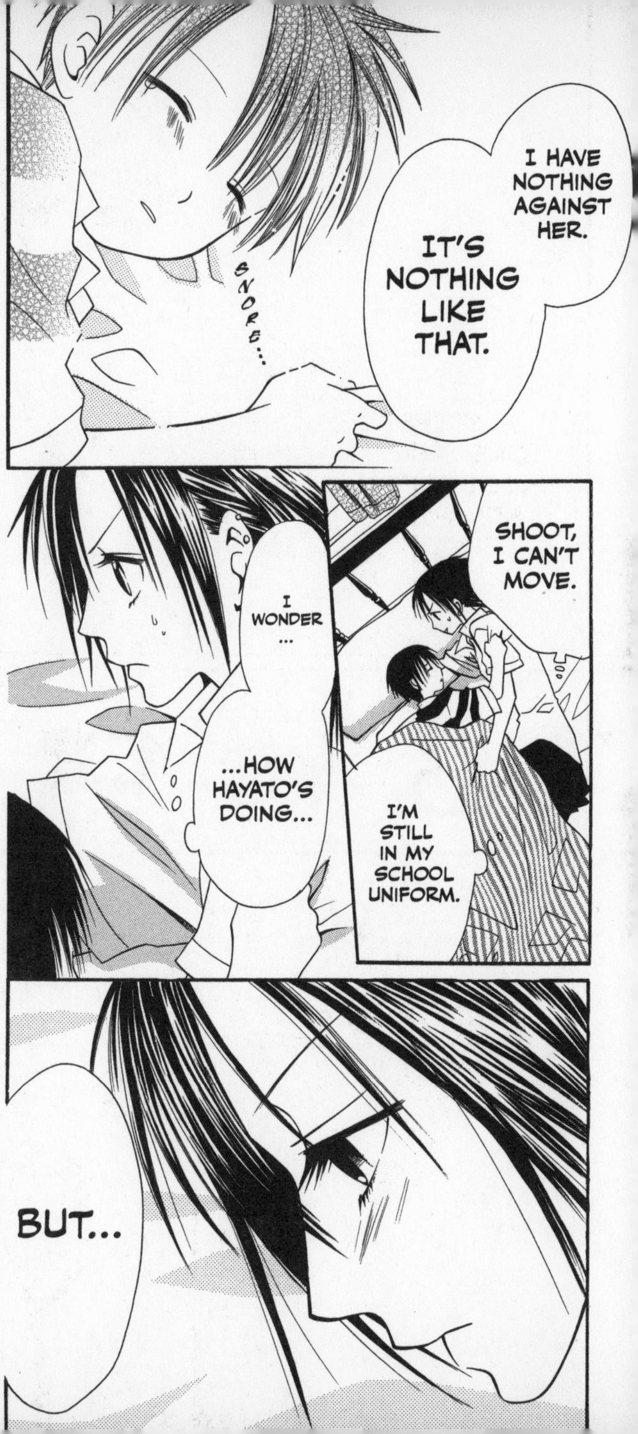
I HAVE NOTHING AGAINST HER.
IT'S NOTHING LIKE THAT.
SNORE...
SHOOT, I CAN'T MOVE.
I'M STILL IN MY SCHOOL UNIFORM.
I WONDER...
...HOW HAYATO'S DOING...
BUT...

Promotion ☆

Between chapters 17 and 18, Margaret magazine let me take a break.

I didn't want to just go, so in that one issue, we had a page titled, "MV Seconds!"

(I illustrated the recipe for Cheese Wrapped in Shiso Leaf.)

And in Margaret's 7th issue of 2006 (MV Chapter 20), "Seconds!" became a regular feature!

It's a corner where readers can participate in all kinds of discussions, and where my (and my editor's) passion for baseball is obvious.

Contributors whose postcards are featured all receive a special Sushidokoro Hyuga teacup!

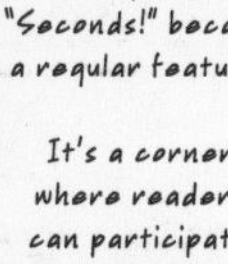
Sushidokoro Hyuga

It's really nice!

All you comic fans, please check out Margaret magazine!

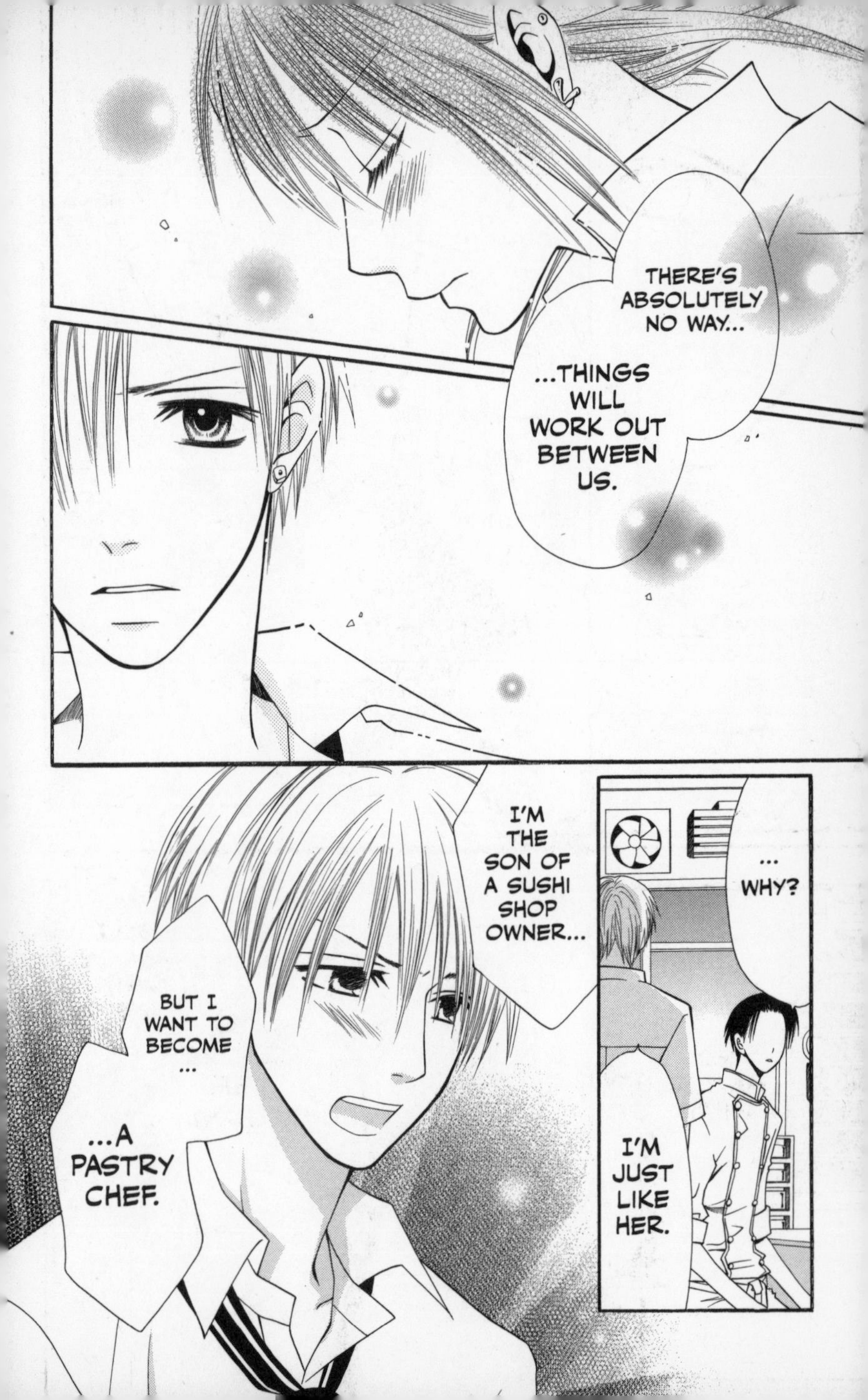
THERE'S ABSOLUTELY NO WAY...
...THINGS WILL WORK OUT BETWEEN US.
...WHY?
I'M JUST LIKE HER.
I'M THE SON OF A SUSHI SHOP OWNER...
BUT I WANT TO BECOME...
...A PASTRY CHEF.

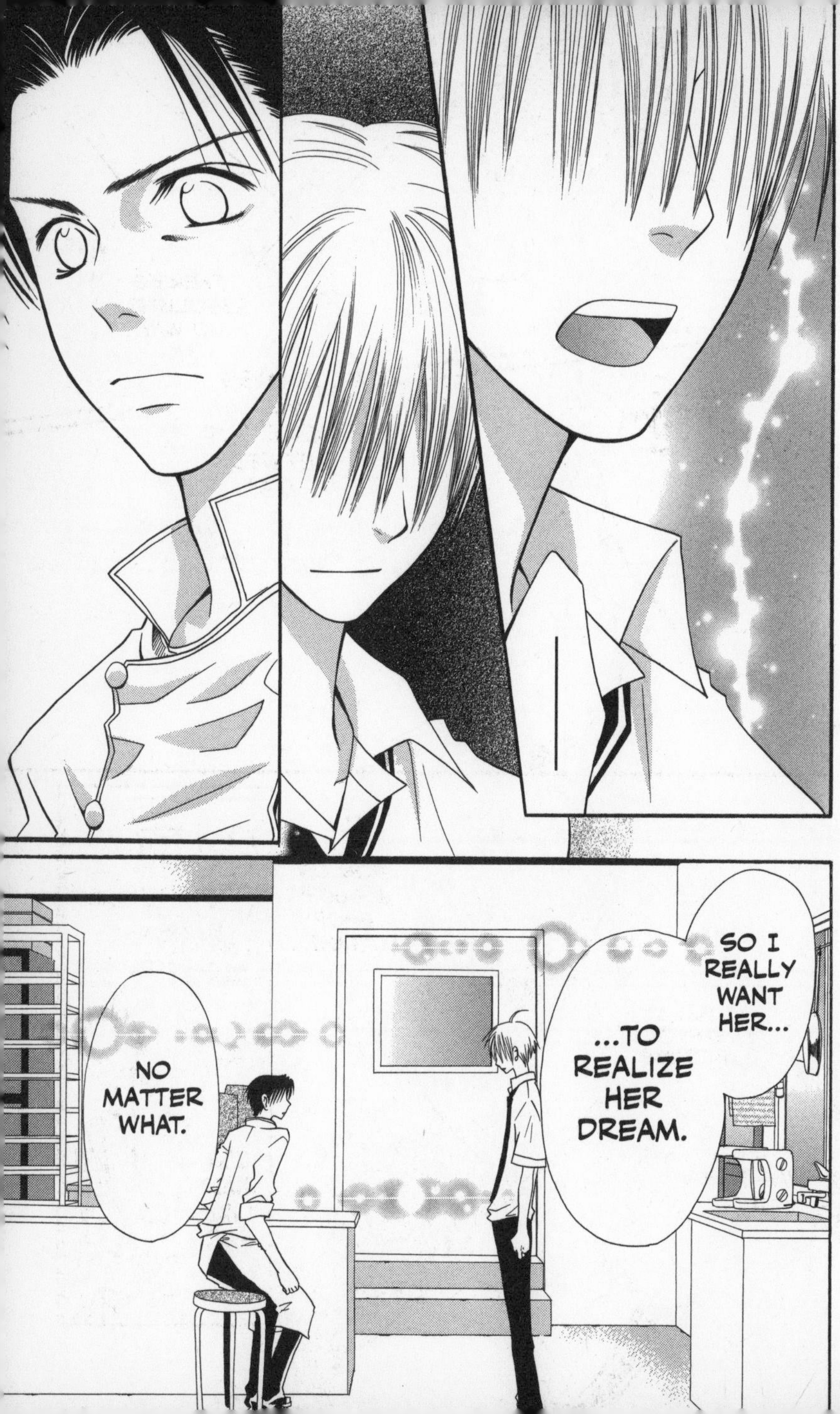
SO I REALLY WANT HER...
...TO REALIZE HER DREAM.
NO MATTER WHAT.

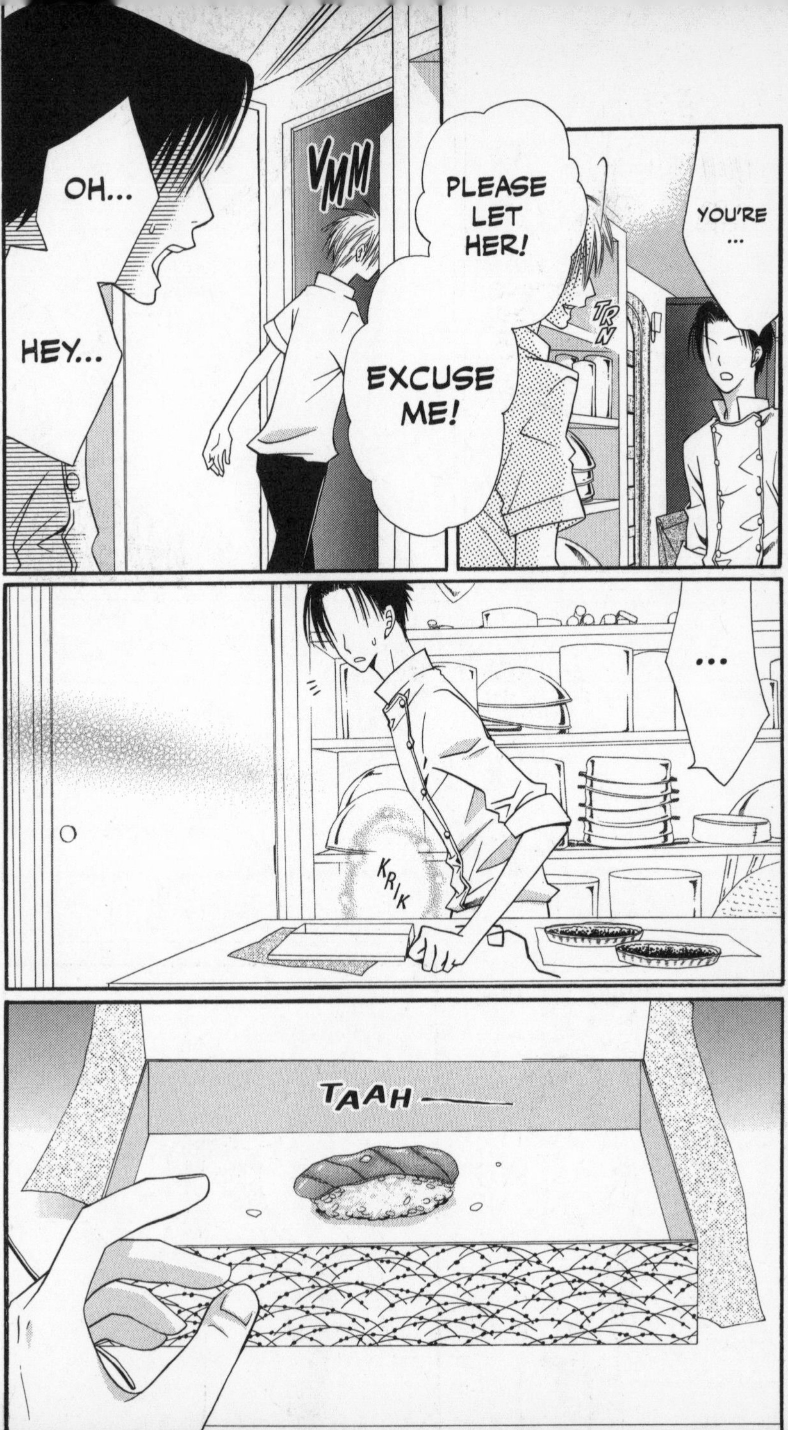
YOU'RE ...
PLEASE LET HER!
TRN
EXCUSE ME!
VMM
OH...
HEY...
...
KRIK
TAAH

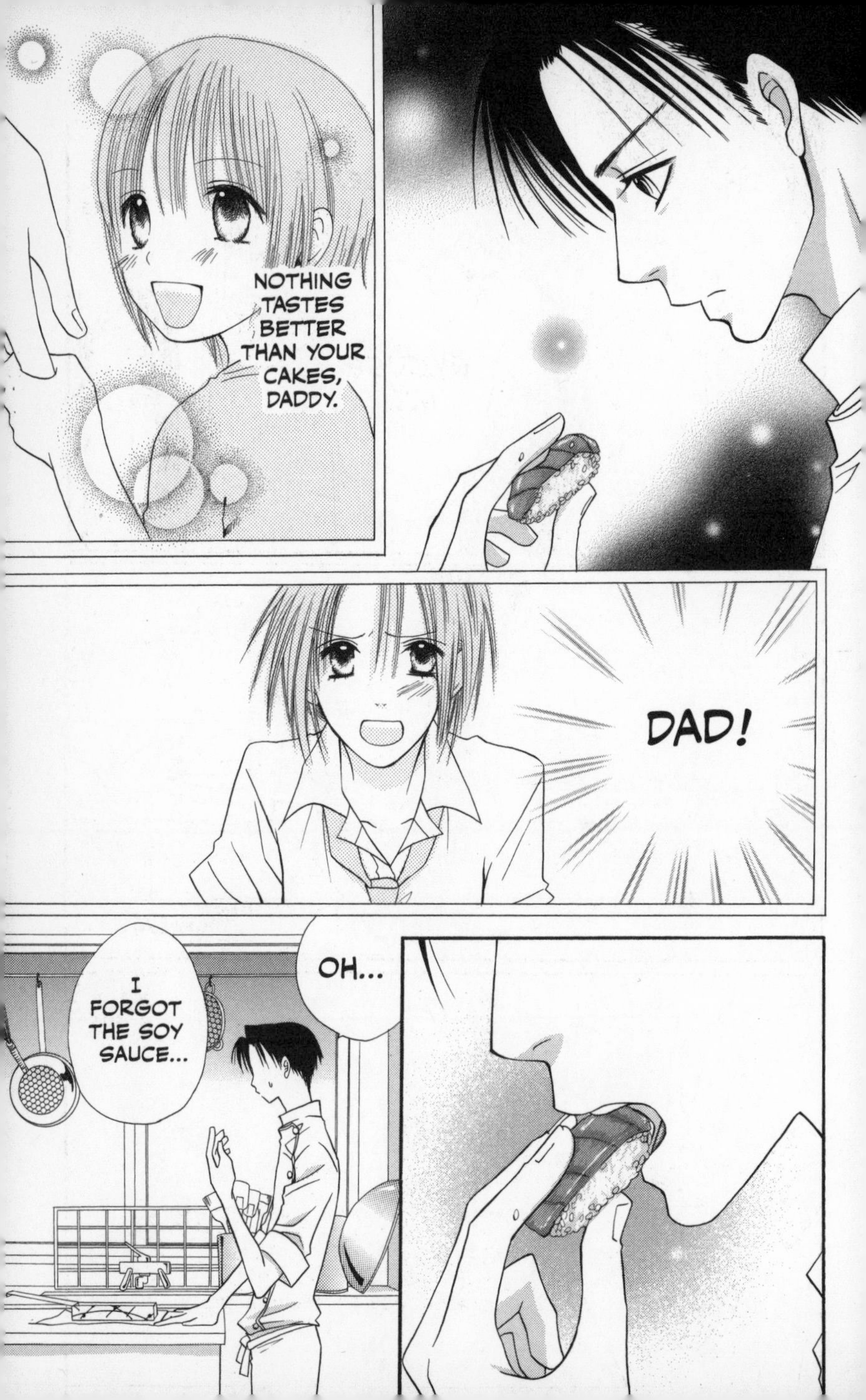
NOTHING TASTES BETTER THAN YOUR CAKES, DADDY.
DAD!
OH...
I FORGOT THE SOY SAUCE...

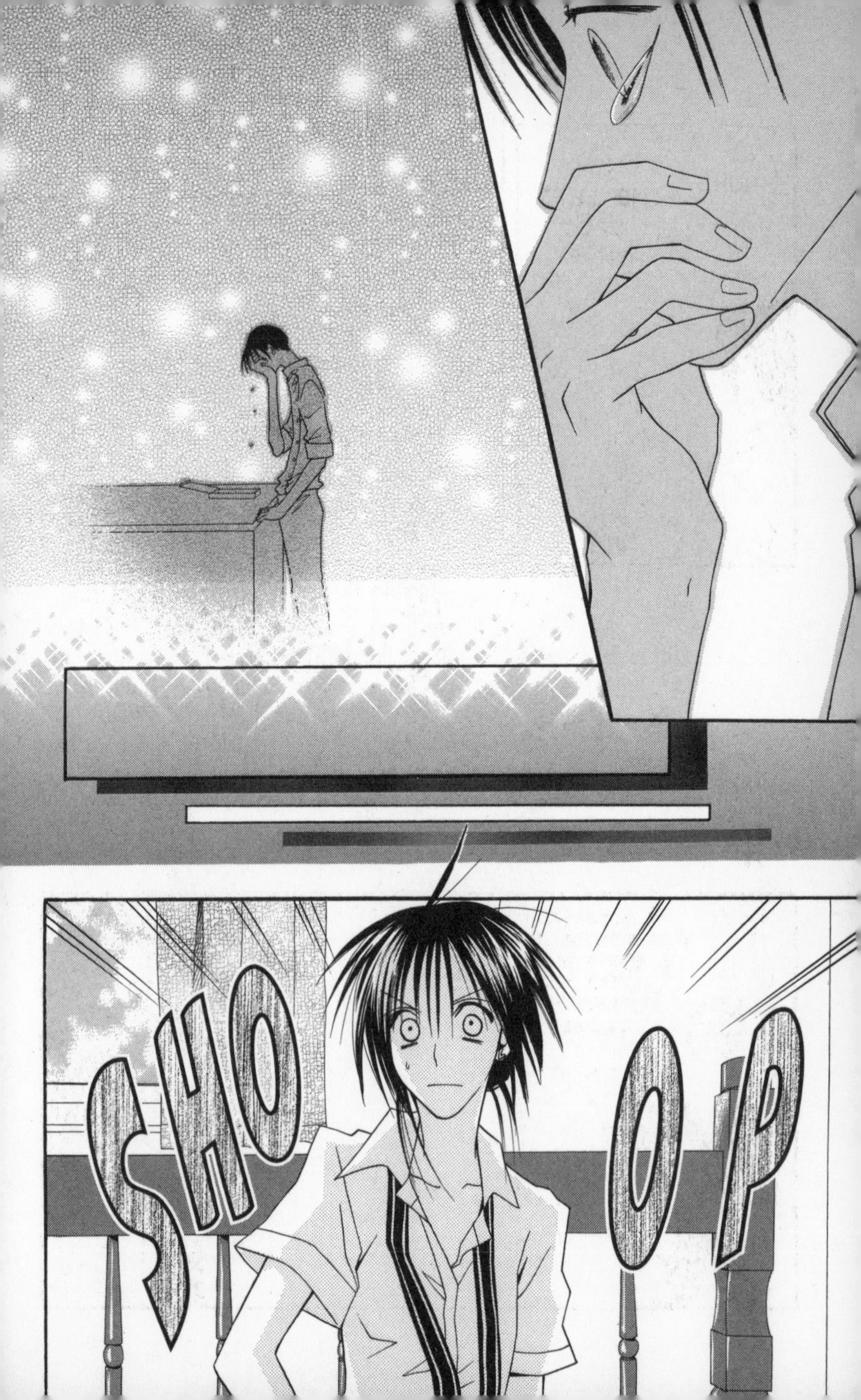
SHOOP

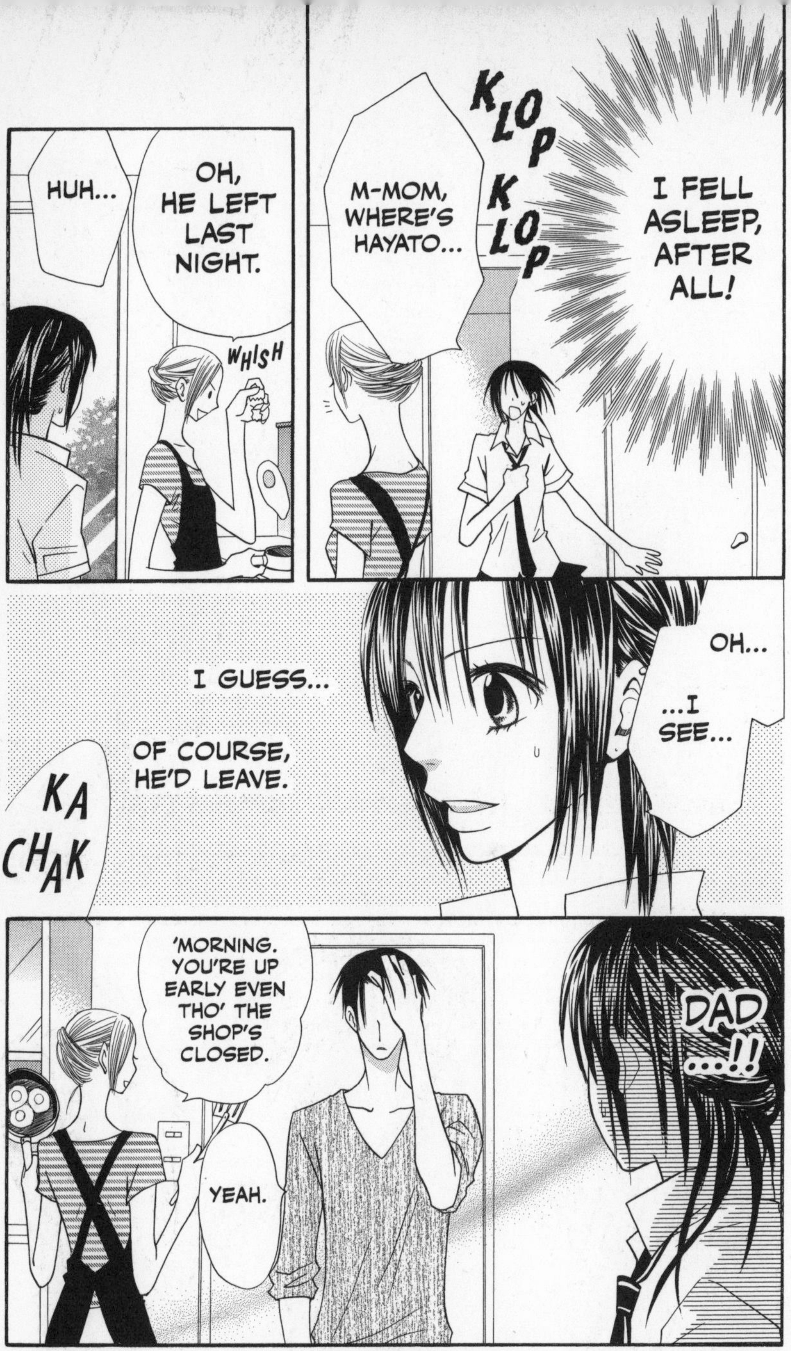
I FELL ASLEEP, AFTER ALL!
KLOP KLOP
M-MOM, WHERE'S HAYATO...
OH, HE LEFT LAST NIGHT.
HUH...
WHISH
OH...
...I SEE...
I GUESS...
OF COURSE, HE'D LEAVE.
KA CHAK
DAD...!!
'MORNING. YOU'RE UP EARLY EVEN THO' THE SHOP'S CLOSED.
YEAH.

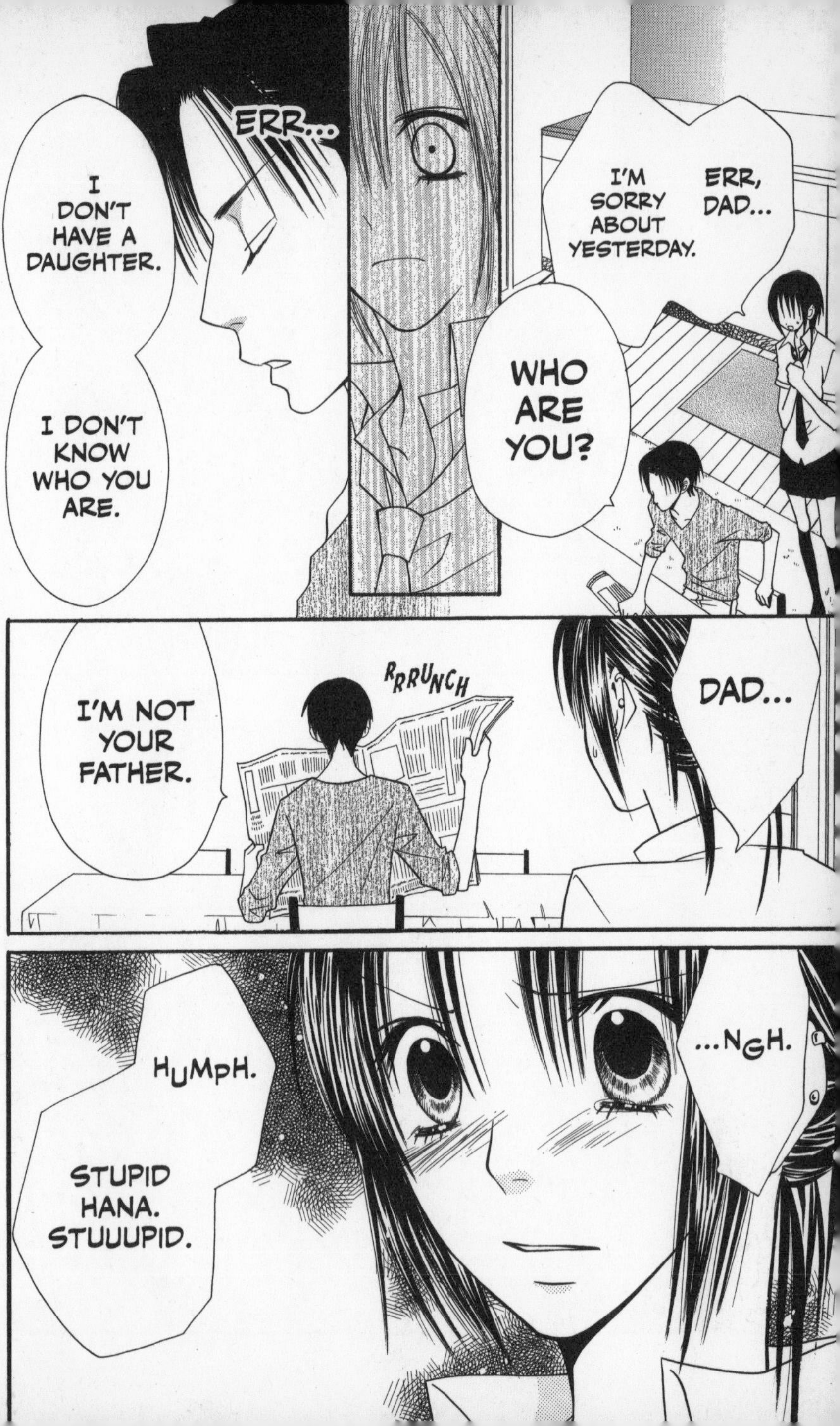
ERR, DAD...
I'M SORRY ABOUT YESTERDAY.
WHO ARE YOU?
ERR...
I DON'T HAVE A DAUGHTER.
I DON'T KNOW WHO YOU ARE.
DAD...
RRRUNCH
I'M NOT YOUR FATHER.
...NGH.
HUMPH.
STUPID HANA. STUUUPID.

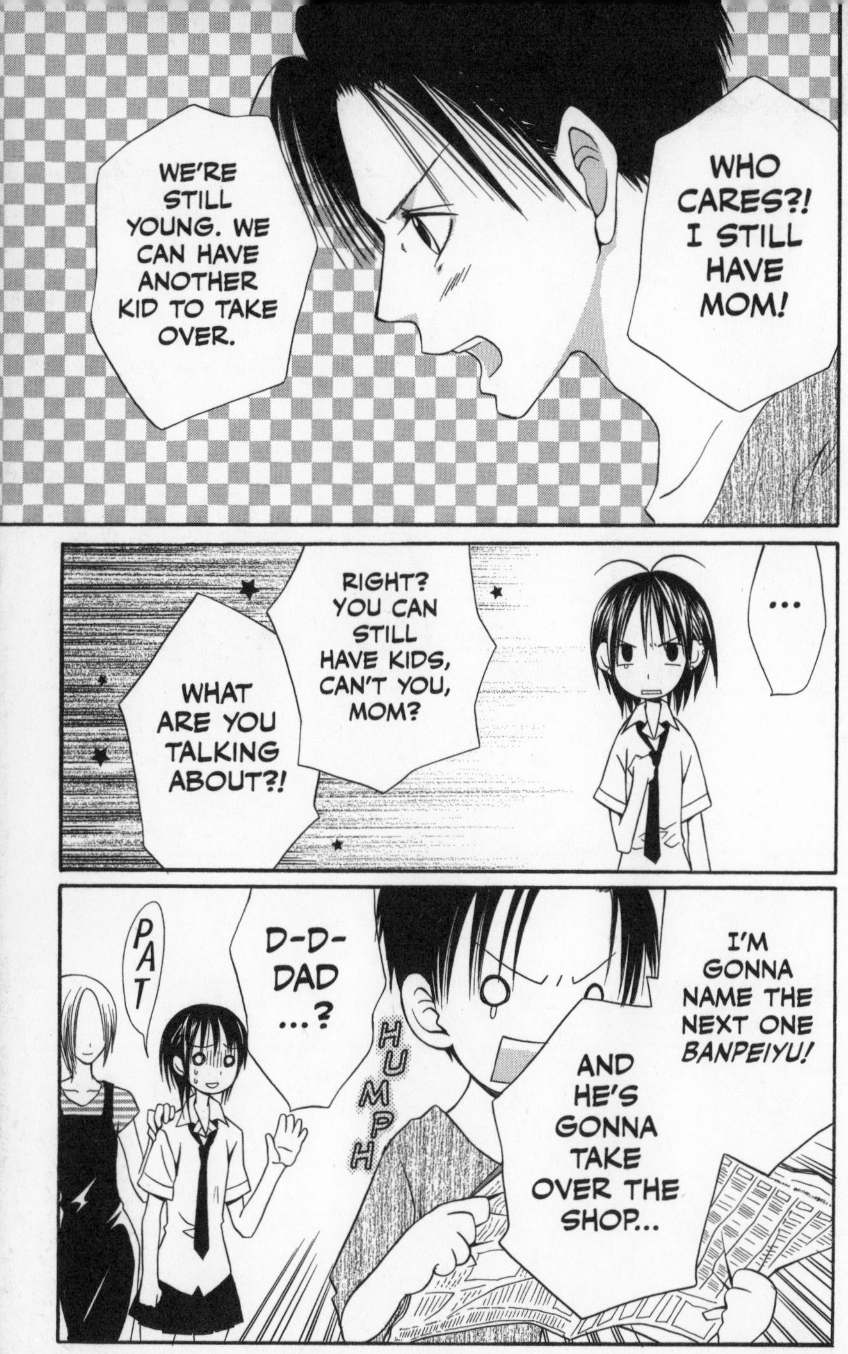
WHO CARES?! I STILL HAVE MOM!
WE'RE STILL YOUNG. WE CAN HAVE ANOTHER KID TO TAKE OVER.
...
RIGHT? YOU CAN STILL HAVE KIDS, CAN'T YOU, MOM?
WHAT ARE YOU TALKING ABOUT?!
I'M GONNA NAME THE NEXT ONE *BANPEIYU!*
AND HE'S GONNA TAKE OVER THE SHOP...
HUMPH
D-D-DAD ...?
PAT

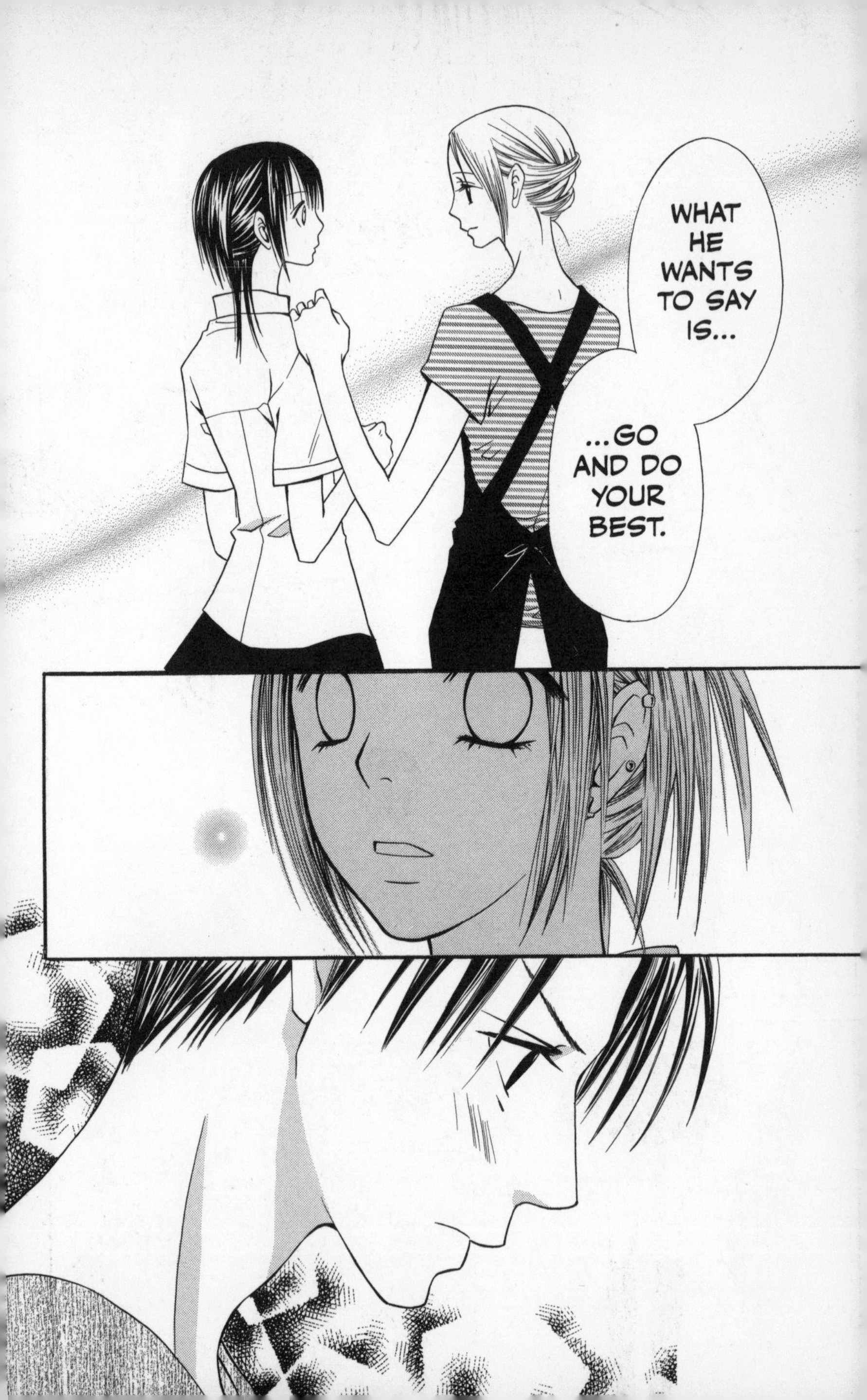
WHAT HE WANTS TO SAY IS...
...GO AND DO YOUR BEST.

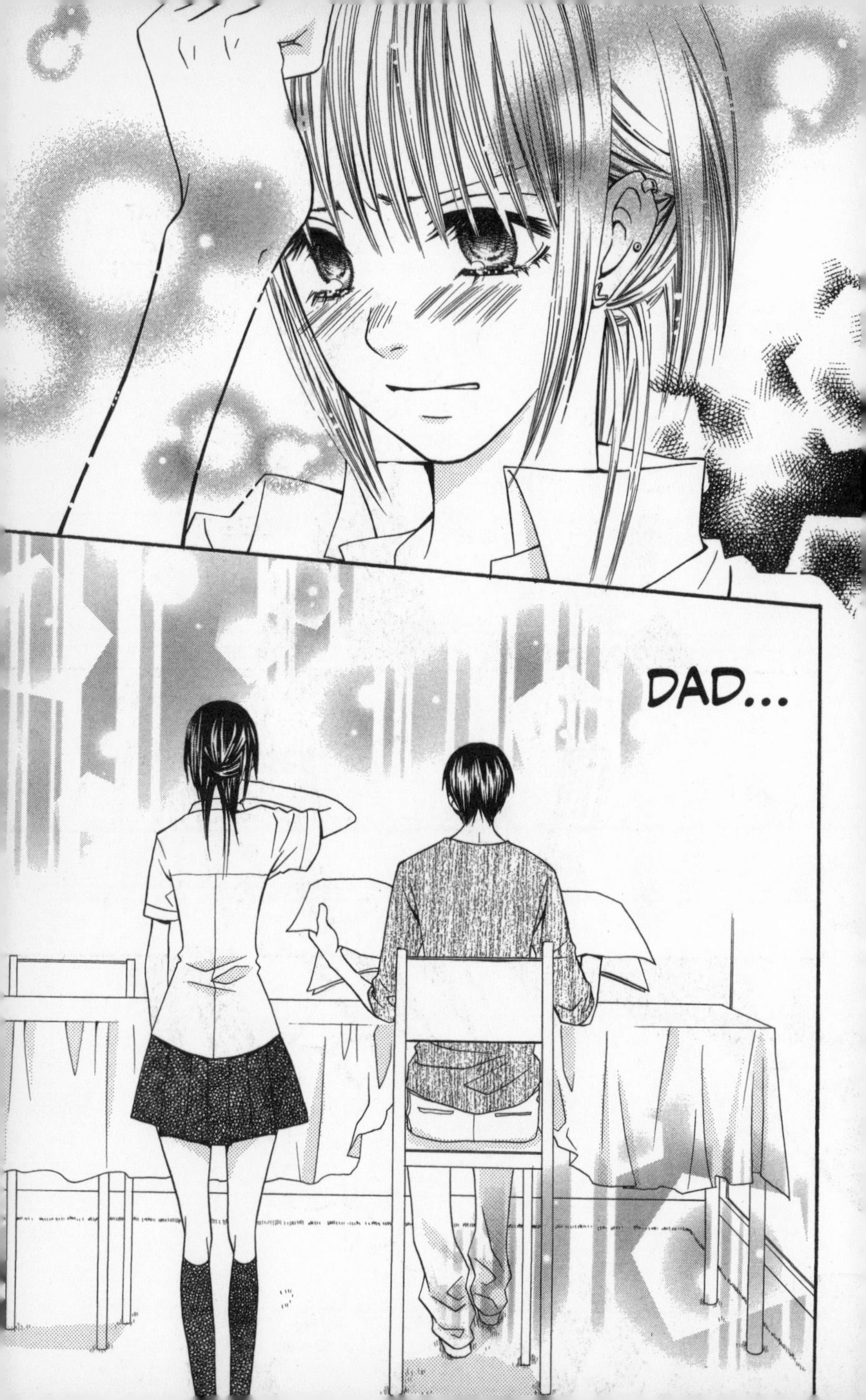
DAD...

SIDE DISH Mixed Vegetables 4

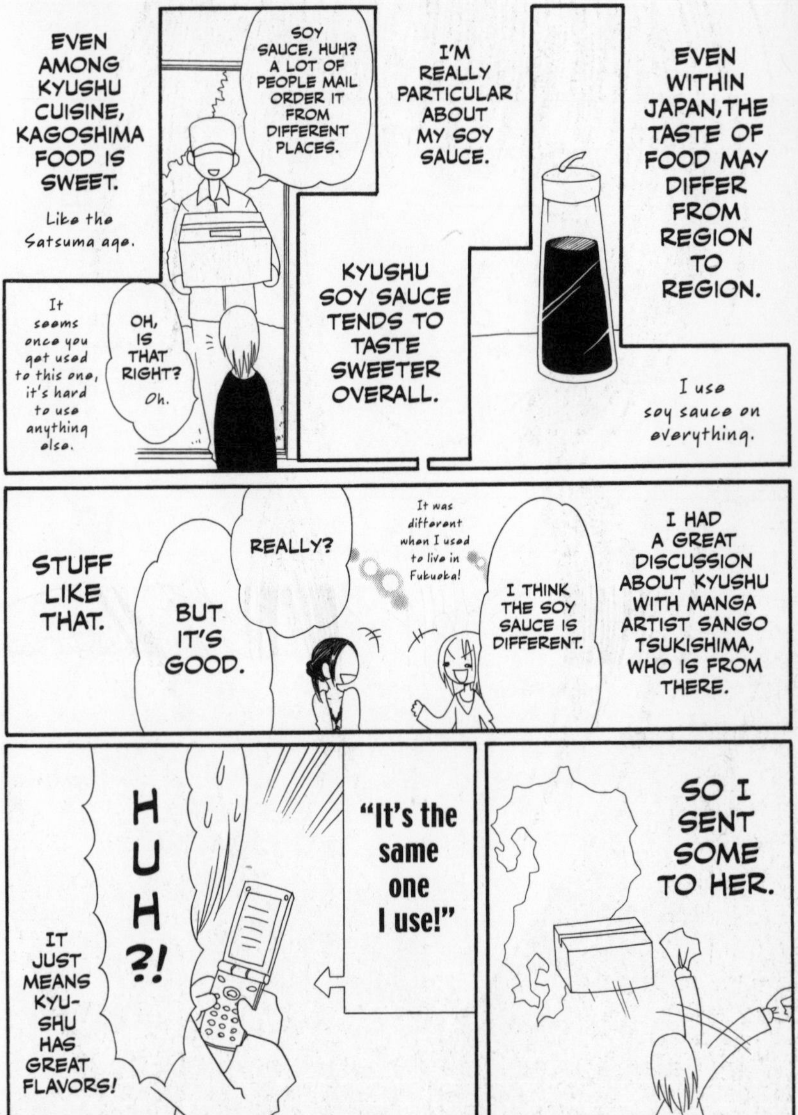
EVEN WITHIN JAPAN, THE TASTE OF FOOD MAY DIFFER FROM REGION TO REGION.
I use soy sauce on everything.
I'M REALLY PARTICULAR ABOUT MY SOY SAUCE.
KYUSHU SOY SAUCE TENDS TO TASTE SWEETER OVERALL.
EVEN AMONG KYUSHU CUISINE, KAGOSHIMA FOOD IS SWEET.
Like the Satsuma age.
SOY SAUCE, HUH? A LOT OF PEOPLE MAIL ORDER IT FROM DIFFERENT PLACES.
OH, IS THAT RIGHT?
Oh.
It seems once you get used to this one, it's hard to use anything else.
I HAD A GREAT DISCUSSION ABOUT KYUSHU WITH MANGA ARTIST SANGO TSUKISHIMA, WHO IS FROM THERE.
I THINK THE SOY SAUCE IS DIFFERENT.
It was different when I used to live in Fukuoka!
REALLY?
BUT IT'S GOOD.
STUFF LIKE THAT.
SO I SENT SOME TO HER.
"It's the same one I use!"
HUH?!
IT JUST MEANS KYU-SHU HAS GREAT FLAVORS!

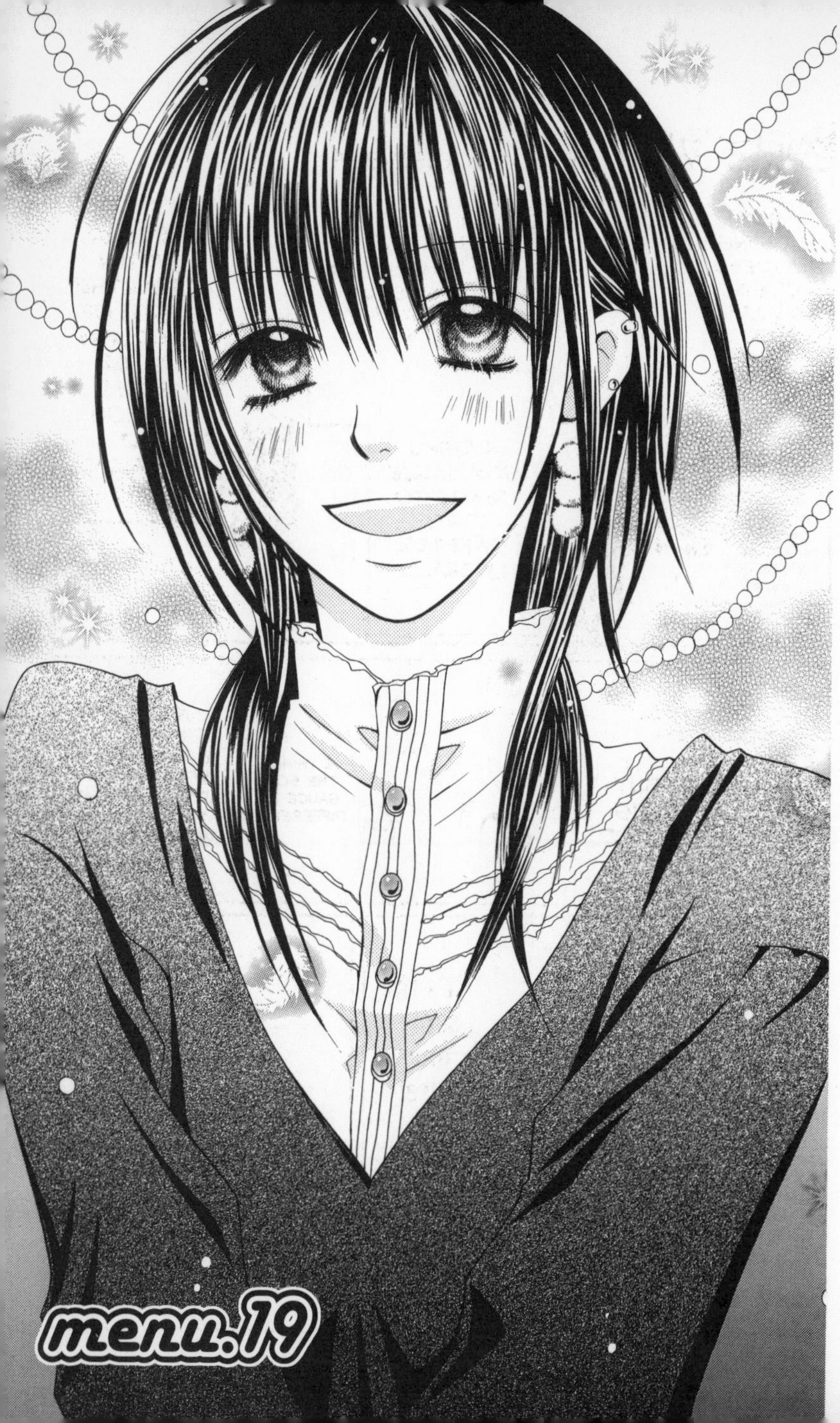
menu.19

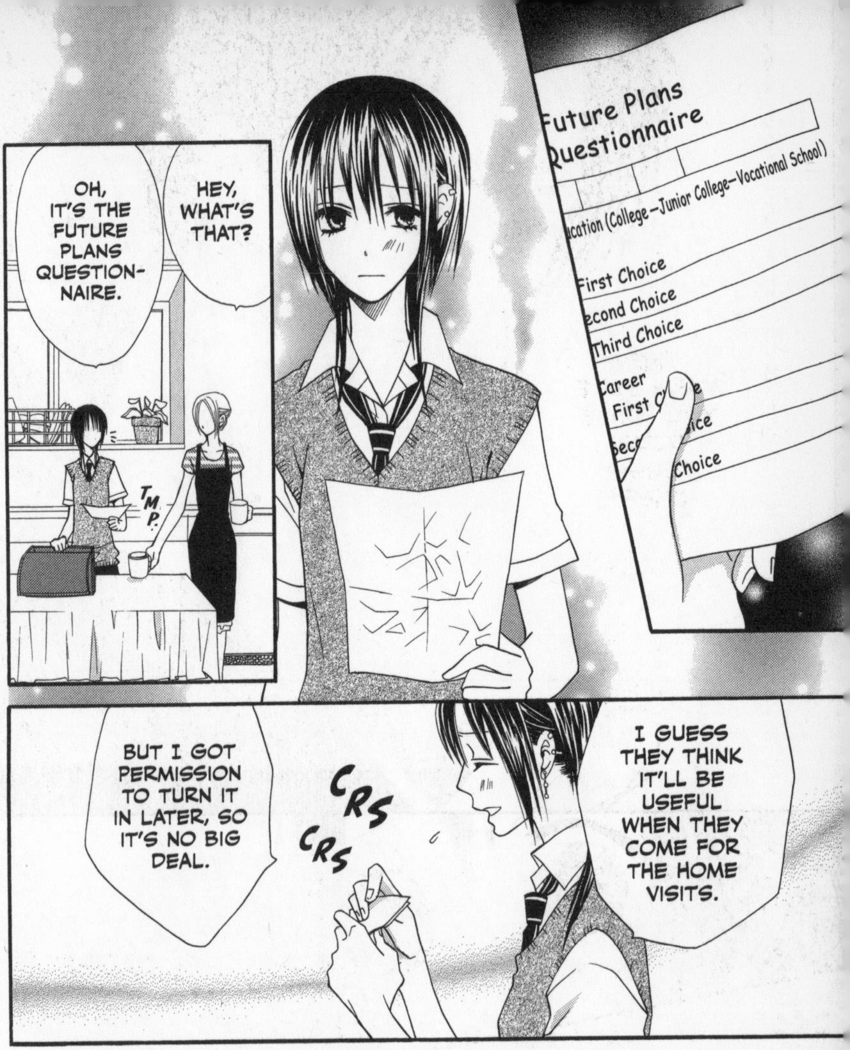
Future Plans Questionnaire
(College–Junior College–Vocational School)
First Choice
Third Choice
Career
Choice
HEY, WHAT'S THAT?
OH, IT'S THE FUTURE PLANS QUESTION-NAIRE.
TMP
I GUESS THEY THINK IT'LL BE USEFUL WHEN THEY COME FOR THE HOME VISITS.
CRS CRS
BUT I GOT PERMISSION TO TURN IT IN LATER, SO IT'S NO BIG DEAL.

menu 19

I don't draw smiling faces very well. Especially full page ones with no lead-in. Although, it's okay if it's a natural progression in the storyline.

Anyway, for this title page, Hana's smile flows naturally from the preceding scene.

The fruit tart that appears is actually something I made in cooking class.

And a reader even noticed that Hayato's piercing eyes change by day! I'm so happy that you're taking a good look at the drawings. ♥

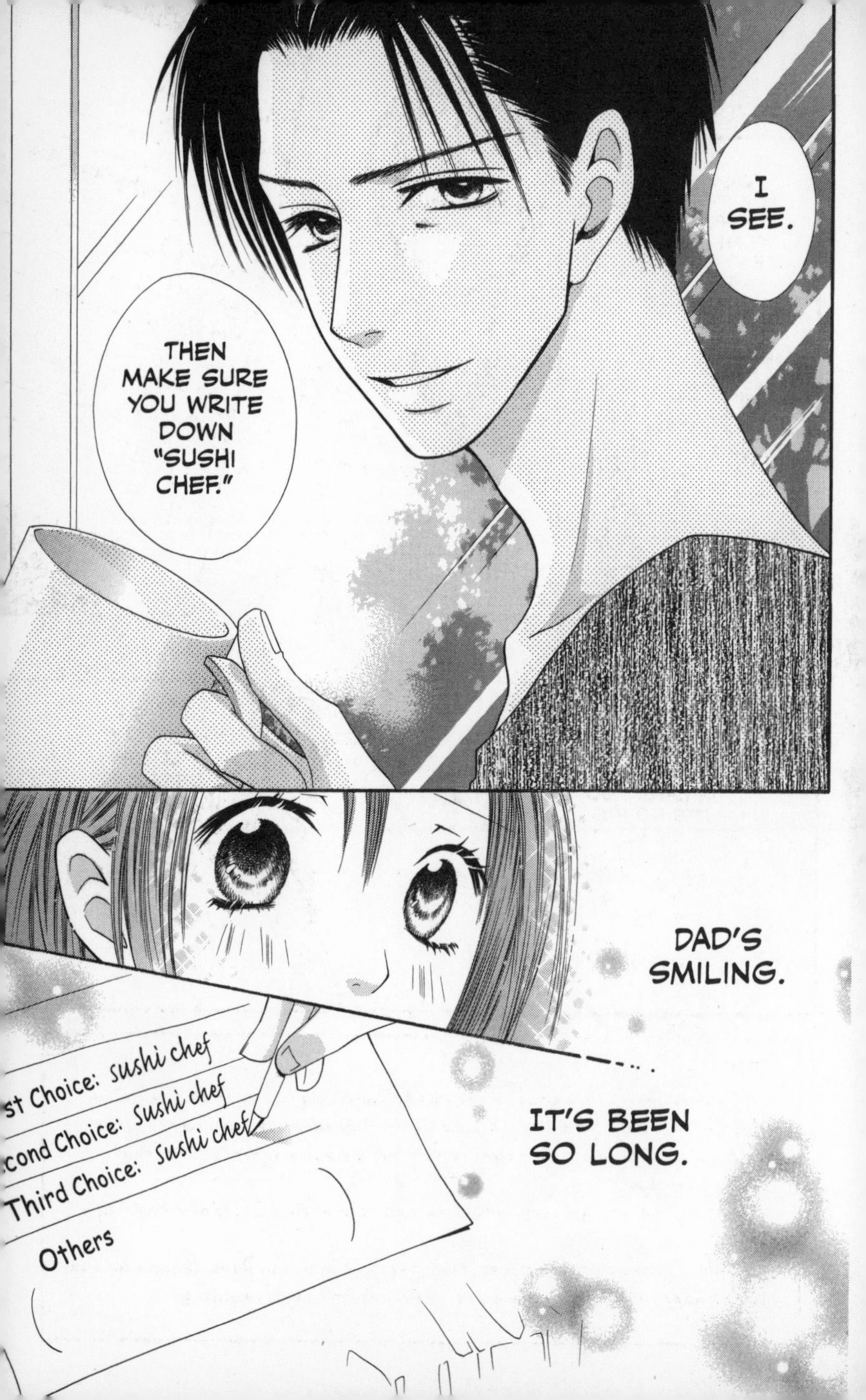

I SEE.
THEN MAKE SURE YOU WRITE DOWN "SUSHI CHEF."
DAD'S SMILING.
st Choice: sushi chef
cond Choice: Sushi chef
Third Choice: Sushi chef
Others
IT'S BEEN SO LONG.

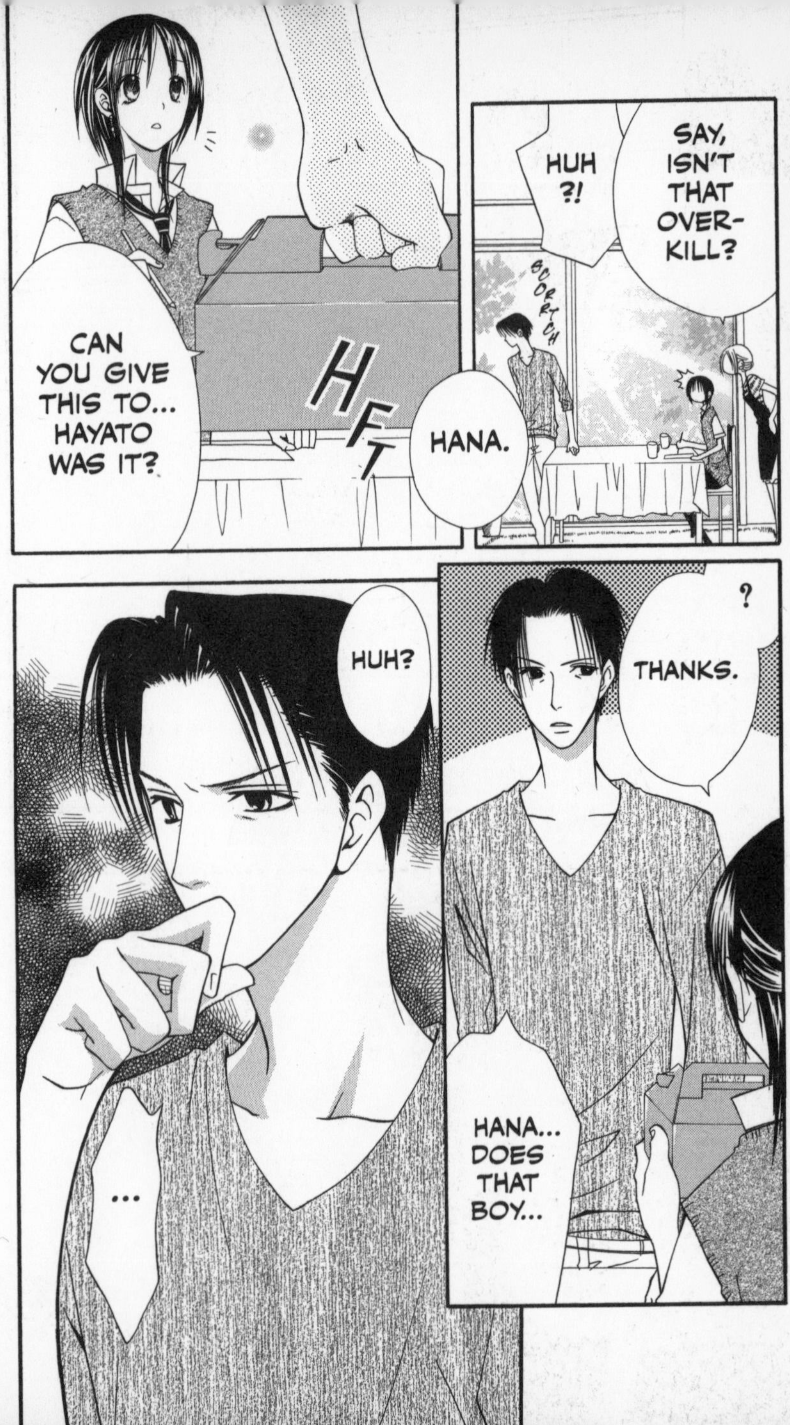
SAY, ISN'T THAT OVER-KILL?
HUH ?!
SCORTCH
HANA.
CAN YOU GIVE THIS TO... HAYATO WAS IT?
HFT
?
THANKS.
HANA... DOES THAT BOY...
HUH?
...

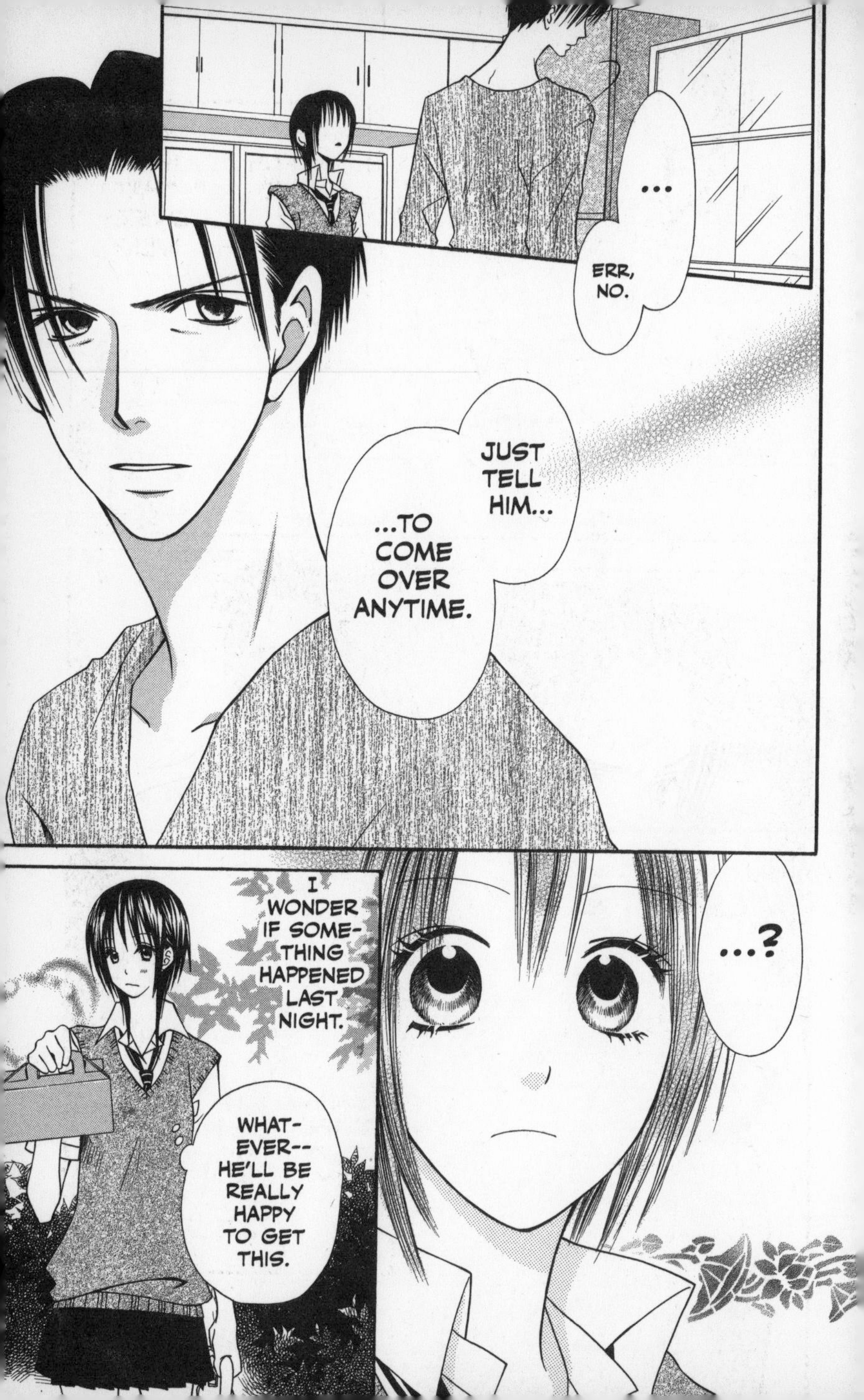
...
ERR, NO.
JUST TELL HIM...
...TO COME OVER ANYTIME.
...?
I WONDER IF SOME-THING HAPPENED LAST NIGHT.
WHAT-EVER-- HE'LL BE REALLY HAPPY TO GET THIS.

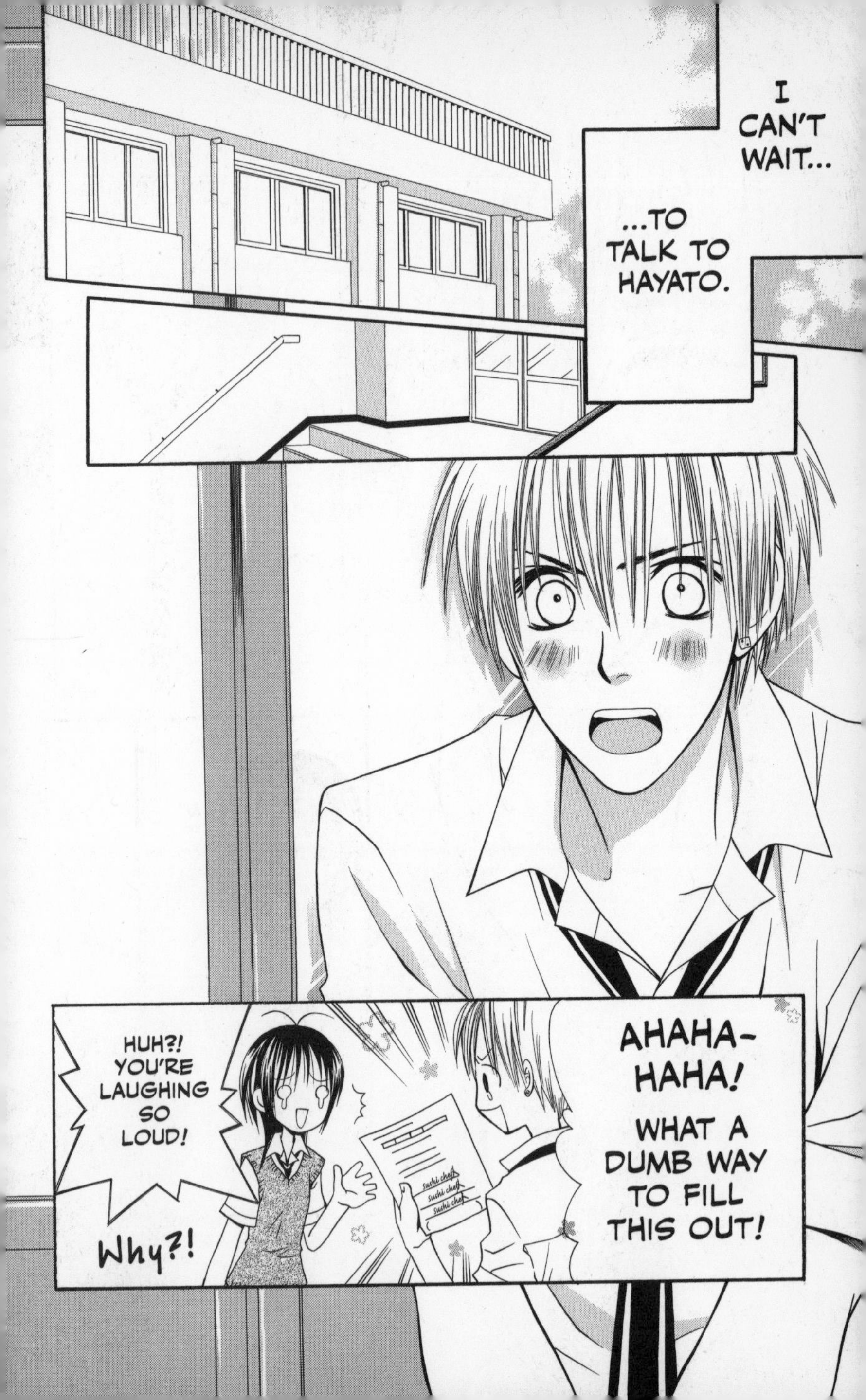
I CAN'T WAIT...
...TO TALK TO HAYATO.
AHAHA-HAHA!
WHAT A DUMB WAY TO FILL THIS OUT!
HUH?! YOU'RE LAUGHING SO LOUD!
Why?!
sushi chef
sushi chef
sushi chef

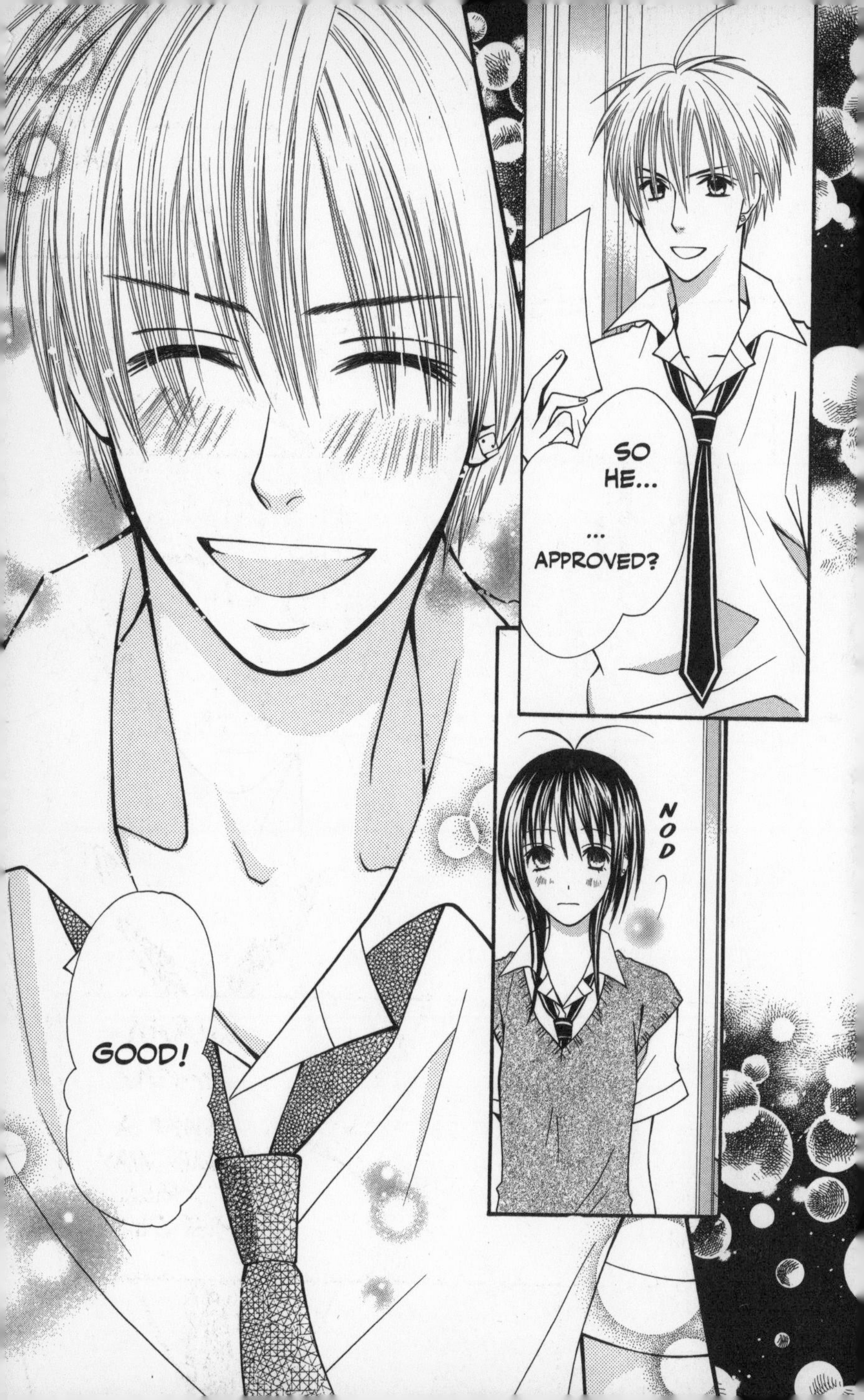
SO HE...
... APPROVED?
NOD
GOOD!

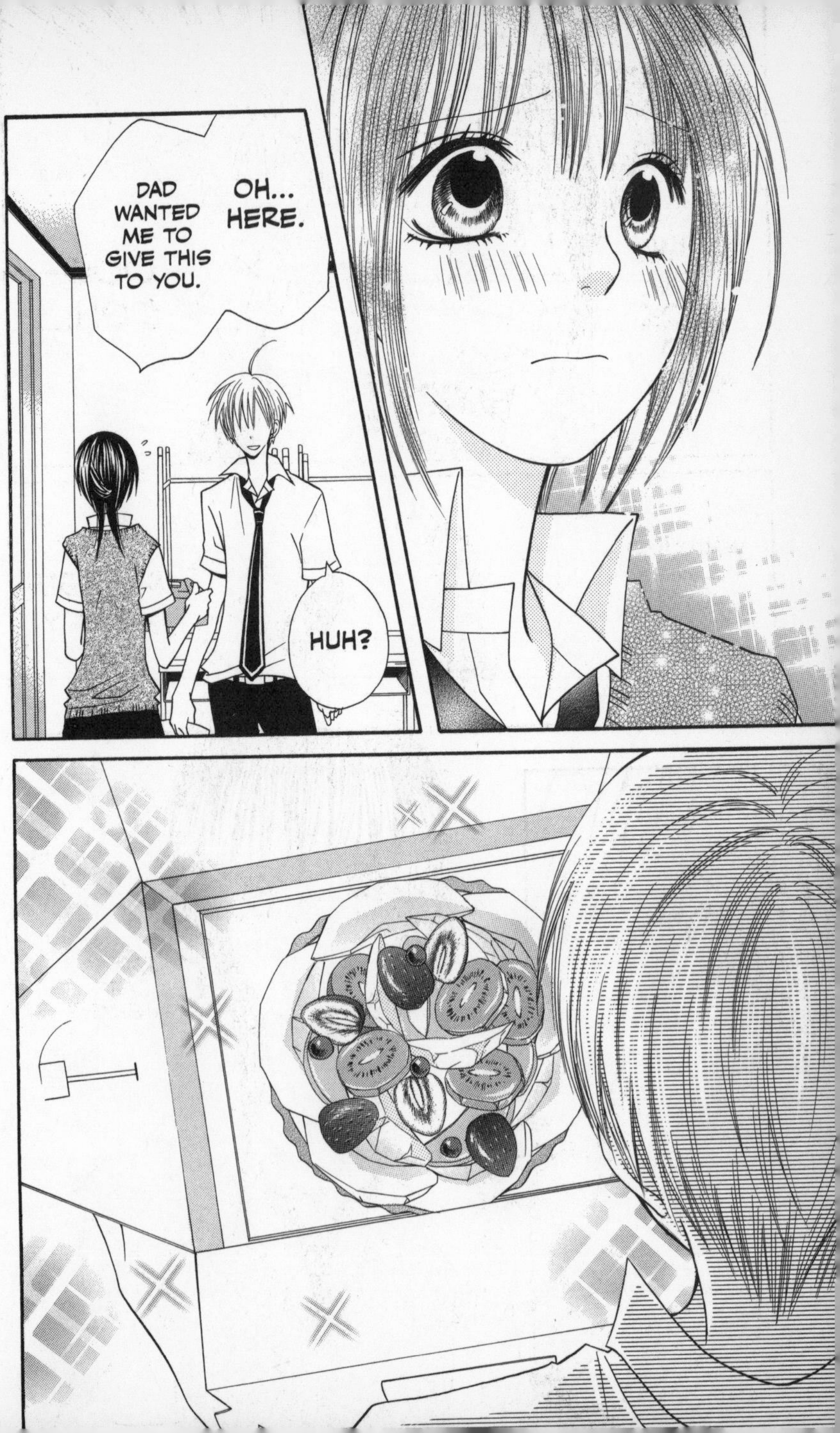
OH... HERE.
DAD WANTED ME TO GIVE THIS TO YOU.
HUH?

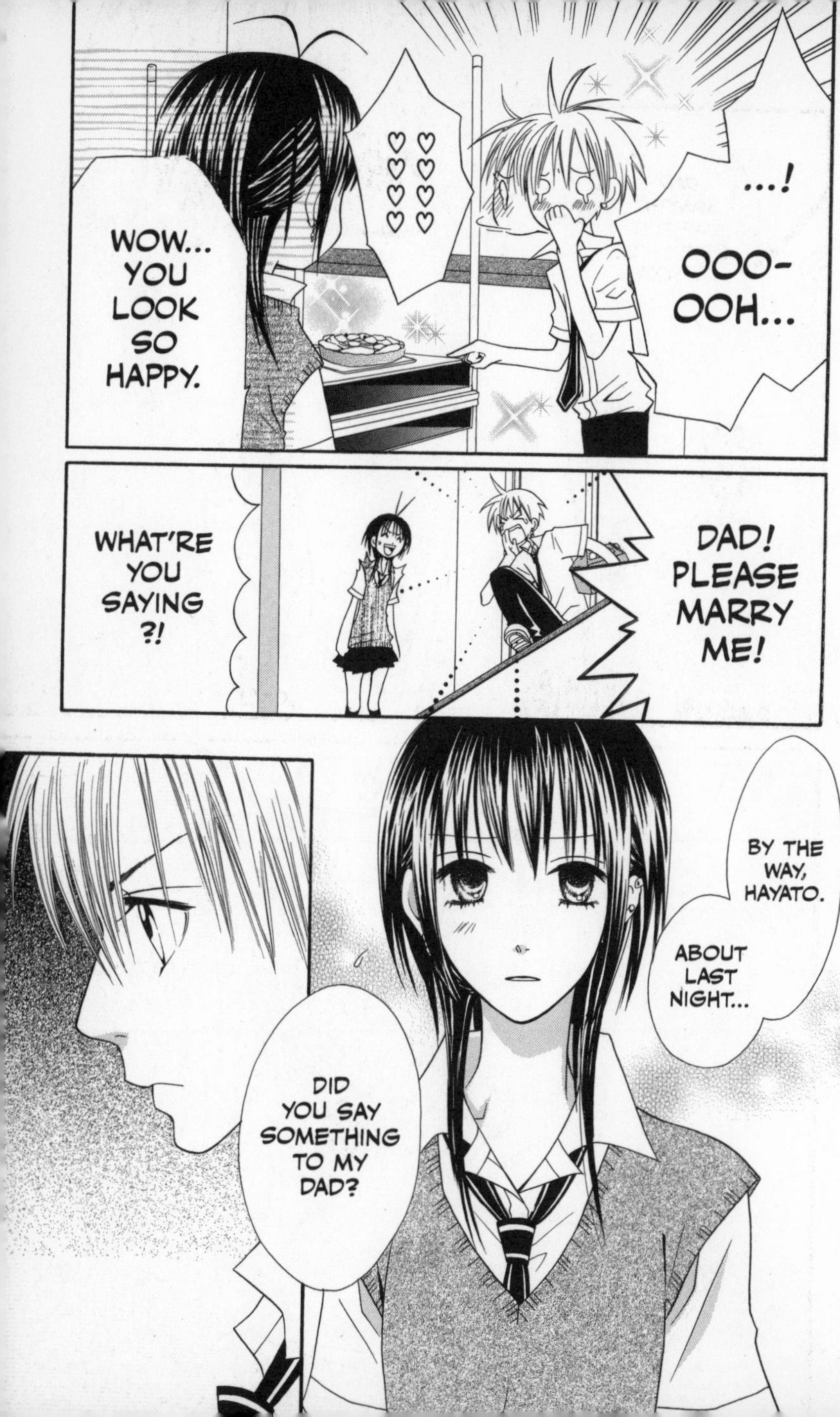
...!
OOO-OOH...
WOW... YOU LOOK SO HAPPY.
DAD! PLEASE MARRY ME!
WHAT'RE YOU SAYING?!
BY THE WAY, HAYATO.
ABOUT LAST NIGHT...
DID YOU SAY SOMETHING TO MY DAD?

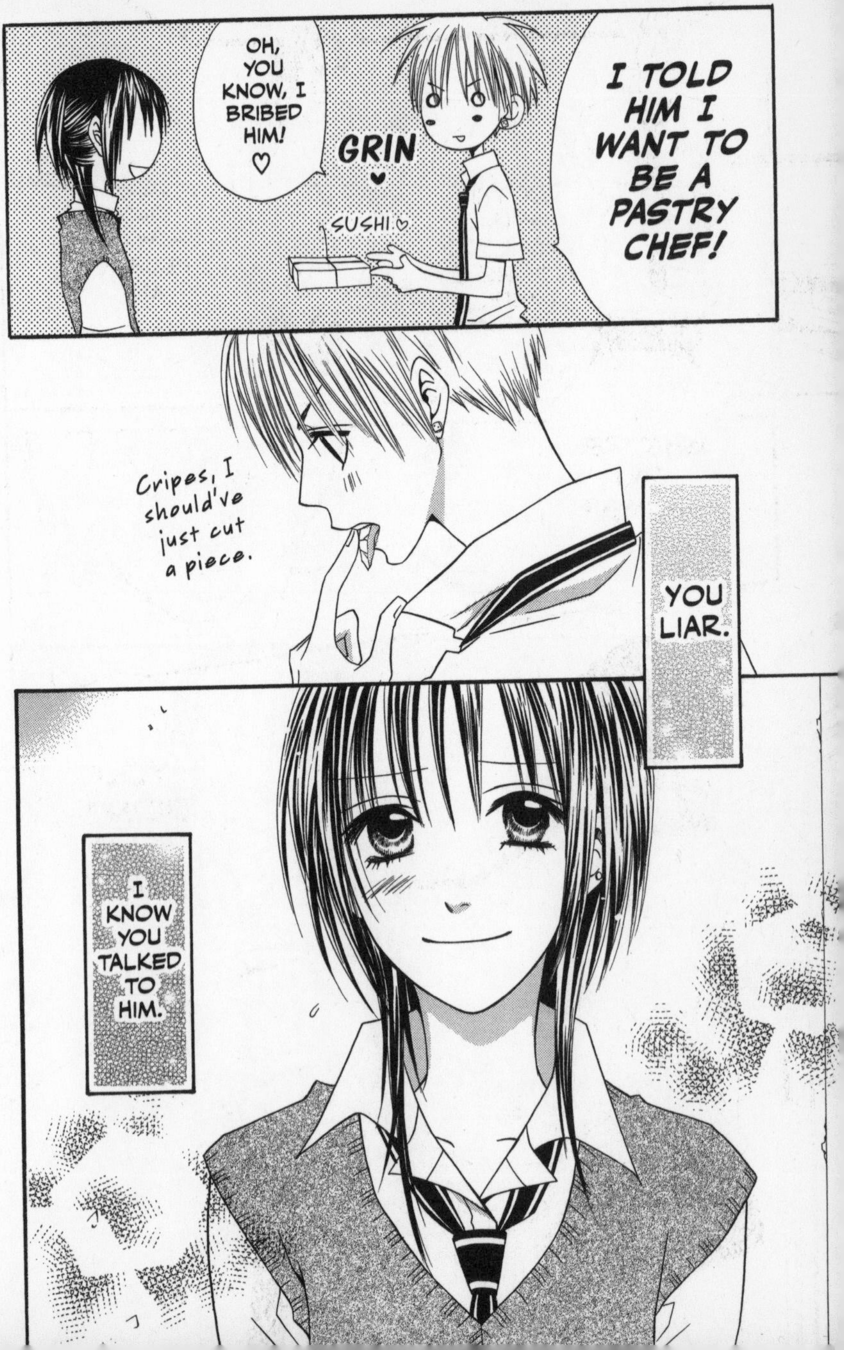
I TOLD HIM I WANT TO BE A PASTRY CHEF!
OH, YOU KNOW, I BRIBED HIM! ♡
GRIN ♥
SUSHI ♡
YOU LIAR.
Cripes, I should've just cut a piece.
I KNOW YOU TALKED TO HIM.

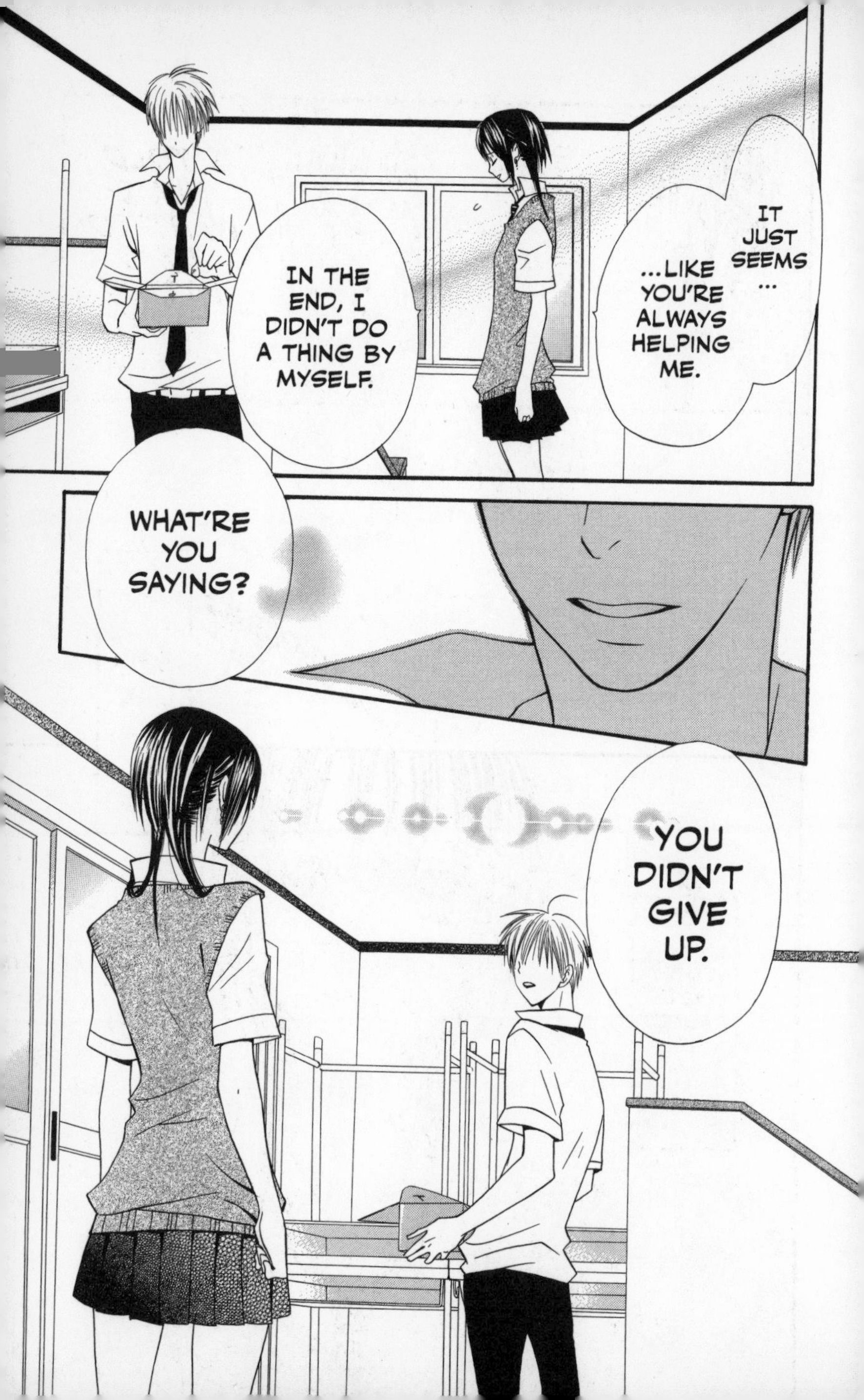
IT JUST SEEMS ...
...LIKE YOU'RE ALWAYS HELPING ME.
IN THE END, I DIDN'T DO A THING BY MYSELF.
WHAT'RE YOU SAYING?
YOU DIDN'T GIVE UP.

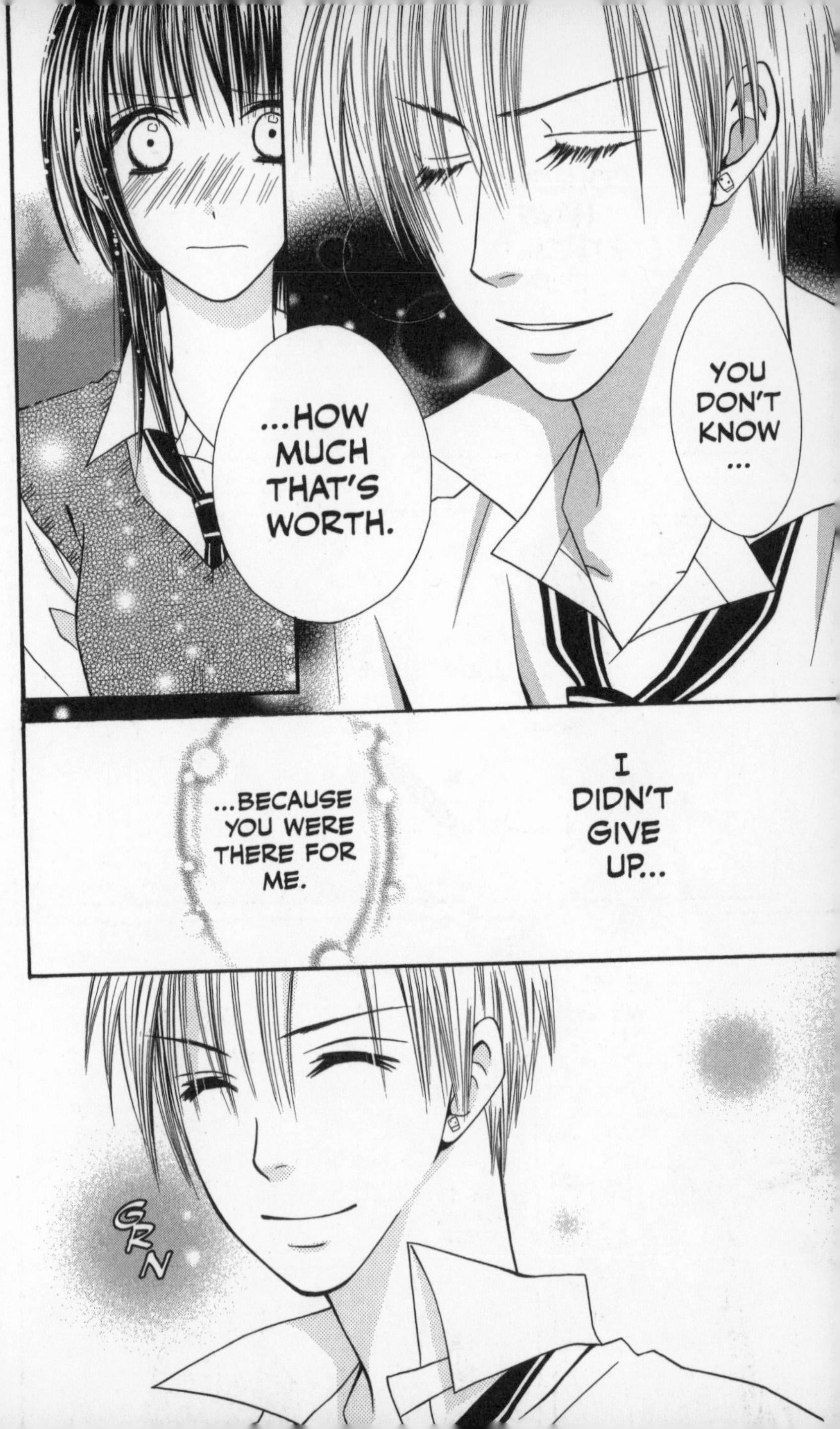
YOU DON'T KNOW ...
...HOW MUCH THAT'S WORTH.
I DIDN'T GIVE UP...
...BECAUSE YOU WERE THERE FOR ME.
GRN

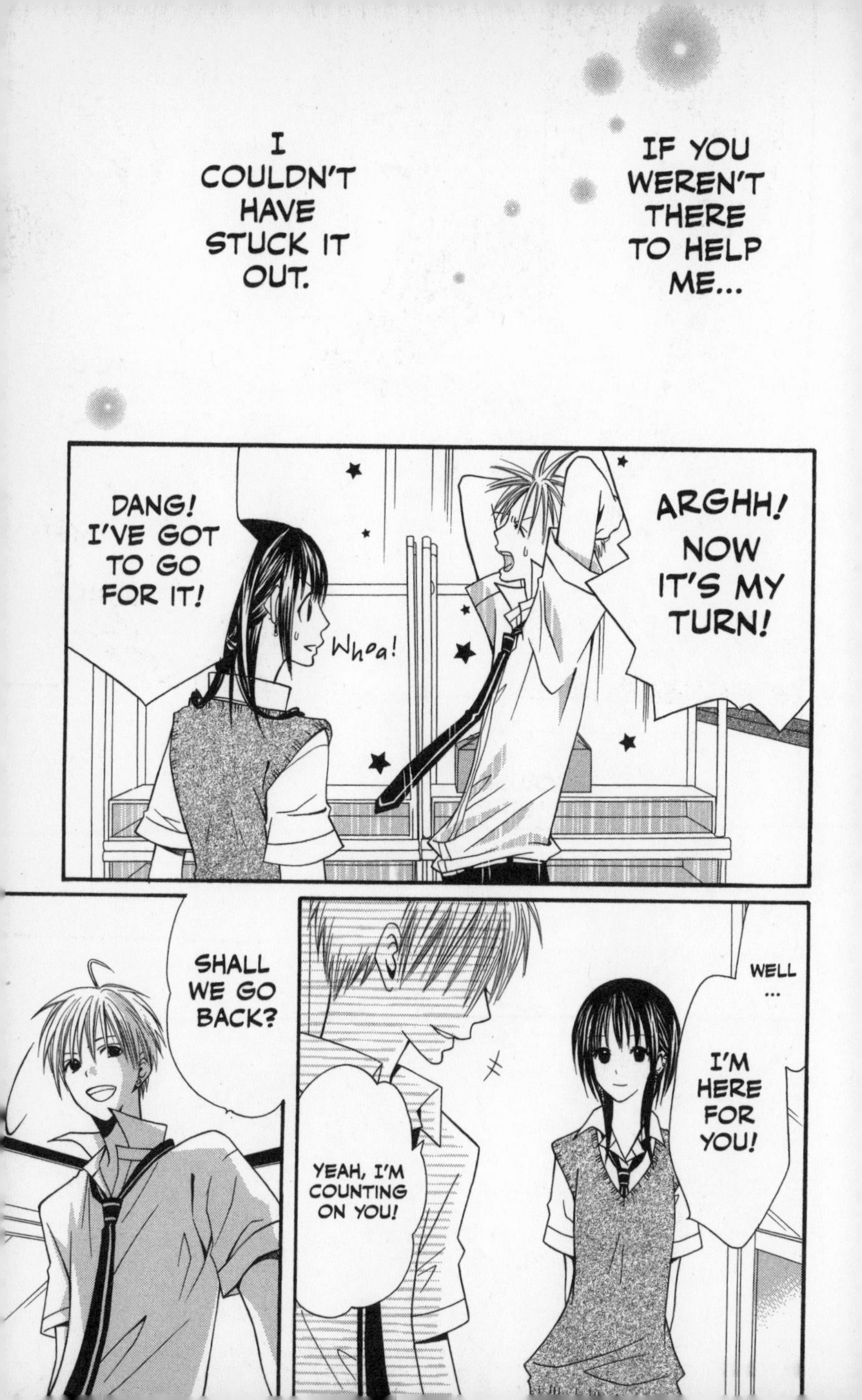
IF YOU WEREN'T THERE TO HELP ME...
I COULDN'T HAVE STUCK IT OUT.
ARGHH! NOW IT'S MY TURN!
Whoa!
DANG! I'VE GOT TO GO FOR IT!
WELL ...
I'M HERE FOR YOU!
YEAH, I'M COUNTING ON YOU!
SHALL WE GO BACK?

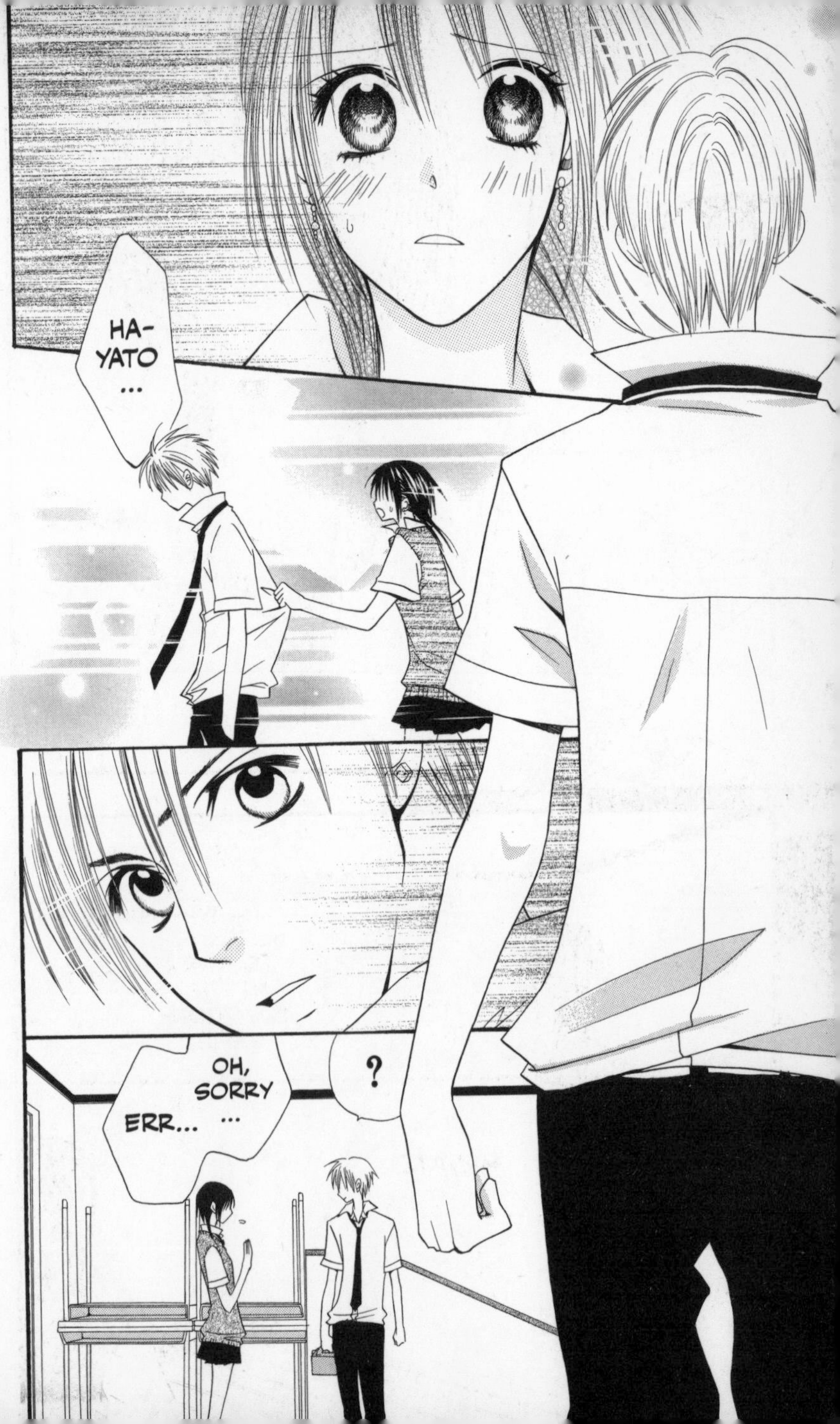
HA-YATO ...
?
OH, SORRY ...
ERR...

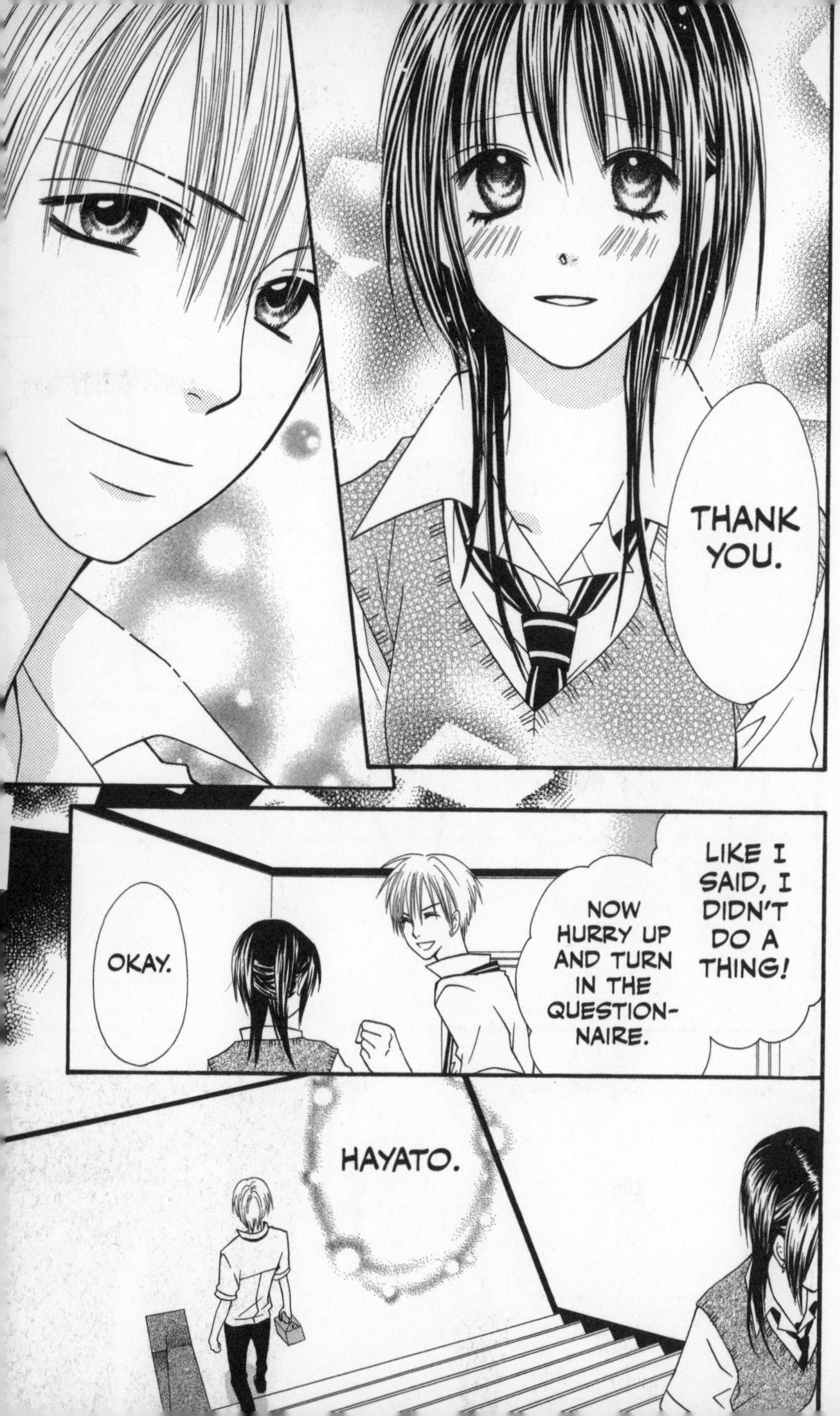
THANK YOU.
LIKE I SAID, I DIDN'T DO A THING!
NOW HURRY UP AND TURN IN THE QUESTION-NAIRE.
OKAY.
HAYATO.

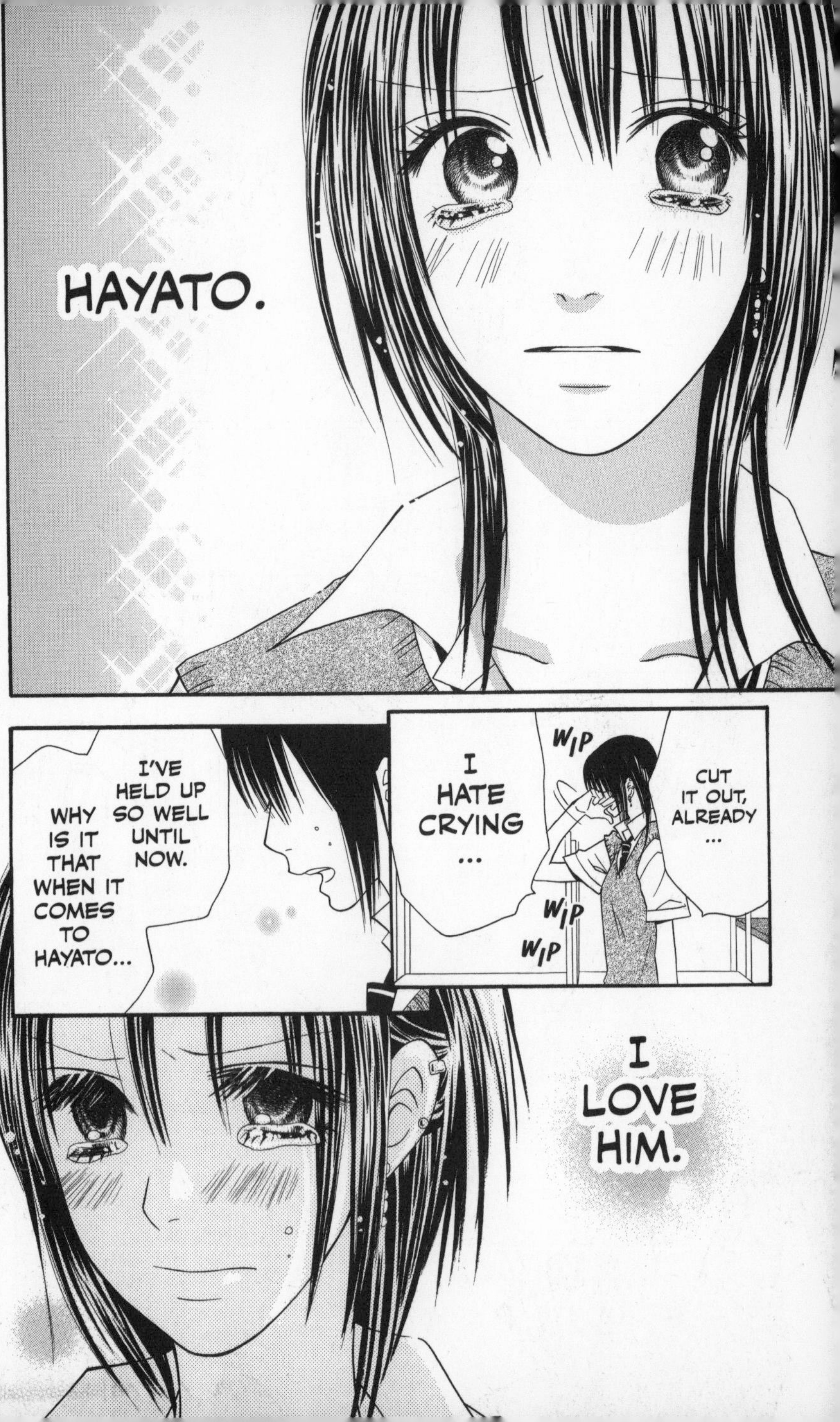
HAYATO.
CUT IT OUT, ALREADY...
WIP
I HATE CRYING...
WIP
WIP
I'VE HELD UP SO WELL UNTIL NOW.
WHY IS IT THAT WHEN IT COMES TO HAYATO...
I LOVE HIM.

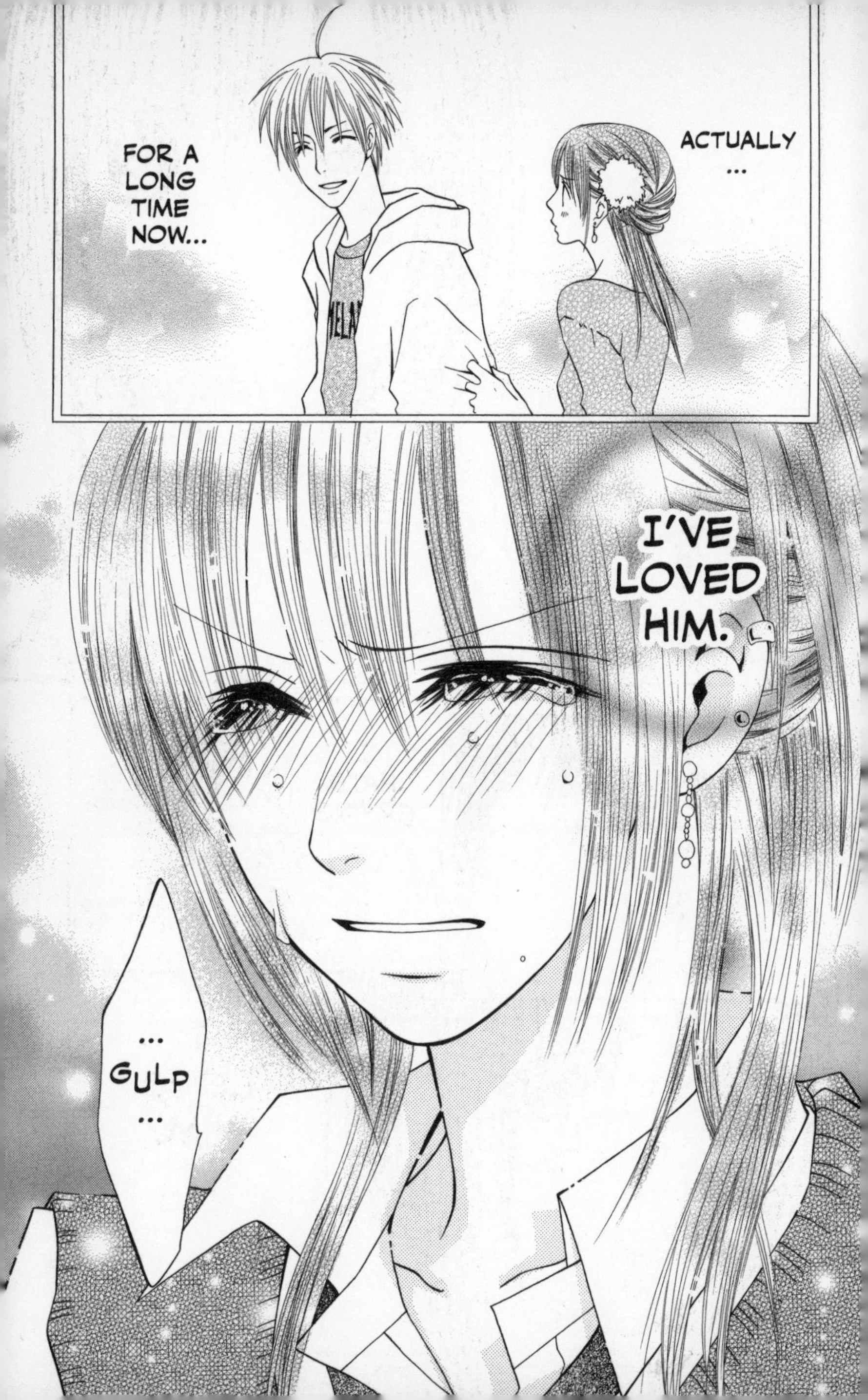
ACTUALLY ...
FOR A LONG TIME NOW...
I'VE LOVED HIM.
... GULP ...

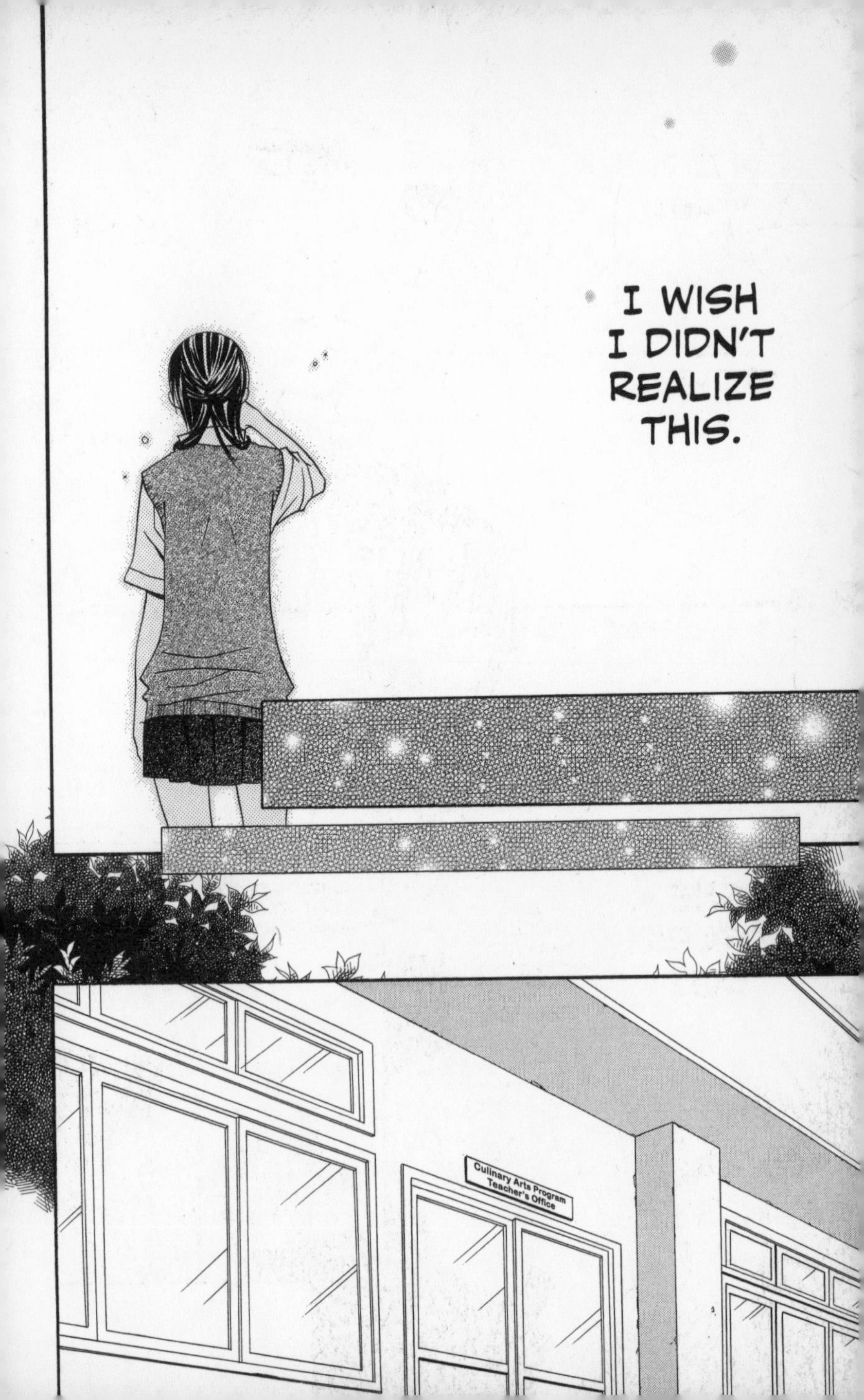
I WISH I DIDN'T REALIZE THIS.
Culinary Arts Program Teacher's Office

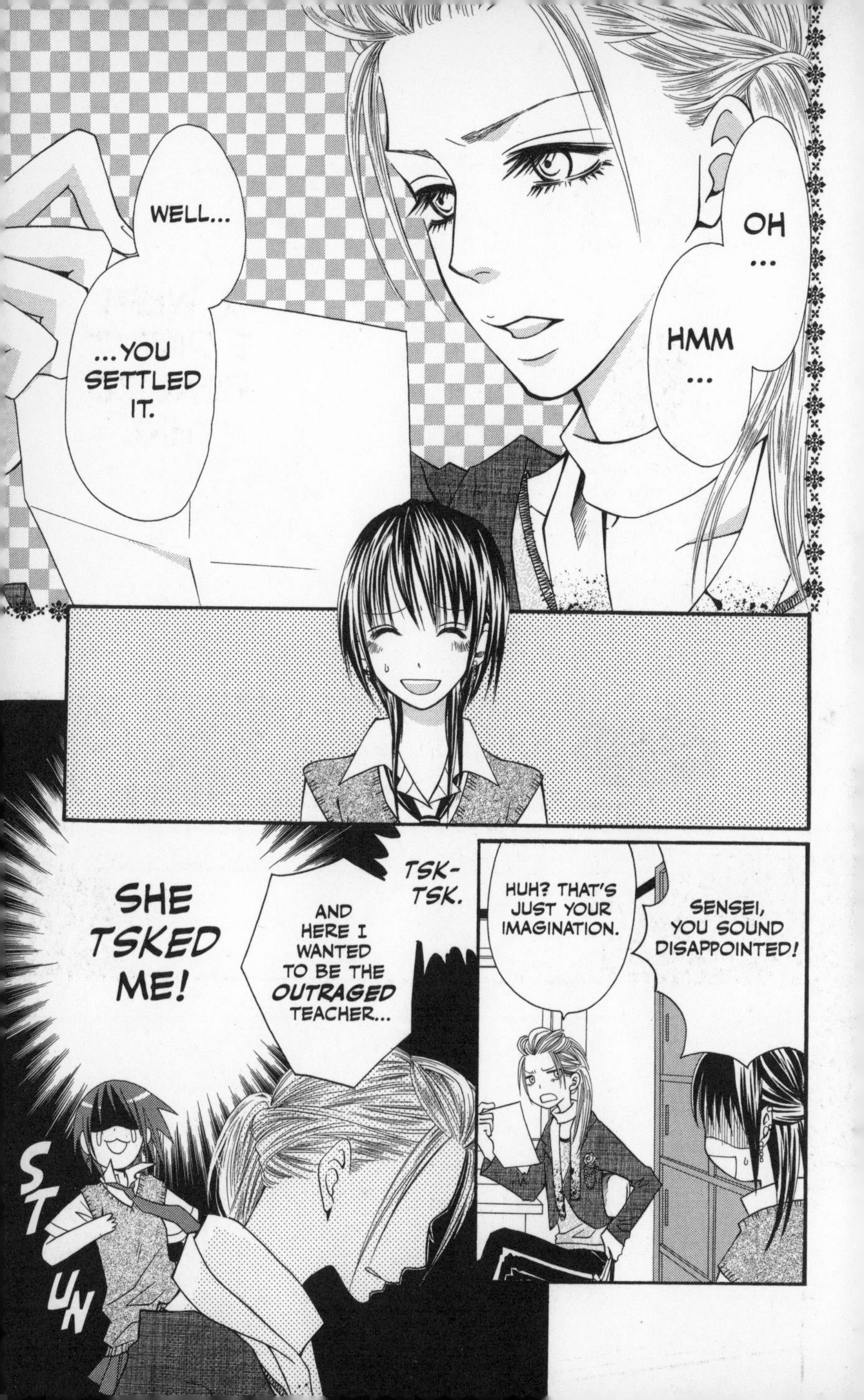
OH ... HMM ...
WELL...
...YOU SETTLED IT.
SENSEI, YOU SOUND DISAPPOINTED!
HUH? THAT'S JUST YOUR IMAGINATION.
TSK-TSK.
AND HERE I WANTED TO BE THE OUTRAGED TEACHER...
SHE TSKED ME!
STUN

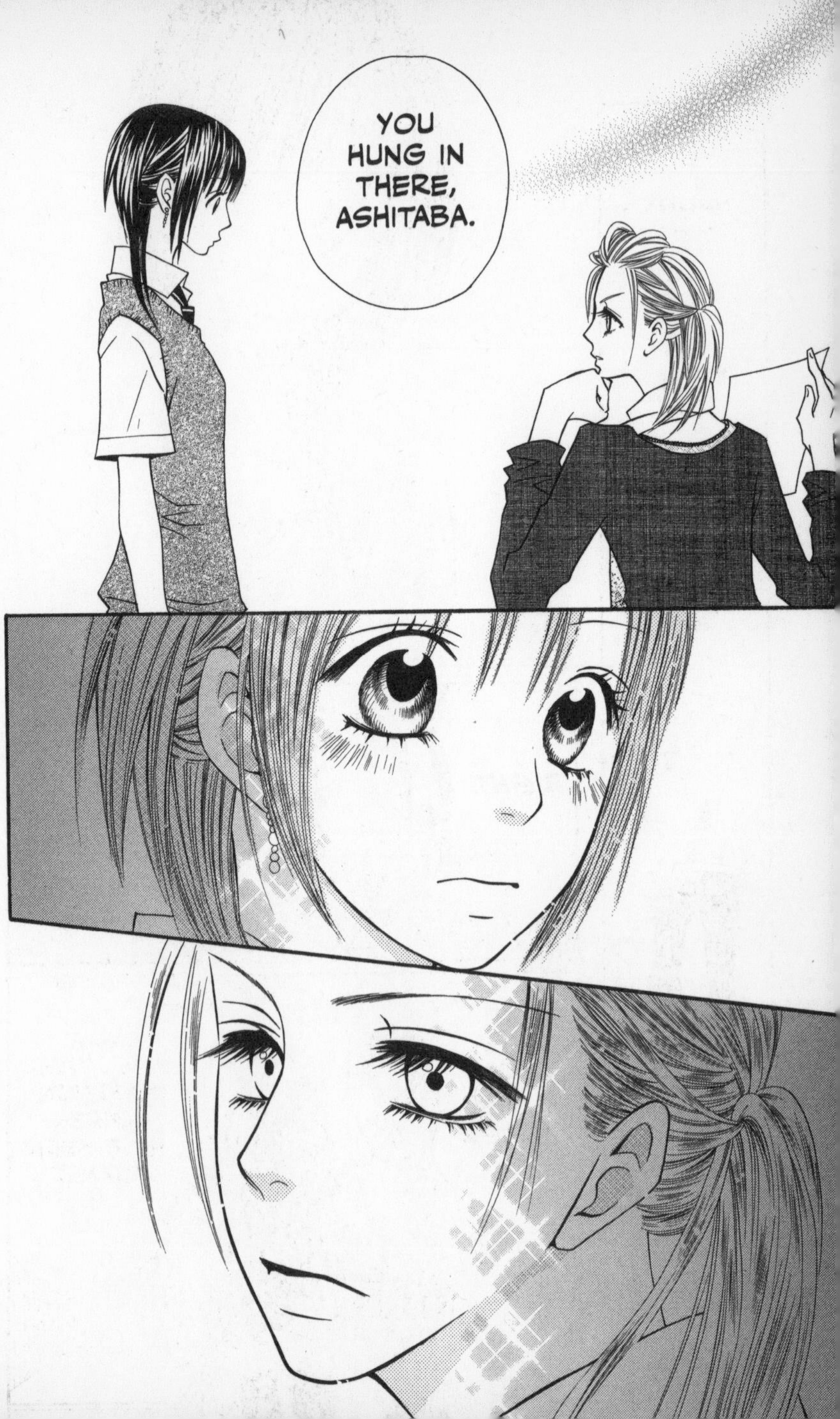
YOU HUNG IN THERE, ASHITABA.

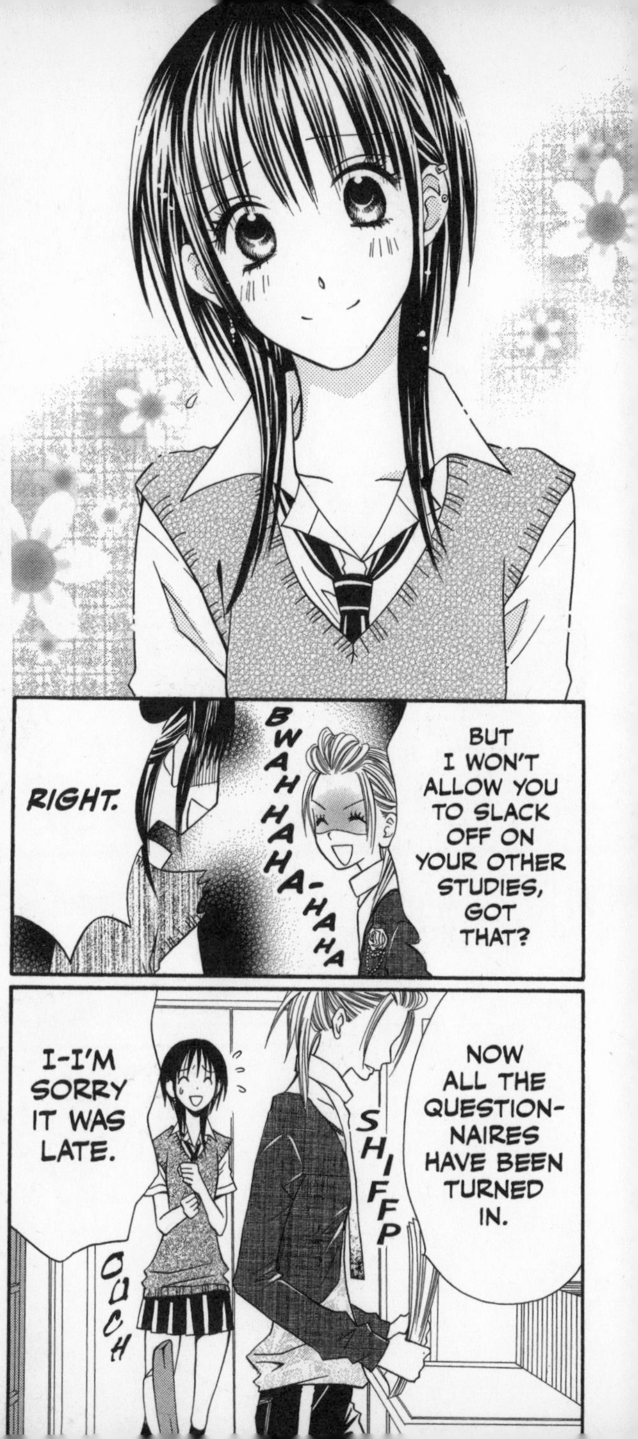
BUT I WON'T ALLOW YOU TO SLACK OFF ON YOUR OTHER STUDIES, GOT THAT?
BWAHAHAHA-HAHAHA
RIGHT.
NOW ALL THE QUESTION-NAIRES HAVE BEEN TURNED IN.
SHIFFP
I-I'M SORRY IT WAS LATE.
OUCH
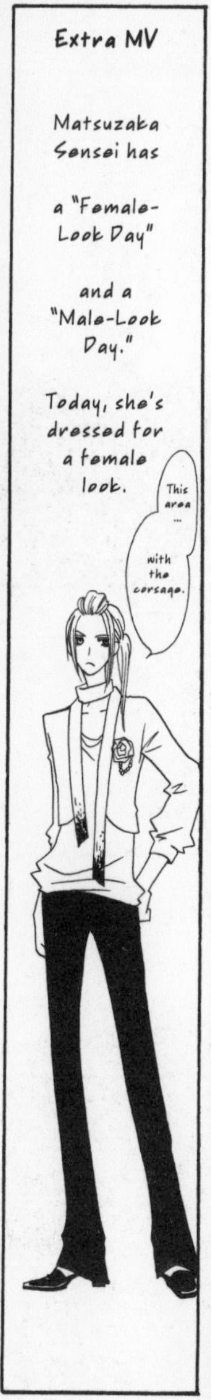
Extra MV
Matsuzaka Sensei has
a "Female-Look Day"
and a "Male-Look Day."
Today, she's dressed for a female look.
This area ... with the corsage.

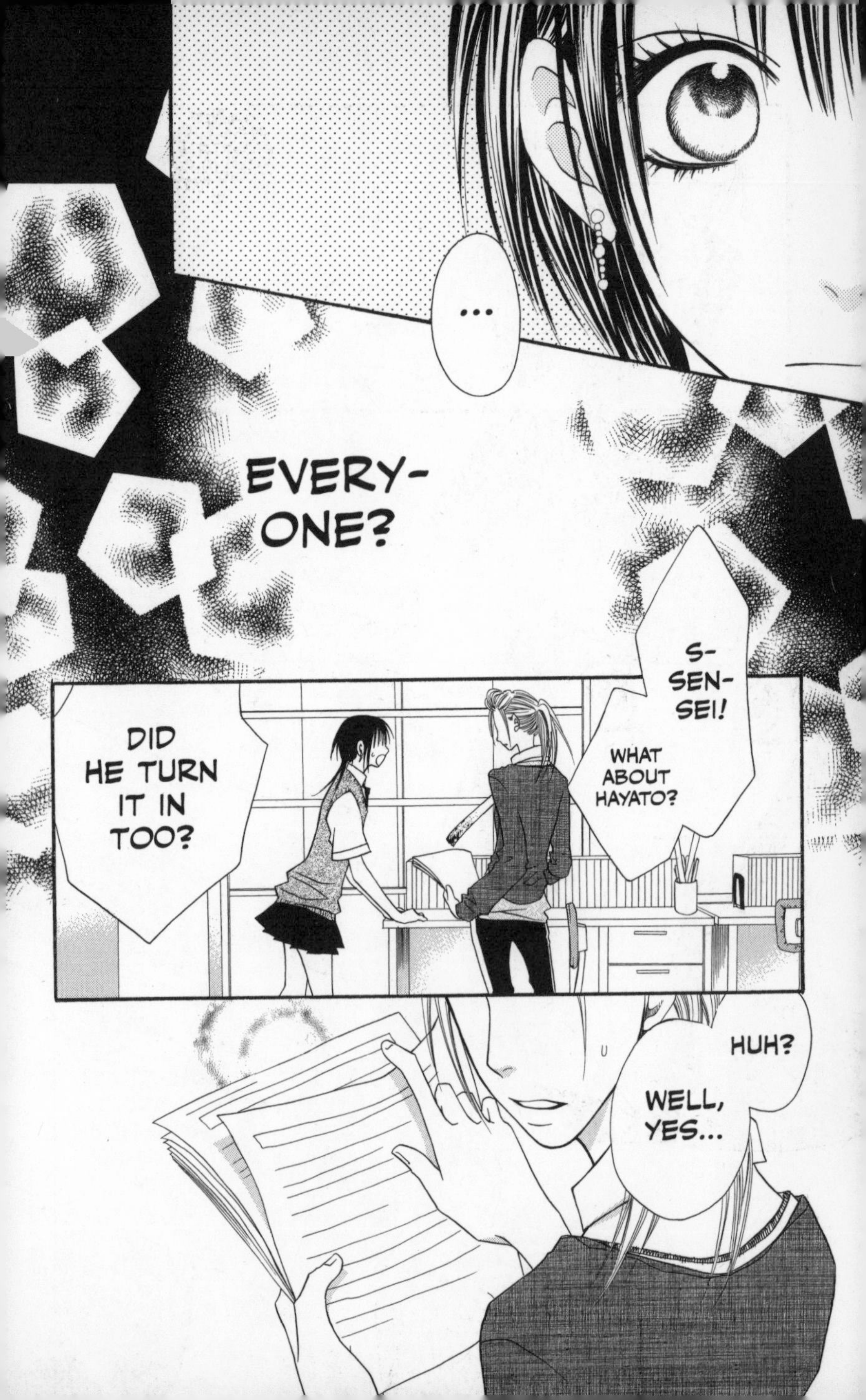
...
EVERY-ONE?
S-SEN-SEI!
WHAT ABOUT HAYATO?
DID HE TURN IT IN TOO?
HUH?
WELL, YES...

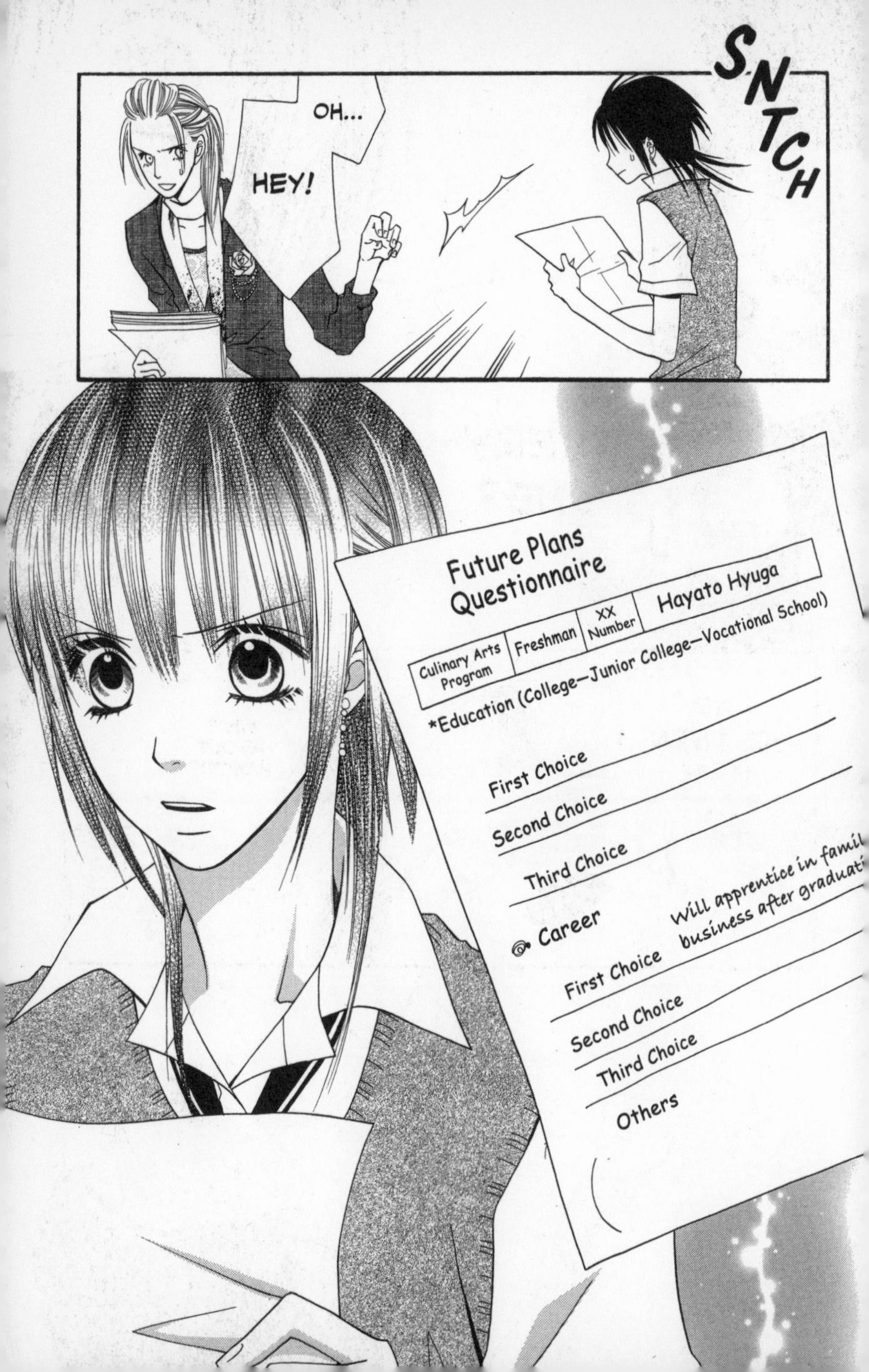
SNTCH
OH...
HEY!
Future Plans Questionnaire
Culinary Arts Program
Freshman
XX Number
Hayato Hyuga
*Education (College—Junior College—Vocational School)
First Choice
Second Choice
Third Choice
Career
First Choice
Will apprentice in famil
business after graduati
Second Choice
Third Choice
Others

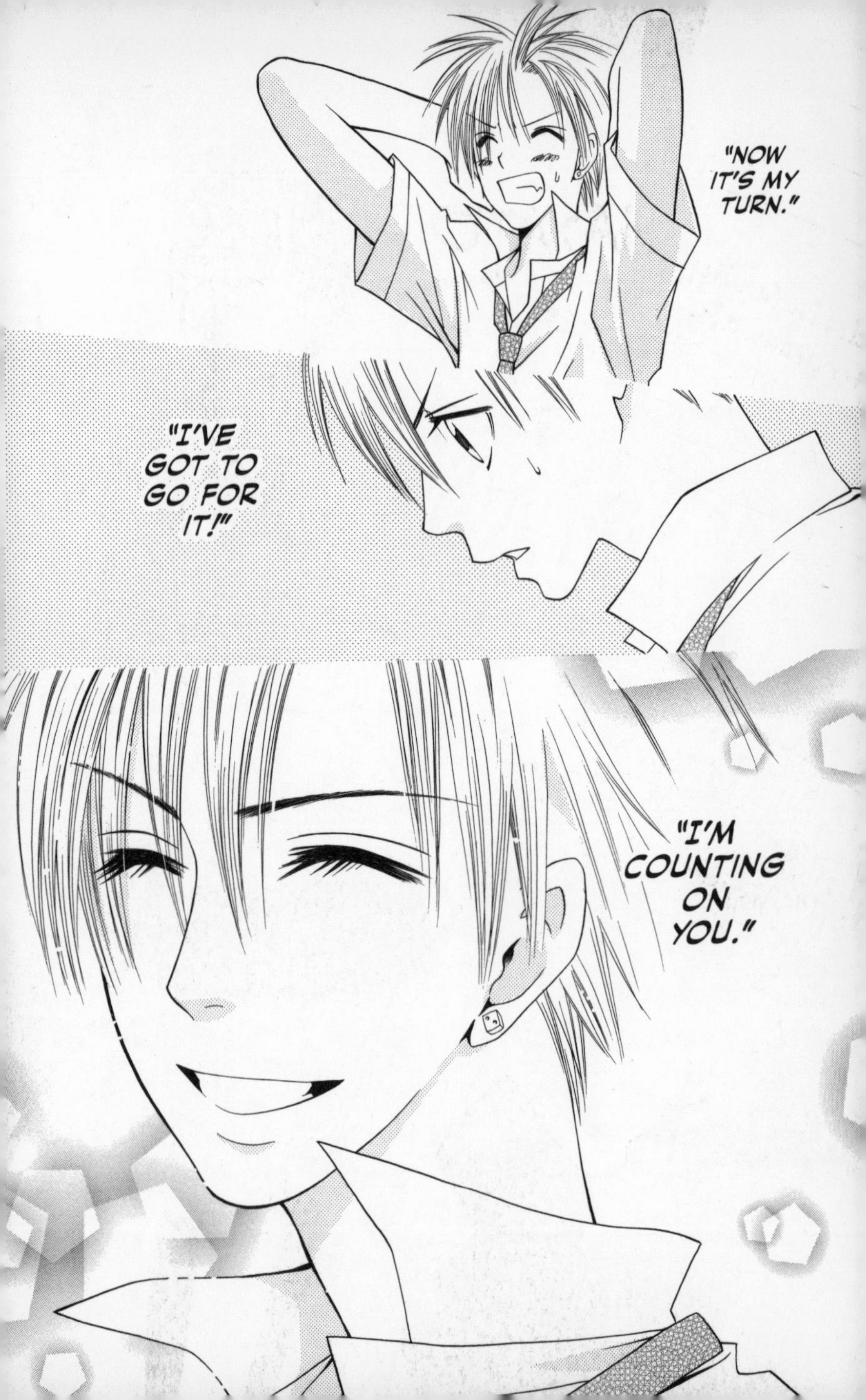
"NOW IT'S MY TURN."
"I'VE GOT TO GO FOR IT!"
"I'M COUNTING ON YOU."

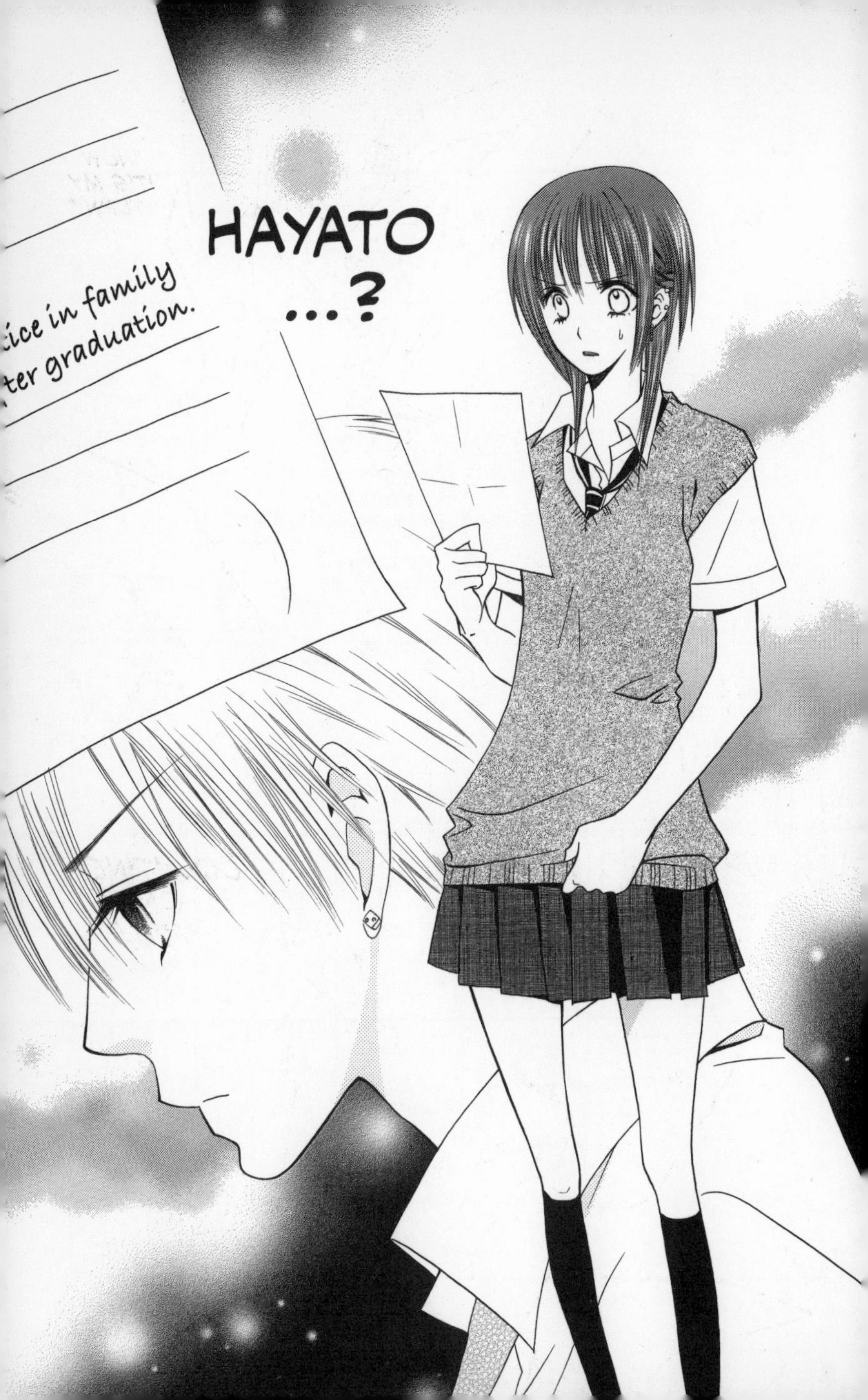
HAYATO ...?
ice in family
ter graduation.

SIDE DISH Mixed Vegetables 5

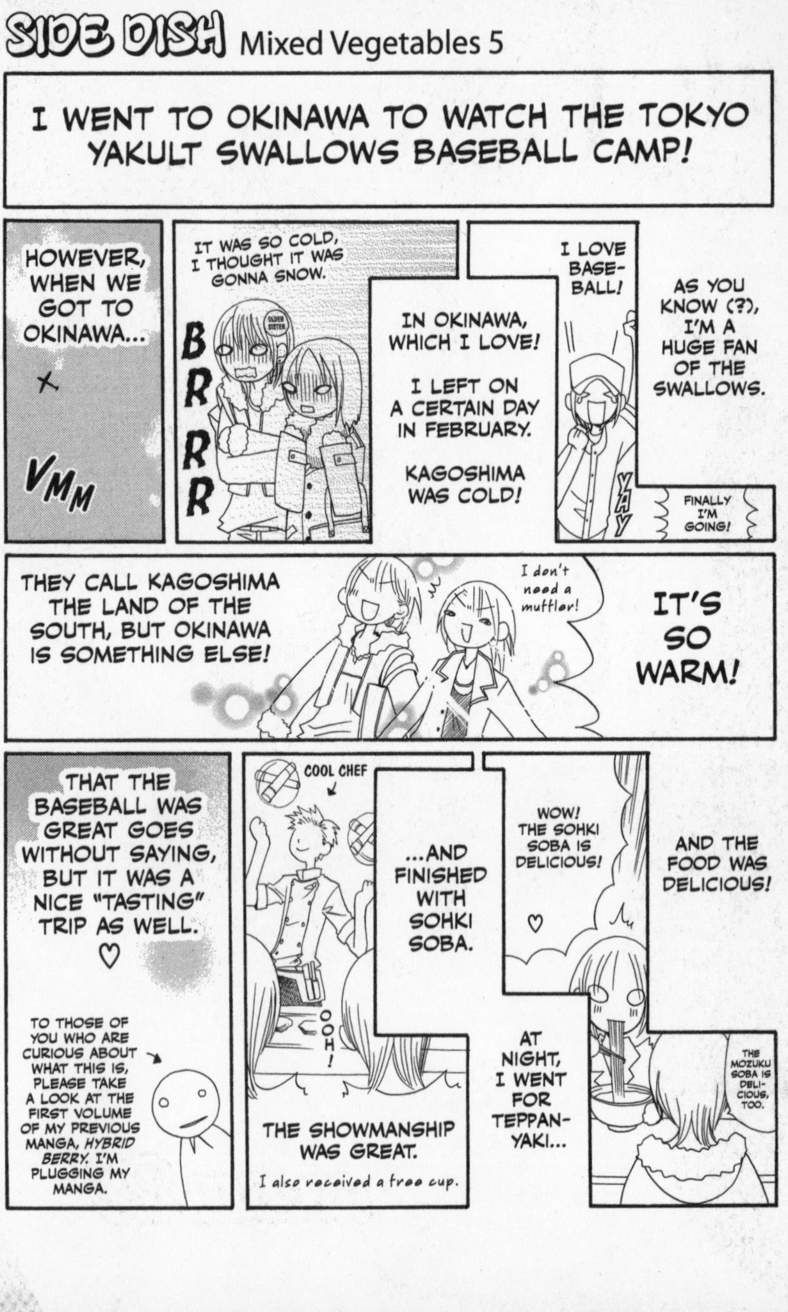
I WENT TO OKINAWA TO WATCH THE TOKYO YAKULT SWALLOWS BASEBALL CAMP!
AS YOU KNOW (?), I'M A HUGE FAN OF THE SWALLOWS.
I LOVE BASE-BALL!
YAY
FINALLY I'M GOING!
IN OKINAWA, WHICH I LOVE!
I LEFT ON A CERTAIN DAY IN FEBRUARY.
KAGOSHIMA WAS COLD!
IT WAS SO COLD, I THOUGHT IT WAS GONNA SNOW.
OLDER SISTER
BRRRR
HOWEVER, WHEN WE GOT TO OKINAWA...
VMM
IT'S SO WARM!
I don't need a muffler!
THEY CALL KAGOSHIMA THE LAND OF THE SOUTH, BUT OKINAWA IS SOMETHING ELSE!
AND THE FOOD WAS DELICIOUS!
WOW! THE SOHKI SOBA IS DELICIOUS!
THE MOZUKU SOBA IS DELI-CIOUS, TOO.
AT NIGHT, I WENT FOR TEPPAN-YAKI...
COOL CHEF
OOH!
THE SHOWMANSHIP WAS GREAT.
I also received a free cup.
...AND FINISHED WITH SOHKI SOBA.
THAT THE BASEBALL WAS GREAT GOES WITHOUT SAYING, BUT IT WAS A NICE "TASTING" TRIP AS WELL. ♡
TO THOSE OF YOU WHO ARE CURIOUS ABOUT WHAT THIS IS, PLEASE TAKE A LOOK AT THE FIRST VOLUME OF MY PREVIOUS MANGA, *HYBRID BERRY*. I'M PLUGGING MY MANGA.

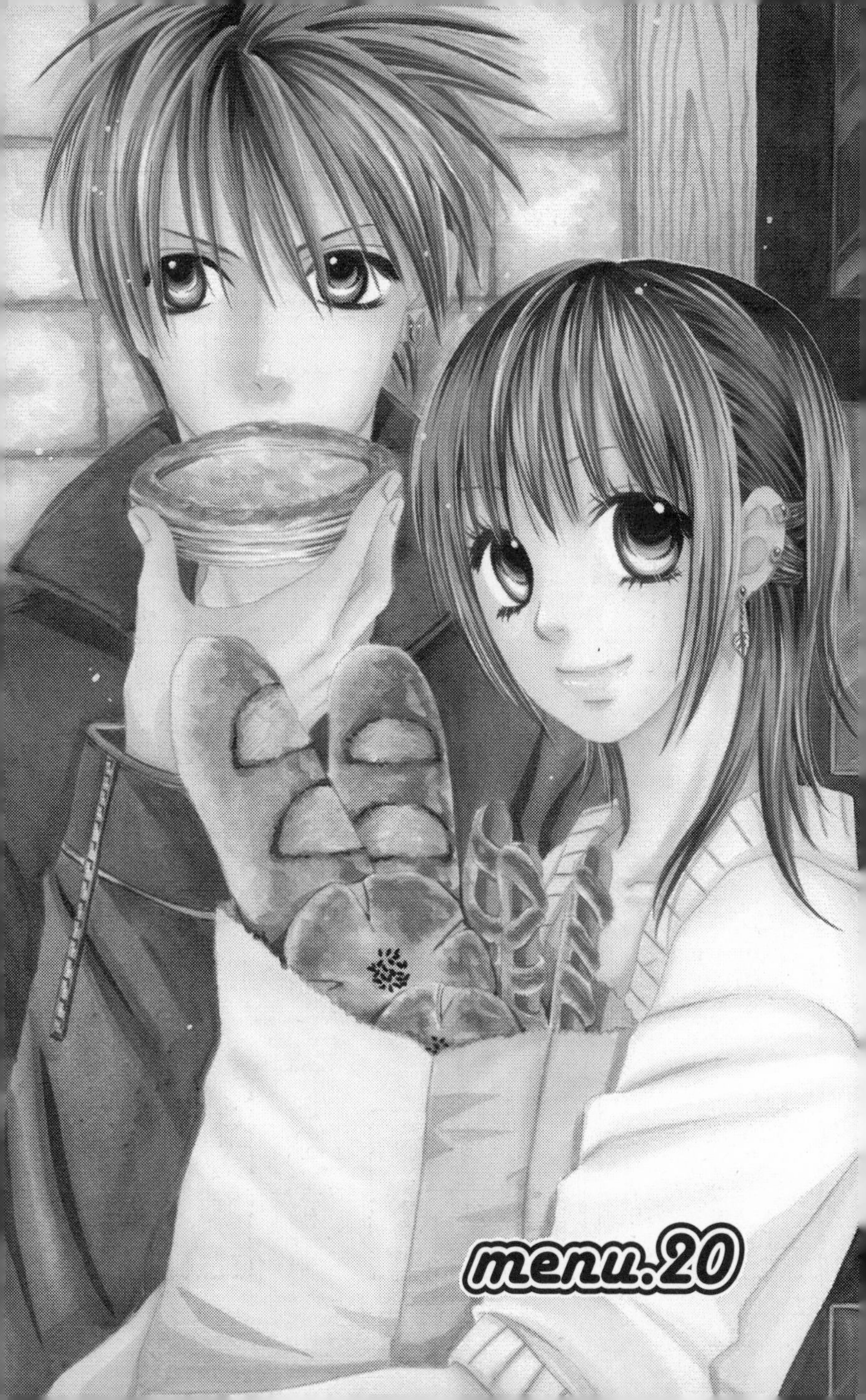
menu.20

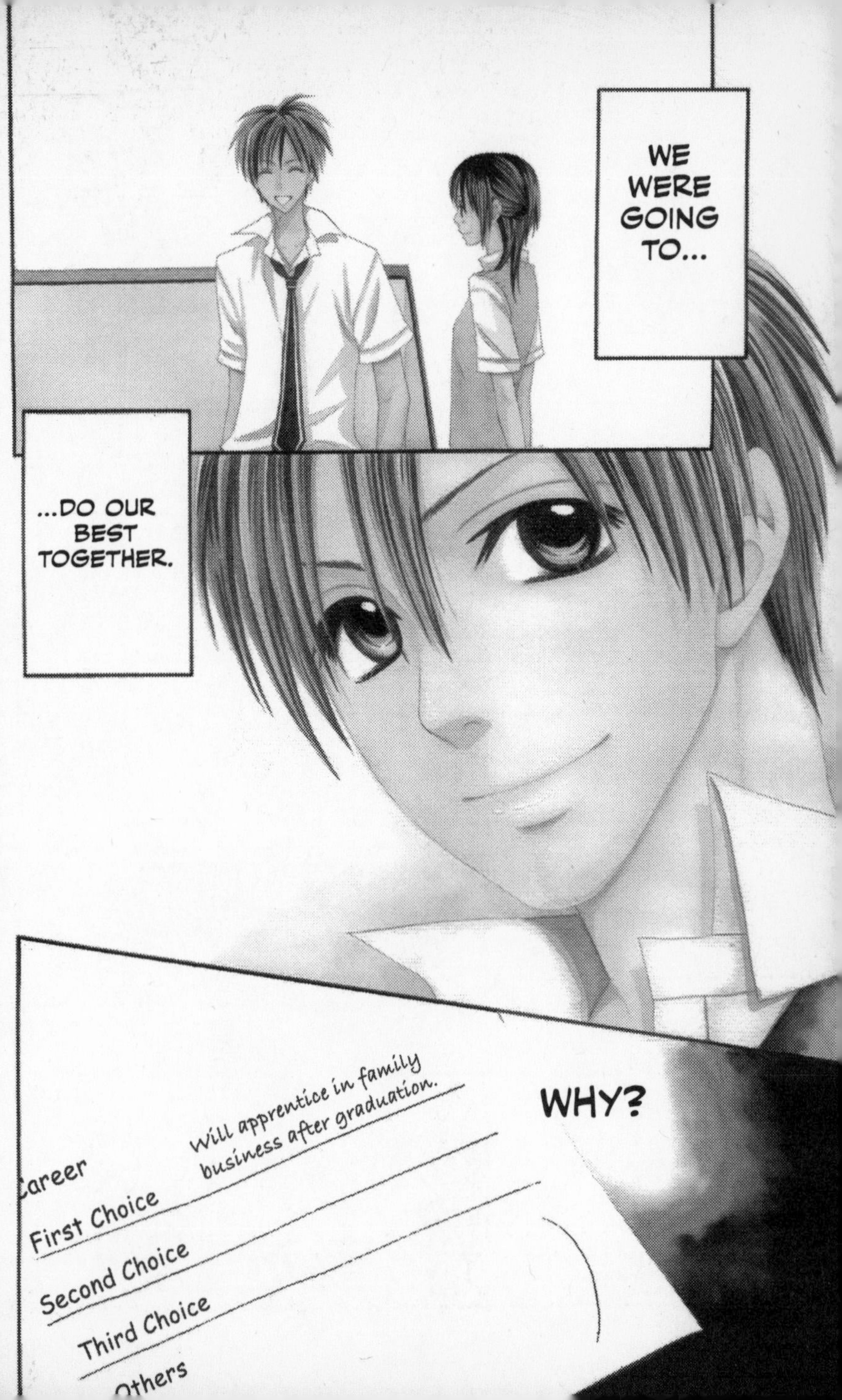
WE WERE GOING TO...
...DO OUR BEST TOGETHER.
WHY?
Career
First Choice
Will apprentice in family business after graduation.
Second Choice
Third Choice
Others

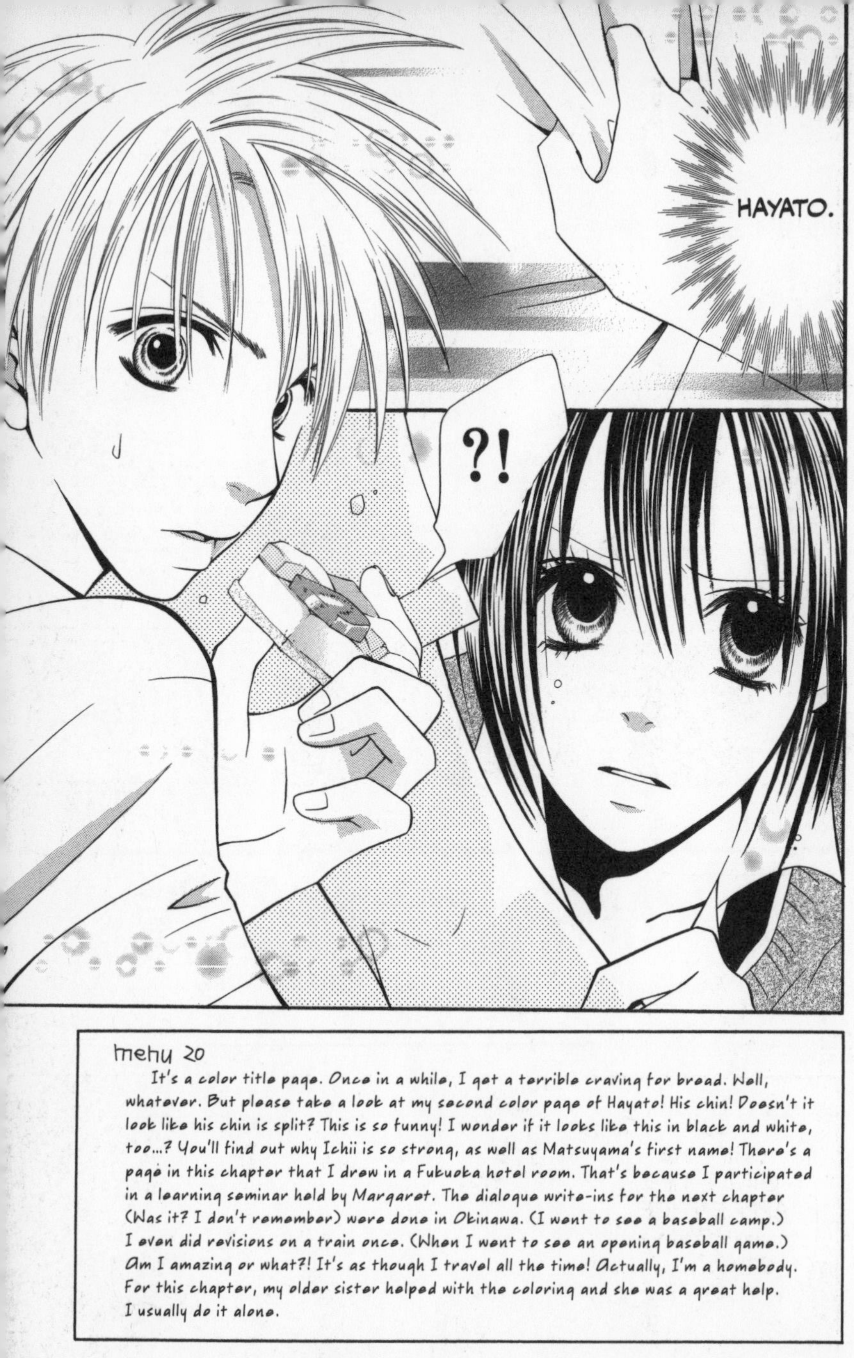
HAYATO.
?!

Menu 20

It's a color title page. Once in a while, I get a terrible craving for bread. Well, whatever. But please take a look at my second color page of Hayato! His chin! Doesn't it look like his chin is split? This is so funny! I wonder if it looks like this in black and white, too...? You'll find out why Ichii is so strong, as well as Matsuyama's first name! There's a page in this chapter that I drew in a Fukuoka hotel room. That's because I participated in a learning seminar held by Margaret. The dialogue write-ins for the next chapter (Was it? I don't remember) were done in Okinawa. (I went to see a baseball camp.) I even did revisions on a train once. (When I went to see an opening baseball game.) Am I amazing or what?! It's as though I travel all the time! Actually, I'm a homebody. For this chapter, my older sister helped with the coloring and she was a great help. I usually do it alone.

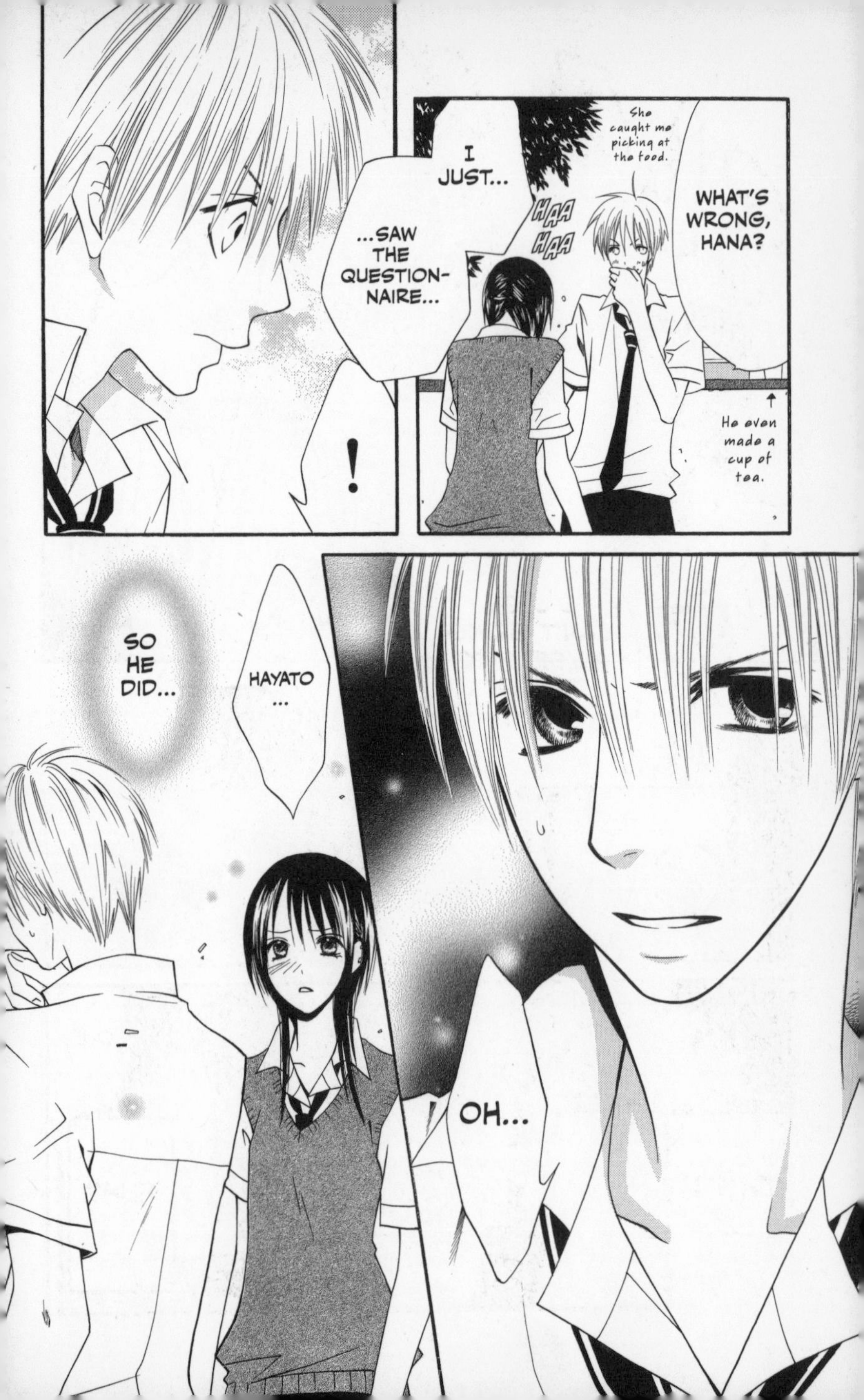

WHAT'S WRONG, HANA?
She caught me picking at the food.
I JUST...
HAA HAA
...SAW THE QUESTION-NAIRE...
He even made a cup of tea.
!
OH...
HAYATO...
SO HE DID...

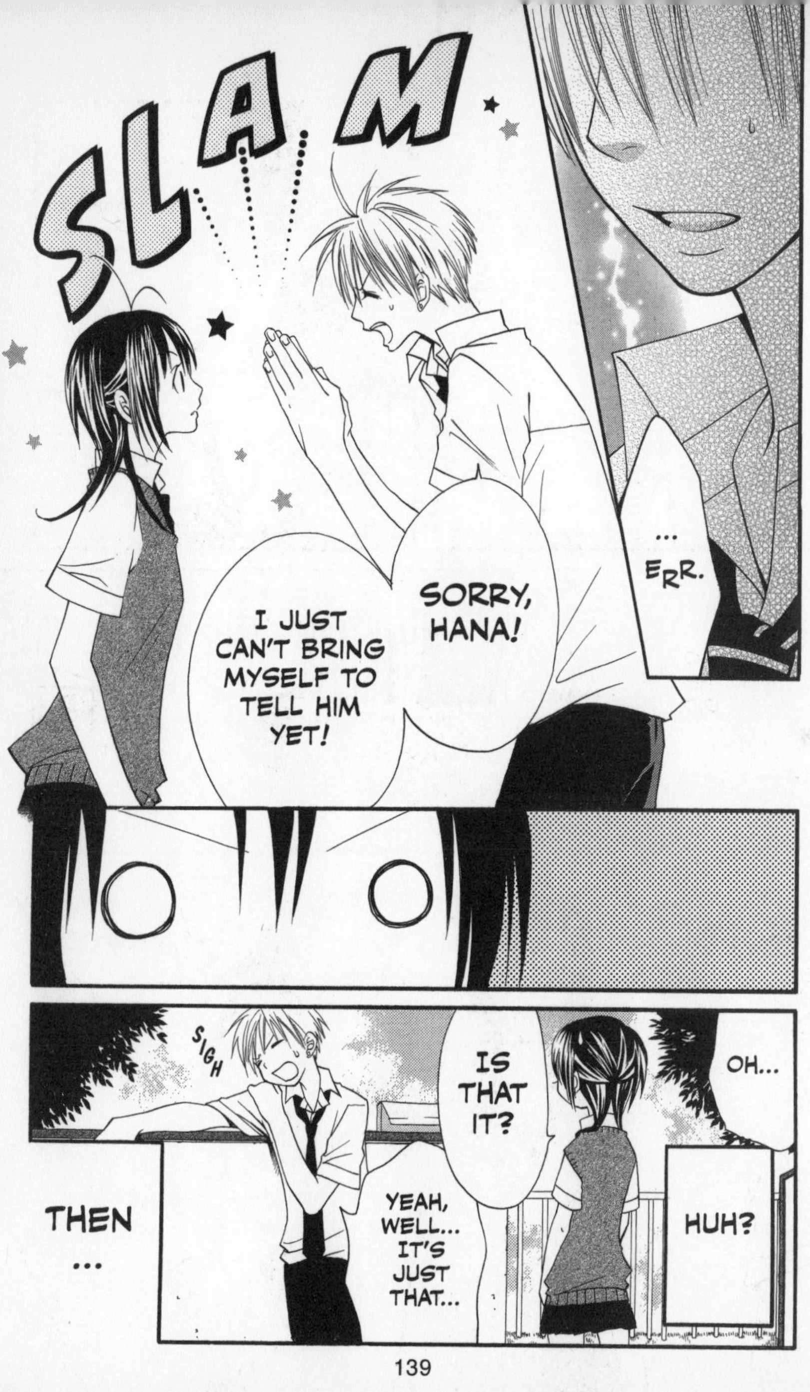
... ERR.
SLAM
SORRY, HANA!
I JUST CAN'T BRING MYSELF TO TELL HIM YET!
OH...
IS THAT IT?
SIGH
HUH?
YEAH, WELL... IT'S JUST THAT...
THEN ...

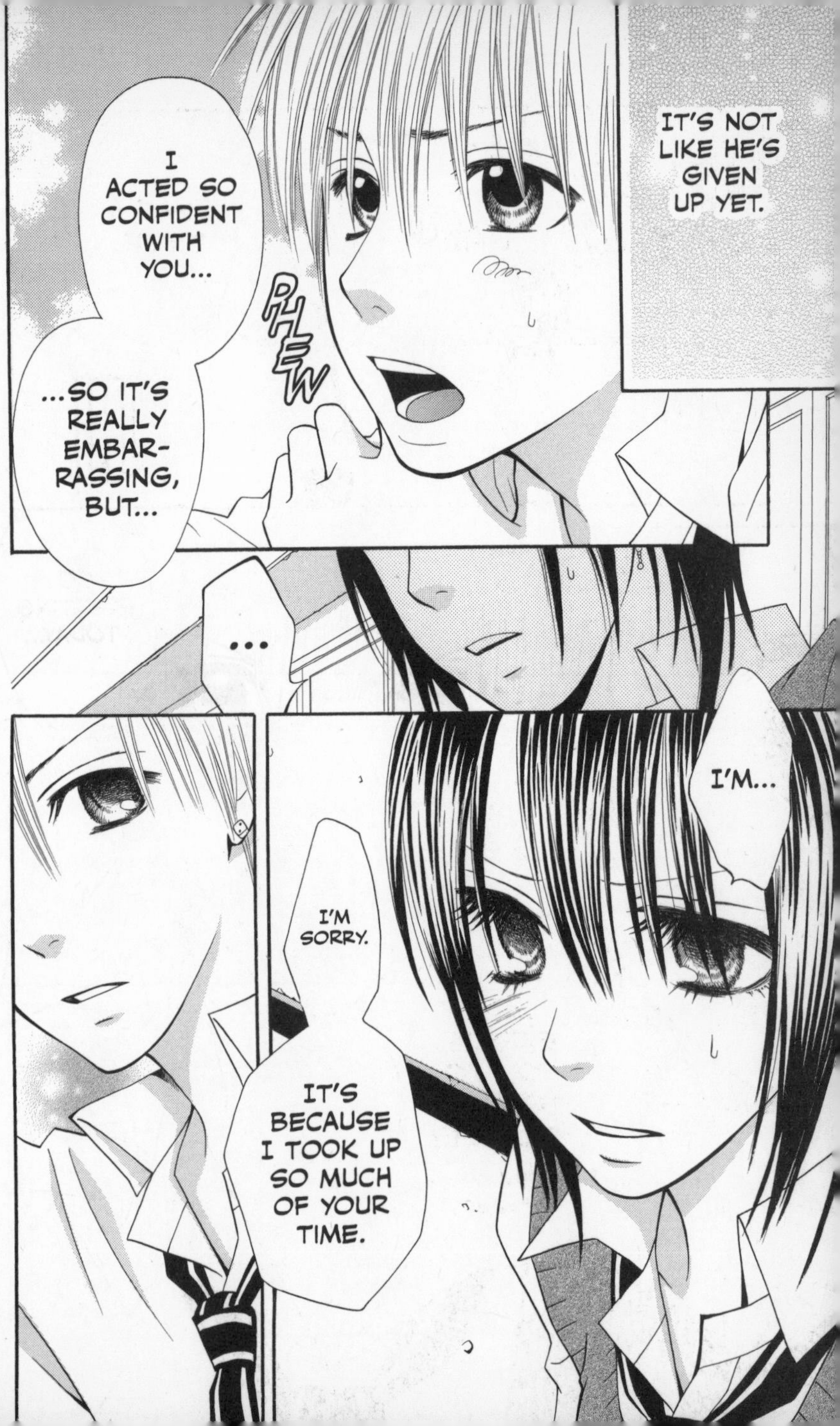
IT'S NOT LIKE HE'S GIVEN UP YET.
I ACTED SO CONFIDENT WITH YOU...
PHEW
...SO IT'S REALLY EMBAR-RASSING, BUT...
...
I'M...
I'M SORRY.
IT'S BECAUSE I TOOK UP SO MUCH OF YOUR TIME.

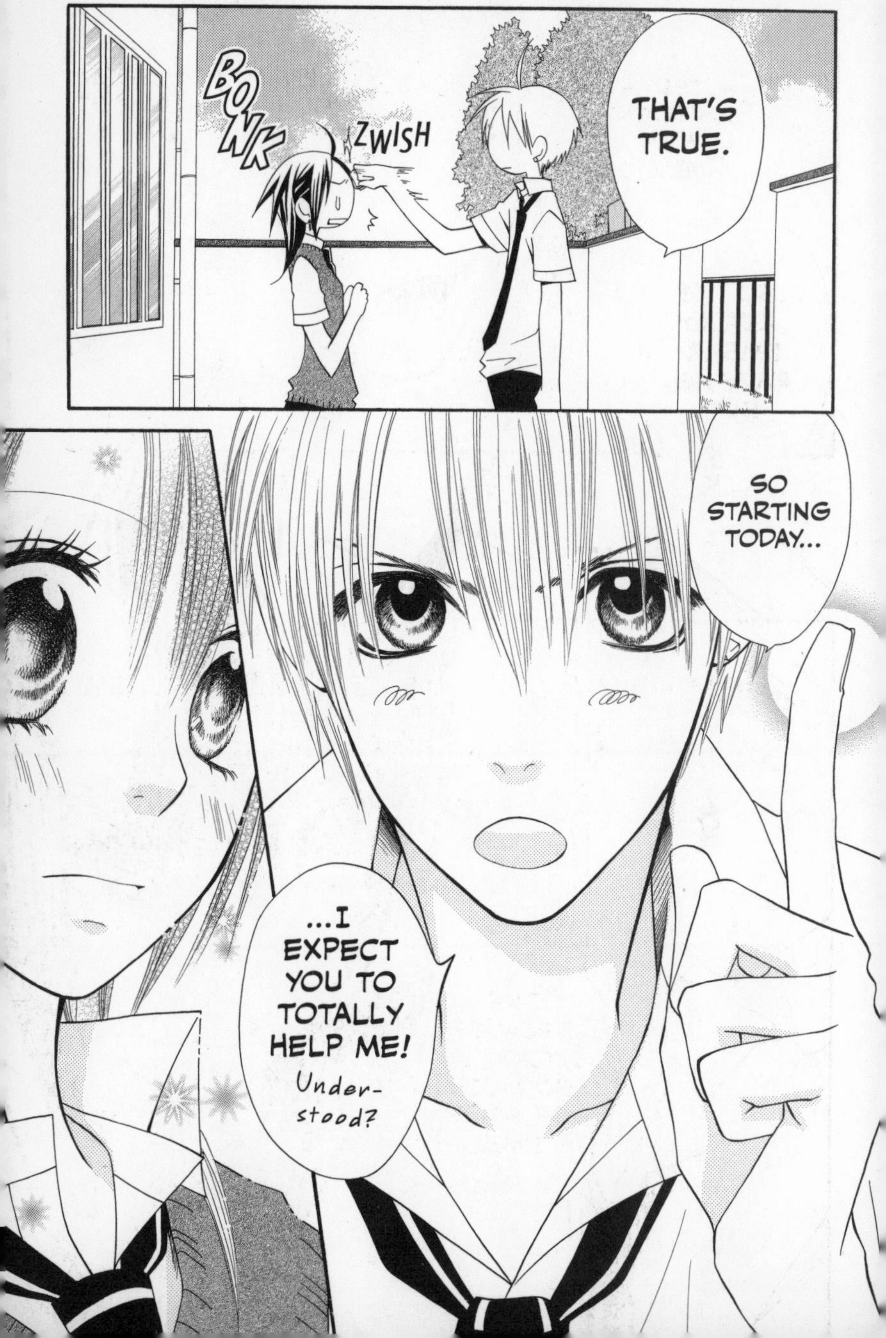
THAT'S TRUE.
ZWISH
BONK
SO STARTING TODAY...
...I EXPECT YOU TO TOTALLY HELP ME!
Under-stood?

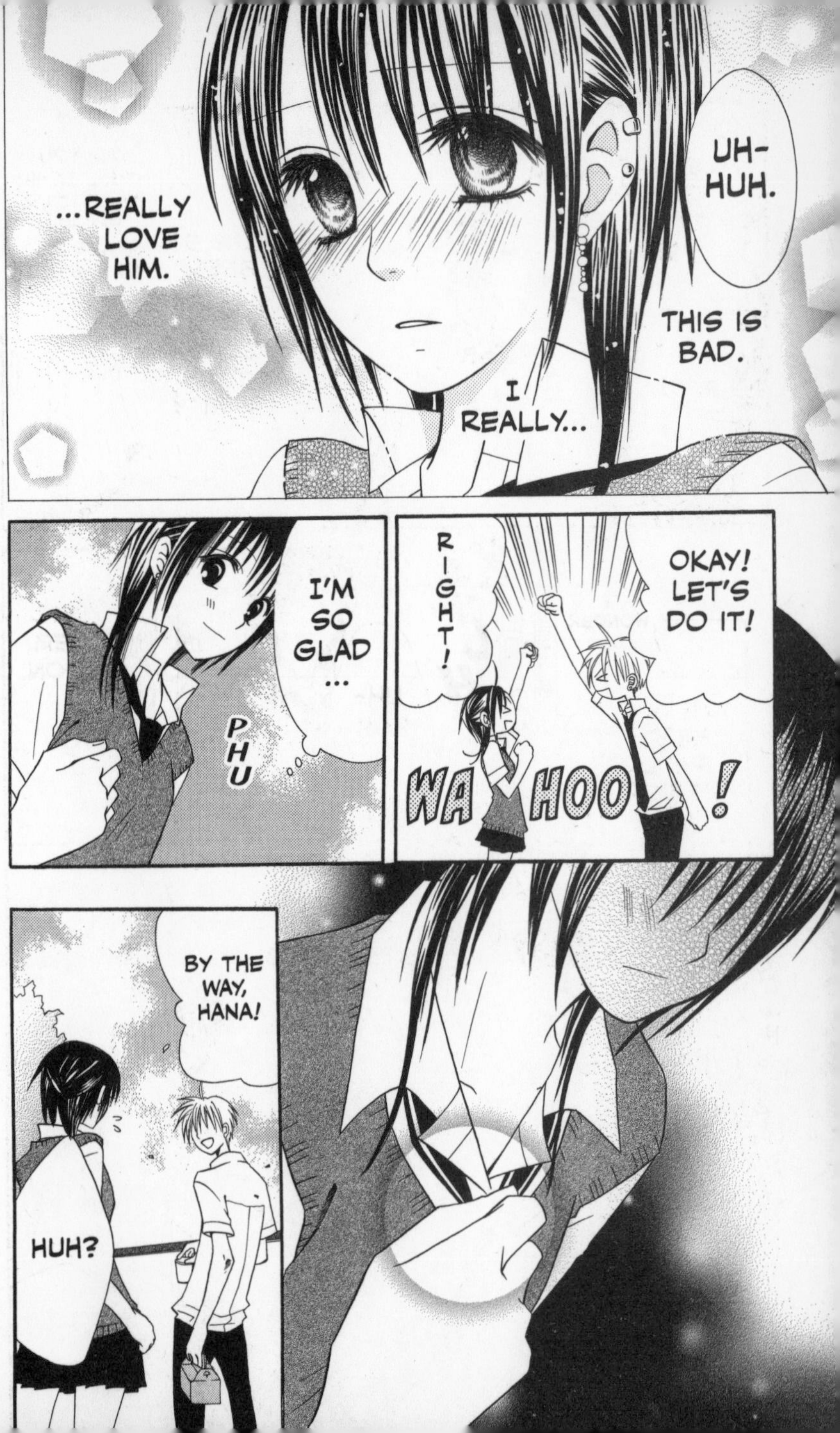
UH-HUH.
THIS IS BAD.
I REALLY...
...REALLY LOVE HIM.
OKAY! LET'S DO IT!
RIGHT!
WAHOO!
I'M SO GLAD...
PHU
BY THE WAY, HANA!
HUH?

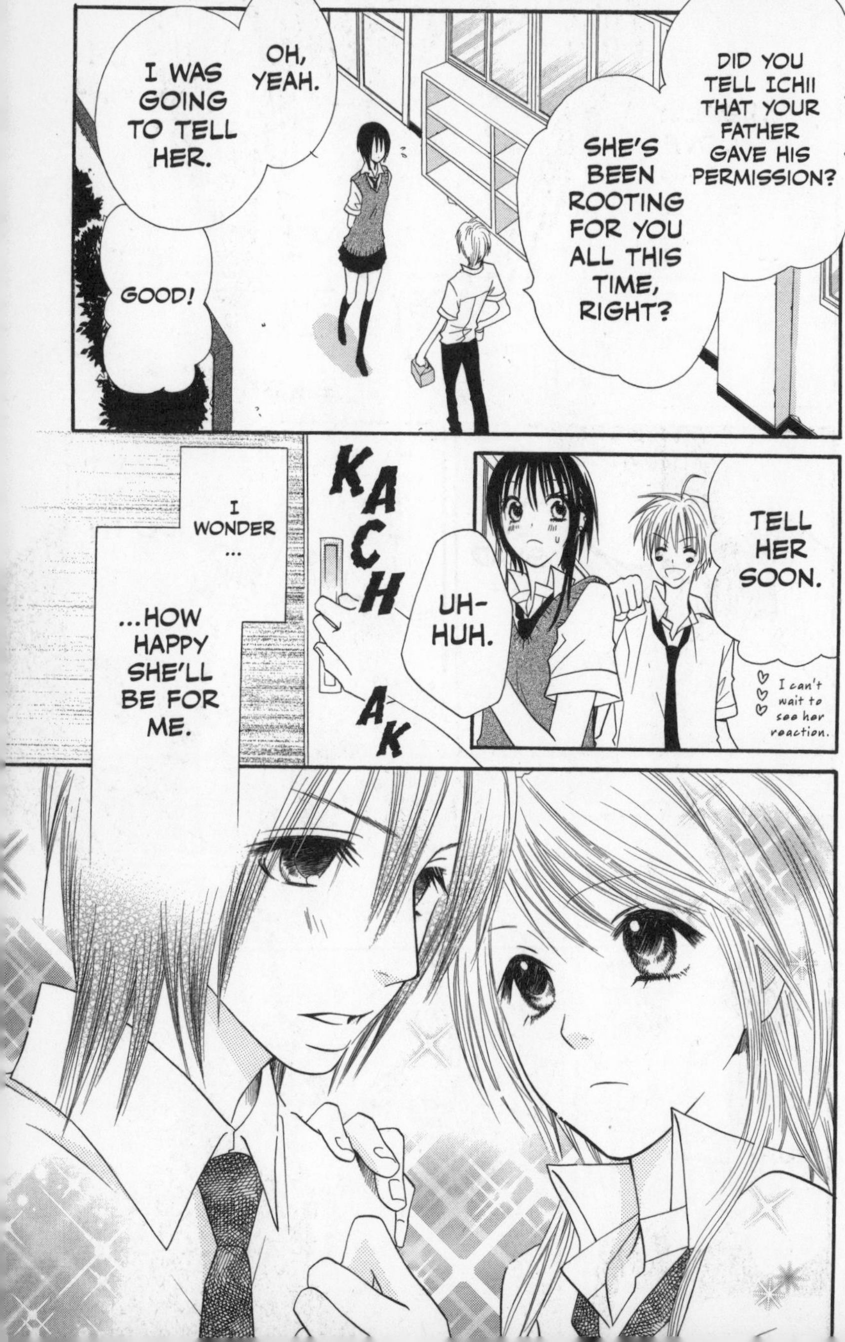
DID YOU TELL ICHII THAT YOUR FATHER GAVE HIS PERMISSION?
SHE'S BEEN ROOTING FOR YOU ALL THIS TIME, RIGHT?
OH, YEAH.
I WAS GOING TO TELL HER.
GOOD!
TELL HER SOON.
I can't wait to see her reaction.
UH-HUH.
KACHAK
I WONDER ...
...HOW HAPPY SHE'LL BE FOR ME.

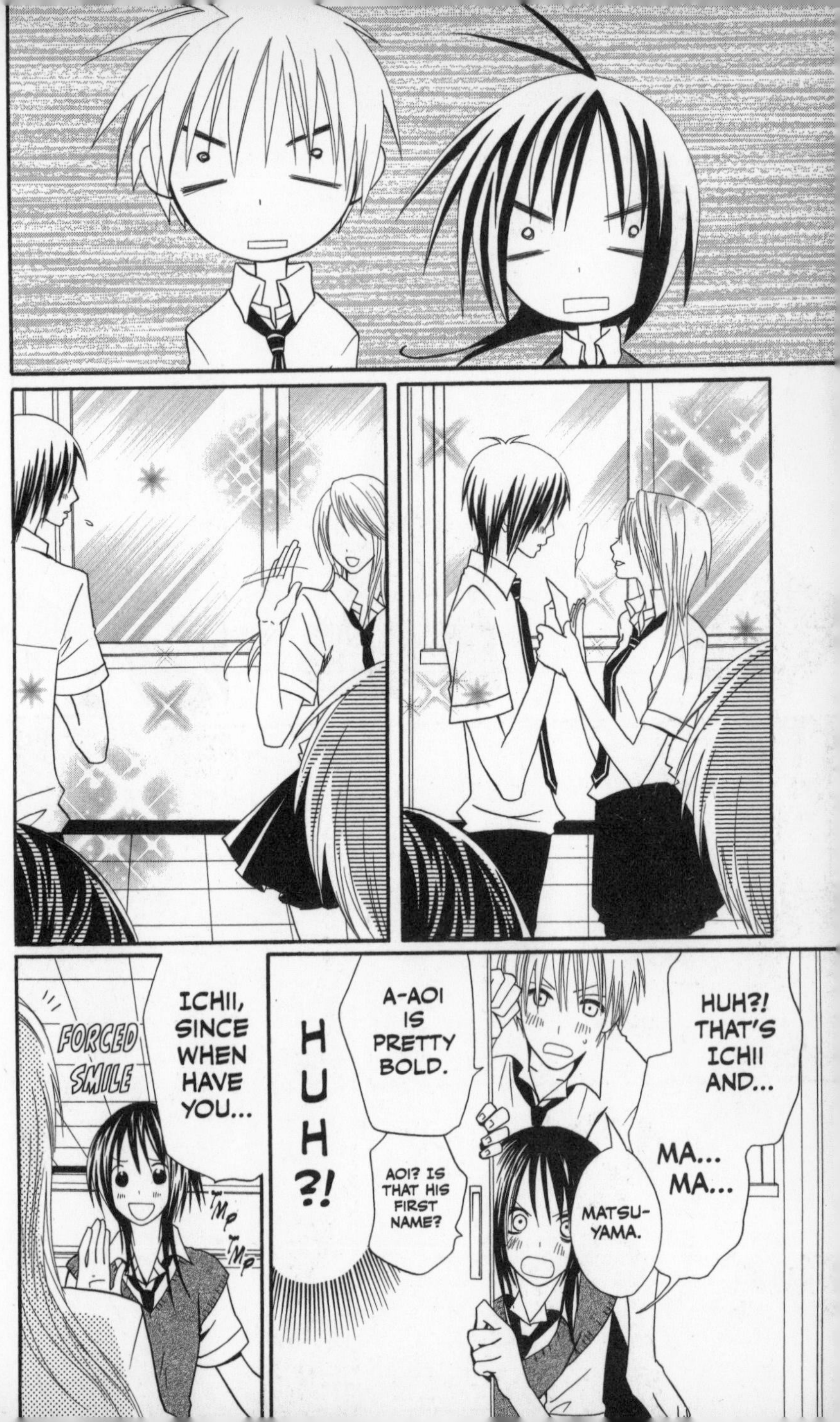
HUH?! THAT'S ICHII AND...
A-AOI IS PRETTY BOLD.
MA... MA...
MATSU-YAMA.
HUH?!
AOI? IS THAT HIS FIRST NAME?
ICHII, SINCE WHEN HAVE YOU...
FORCED SMILE
TMP TMP

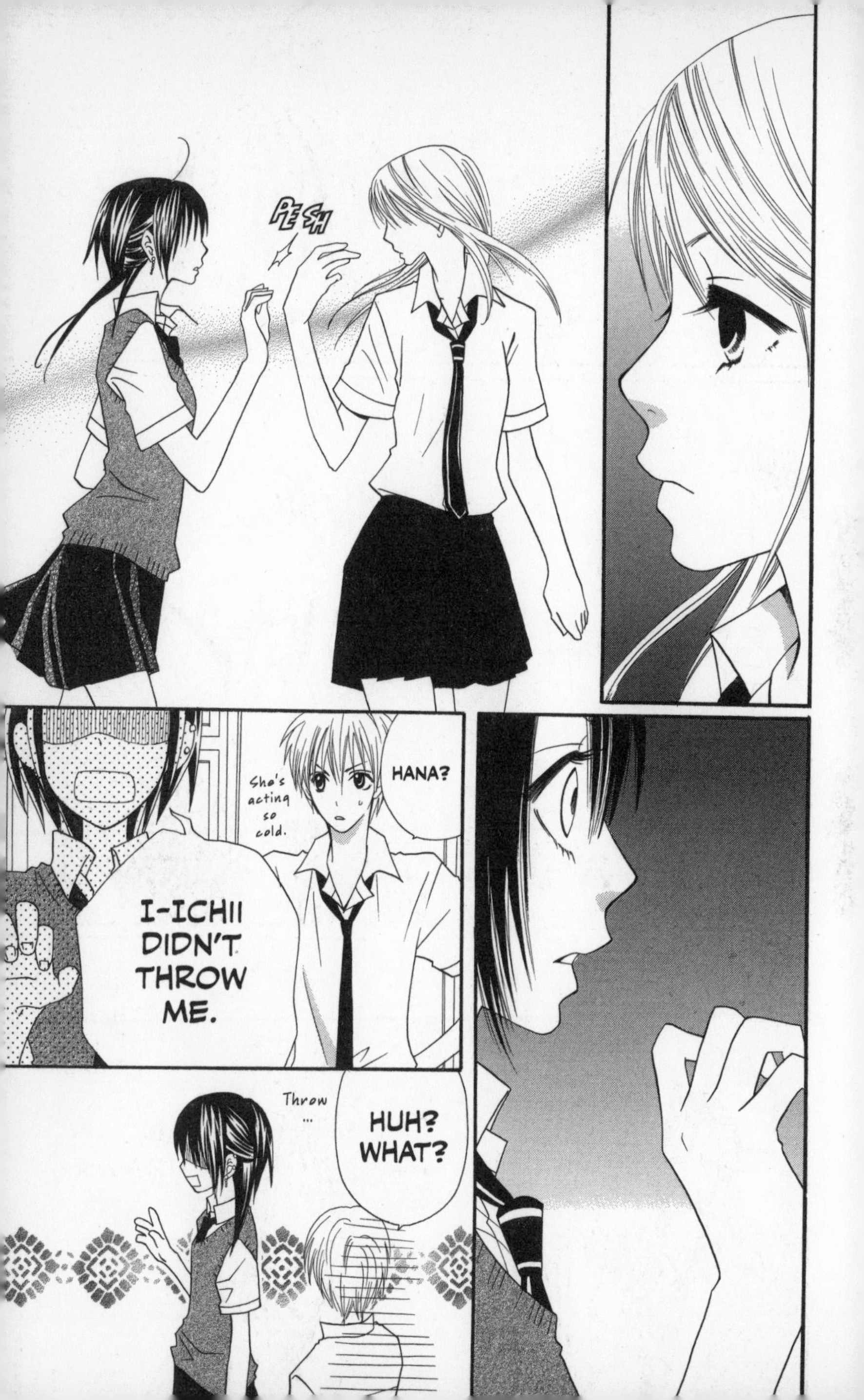
PESH
HANA?
She's acting so cold.
I-ICHII DIDN'T THROW ME.
HUH? WHAT?
Throw ...

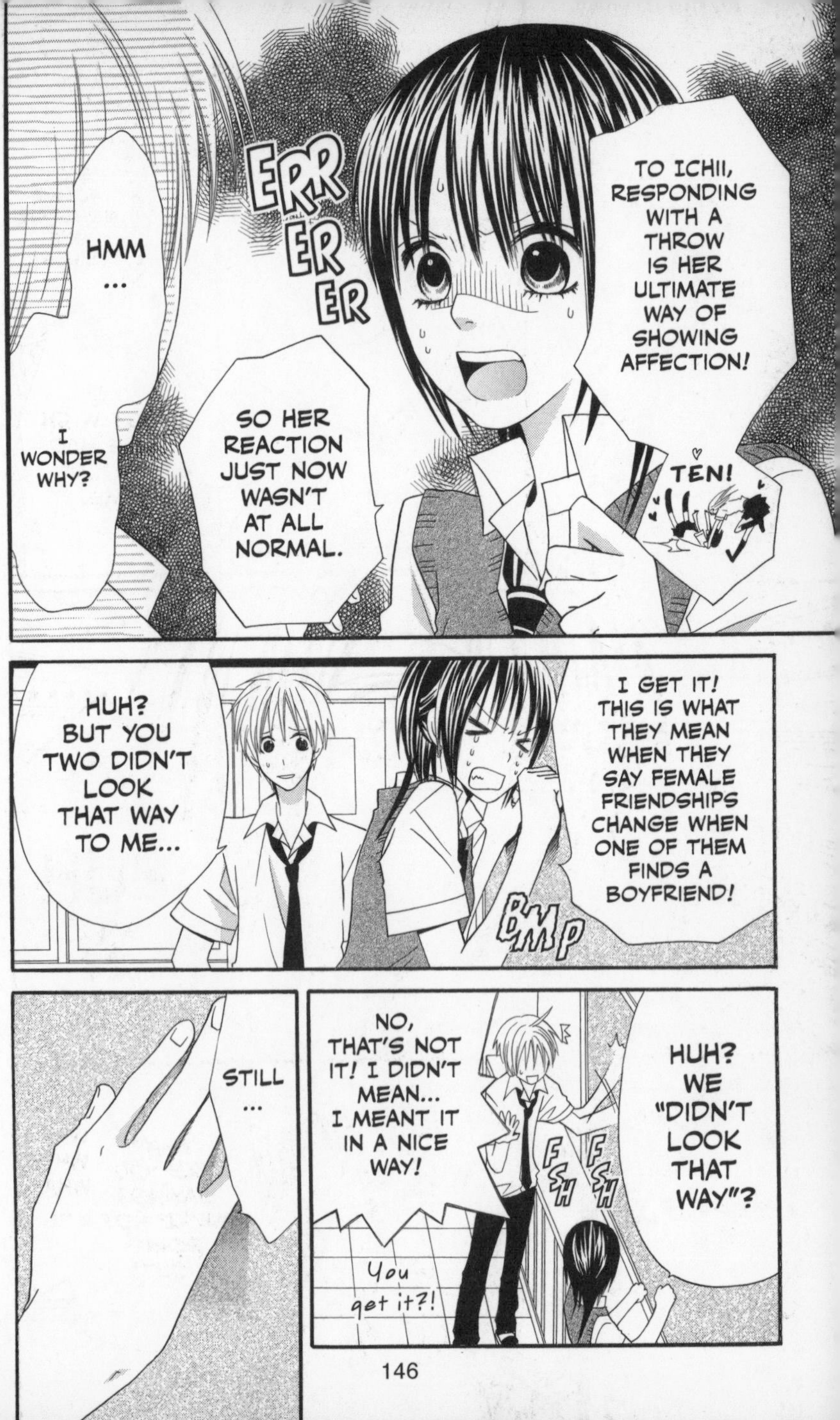
TO ICHII, RESPONDING WITH A THROW IS HER ULTIMATE WAY OF SHOWING AFFECTION!
TEN!
ERR ER ER
SO HER REACTION JUST NOW WASN'T AT ALL NORMAL.
HMM ...
I WONDER WHY?
I GET IT! THIS IS WHAT THEY MEAN WHEN THEY SAY FEMALE FRIENDSHIPS CHANGE WHEN ONE OF THEM FINDS A BOYFRIEND!
BMP
HUH? BUT YOU TWO DIDN'T LOOK THAT WAY TO ME...
HUH? WE "DIDN'T LOOK THAT WAY"?
FSH FSH
NO, THAT'S NOT IT! I DIDN'T MEAN... I MEANT IT IN A NICE WAY!
You get it?!
STILL ...

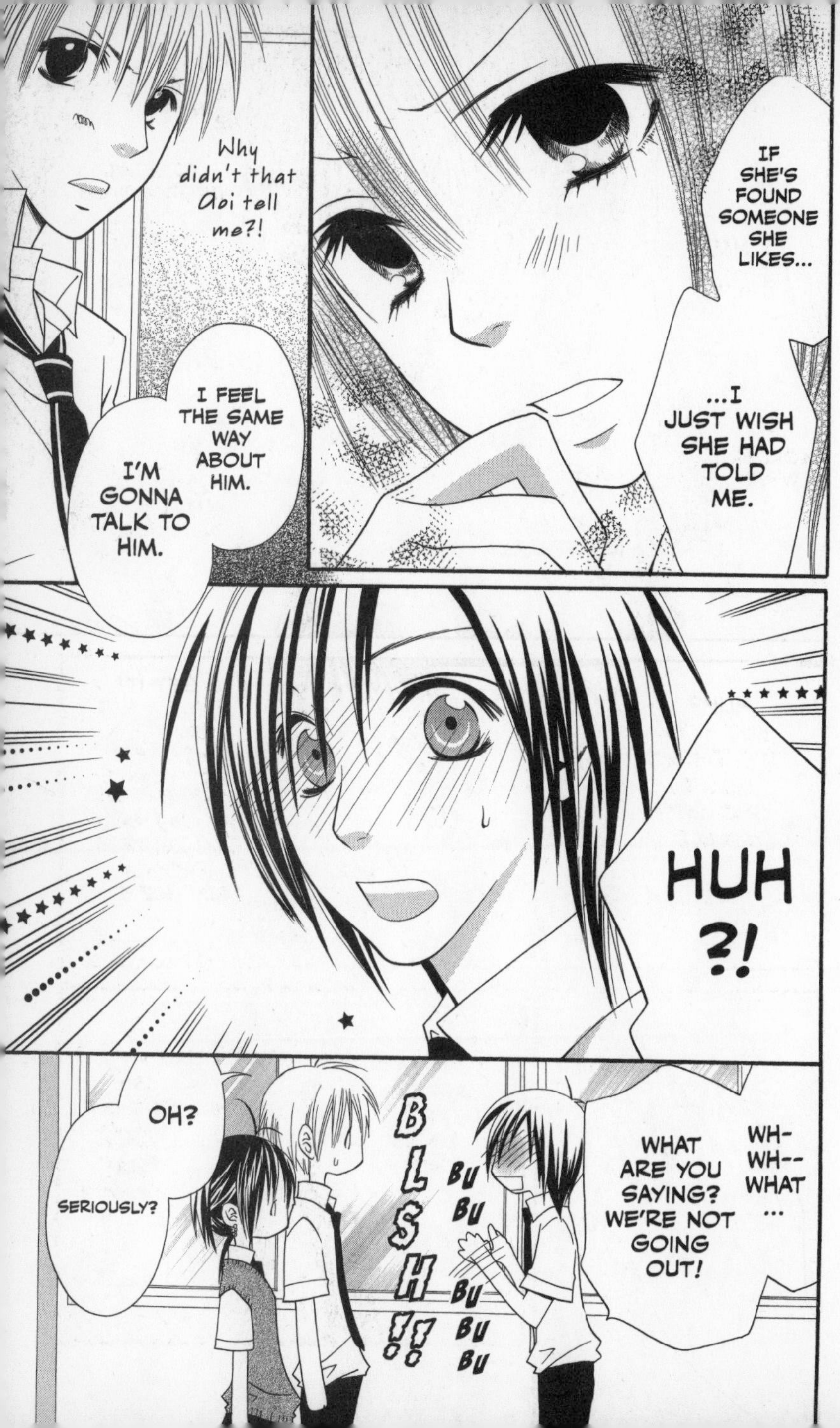
IF SHE'S FOUND SOMEONE SHE LIKES...
...I JUST WISH SHE HAD TOLD ME.
Why didn't that Aoi tell me?!
I FEEL THE SAME WAY ABOUT HIM. I'M GONNA TALK TO HIM.
HUH ?!
WH-WH--WHAT...
WHAT ARE YOU SAYING? WE'RE NOT GOING OUT!
BU BU BU BU BU
BLSH!!
OH?
SERIOUSLY?

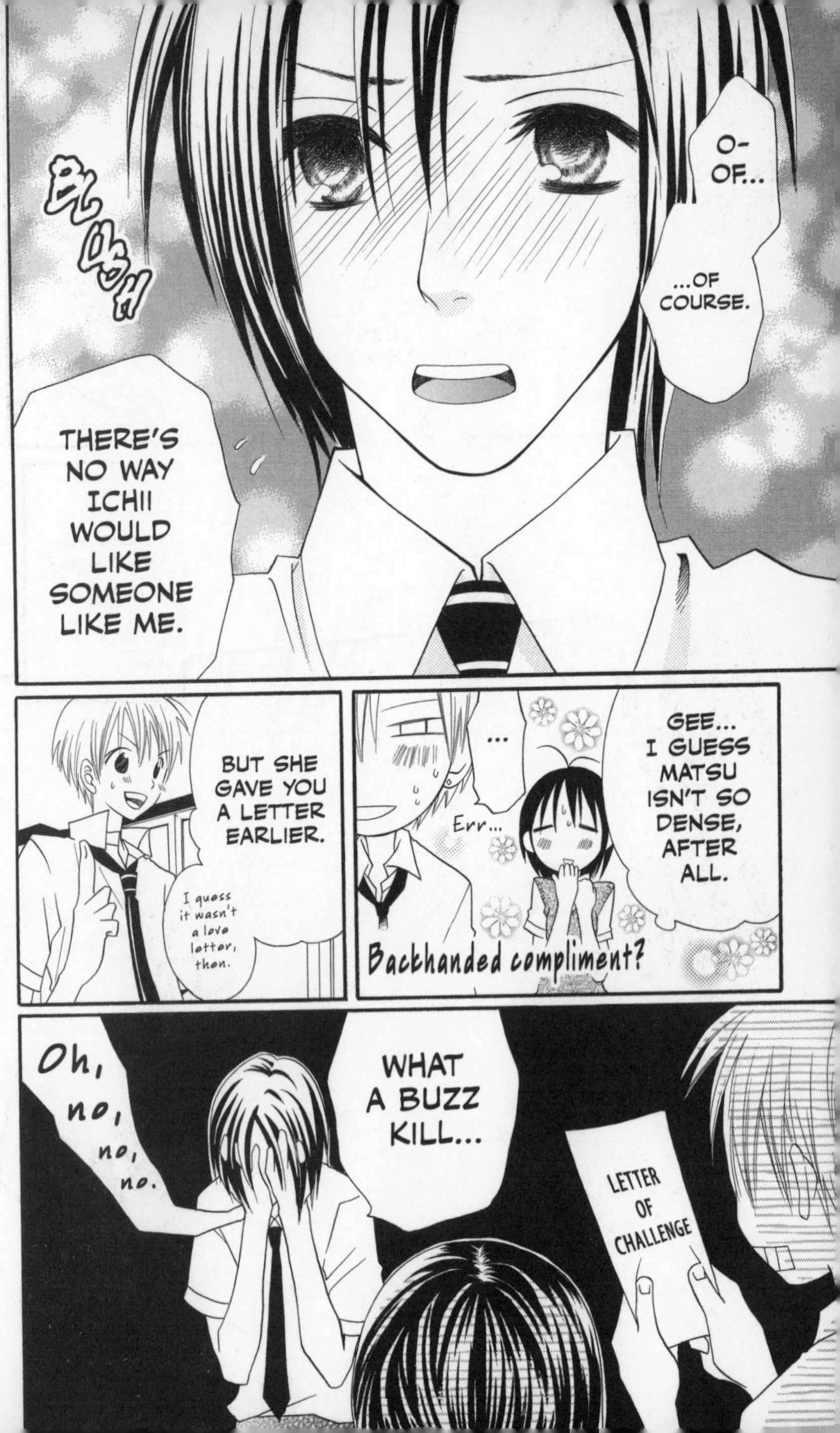
O- OF...
...OF COURSE.
BLUSH
THERE'S NO WAY ICHII WOULD LIKE SOMEONE LIKE ME.
GEE... I GUESS MATSU ISN'T SO DENSE, AFTER ALL.
...
Err...
Backhanded compliment?
BUT SHE GAVE YOU A LETTER EARLIER.
I guess it wasn't a love letter, then.
LETTER OF CHALLENGE
WHAT A BUZZ KILL...
Oh, no, no, no.

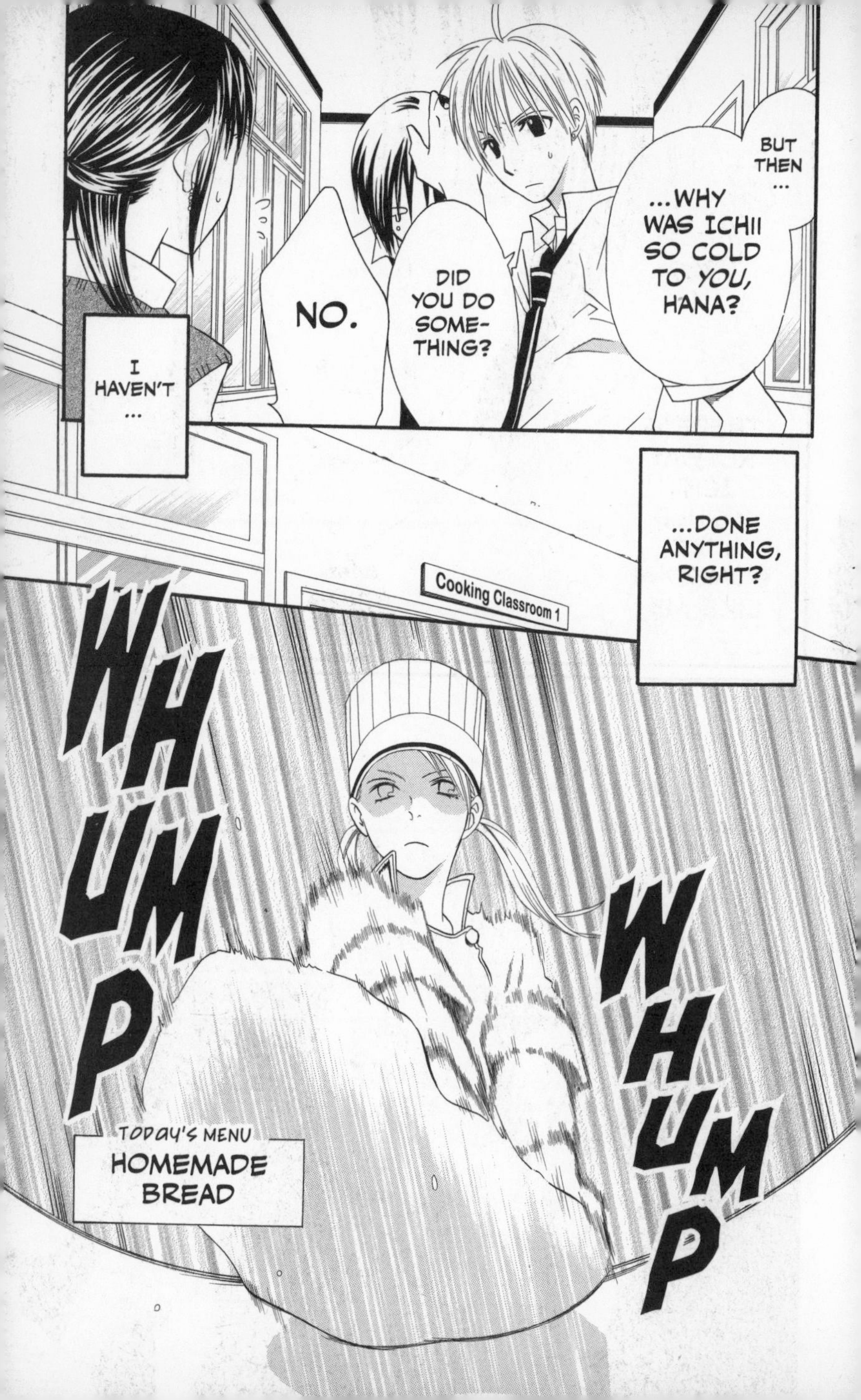
BUT THEN ...
...WHY WAS ICHII SO COLD TO YOU, HANA?
DID YOU DO SOME-THING?
NO.
I HAVEN'T ...
...DONE ANYTHING, RIGHT?
Cooking Classroom 1
WHUMP
WHUMP
TODAY'S MENU
HOMEMADE BREAD

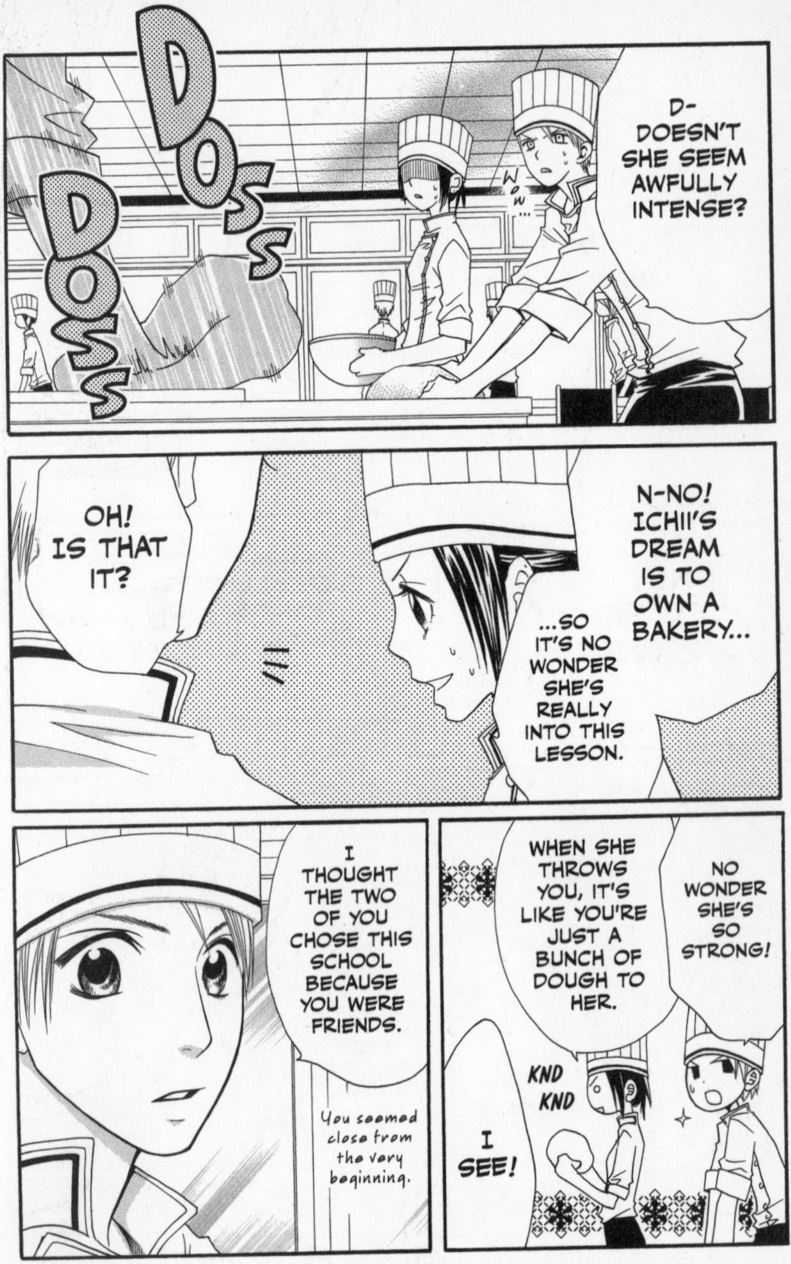
D- DOESN'T SHE SEEM AWFULLY INTENSE?
WOW...
DOSS DOSS
N-NO! ICHII'S DREAM IS TO OWN A BAKERY...
...SO IT'S NO WONDER SHE'S REALLY INTO THIS LESSON.
OH! IS THAT IT?
NO WONDER SHE'S SO STRONG!
WHEN SHE THROWS YOU, IT'S LIKE YOU'RE JUST A BUNCH OF DOUGH TO HER.
KND KND
I SEE!
I THOUGHT THE TWO OF YOU CHOSE THIS SCHOOL BECAUSE YOU WERE FRIENDS.
You seemed close from the very beginning.

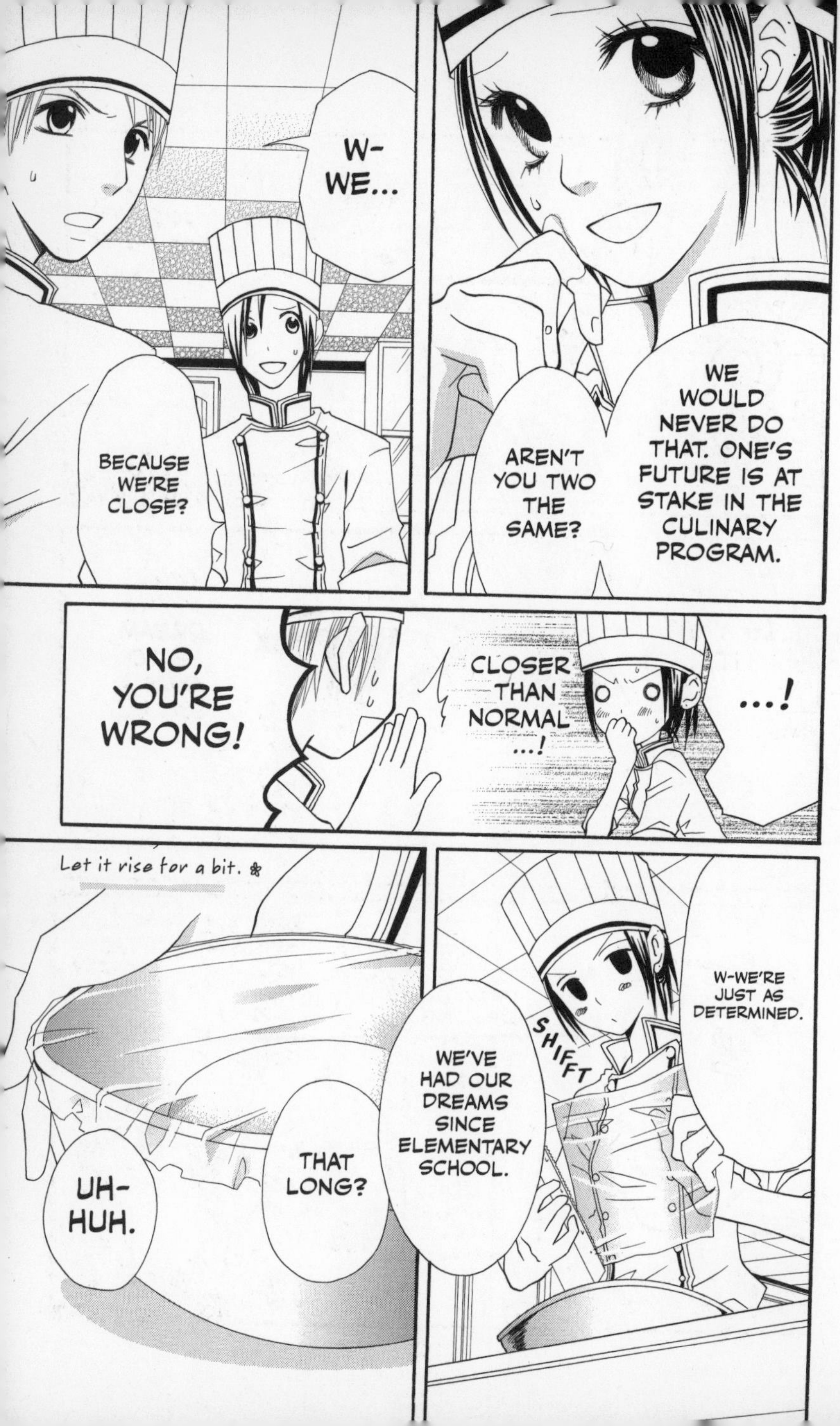
WE WOULD NEVER DO THAT. ONE'S FUTURE IS AT STAKE IN THE CULINARY PROGRAM.
AREN'T YOU TWO THE SAME?
W-WE...
BECAUSE WE'RE CLOSE?
...!
CLOSER THAN NORMAL ...!
NO, YOU'RE WRONG!
W-WE'RE JUST AS DETERMINED.
SHIFFT
WE'VE HAD OUR DREAMS SINCE ELEMENTARY SCHOOL.
Let it rise for a bit.
THAT LONG?
UH-HUH.

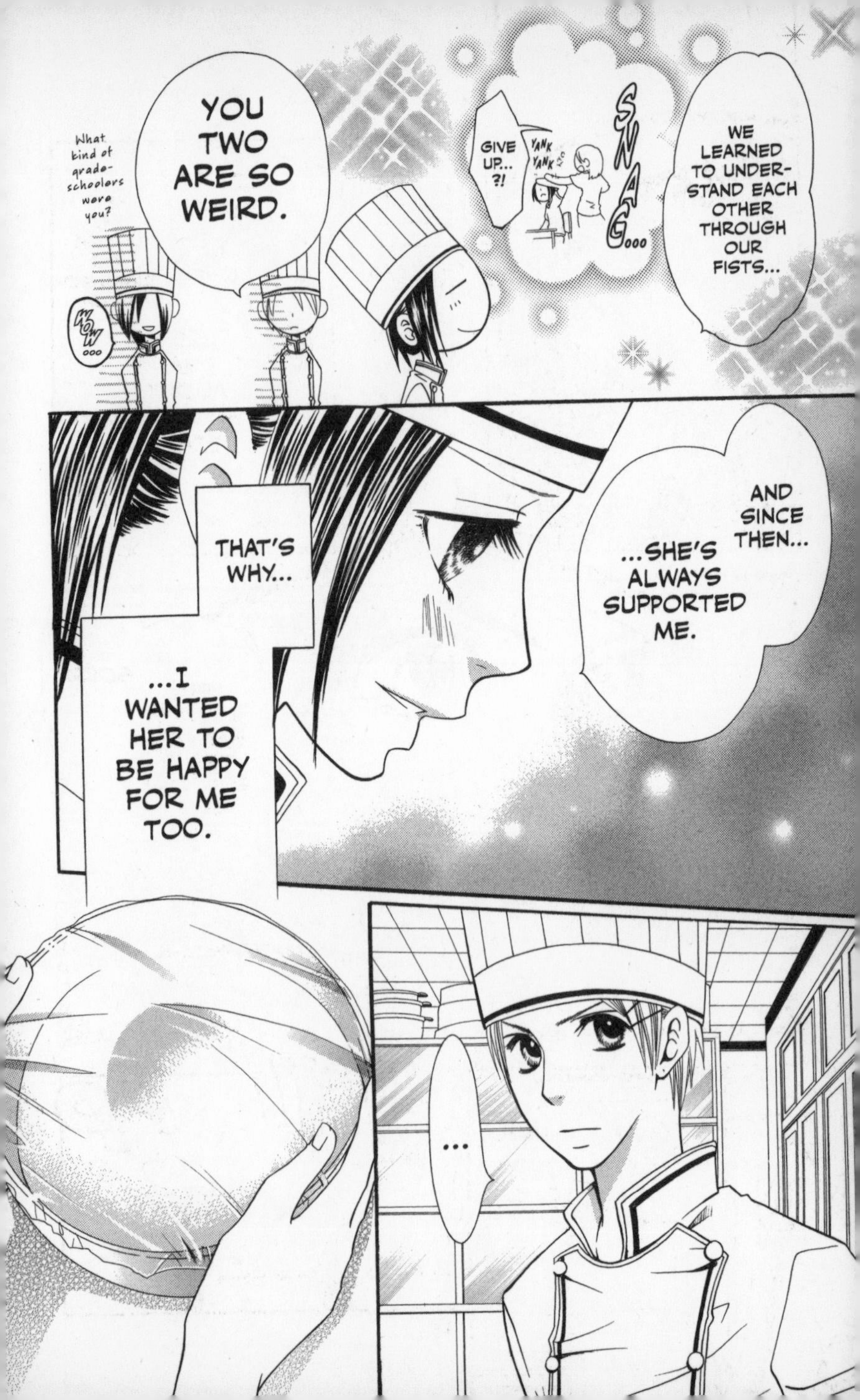
WE LEARNED TO UNDER-STAND EACH OTHER THROUGH OUR FISTS...
SNAG...
GIVE UP... ?!
YANK YANK
YOU TWO ARE SO WEIRD.
What kind of grade-schoolers were you?
WOW...
AND SINCE THEN...
...SHE'S ALWAYS SUPPORTED ME.
THAT'S WHY...
...I WANTED HER TO BE HAPPY FOR ME TOO.
...

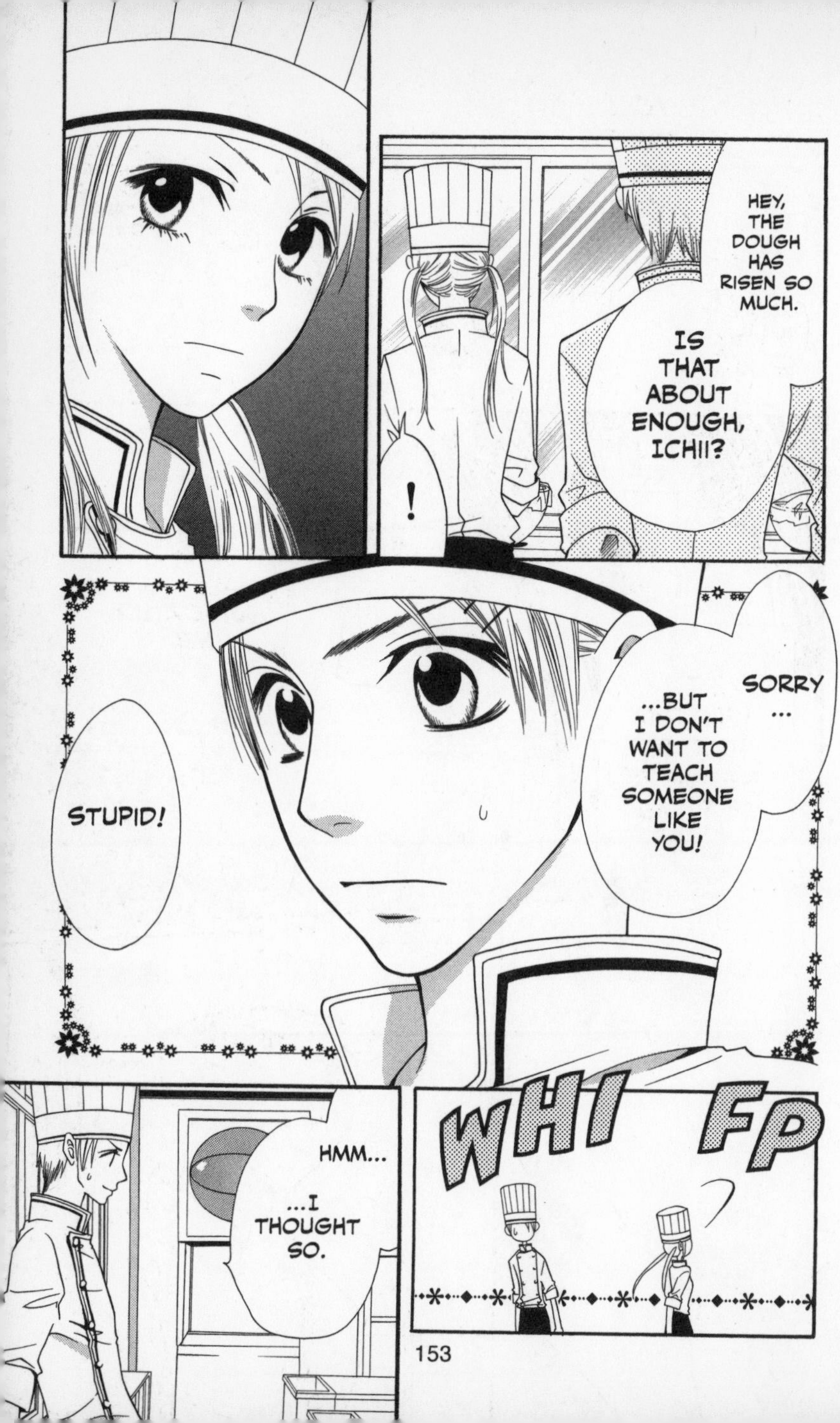
HEY, THE DOUGH HAS RISEN SO MUCH.
IS THAT ABOUT ENOUGH, ICHII?
!
SORRY...
...BUT I DON'T WANT TO TEACH SOMEONE LIKE YOU!
STUPID!
WHI FP
HMM...
...I THOUGHT SO.

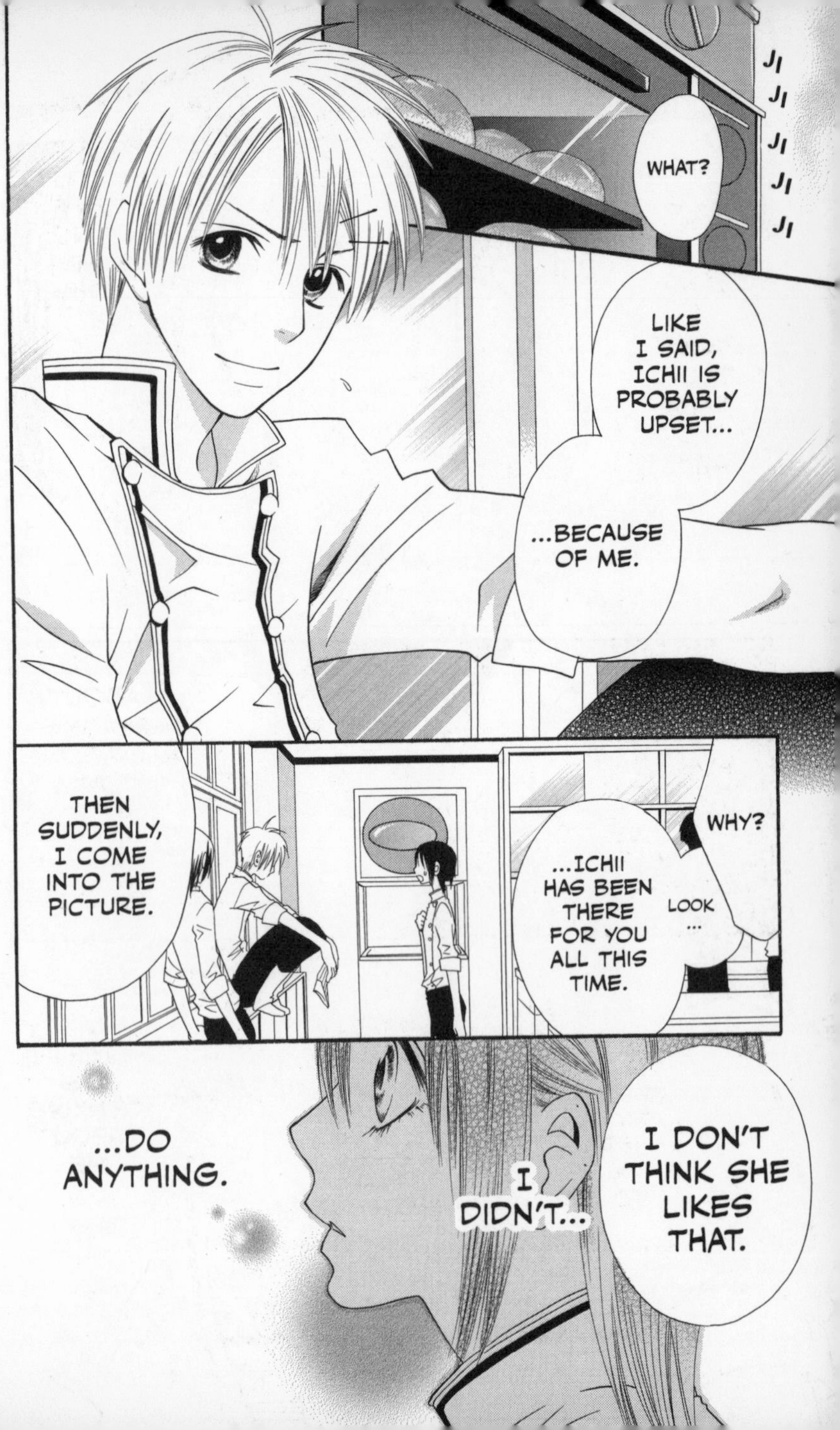
JI JI JI JI JI
WHAT?
LIKE I SAID, ICHII IS PROBABLY UPSET...
...BECAUSE OF ME.
WHY?
LOOK ...
...ICHII HAS BEEN THERE FOR YOU ALL THIS TIME.
THEN SUDDENLY, I COME INTO THE PICTURE.
I DON'T THINK SHE LIKES THAT.
I DIDN'T...
...DO ANYTHING.

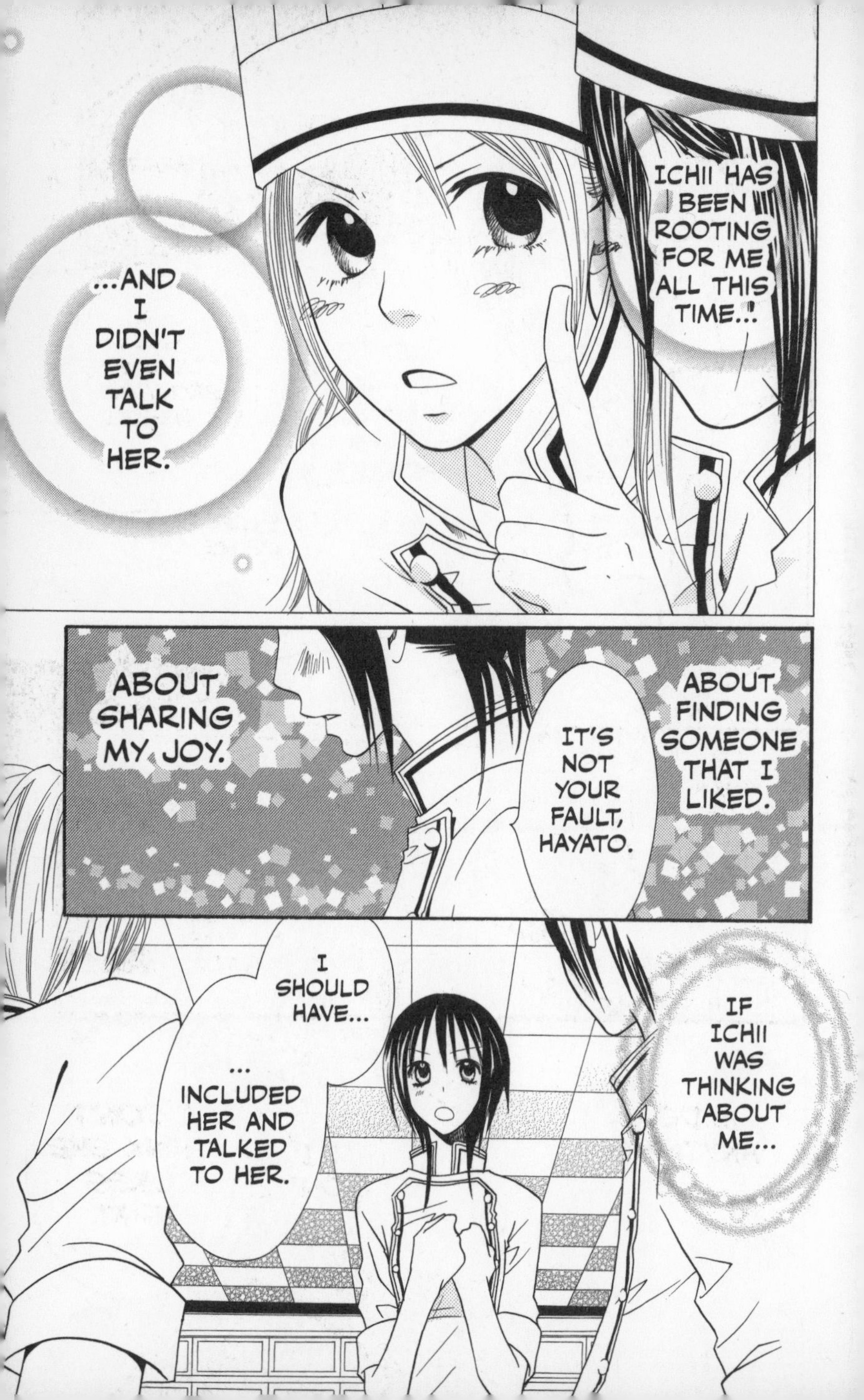
ICHII HAS BEEN ROOTING FOR ME ALL THIS TIME...!
...AND I DIDN'T EVEN TALK TO HER.
ABOUT FINDING SOMEONE THAT I LIKED.
IT'S NOT YOUR FAULT, HAYATO.
ABOUT SHARING MY JOY.
IF ICHII WAS THINKING ABOUT ME...
I SHOULD HAVE...
...INCLUDED HER AND TALKED TO HER.

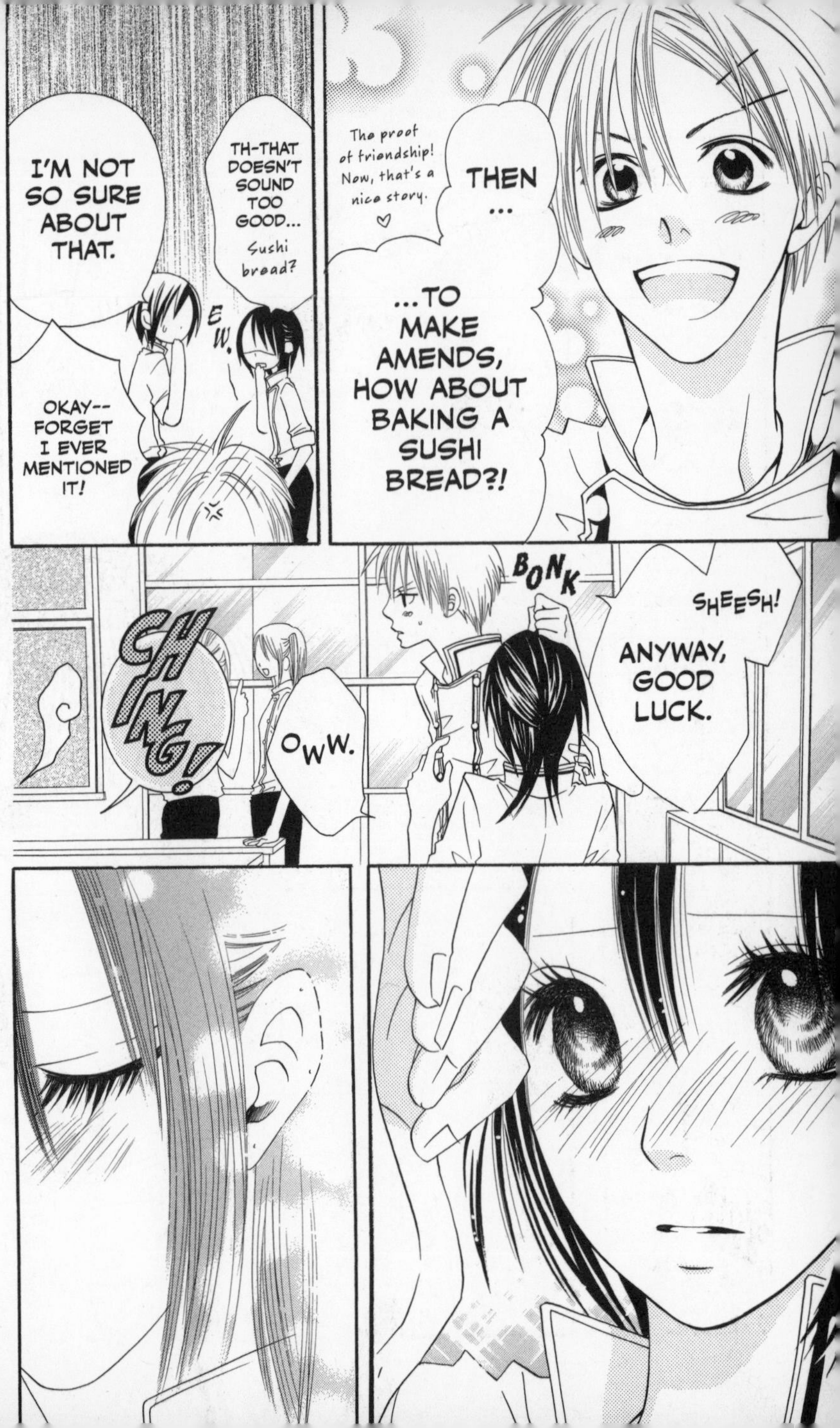
The proof of friendship! Now, that's a nice story.
THEN ...
...TO MAKE AMENDS, HOW ABOUT BAKING A SUSHI BREAD?!
TH-THAT DOESN'T SOUND TOO GOOD...
Sushi bread?
EW.
I'M NOT SO SURE ABOUT THAT.
OKAY-- FORGET I EVER MENTIONED IT!
SHEESH!
ANYWAY, GOOD LUCK.
BONK
OWW.
CHING!

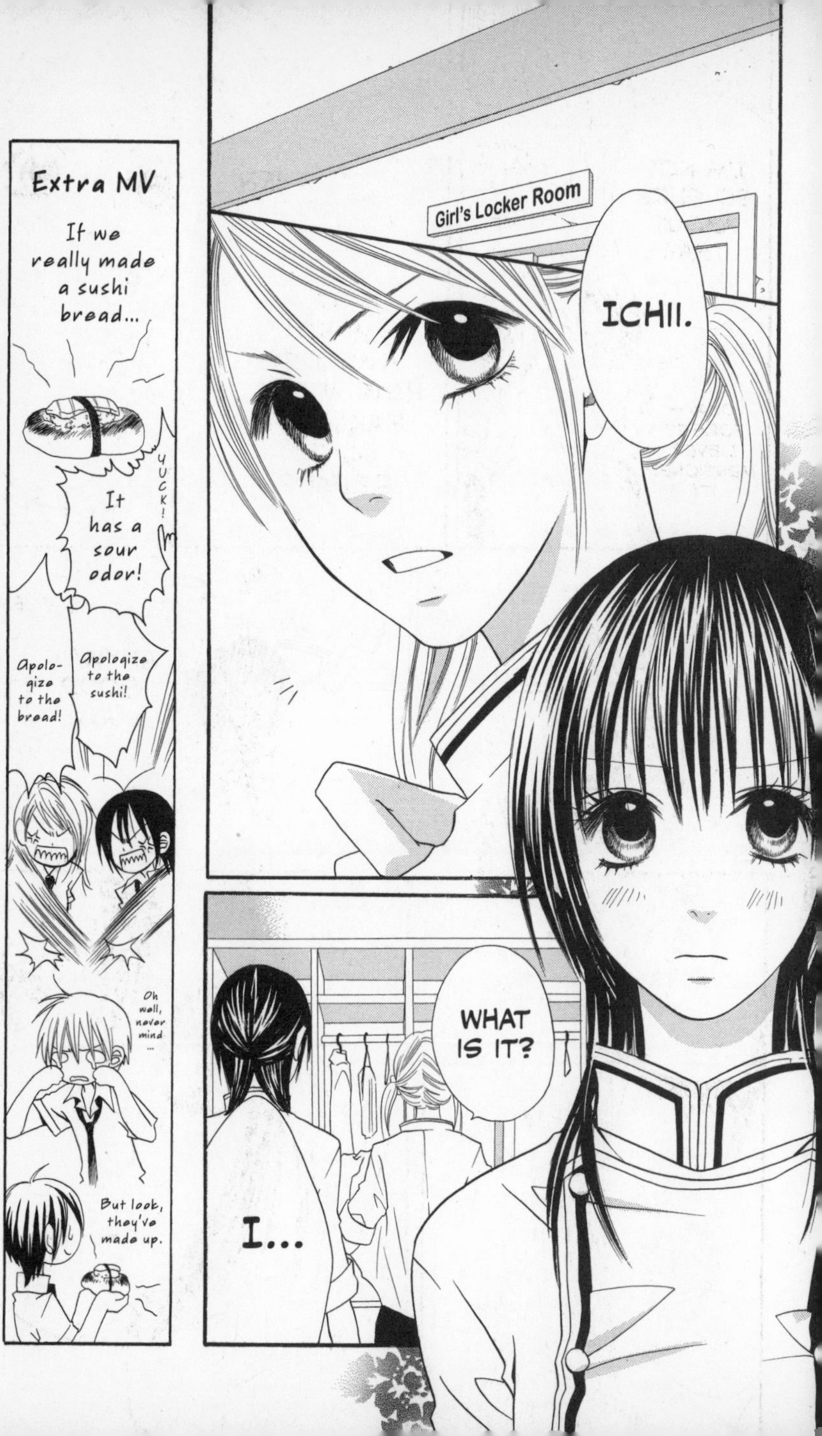
Girl's Locker Room
ICHII.
WHAT IS IT?
I...
Extra MV
If we really made a sushi bread...
YUCK!
It has a sour odor!
Apologize to the sushi!
Apolo-gize to the bread!
Oh well, never mind...
But look, they've made up.

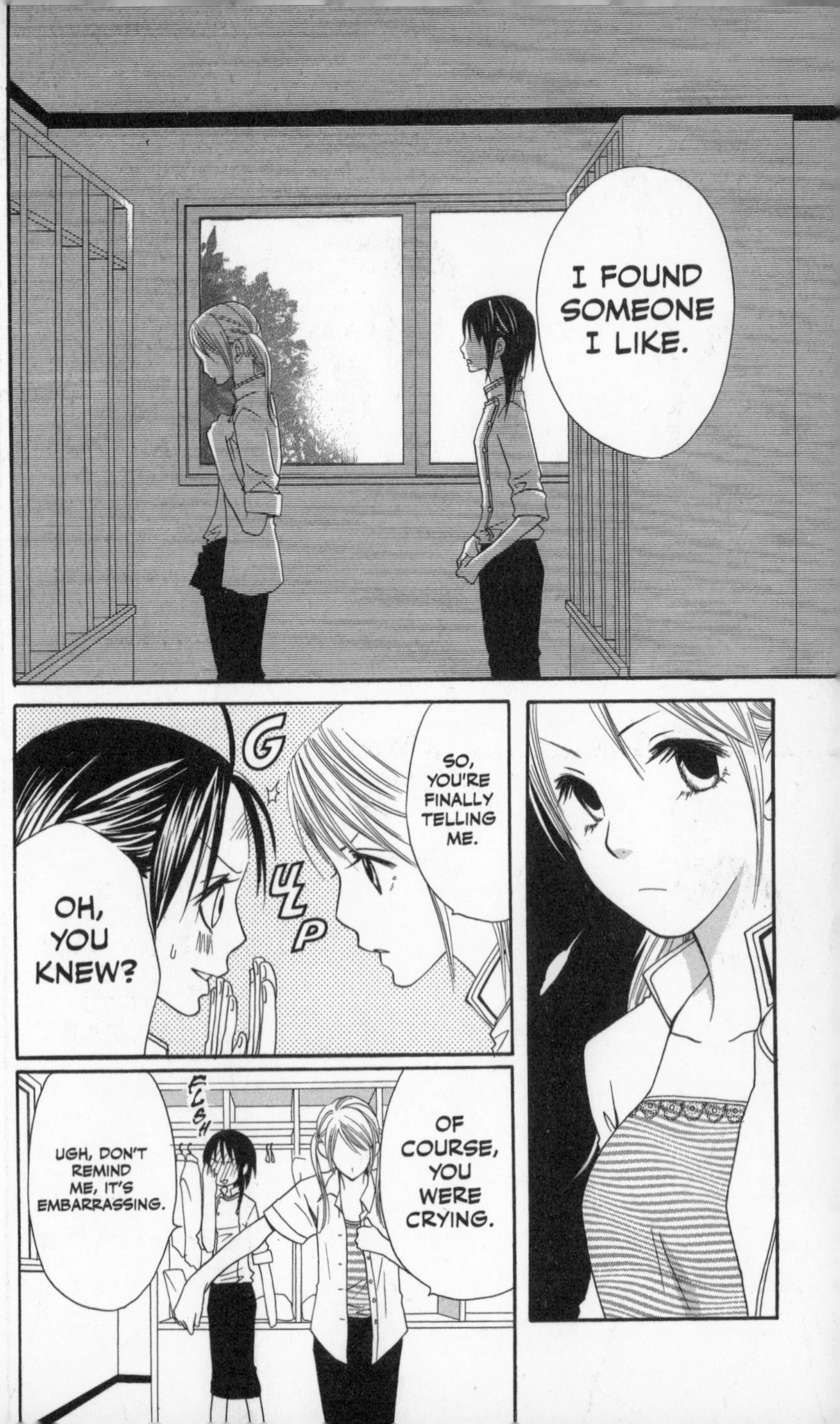
I FOUND SOMEONE I LIKE.
SO, YOU'RE FINALLY TELLING ME.
GULP
OH, YOU KNEW?
OF COURSE, YOU WERE CRYING.
FLSH
UGH, DON'T REMIND ME, IT'S EMBARRASSING.

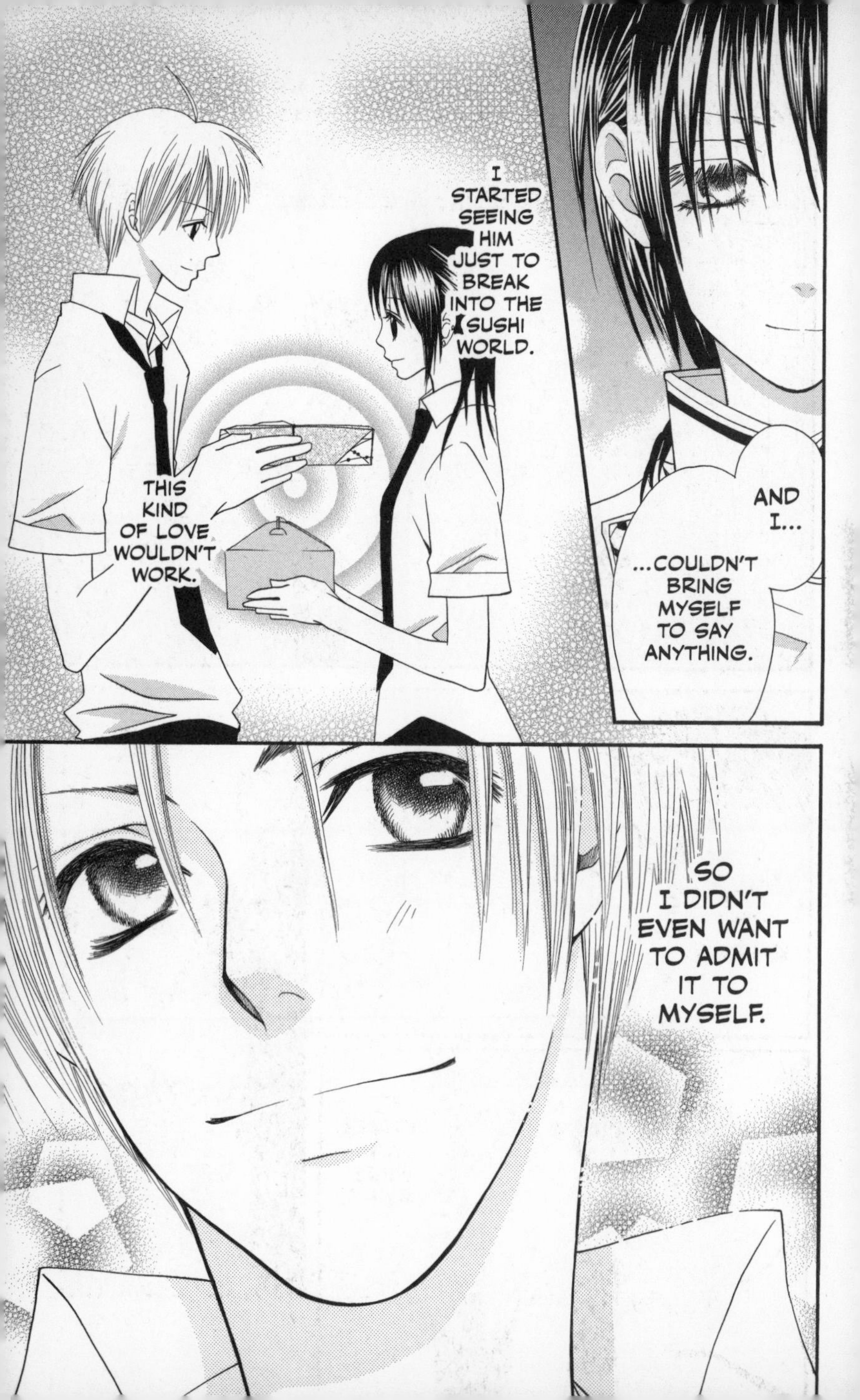
AND I...
...COULDN'T BRING MYSELF TO SAY ANYTHING.
I STARTED SEEING HIM JUST TO BREAK INTO THE SUSHI WORLD.
THIS KIND OF LOVE WOULDN'T WORK.
SO I DIDN'T EVEN WANT TO ADMIT IT TO MYSELF.

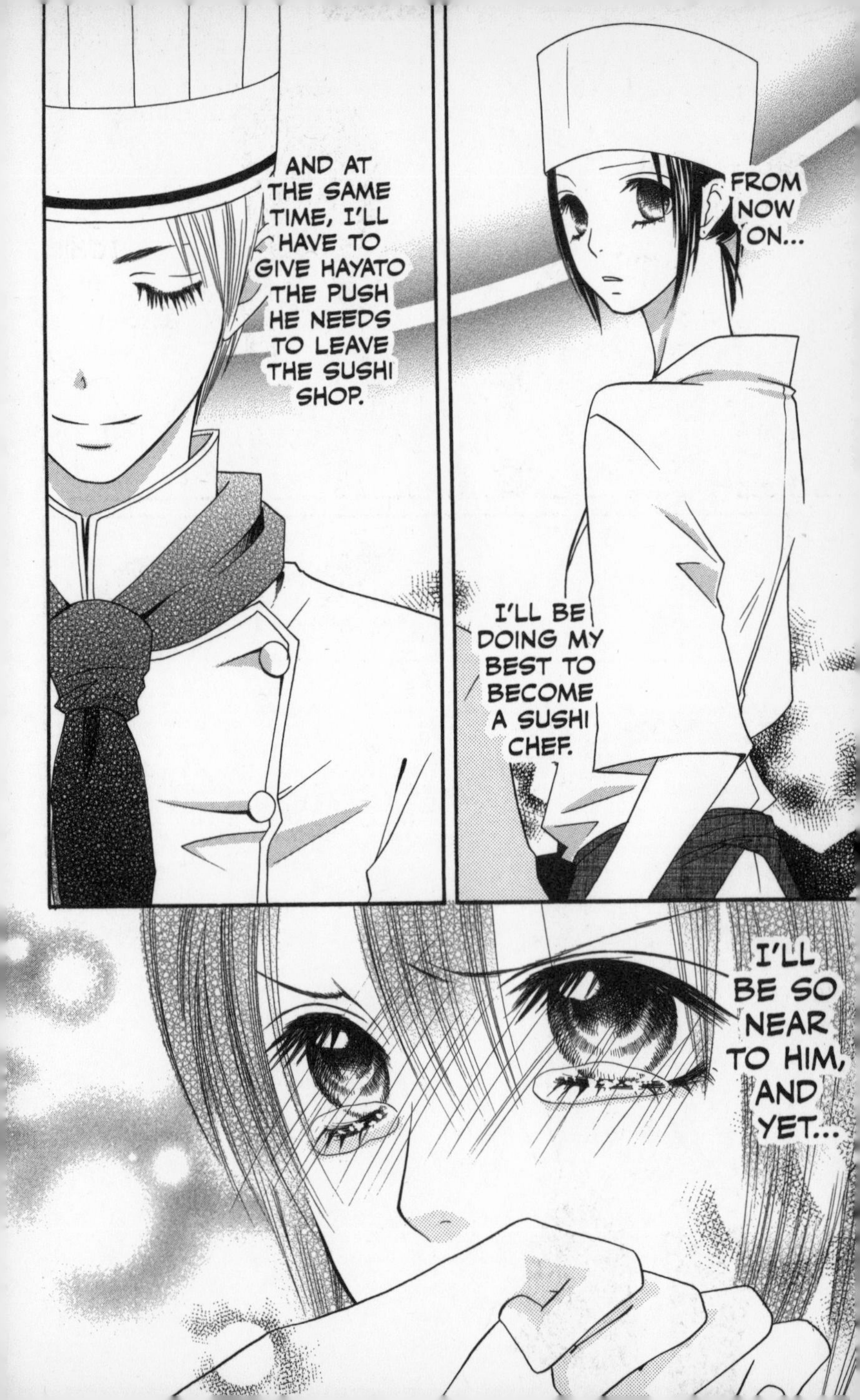
FROM NOW ON...
I'LL BE DOING MY BEST TO BECOME A SUSHI CHEF.
AND AT THE SAME TIME, I'LL HAVE TO GIVE HAYATO THE PUSH HE NEEDS TO LEAVE THE SUSHI SHOP.
I'LL BE SO NEAR TO HIM, AND YET...

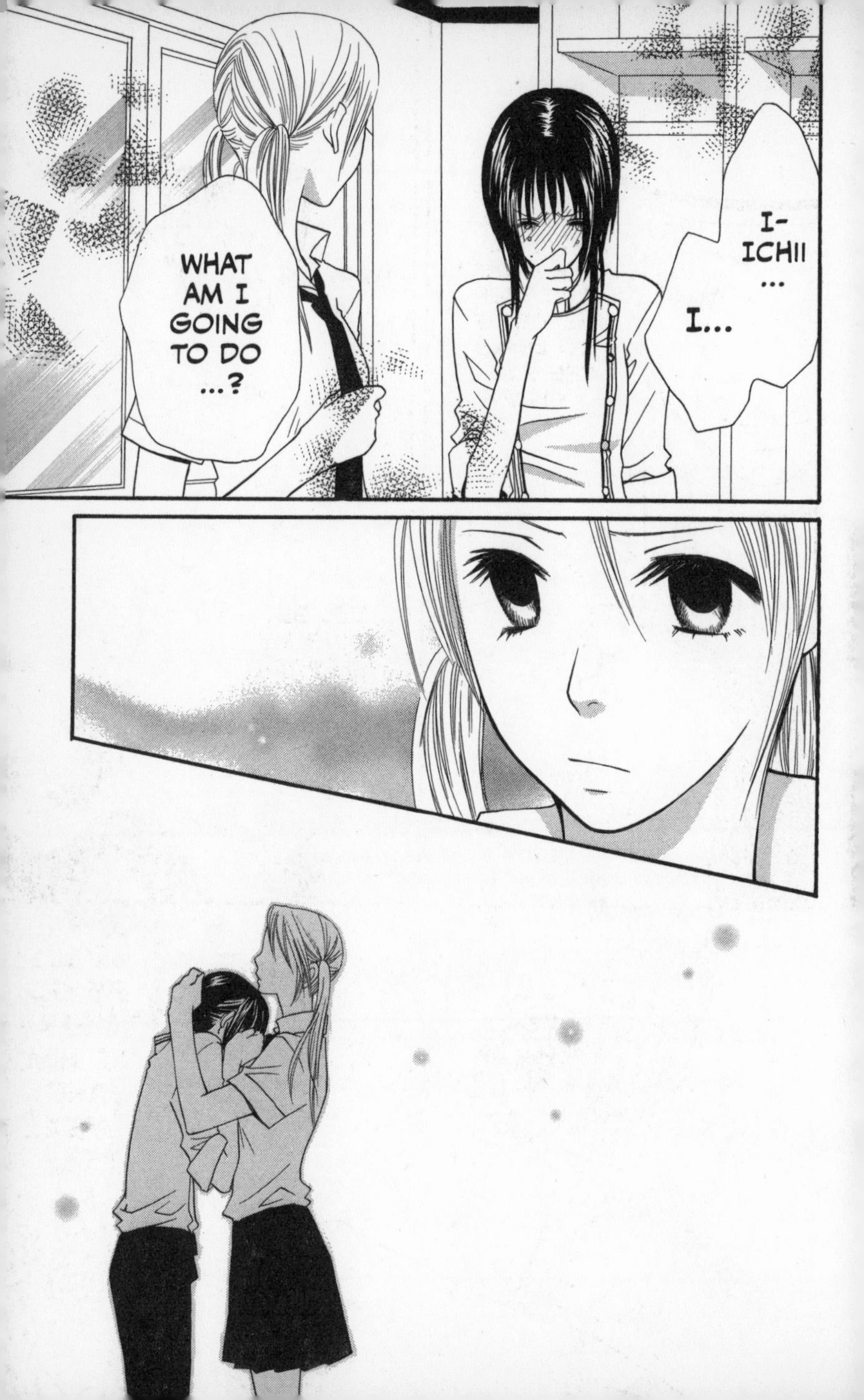
I-ICHII ...
I...
WHAT AM I GOING TO DO ...?

SIDE DISH Mixed Vegetables 6

FROM THE BOTTOM OF MY STOMACH, WITH ALL MY MIGHT,
A HEARTY THANK YOU!

I'M BEHOLDEN TO SO MANY PEOPLE AGAIN.

- MY EDITOR (WE ALWAYS TALK ABOUT BASEBALL)
- THE EDITORIAL STAFF AT *MARGARET* MAGAZINE
- SHUEISHA
- MY FELLOW MANGA ARTISTS
  (THANK YOU FOR LISTENING! YOU'RE ALL SO KIND...)
- EVERYONE WHO WAS SO COOPERATIVE AT THE STORES
  (I'M SO SORRY I COULDN'T GO MORE OFTEN)
- MY FAMILY (THEY NEVER BLAME ME WHEN THEY GAIN WEIGHT!)

AND FIRST AND FOREMOST, *MY READERS!*
YOU ARE SOOO KIND...!

WHEN YOU READ MY MANGA, IT BRINGS MEANING TO MY WORK.

AS LONG AS ONE PERSON READS MY MANGA,
I WILL CONTINUE DRAWING!

I'LL DO MY BEST!

PLEASE CONTINUE TO SUPPORT ME!

I LOVE HEARING YOUR IMPRESSIONS.

TO: AYUMI KOMURA/MIXED VEGETABLES
C/O SHOJO BEAT MANGA
VIZ MEDIA, LLC
P.O. BOX 77010
SAN FRANCISCO, CA 94107

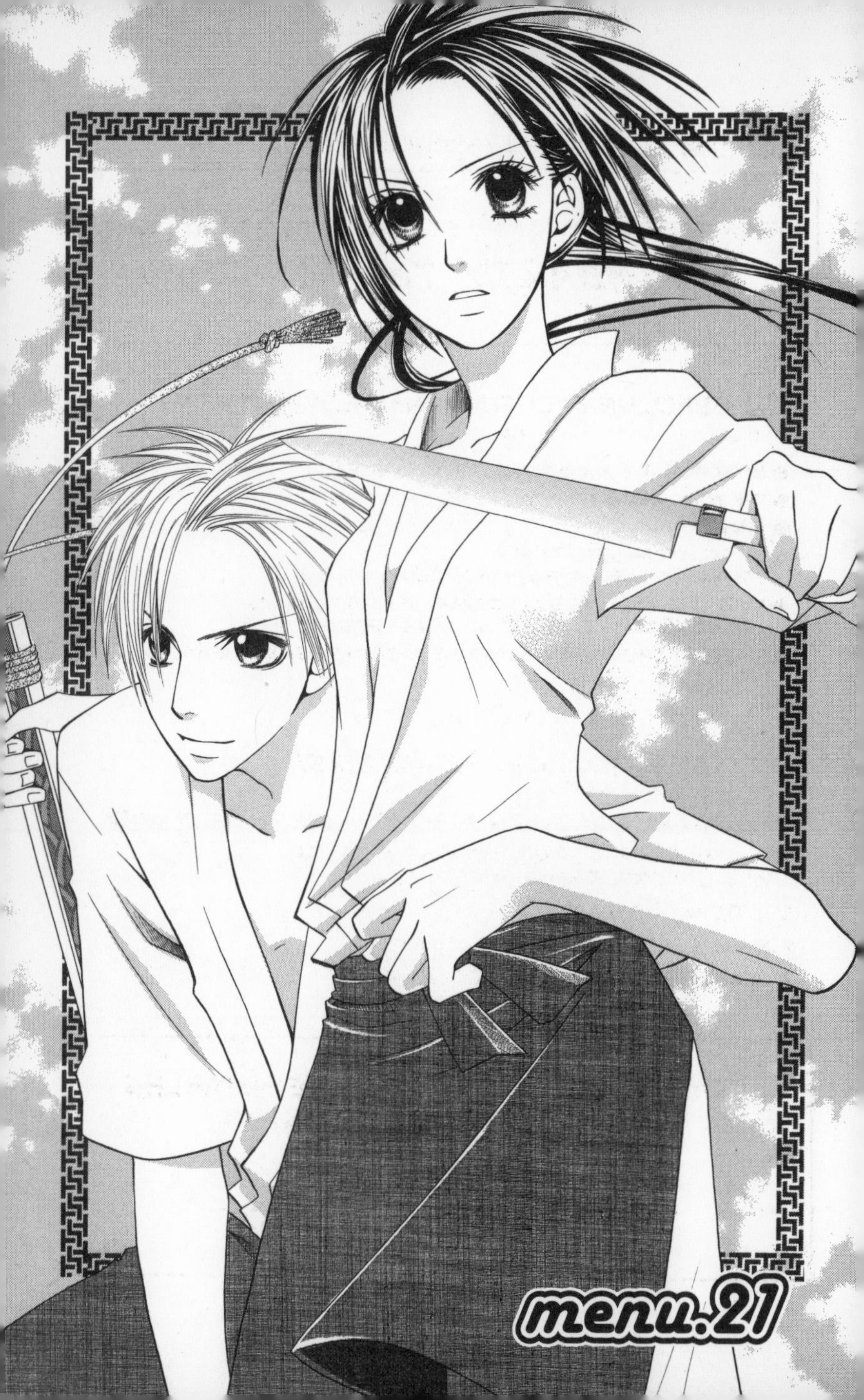
menu.21

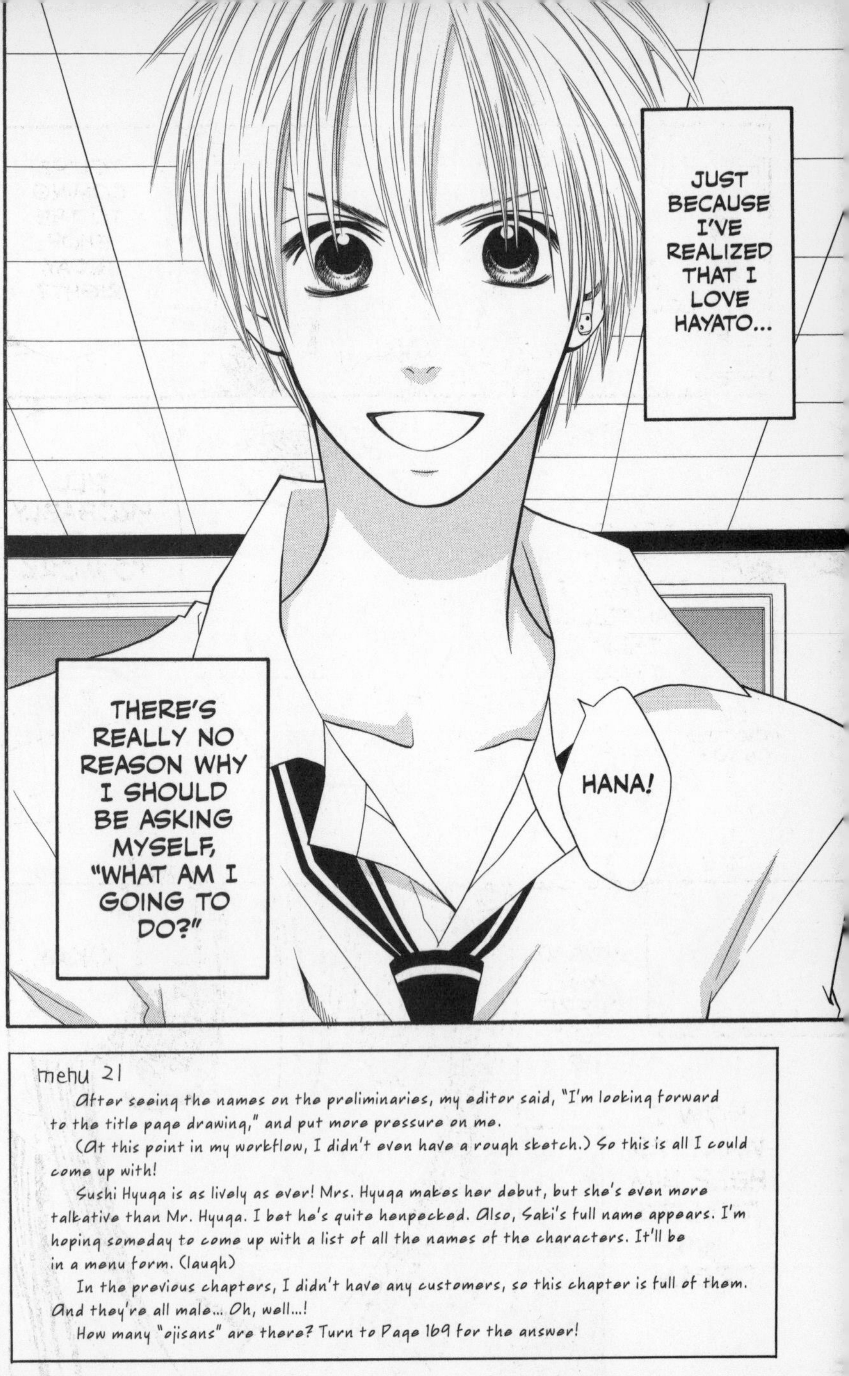
JUST BECAUSE I'VE REALIZED THAT I LOVE HAYATO...
THERE'S REALLY NO REASON WHY I SHOULD BE ASKING MYSELF, "WHAT AM I GOING TO DO?"
HANA!

menu 21

After seeing the names on the preliminaries, my editor said, "I'm looking forward to the title page drawing," and put more pressure on me.

(At this point in my workflow, I didn't even have a rough sketch.) So this is all I could come up with!

Sushi Hyuga is as lively as ever! Mrs. Hyuga makes her debut, but she's even more talkative than Mr. Hyuga. I bet he's quite henpecked. Also, Saki's full name appears. I'm hoping someday to come up with a list of all the names of the characters. It'll be in a menu form. (laugh)

In the previous chapters, I didn't have any customers, so this chapter is full of them. And they're all male... Oh, well...!

How many "ojisans" are there? Turn to Page 169 for the answer!

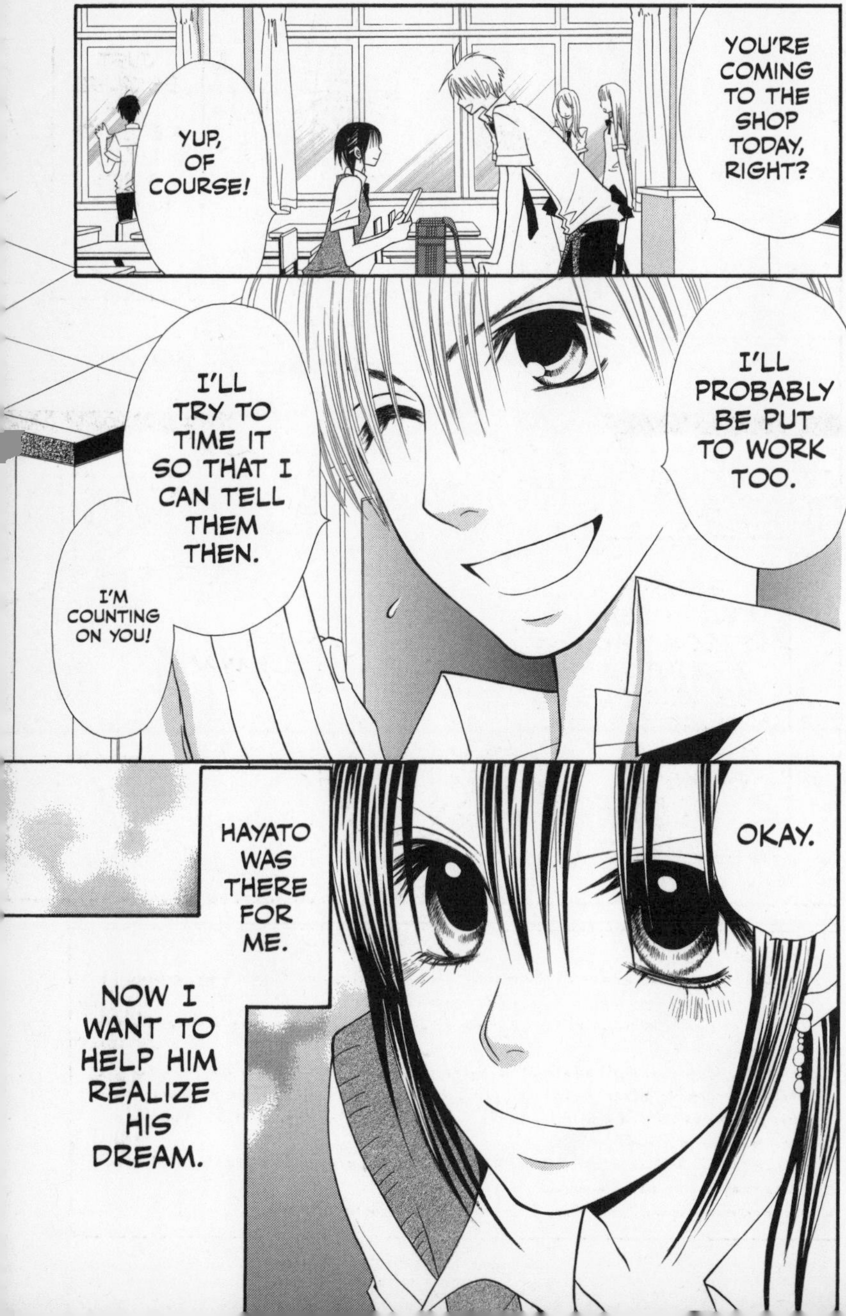
YOU'RE COMING TO THE SHOP TODAY, RIGHT?
YUP, OF COURSE!
I'LL PROBABLY BE PUT TO WORK TOO.
I'LL TRY TO TIME IT SO THAT I CAN TELL THEM THEN.
I'M COUNTING ON YOU!
OKAY.
HAYATO WAS THERE FOR ME.
NOW I WANT TO HELP HIM REALIZE HIS DREAM.

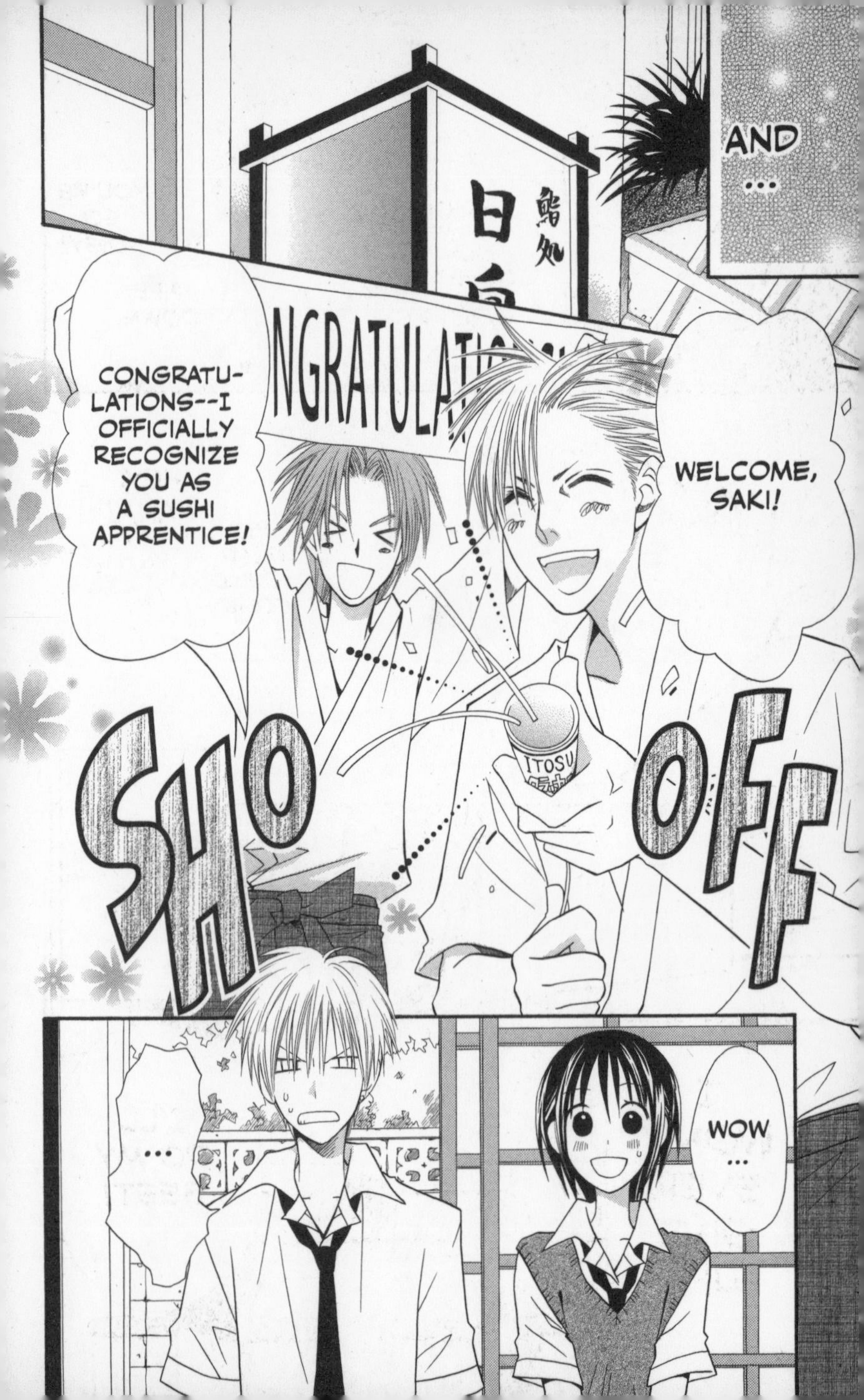
AND ...
WELCOME, SAKI!
CONGRATU-LATIONS--I OFFICIALLY RECOGNIZE YOU AS A SUSHI APPRENTICE!
ITOSU
SHO OFF
WOW ...
...

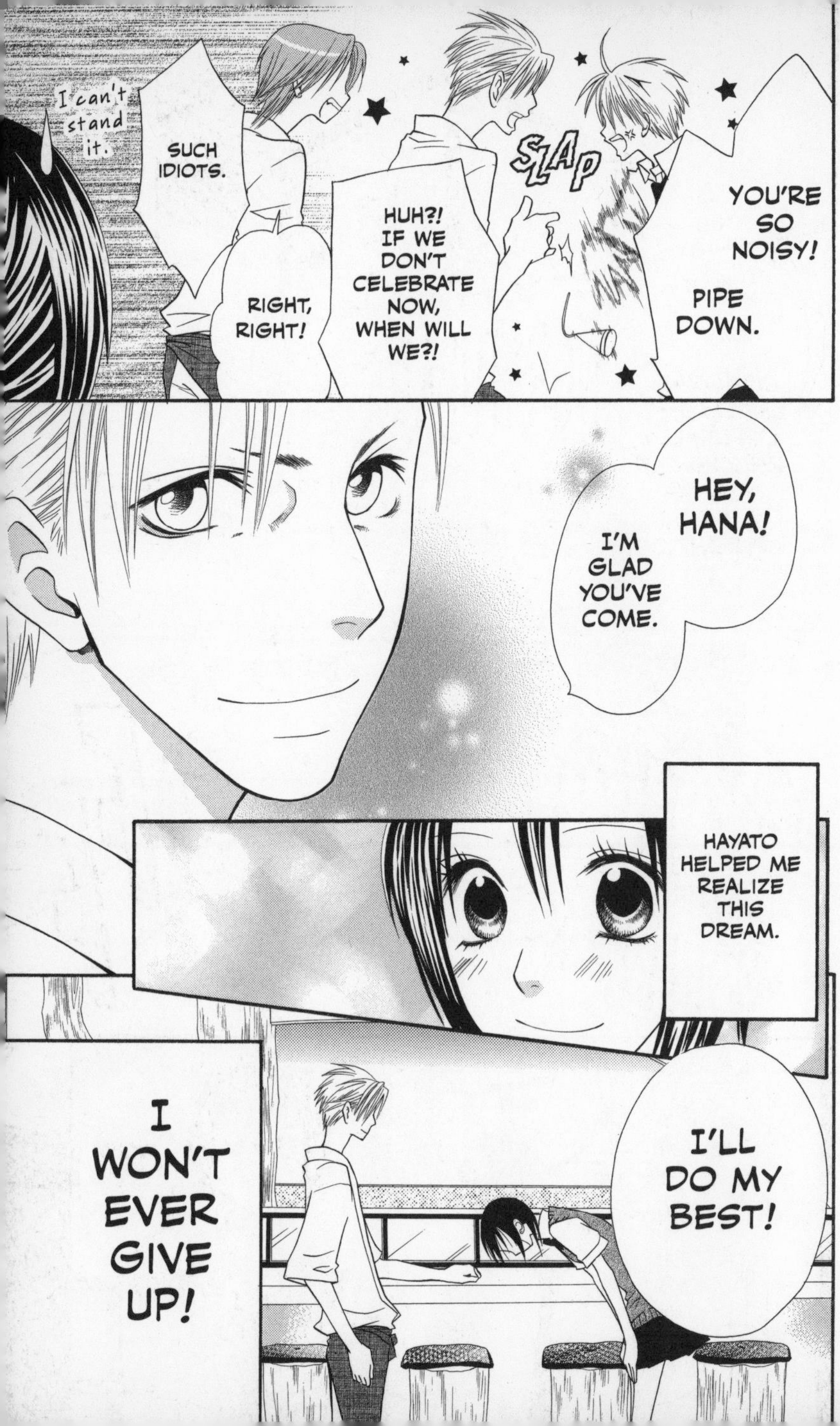
YOU'RE SO NOISY!
PIPE DOWN.
SLAP
HUH?! IF WE DON'T CELEBRATE NOW, WHEN WILL WE?!
RIGHT, RIGHT!
SUCH IDIOTS.
I can't stand it.
HEY, HANA!
I'M GLAD YOU'VE COME.
HAYATO HELPED ME REALIZE THIS DREAM.
I'LL DO MY BEST!
I WON'T EVER GIVE UP!

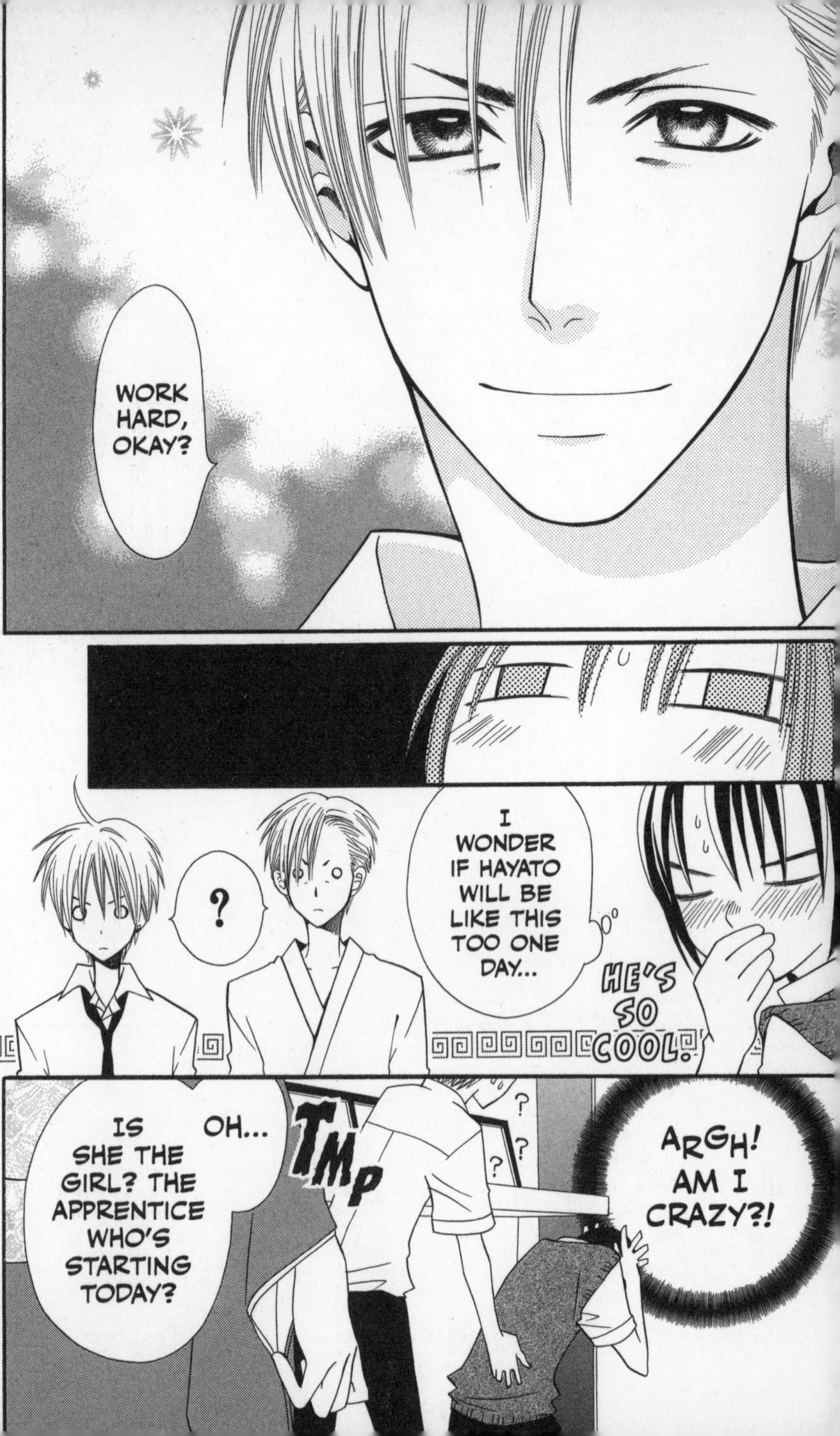
WORK HARD, OKAY?
HE'S SO COOL!
I WONDER IF HAYATO WILL BE LIKE THIS TOO ONE DAY...
?
ARGH! AM I CRAZY?!
?
?
?
TMP
OH...
IS SHE THE GIRL? THE APPRENTICE WHO'S STARTING TODAY?

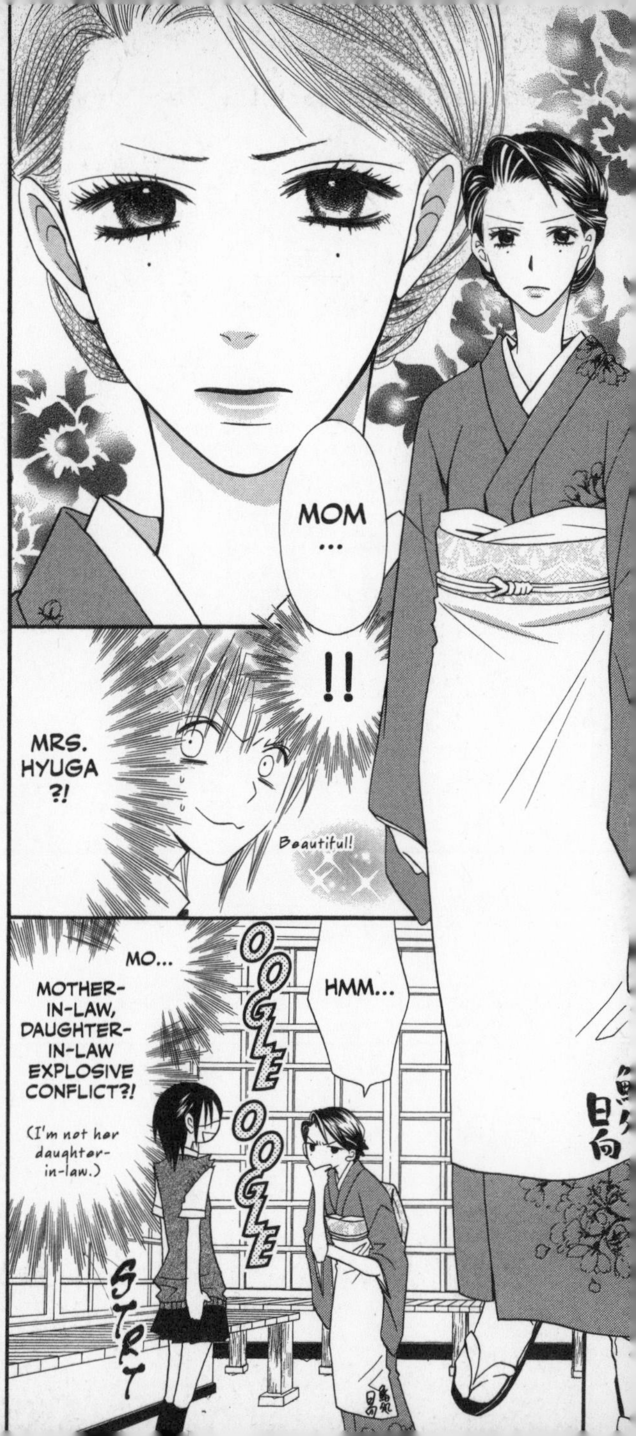

日向
MOM ...
!!
MRS. HYUGA ?!
Beautiful!
HMM...
OOGLE OOGLE
MO...
MOTHER-IN-LAW, DAUGHTER-IN-LAW EXPLOSIVE CONFLICT?!
(I'm not her daughter-in-law.)
STRT

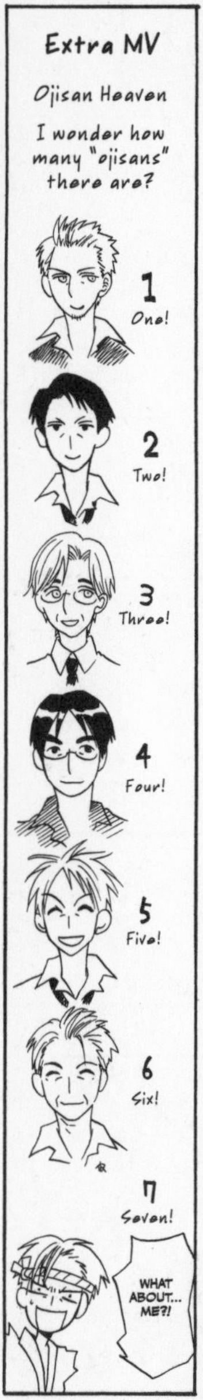

Extra MV
Ojisan Heaven
I wonder how many "ojisans" there are?
1
One!
2
Two!
3
Three!
4
Four!
5
Five!
6
Six!
7
Seven!
WHAT ABOUT... ME?!

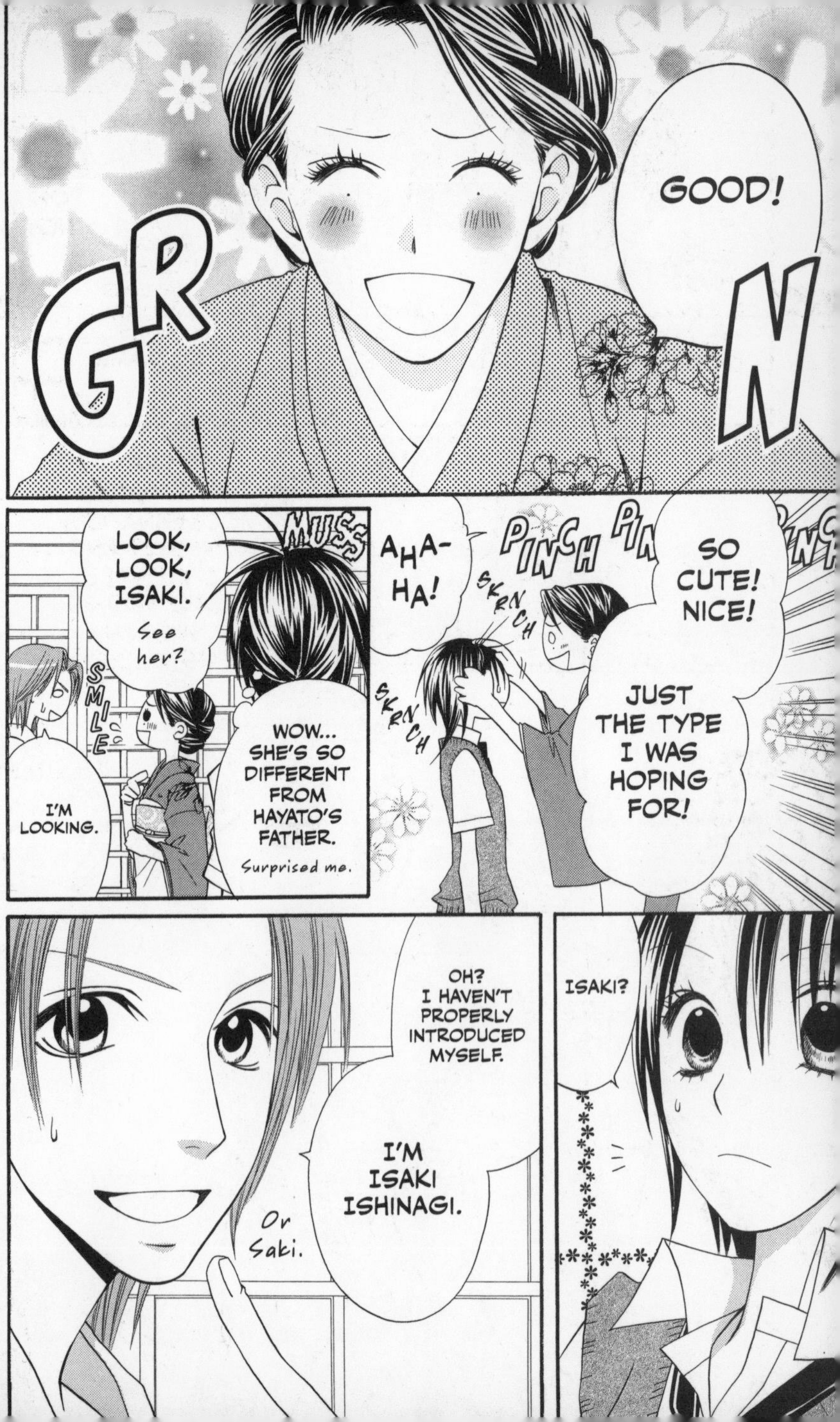
GOOD!
GR
N
PINCH
SO CUTE! NICE!
JUST THE TYPE I WAS HOPING FOR!
SKRNCH
SKRNCH
AHA-HA!
MUSS
LOOK, LOOK, ISAKI.
See her?
WOW... SHE'S SO DIFFERENT FROM HAYATO'S FATHER.
Surprised me.
SMILE
I'M LOOKING.
ISAKI?
OH? I HAVEN'T PROPERLY INTRODUCED MYSELF.
I'M ISAKI ISHINAGI.
Or Saki.

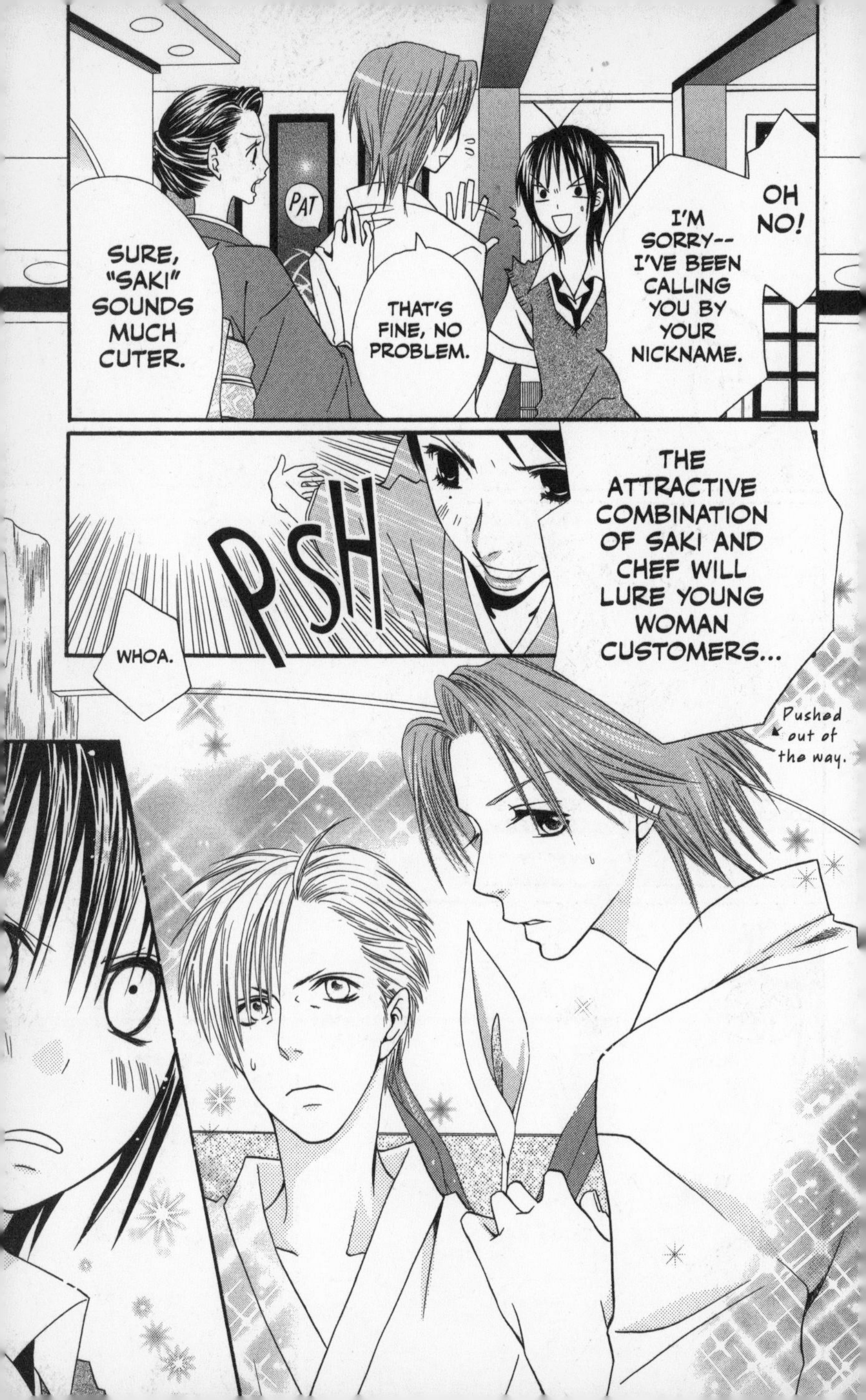
OH NO!
I'M SORRY-- I'VE BEEN CALLING YOU BY YOUR NICKNAME.
PAT
THAT'S FINE, NO PROBLEM.
SURE, "SAKI" SOUNDS MUCH CUTER.
THE ATTRACTIVE COMBINATION OF SAKI AND CHEF WILL LURE YOUNG WOMAN CUSTOMERS...
PSH
WHOA.
Pushed out of the way.

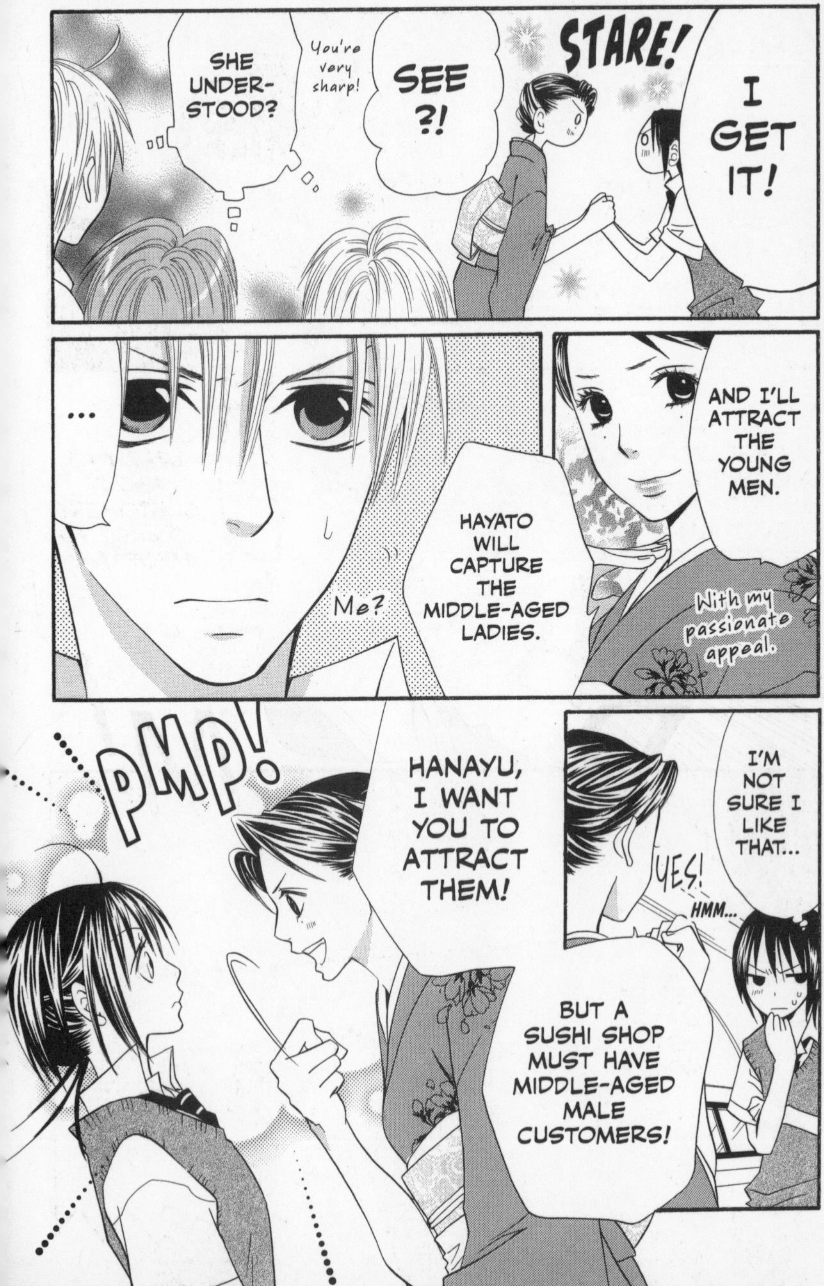
I GET IT!
STARE!
SEE ?!
You're very sharp!
SHE UNDER-STOOD?
AND I'LL ATTRACT THE YOUNG MEN.
With my passionate appeal.
HAYATO WILL CAPTURE THE MIDDLE-AGED LADIES.
Me?
...
I'M NOT SURE I LIKE THAT...
YES!
HMM...
BUT A SUSHI SHOP MUST HAVE MIDDLE-AGED MALE CUSTOMERS!
HANAYU, I WANT YOU TO ATTRACT THEM!
PMP!

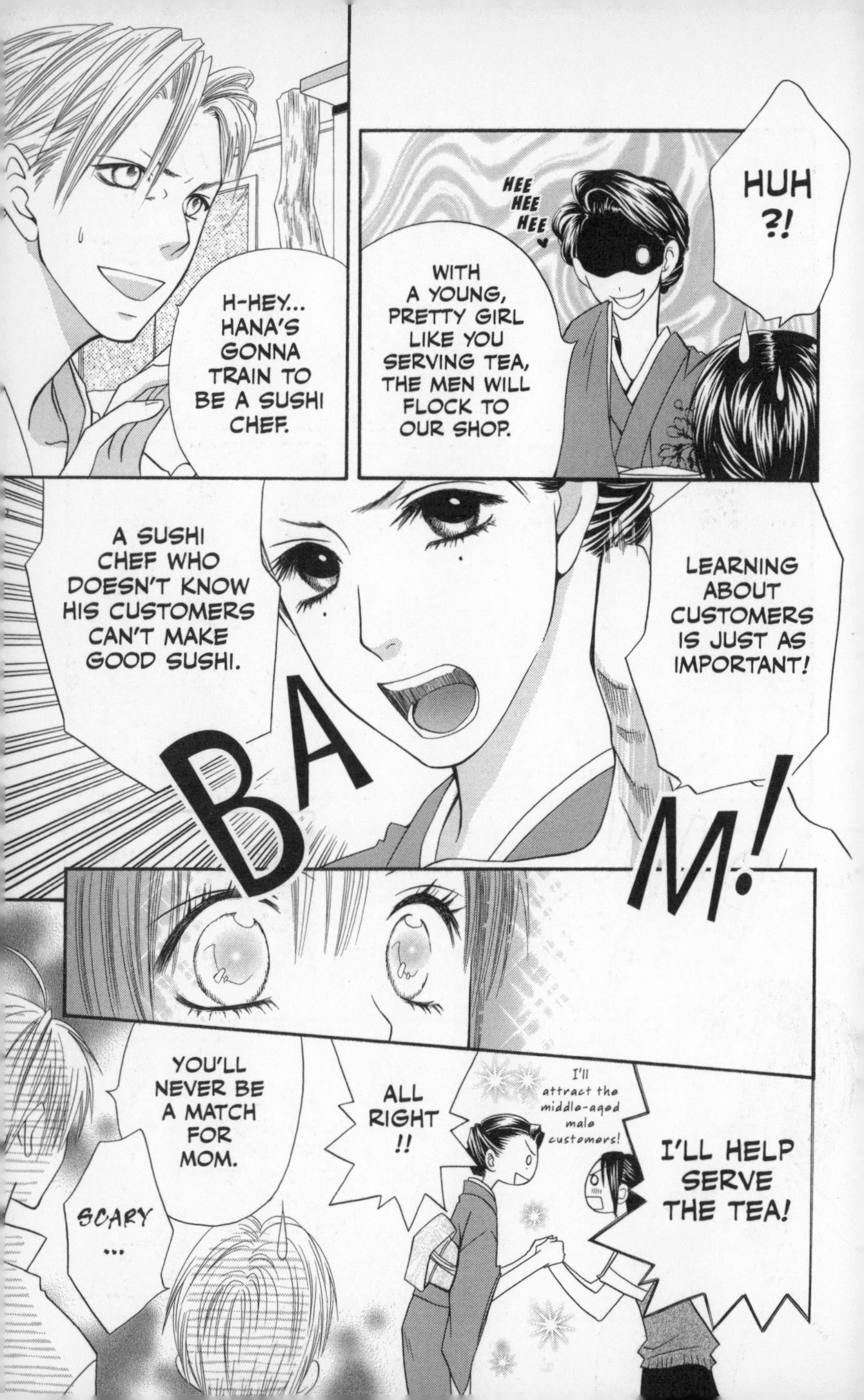
HUH ?!
HEE HEE HEE
WITH A YOUNG, PRETTY GIRL LIKE YOU SERVING TEA, THE MEN WILL FLOCK TO OUR SHOP.
H-HEY... HANA'S GONNA TRAIN TO BE A SUSHI CHEF.
LEARNING ABOUT CUSTOMERS IS JUST AS IMPORTANT!
A SUSHI CHEF WHO DOESN'T KNOW HIS CUSTOMERS CAN'T MAKE GOOD SUSHI.
BAM!
I'LL HELP SERVE THE TEA!
I'll attract the middle-aged male customers!
ALL RIGHT !!
YOU'LL NEVER BE A MATCH FOR MOM.
SCARY ...

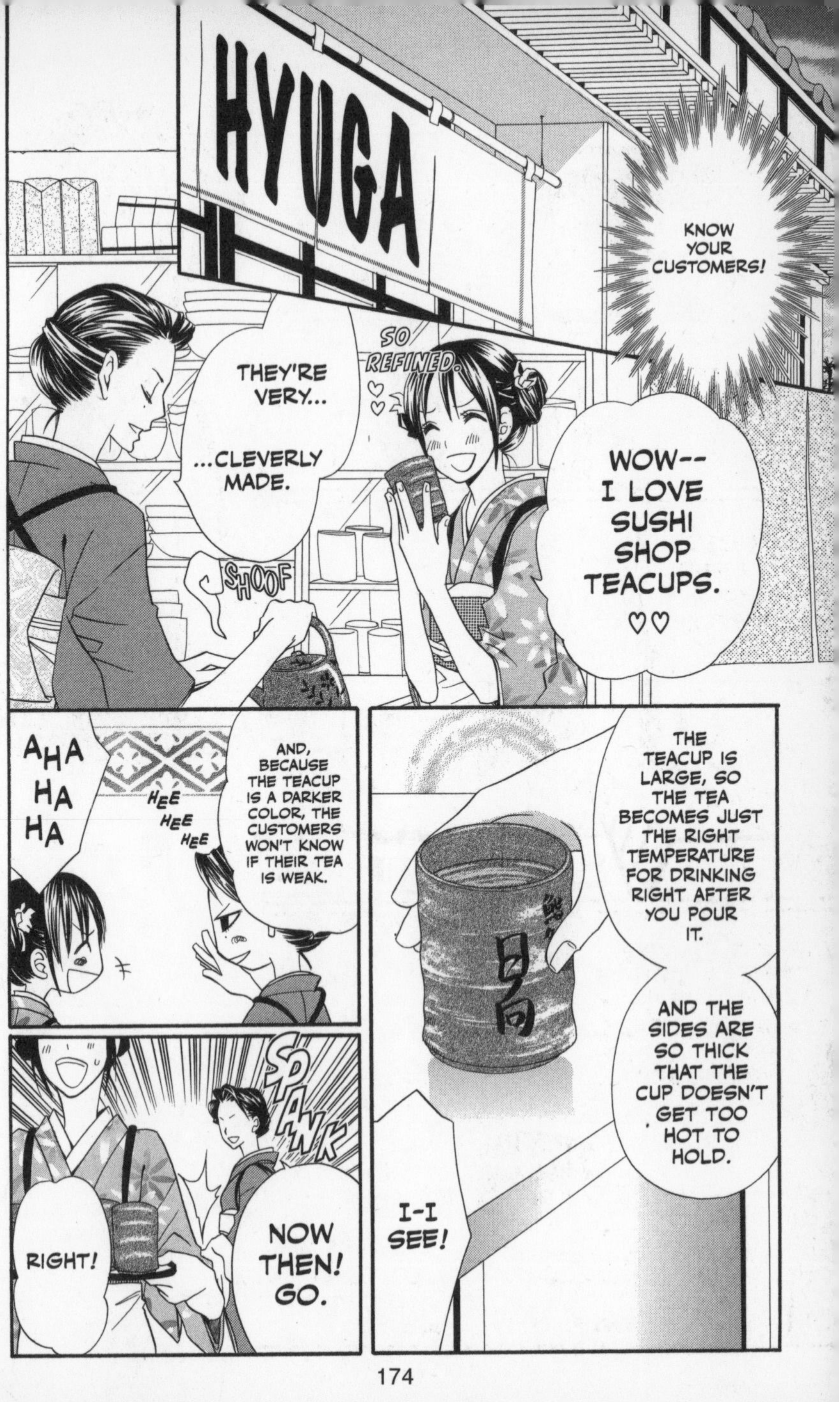
HYUGA
KNOW YOUR CUSTOMERS!
WOW-- I LOVE SUSHI SHOP TEACUPS. ♡♡
SO REFINED. ♡♡
THEY'RE VERY...
...CLEVERLY MADE.
SHOOF
THE TEACUP IS LARGE, SO THE TEA BECOMES JUST THE RIGHT TEMPERATURE FOR DRINKING RIGHT AFTER YOU POUR IT.
AND THE SIDES ARE SO THICK THAT THE CUP DOESN'T GET TOO HOT TO HOLD.
I-I SEE!
AND, BECAUSE THE TEACUP IS A DARKER COLOR, THE CUSTOMERS WON'T KNOW IF THEIR TEA IS WEAK.
HEE HEE HEE
AHA HA HA
SPANK
NOW THEN! GO.
RIGHT!

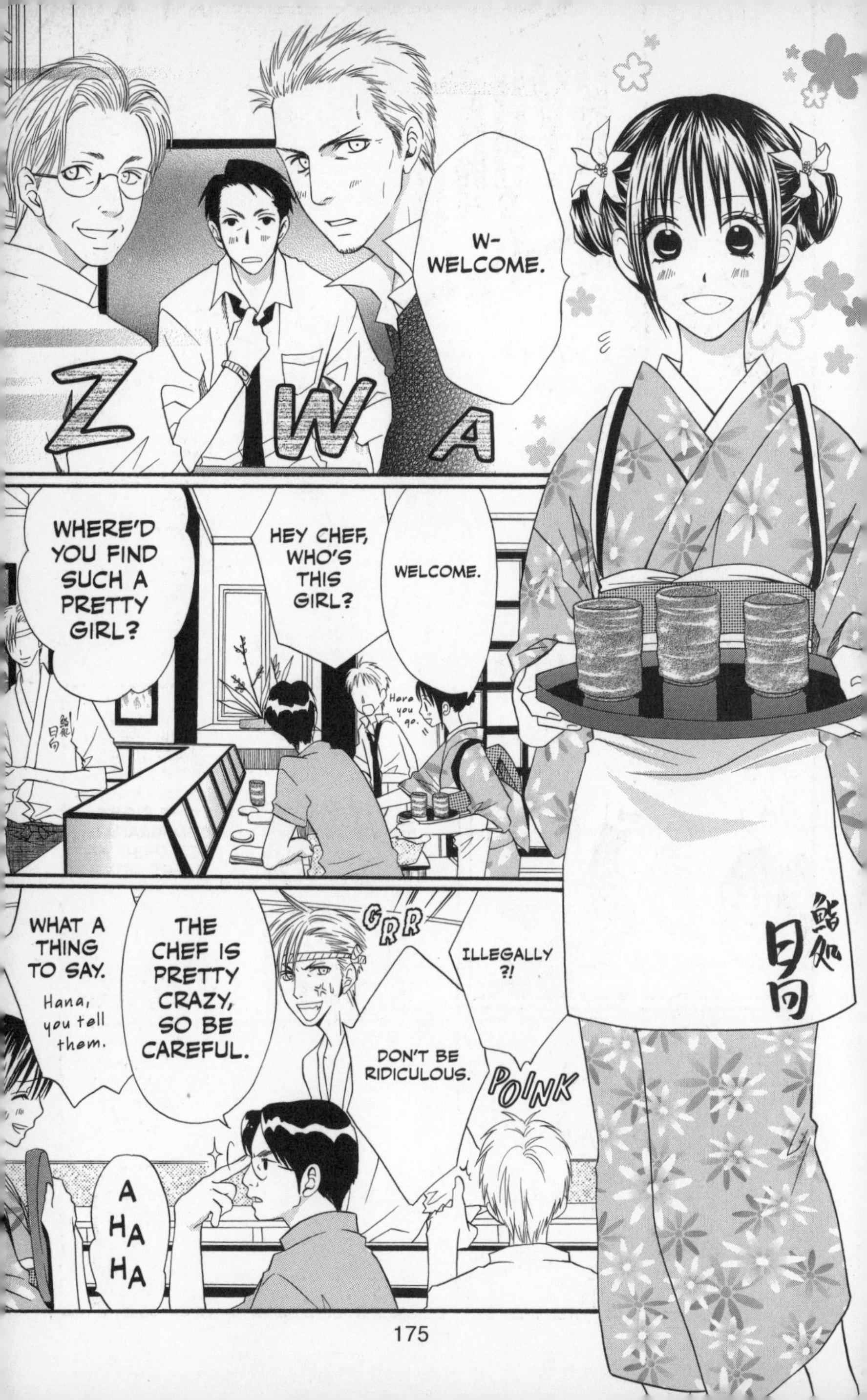
鮨処 日向
W- WELCOME.
ZWA
WELCOME.
HEY CHEF, WHO'S THIS GIRL?
WHERE'D YOU FIND SUCH A PRETTY GIRL?
Here you go.
ILLEGALLY ?!
GRR
THE CHEF IS PRETTY CRAZY, SO BE CAREFUL.
WHAT A THING TO SAY.
Hana, you tell them.
DON'T BE RIDICULOUS.
POINK
A HA HA HA

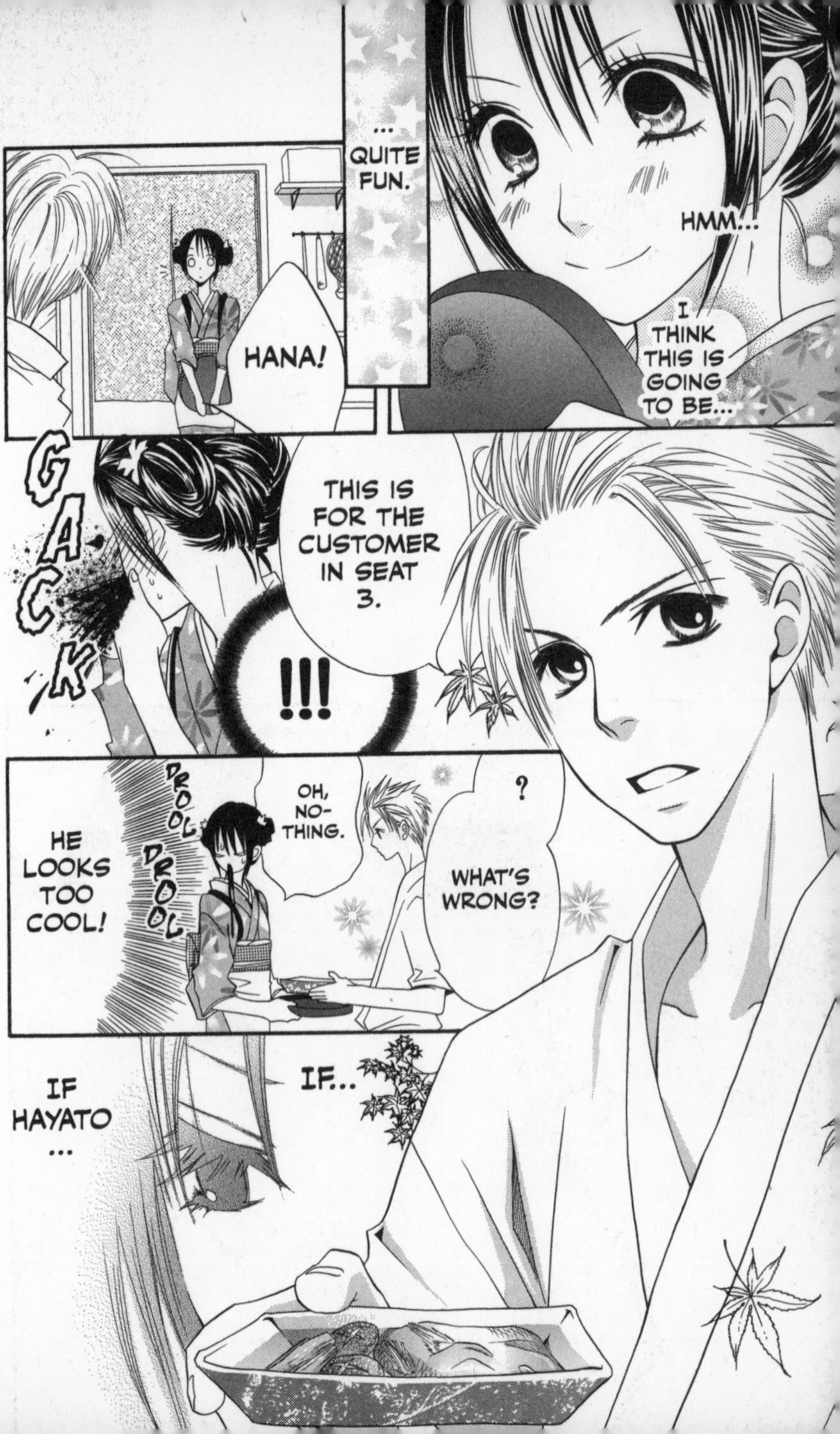
HMM...
I THINK THIS IS GOING TO BE...
... QUITE FUN.
HANA!
THIS IS FOR THE CUSTOMER IN SEAT 3.
GACK
!!!
?
WHAT'S WRONG?
OH, NO-THING.
DROOL DROOL DROOL
HE LOOKS TOO COOL!
IF...
IF HAYATO ...

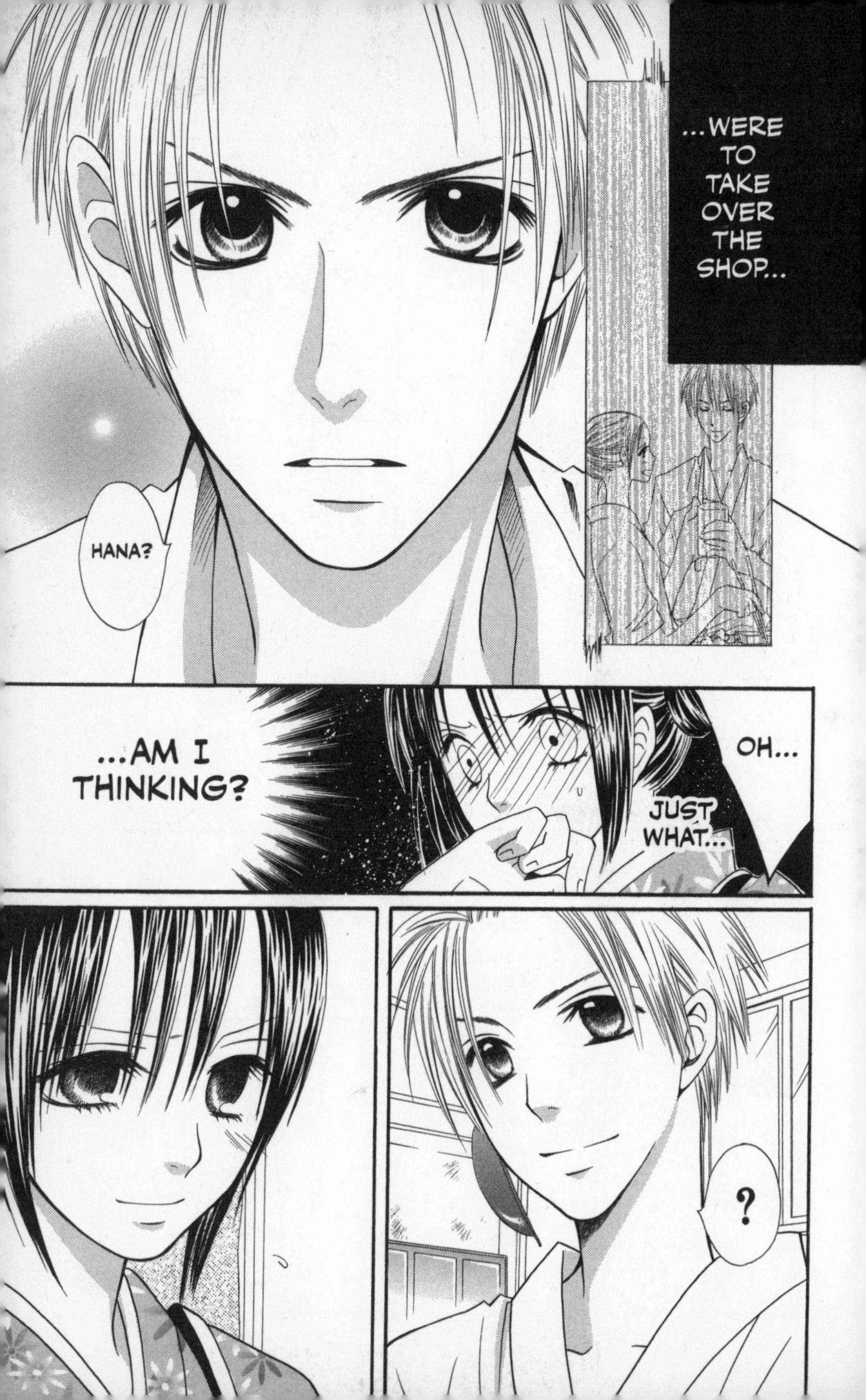
...WERE TO TAKE OVER THE SHOP...
HANA?
OH...
JUST WHAT...
...AM I THINKING?
?

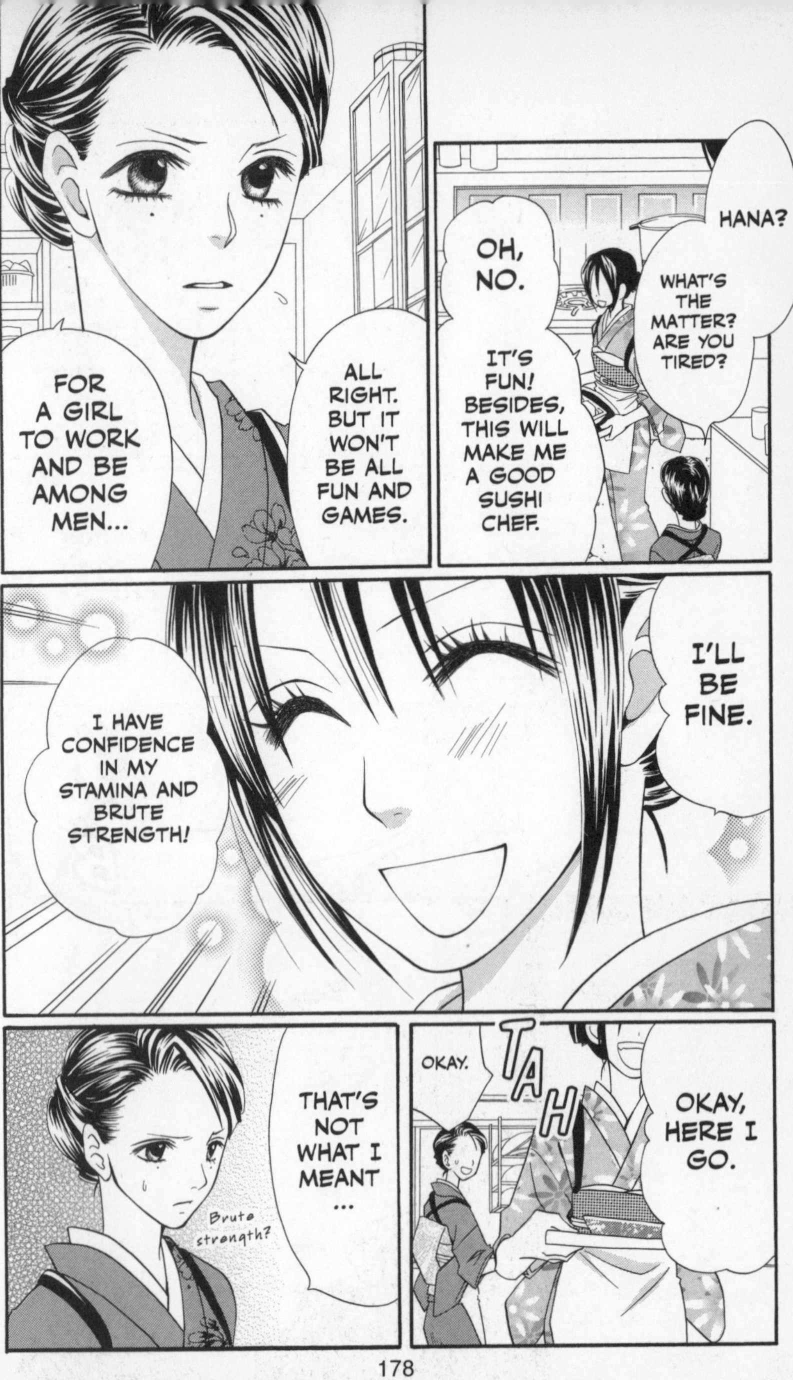
HANA?
WHAT'S THE MATTER? ARE YOU TIRED?
OH, NO.
IT'S FUN! BESIDES, THIS WILL MAKE ME A GOOD SUSHI CHEF.
ALL RIGHT. BUT IT WON'T BE ALL FUN AND GAMES.
FOR A GIRL TO WORK AND BE AMONG MEN...
I'LL BE FINE.
I HAVE CONFIDENCE IN MY STAMINA AND BRUTE STRENGTH!
OKAY, HERE I GO.
TAH
OKAY.
THAT'S NOT WHAT I MEANT ...
Brute strength?

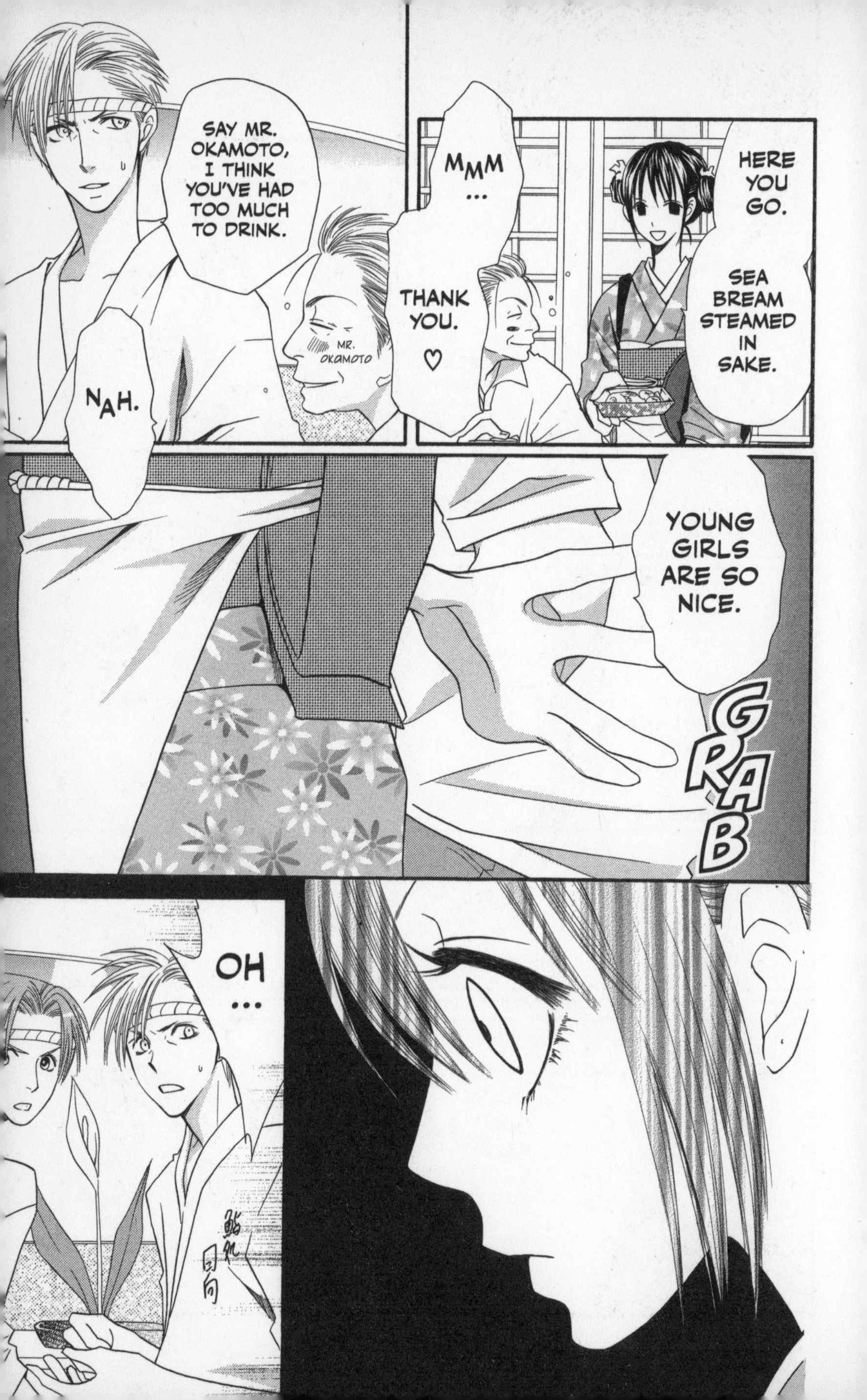
HERE YOU GO.
SEA BREAM STEAMED IN SAKE.
MMM ...
THANK YOU. ♡
SAY MR. OKAMOTO, I THINK YOU'VE HAD TOO MUCH TO DRINK.
MR. OKAMOTO
NAH.
YOUNG GIRLS ARE SO NICE.
GRAB
OH ...

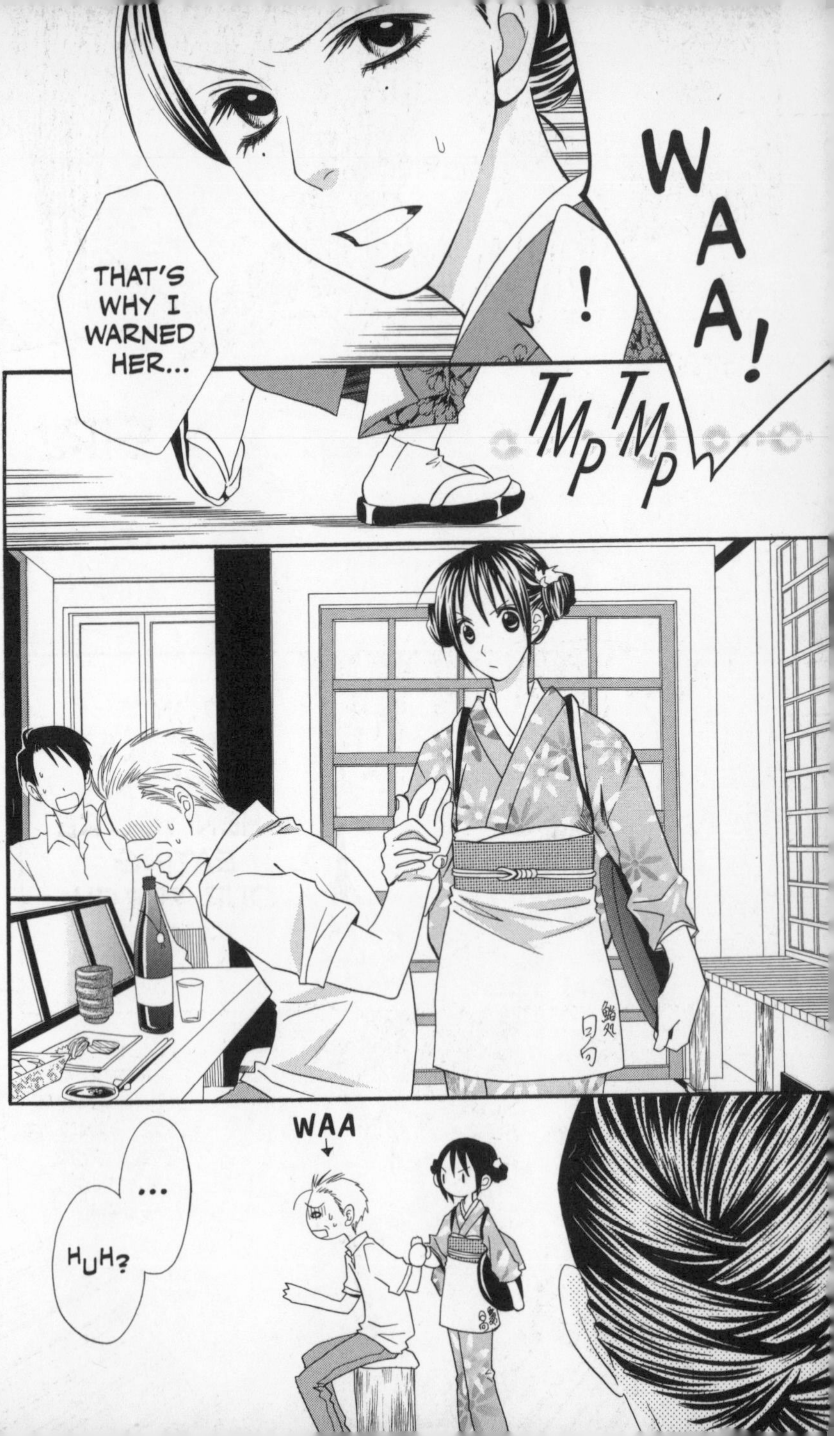
WAA!
!
THAT'S WHY I WARNED HER...
TMP TMP
WAA
...
HUH?

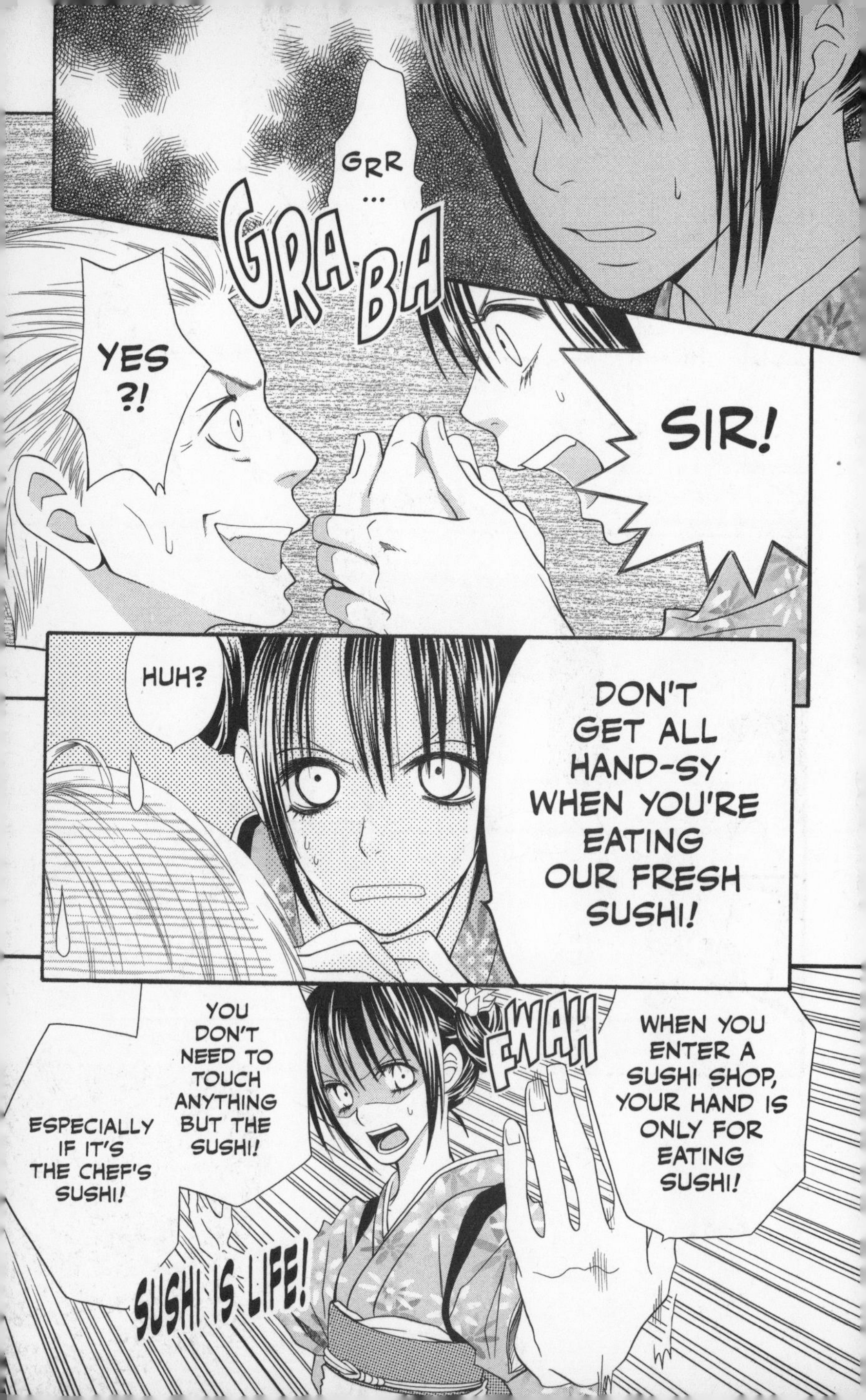
GRR ...
GRABA
SIR!
YES ?!
DON'T GET ALL HAND-SY WHEN YOU'RE EATING OUR FRESH SUSHI!
HUH?
WHEN YOU ENTER A SUSHI SHOP, YOUR HAND IS ONLY FOR EATING SUSHI!
FWAH
YOU DON'T NEED TO TOUCH ANYTHING BUT THE SUSHI!
ESPECIALLY IF IT'S THE CHEF'S SUSHI!
SUSHI IS LIFE!

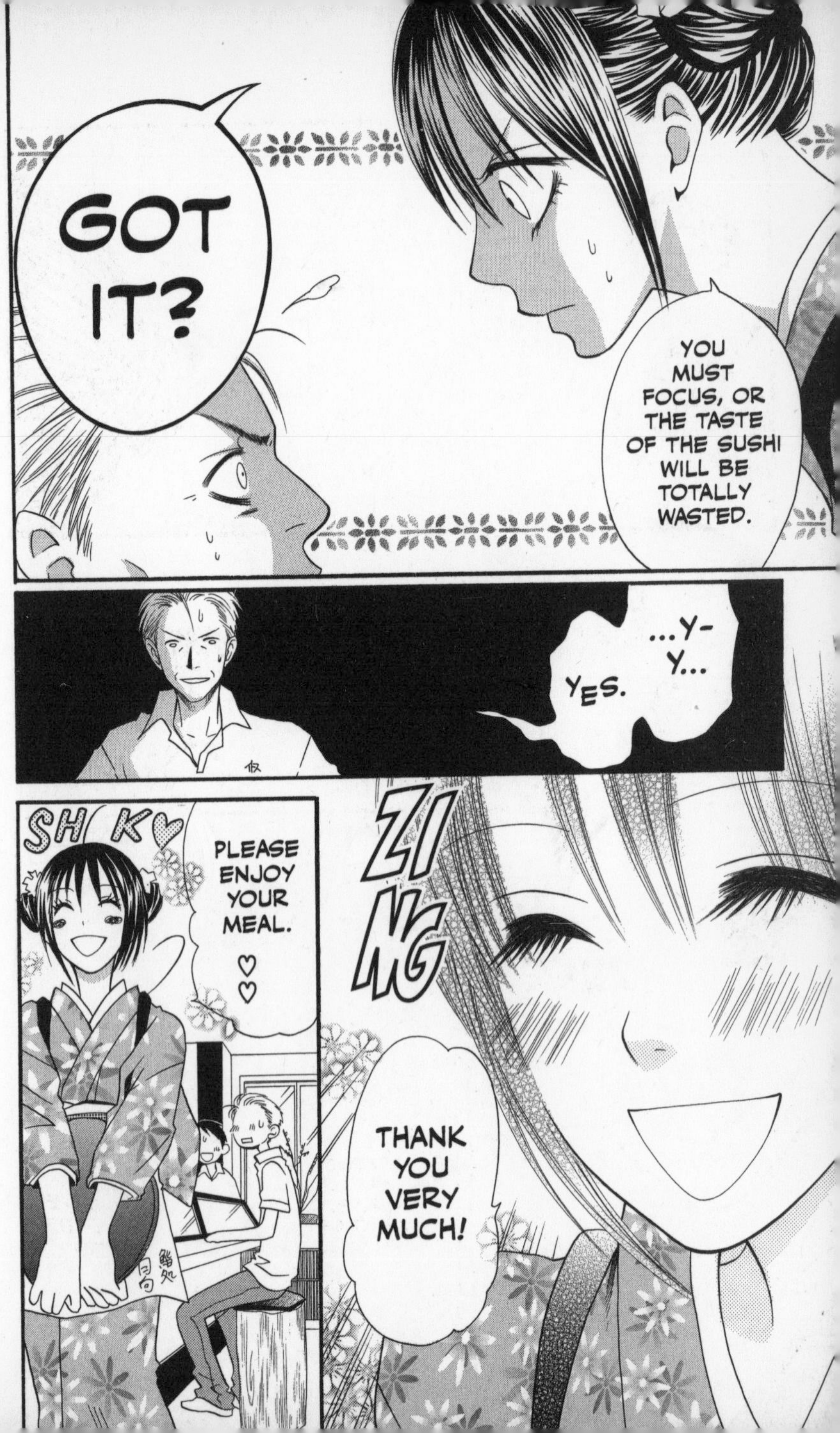
YOU MUST FOCUS, OR THE TASTE OF THE SUSHI WILL BE TOTALLY WASTED.
GOT IT?
...Y- Y... YES.
ZING
THANK YOU VERY MUCH!
SH K♥
PLEASE ENJOY YOUR MEAL. ♡ ♡

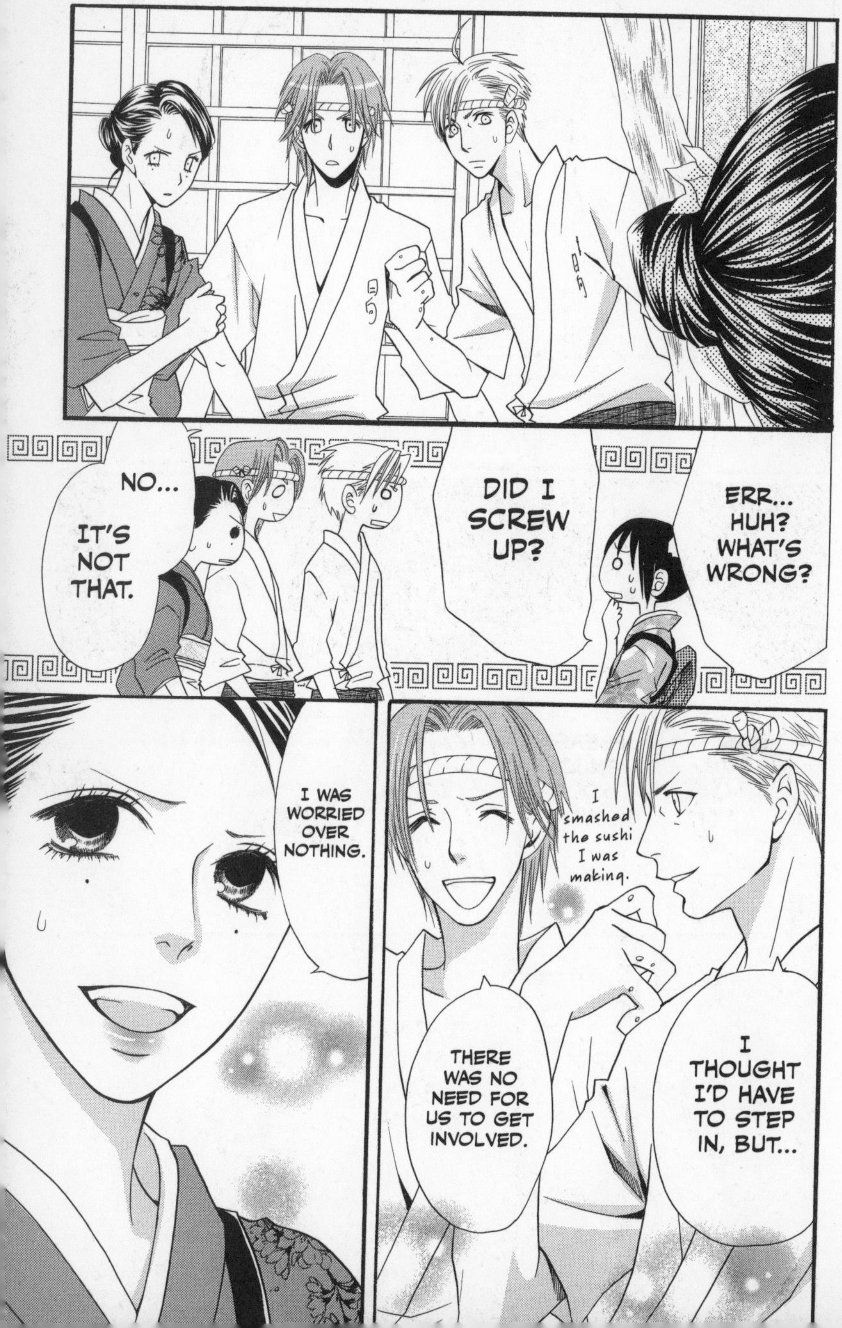
ERR... HUH? WHAT'S WRONG?
DID I SCREW UP?
NO... IT'S NOT THAT.
I THOUGHT I'D HAVE TO STEP IN, BUT...
THERE WAS NO NEED FOR US TO GET INVOLVED.
I smashed the sushi I was making.
I WAS WORRIED OVER NOTHING.

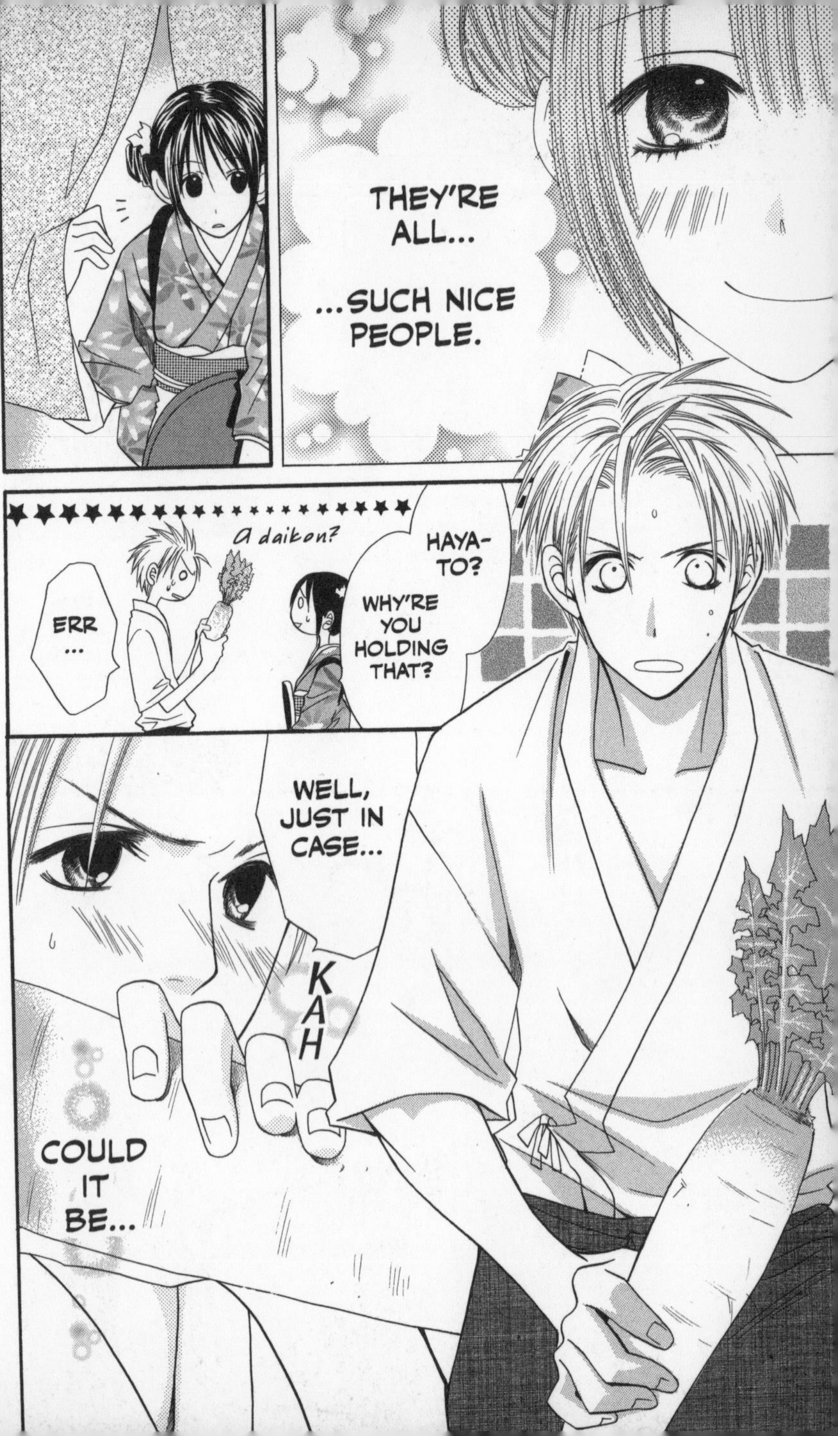
THEY'RE ALL...
...SUCH NICE PEOPLE.
HAYA-TO?
WHY'RE YOU HOLDING THAT?
A daikon?
ERR ...
WELL, JUST IN CASE...
KAH
COULD IT BE...

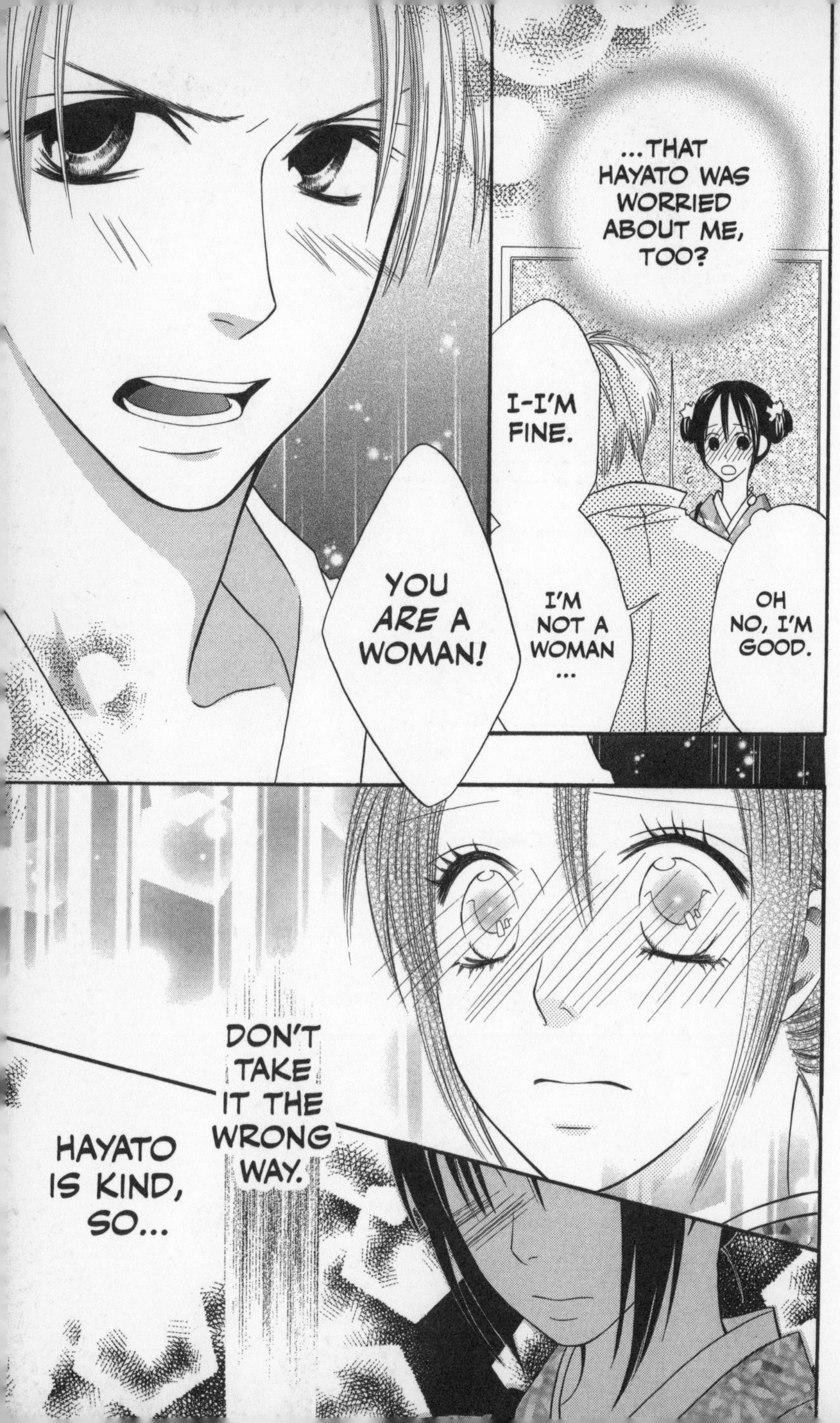
...THAT HAYATO WAS WORRIED ABOUT ME, TOO?
I-I'M FINE.
OH NO, I'M GOOD.
I'M NOT A WOMAN ...
YOU *ARE* A WOMAN!
DON'T TAKE IT THE WRONG WAY.
HAYATO IS KIND, SO...

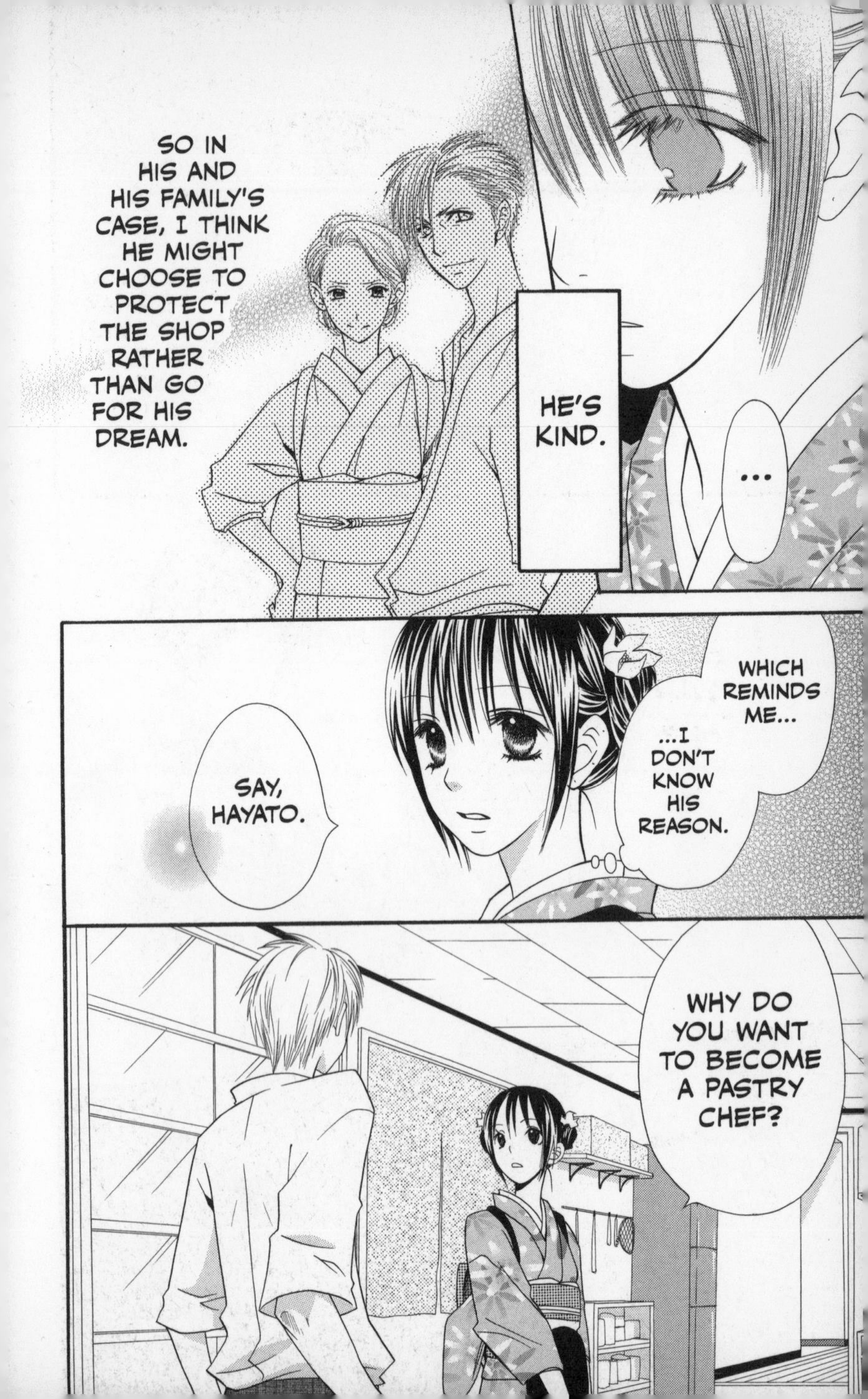
...
HE'S KIND.
SO IN HIS AND HIS FAMILY'S CASE, I THINK HE MIGHT CHOOSE TO PROTECT THE SHOP RATHER THAN GO FOR HIS DREAM.
WHICH REMINDS ME...
...I DON'T KNOW HIS REASON.
SAY, HAYATO.
WHY DO YOU WANT TO BECOME A PASTRY CHEF?

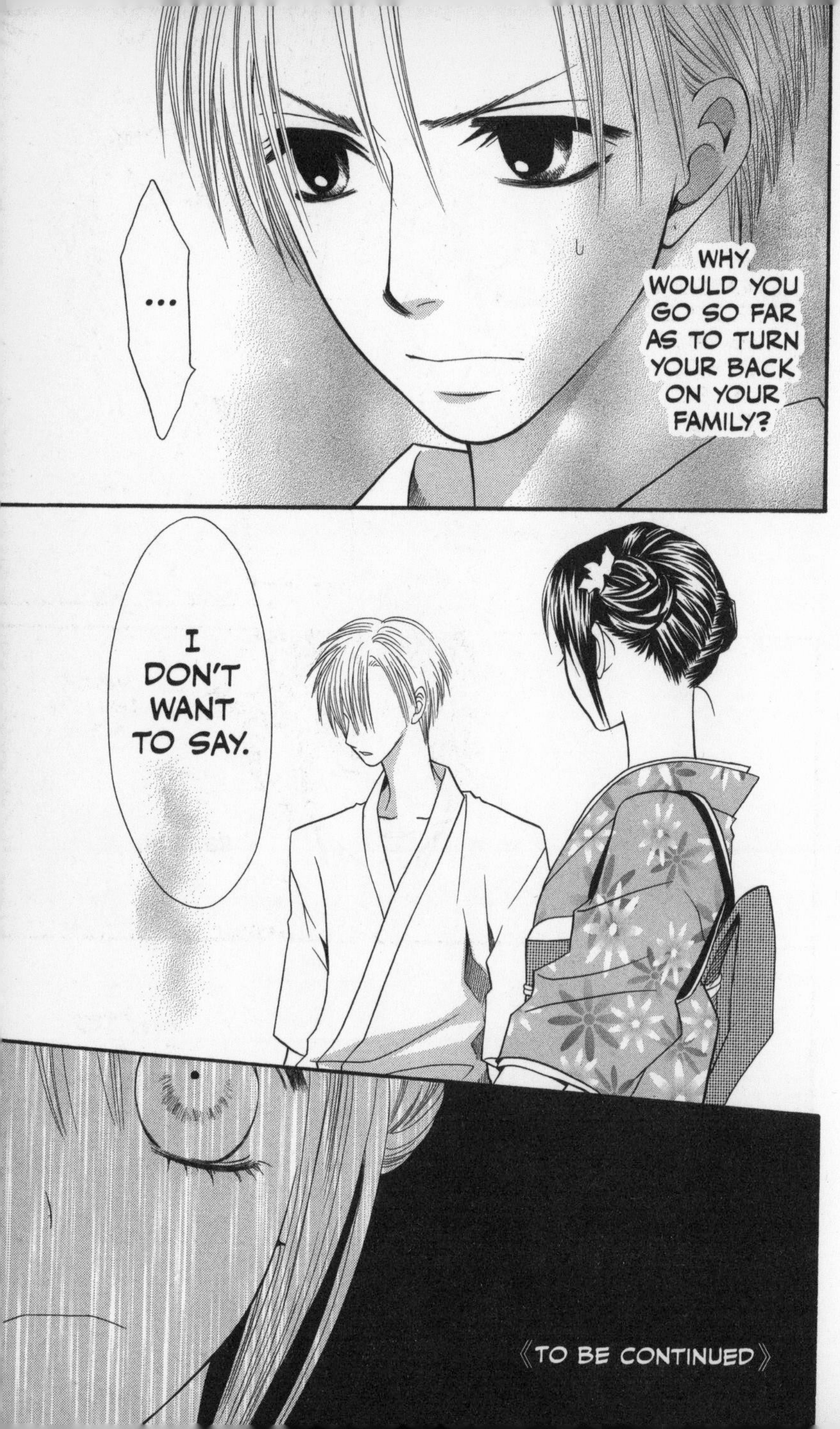
WHY WOULD YOU GO SO FAR AS TO TURN YOUR BACK ON YOUR FAMILY?
...
I DON'T WANT TO SAY.
《TO BE CONTINUED》

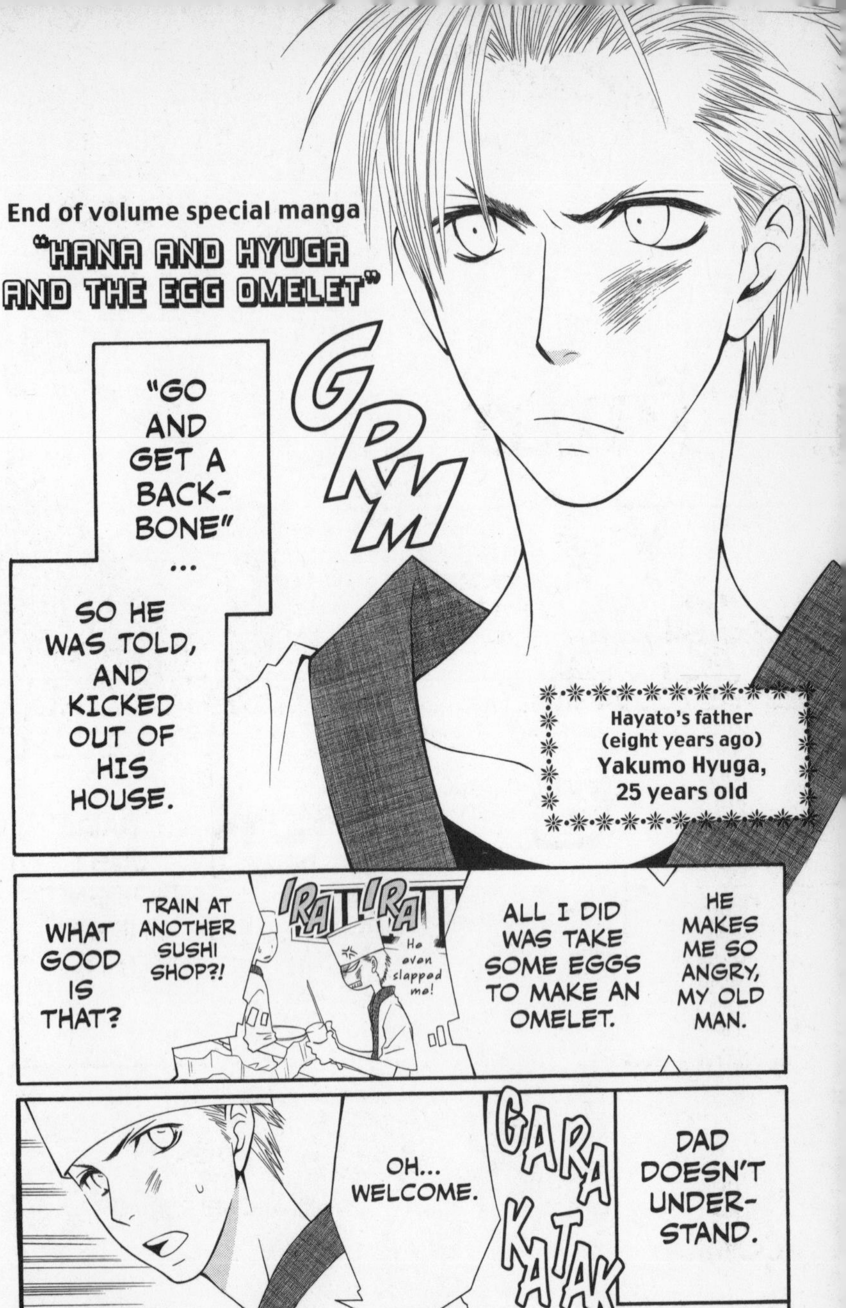
End of volume special manga
"HANA AND HYUGA AND THE EGG OMELET"
GRM
"GO AND GET A BACKBONE"... SO HE WAS TOLD, AND KICKED OUT OF HIS HOUSE.
Hayato's father (eight years ago) Yakumo Hyuga, 25 years old
HE MAKES ME SO ANGRY, MY OLD MAN.
ALL I DID WAS TAKE SOME EGGS TO MAKE AN OMELET.
IRA IRA
He even slapped me!
TRAIN AT ANOTHER SUSHI SHOP?!
WHAT GOOD IS THAT?
DAD DOESN'T UNDER-STAND.
GARA KATAK
OH... WELCOME.

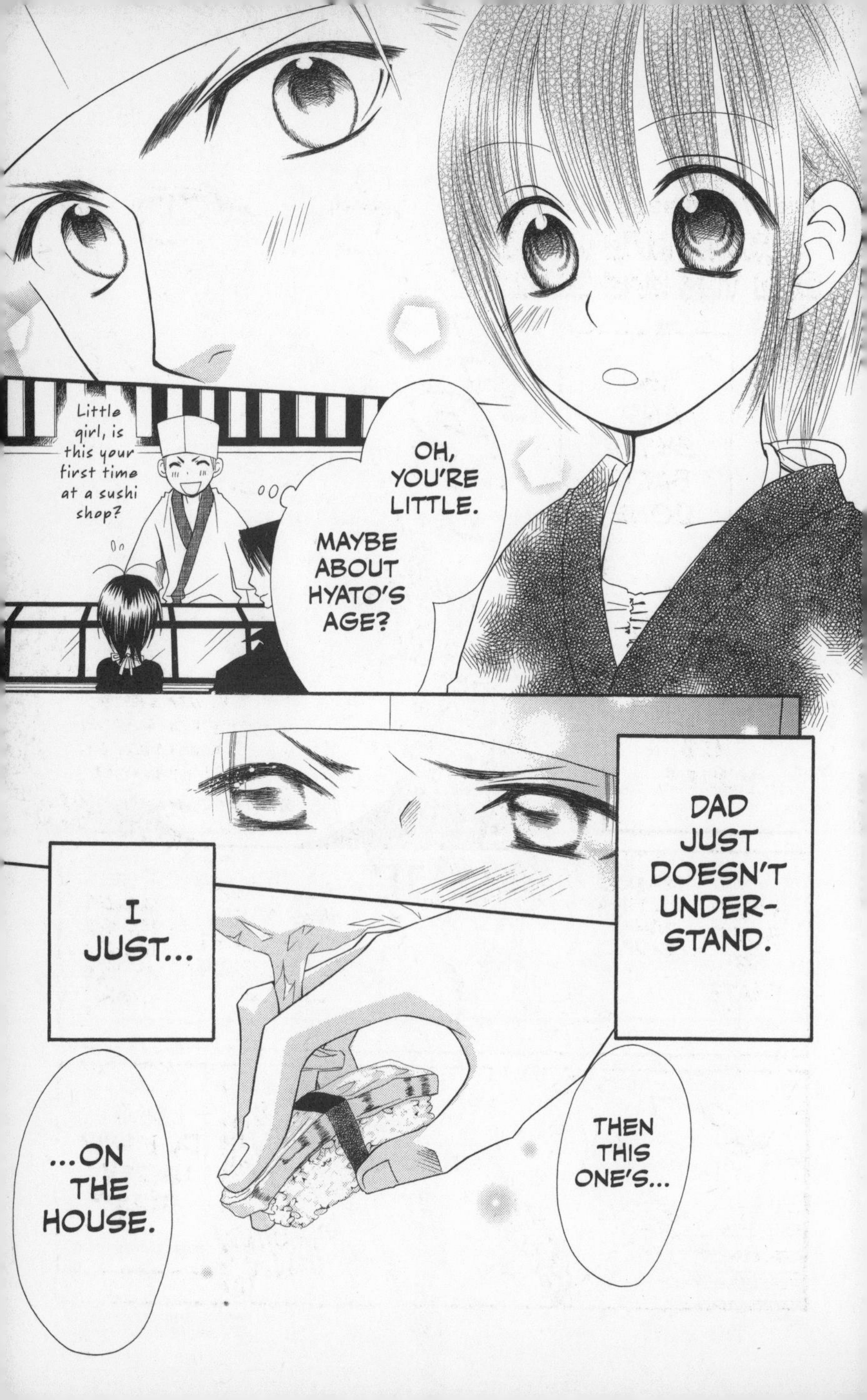
OH, YOU'RE LITTLE. MAYBE ABOUT HYATO'S AGE?
Little girl, is this your first time at a sushi shop?
DAD JUST DOESN'T UNDER-STAND.
I JUST...
THEN THIS ONE'S...
...ON THE HOUSE.

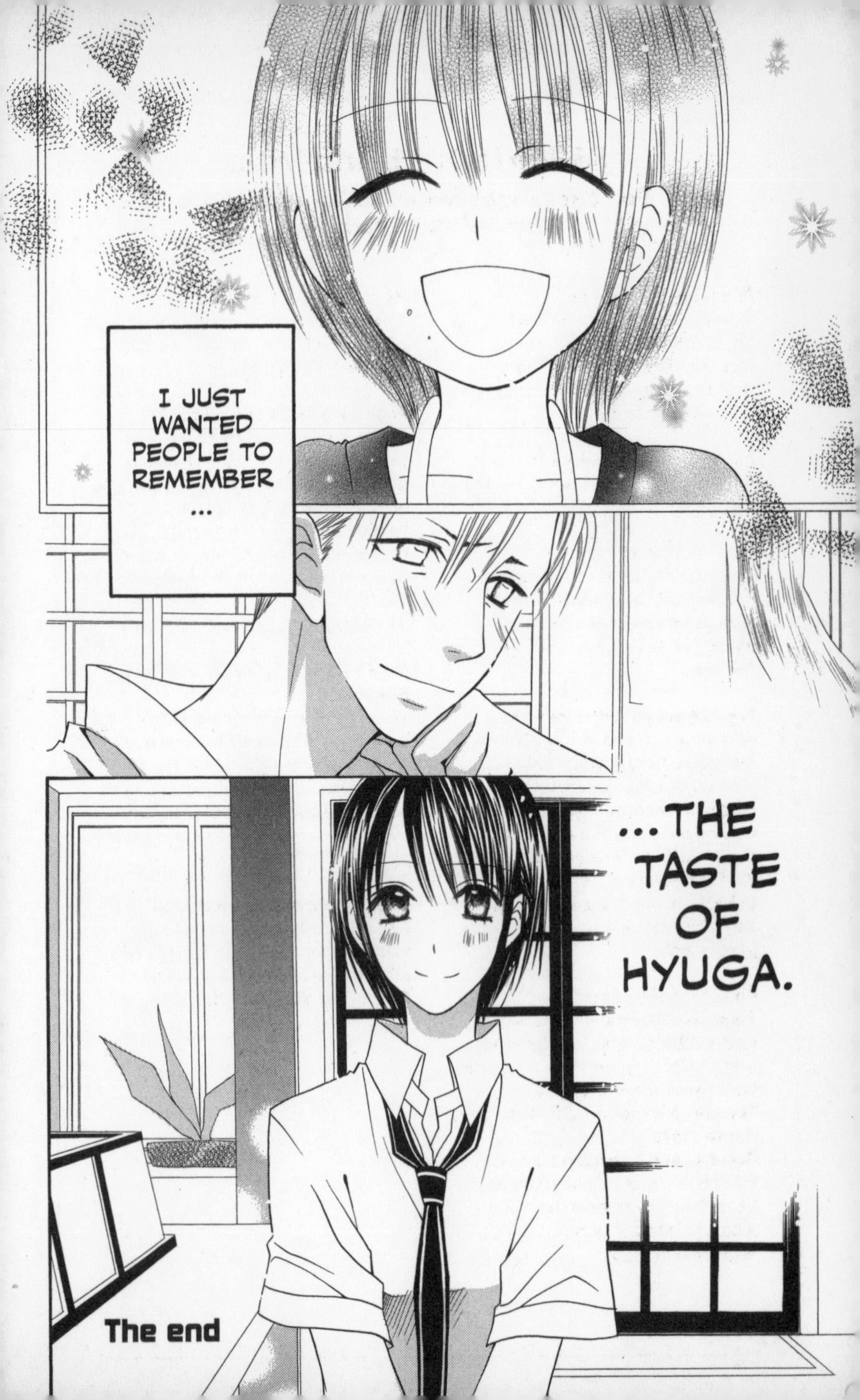
I JUST WANTED PEOPLE TO REMEMBER ...
...THE TASTE OF HYUGA.
The end

Side Dish—End Notes
For those who want to know a little more about the menu.

Page 6, panel 1: Noren
A short cotton or linen curtain hung in the doorway of some Japanese restaurants and shops. Putting the noren out signals that the establishment is open for business.

Page 13, panel 1: Hokkaido
Japan's second largest island. Hokkaido's capital is Sapporo.

Page 14, panel 3: Yanki
Term used for a youth subculture in Japan associated with juvenile delinquency. Hanayu is basically asking if Hayato's father was a juvenile delinquent.

Page 28, panel 1: Alex Ramírez
Alex Ramírez is a baseball player from Venezuela. He was a right fielder for the Cleveland Indians and Pittsburgh Pirates in America's major league before moving on to play as a cleanup hitter for the Tokyo Yakult Swallows from 2002 to 2007 (when he wore jersey number 3). In 2008, Ramírez signed with the Tokyo-based Yomiuri Giants, where he wears jersey number 5.

Page 37, author notes
Sango Tsukishima: A fellow manga artist published in Japan's *Margaret* comic anthology (the same magazine that *Mixed Vegetables* is serialized in). Tsukishima is known for her series titled *Otonari wa XX.*
Fukuoka and Kyushu: Fukuoka is the capital city of Fukuoka Prefecture, located on the northern shore of the Japanese island of Kyushu, Japan's third largest island.

Page 49, panel 2: Mont Blanc
A dessert made of puréed chestnut paste and whipped cream, generally topping a meringue base.

Page 54, panel 3: Durian candy
Durian candy is made from the large, thorn-covered, and highly odoriferous durian fruit. Durian is known as the "king of fruits" in Southeast Asia, but has been banned from some hotels and public transportation in that area because of its overpowering and often offensive smell. The fruit's flesh is used to flavor both sweet and savory foods.

Page 63, panel 1: "You sound like a drunk."
This crack alludes to the Japanese stereotype of businessmen who go drinking after work and then bring home a box of sushi or dumplings to get back in the good graces of their families. *(The joke recurs on page 83, panel 1, and page 93, panel 4—Ed.)*

Page 63, panel 1: Pressed sushi
Also called *oshizushi*. A kind of sushi made by pressing rice and vinegared fish into a small wooden box mold. Oshizushi is a specialty of Osaka.

Page 80, author notes
Okonomiyaki: A cross between a pizza and a pancake, this dish is usually made up of several ingredients—such as meats, shredded cabbage and other vegetables—mixed into an egg and flour-based batter and poured on a grill. *Okonomi* means "as you like," referring to the tradition of using whatever ingredients you want, and *yaki* means "grilled" or "cooked."

Yamaimo: Sometimes called "Japanese mountain yam," yamaimo is a kind of yam that can be consumed raw and is commonly used in Japanese cooking.

Page 97, author note: Shiso
A variety of the strongly flavored herb known variously as perilla, aojiso, or shiso around the world. Shiso is eaten with sashimi or sliced into strips and used in salads and other dishes.

Page 105, panel 3: Banpeiyu
Banpeiyu is another name for pomelo, which is a large citrus fruit that looks like an oversized grapefruit. Hana's father is using wordplay to come up with a name that is similar to Hanayu's.

Page 108, panel 3
Kagoshima: The capital city of Kagoshima Prefecture, located at the southwestern tip of the island of Kyushu.

Satsuma age: Fried fishcake from Kagoshima. White fish flesh is mashed with flour to form a paste, then fried.

Page 134, author notes
Sohki soba: Okinawan noodles with braised pork. Pork spare ribs (*sohki*) are simmered slowly for several hours until very tender with sugar, soy sauce, and *awamori* (distilled rice-based liquor from Japan's southern island of Okinawa). The resulting meat is then combined with thin buckwheat noodles (soba). It is one of the most popular kinds of soba in Okinawa.

Mozuku soba: Fine strands of seaweed eaten like noodles.

Teppanyaki: Meat and vegetables cooked at the table on a flat, smooth iron grill. Teppanyaki was made famous in the United States by the Benihana restaurant chain.

Page 164, author note: Ojisan
The Japanese term *ojisan* can mean "uncle" or can be used as a term of address for any older male. *(See page 169 for more ojisans!—Ed.)*

Page 174, panel 2: Sushi teacups
Sushi shop teacups are larger than usual teacups and hold about as much as a one-cup measuring cup.

Page 184, panel 3: Daikon
A large East Asian white radish with a subtle, gentle flavor. Important in Japanese cuisine, daikon is crunchy and often served raw in salads or as a sashimi garnish. Daikon can also be cooked and eaten in miso soup or cooked with seafood or meat.

I put my heart and soul into volume 3 and would really love for you to read it. I'm glad I feel this way!

-Ayumi Komura

Ayumi Komura was born in Kagoshima Prefecture. Her favorite number is 22, and her hobbies include watching baseball. Her previous title is *Hybrid Berry*, about a high school girl who ends up posing as a boy on her school's baseball team.

MIXED VEGETABLES
VOL. 3
The Shojo Beat Manga Edition

STORY AND ART BY
AYUMI KOMURA

English Translation/JN Productions
English Adaptation/Stephanie V.W. Lucianovic
Touch-up Art & Lettering/Jim Keefe
Design/Yukiko Whitley
Editor/Megan Bates

Editor in Chief, Books/Alvin Lu
Editor in Chief, Magazines/Marc Weidenbaum
VP, Publishing Licensing/Rika Inouye
VP, Sales & Product Marketing/Gonzalo Ferreyra
VP, Creative/Linda Espinosa
Publisher/Hyoe Narita

Printed in Canada

Published by VIZ Media, LLC
P.O. Box 77010
San Francisco, CA 94107

Shojo Beat Manga Edition
10 9 8 7 6 5 4 3 2 1
First printing, March 2009

store.viz.com

RATED T FOR TEEN
PARENTAL ADVISORY
MIXED VEGETABLES is rated T for Teen and is recommended for ages 13 and up.
ratings.viz.com

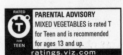

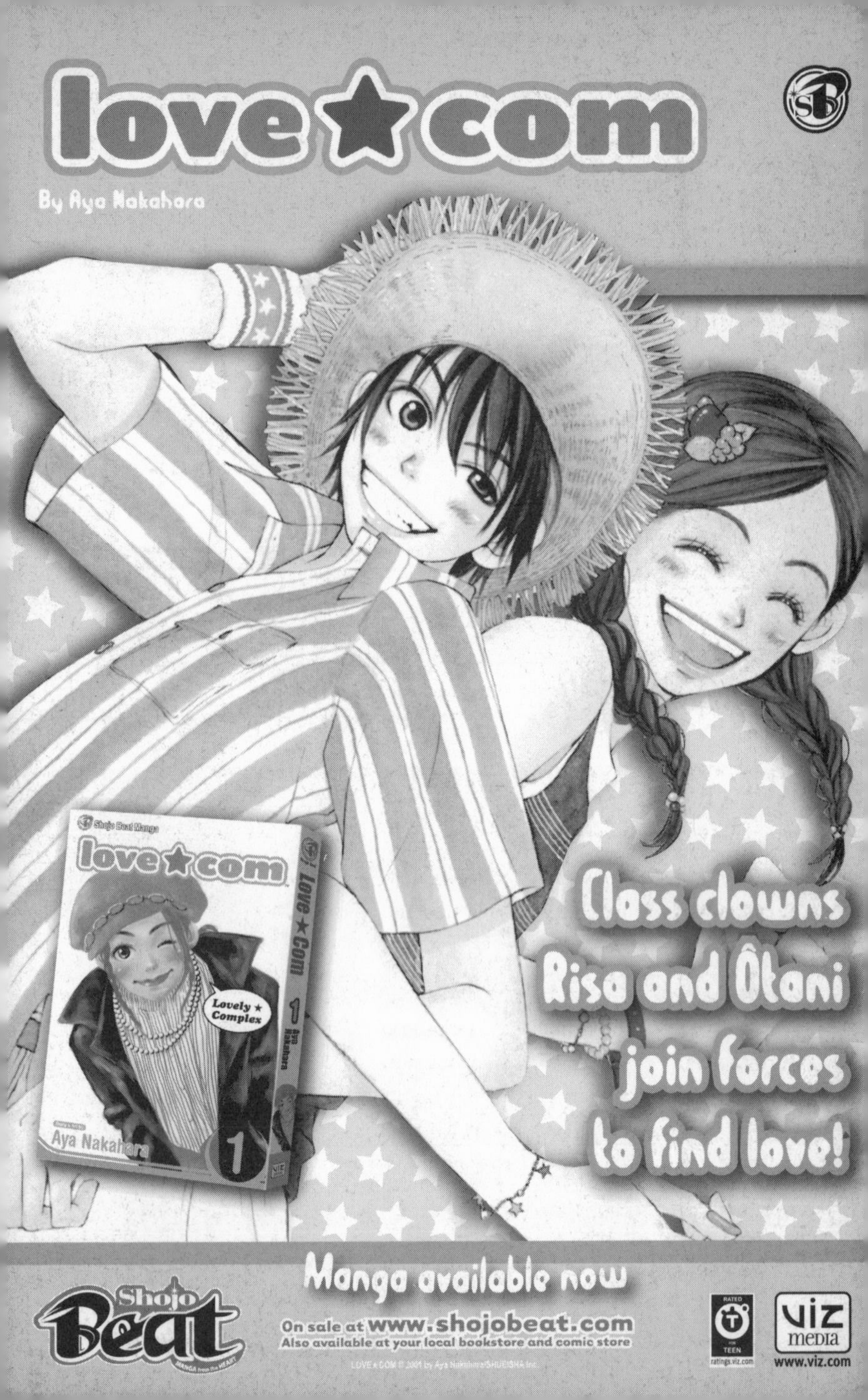
love★com
By Aya Nakahara
Shojo Beat Manga
love★com
Lovely ★ Complex
Aya Nakahara
1
Class clowns Risa and Ôtani join forces to find love!
Manga available now
Shojo Beat
On sale at www.shojobeat.com
Also available at your local bookstore and comic store
RATED T FOR TEEN
ratings.viz.com
VIZ media
www.viz.com

Shojo Beat™

MANGA from the HEART

The Shojo Manga Authority

12 GIANT issues for ONLY $34.99*

The most **ADDICTIVE** shojo manga stories from Japan **PLUS** unique editorial coverage on the arts, music, culture, fashion, and much more!

That's 51% OFF the cover price!

Subscribe NOW and become a member of the Sub Club!

- **SAVE** 51% OFF the cover price
- **ALWAYS** get every issue
- **ACCESS** exclusive areas of www.shojobeat.com
- **FREE** members-only gifts several times a year

Strictly VIP!

3 EASY WAYS TO SUBSCRIBE!

1) Send in the subscription order form from this book OR
2) Log on to: www.shojobeat.com OR
3) Call 1-800-541-7876